Identical Twins
Reared Apart

IDENTICAL

TWINS

REARED APART

A Reanalysis

Susan L. Farber

Basic Books, Inc., Publishers   New York

Grateful acknowledgment is made for permission to reprint material from the following:

Niels Juel-Nielsen, *Individual and Environment*, copyright © 1965 by Niels Juel-Nielsen, © 1980, rev. ed., International Universities Press, by permission of International Universities Press.

James Shields, *Monozygotic Twins Brought Up Apart and Brought Up Together*, copyright © 1962 by Oxford University Press, by permission of Oxford University Press.

H. H. Newman, F. N. Freeman, and K. J. Holzinger, *Twins: A Study of Heredity and Environment*, copyright © 1937 by The University of Chicago, © 1965 by Marie E. Newman, by permission of The University of Chicago Press.

I. I. Gottesman and James Shields, *Schizophrenia and Genetics*, copyright © 1972 by Academic Press, Inc., by permission of Academic Press and the authors.

R. Wilson, "Synchronies in Mental Development: An Epigenetic Perspective," *Science* 202 (1 December 1978): 939–948, copyright © 1978 by the American Association for the Advancement of Science.

P. Popenoe, "Twins Reared Apart," *Journal of Heredity* 5 (1922): 142–144, by permission of the American Genetic Association.

H. J. Muller, "Mental Traits and Heredity," *Journal of Heredity* 16 (1925): 433–448, by permission of the American Genetic Association.

Copeman's Textbook of Rheumatic Diseases, 5th ed., by permission of the publisher, Churchill Livingstone.

"Twins: After 40 Years, 'A Mirror,'" *New York Post*, 9 May 1979, by permission of United Press International.

Library of Congress Cataloging in Publication Data

Farber, Susan L   1945-
    Identical twins reared apart.

    Bibliography: p. 363
    Includes index.
    1. Twins—Psychology.   2.   Nature and nurture.
I. Title.
√ BF723.T9F37   155.7   79–3085
    ISBN: 0–465–03228–1

To my family

Contents

Preface

Many times while writing this book I felt a kinship with the ancient supplicant to Delphi who, seeking guidance, asked the oracle to which gods to make sacrifice. Supposedly, after a silence, the oracle answered only, "To the appropriate ones."

This book offers a survey and reanalysis of all published cases of identical twins separated and reared apart. My dilemma in analyzing the material was that there are many disciplines with widely varying methodologies to be propitiated. My dilemma in writing the manuscript was that there is no single, homogeneous audience to assume as readers. My solution was to write descriptively and assume an audience who had curiosity but no specialized training in behavior genetics. Thus, though I present a reanalysis, sometimes resting on statistical procedures, sometimes drawing on clinical judgment, I have come to the conclusion that the book is more a chronicle than anything else. As such, it will serve its purpose if it introduces readers to territory they had not previously considered and if it gives easy access to appropriate cases for anyone who wishes to explore them further.

The study began when I naively attempted to find one similar to it. I am a clinical psychologist, trained, by choice, in a psychodynamic developmental tradition. The child development literature, psychoanalytic and nonanalytic alike, is imbued with the assumption of innate styles, predispositions, and developmental patterns. Child clinical work, which I do, is unwaveringly persuasive that each child is uniquely his own individual, influencing his family as much as it influences him. I went to the twin literature, thinking it could give me more specific information on inherent developmental styles, and ended in the literature on twins reared apart, the best experiment of nature to explicate the nature-nurture question. What I discovered was a provocative series of case reports and a voluminous literature on IQ, but no comprehensive and detailed summary of all facets of all cases. First and foremost I offer the housecleaning and organization I so sorely missed. The "sense" I make of what I found is influenced strongly by my orientation, but I also found my training immeasurably enriched, for frequently I was taken far afield from my own discipline. Because of this experience, I decided to aim for a diverse audience. The questions are important enough and the data so provocative that they should be viewed from many angles.

Though I know of no other overall summary, there are a few extraor-

dinarily specialized analyses of portions of the twin-reared-apart literature. Most are reputable, a few even brilliant. However, some are neither, and the issue of how some have used or, as Shields (1978) says,
abused twin data is an interesting one. The fundamental issue confronted in studies of twins reared apart is, of course, the nature-nurture question. What I find astounding is how such important questions should
sometimes have been approached in such a haphazard way. How is it
possible, for example, that the IQ controversy should have raged with
such fury for so long without someone doing the drudgery we all were
trained to do—without someone, for example, organizing all the cases,
not just the easily accessible ones, into a listing that specifically stated
the twins' rearing status, degree of separation, psychiatric status, and
test validity? Since when do we take such socially important questions
(or socially irrelevant ones, for that matter) and essentially debate conclusions without taking apart and rebuilding bit by bit the scaffolding
of original data on which they are based? Though some have examined
the framework of assumptions and data, I hope I have taken the analysis a step further. Most of all, since I have discovered that the vast majority of even educated readers are baffled by the complex statistics of
behavior genetics, my aim has been to emphasize the questionable nature of every assumption and almost all available data. None of the
data closes the door on the question of the relative contributions of heredity or environment to any trait, nor do they resolve the troublesome
questions concerning such a complicated construct as IQ. Quite the
contrary, the data open the issue. One problem, I suspect, is that prior
statistical analyses of these data *look* so scientific that readers lose sight
of whether the data themselves are questionable or whether alternative
analyses should be proposed. What we probably need is a little less
wheel spinning with statistics and a little more hard work collecting
good information. A touch of clinical intuition, skepticism, and common sense might not hurt either.

I do not wish to convey the impression that this book is merely a
critical lambasting of previous work. The data organize in ways suggestive to me, and I suspect others will find patterns I missed. Physical
characteristics ranging from height, to weight, to menstrual symptoms
are greatly alike among the twins—perhaps not surprisingly, since at
least some of these traits are presumed to have significant degrees of
genetic determination. It is a little more eerie to discover that traits
such as smoking, drinking, nail biting, or gestures and mannerisms are
alike despite environmental differences and lack of contact. If any of
us talk or move like our parents, perhaps identification is not the fully
acceptable explanation of choice. Similarly, perhaps our physical or
psychological illnesses are not as unequivocally environmental as some
would like to think. I have been so challenged by the data that I have
become wary of glib assumptions that any symptom or behavior that

includes substantial somatic components in its expression is "psychoso-matic" rather than "somatopsychic."

However, the data are a little more complicated and intriguing even than this. For example, IQ—if one insists on analyzing dated and ques-tionable tests—may have a genetic component, but it is a component lower than previous studies have estimated, and it is far too low to sup-port the idea of race differences in intelligence (if that idea had merit on other grounds anyway). We already know that macroscopic envi-ronmental parameters such as socioeconomic status (SES) can affect IQ. What these twin cases highlight is the fact that microscopic environ-mental factors such as interaction and probably even motivation and the intrapsychic arena are equally as potent—accounting for some-where around 25 percent of the variance. Now, if "microscopic envi-ronment" is not just another way of describing the nuances of respect or contempt with which we treat each other and ourselves, I do not know what is. Evidently how we raise our children or think about our-selves does affect IQ, and it affects cognition in such subtle ways that it is hard to distinguish from what we transmit to our children in the nu-cleus of our cells.

Personality, too, clearly is affected by microscopic as well as macro-scopic environmental influences. Twins with more contact are *more dif-ferent* from each other in global personality assessment than twins with less contact. Since I assume that motivation as well as overt interaction must be involved in any process of twins making themselves "artifi-cially" different, it seems that intrapsychic events must be singularly potent. All in all, there are enough paradoxes in the data to suggest that we have been asking the wrong kinds of questions. We need to re-define levels of "environment," probably casting them in developmen-tal terms. I speculate that some traits, such as temperament, which are highly imbued with neurobiological patterning (and hence possibly highly genetically determined), may be precisely those that are most affected by minute environmental interactions early in life and must be reexamined from a developmental perspective.

Put another way, the cases analyzed in this book speak forcefully to the influence of both heredity *and* environment—though I speak of en-vironment in broader and more developmental terms than usual. The problem is that it is extraordinarily difficult to have a full conviction of *both* influences—and, in particular, to have a full realization of the influence of microscopic interpersonal and intrapsychic events on something as removed from mentation as genetic determinism (and vice versa). It is easier to slip or slide in one direction or the other. Un-til recently we could not begin to map genes. We will never see the psyche. But we have to believe in the influence of both, just as we have to believe in gravity, which we cannot see either. Too much is left un-explained otherwise.

Freud (1900) once used the metaphor of gravitation in discussing primary and secondary processes of mentation. He was a master of inferring and describing process, and to the end of his life he retained his biologist's heritage. However, he also rose to counter the idea that "hereditary taint" was the immutable cause of mental distress, and, as Sulloway (1979) described, he steadfastly kept his inner circle from linking his concepts with biology, probably as a protection for his nascent discipline. Strategically, he may have been correct. I suspect he was. However, the time for protection is long since past; yet his followers, with the exception of some psychologists and a few child analysts, continue to psychologize in ever more esoteric ways when they belong, in fact, to the psychological tradition most rooted in biology and most capable of building links between psychic and somatic processes. History's lessons of depravity in the guise of "genetic determinism" are not to be forgotten. I submit that the public will continue to be swayed by whichever "hereditarian" or "environmentalist" view currently is popular until those who best understand minute shifts in the psychic and interpersonal sphere begin communicating with those who best understand biology. I believe this to be true particularly in light of my earlier speculation that some traits that are highly somatically based are also those most influenced by minute interactions early in life. When Michelangelo shaped his unyielding marble, he used small, sharp instruments to bring it to life. I suggest that small, hidden events shape people too, sometimes more effectively than large ones. In that sense, this book is a request, backed up by data, that the doors be kept open—more open than they are now. We have to *look* for things, not just state that they are there. I hope this study is a small step in that direction.

Just as Freud's followers became more "psychological" than he probably intended his discipline eventually to be, it usually is the second-generation analyzers of twin-reared-apart data who are the most "hereditarian." The investigators who actually saw the twins were modest in their claims, and they were the most emphatic in asking that future samples be found. They also appear almost uniformly open to asking for reevaluation and further analysis of the data. Newman, Freeman, and Holzinger (1937) closed their well-known study by noting that they left their data in a form suitable for reanalysis. Shields (1962), in a brief and treasured correspondence with me before he died, was encouraging about my plan to reanalyze the data, including his cases, though he did not know in what direction the analysis would take me. Juel-Nielsen (1965), too, has remained unwaveringly supportive though he did not know what I would conclude. Would that all who dealt with this topic had their integrity.

I find it interesting that, of the multitude of themes in this material, the one most forceful idea communicated to me is individuality. Paradoxically, it is best communicated by the similarities within sets and the differences that seem to arise from factors associated with their meeting each other. If separated twins remain similar in many ways despite different homes and social milieus, how much must each of us also be unique in our perceptions, our feelings, and our way of shaping the world? If twins, consciously or unconsciously, make themselves different after meeting, what more do we need to underscore the need of each individual to be an individual? It seems to me to be one of the few simple and unequivocal themes in this literature. Good parents and seasoned clinicians share a relaxed acceptance, even joy, in experiencing other people as different from themselves. Perhaps life gets most of us to that point. Perhaps these cases make it easier to absorb.

In the work that follows I have tried to be straightforward and primarily descriptive. In all instances I have tried to present the data so they may be easily checked by others. With so many case histories, some errors probably will emerge despite my best attempts. I hope readers will bring them to my attention. What concerns me more are the instances in which I may have failed to cite work done by others. As I noted before, the field is new and interdisciplinary. Where I have missed someone's work, I hope others will rectify the omission. Any errors, of course, are entirely my own.

Susan L. Farber
New York City, 1980

Acknowledgments

I owe a debt of gratitude to many who helped with this study. Perhaps the greatest is to Niels Juel-Nielsen and James Shields. Both offered friendly correspondence, information, and encouragement. Shields arranged for the British ratings on one of the cases presented in chapter 6 and, after his death, the Institute of Psychiatry sent information from his private files on IQ tests. Juel-Nielsen has been unstinting in response to my requests for information and took the time to read the full manuscript when it was still in rough draft. Many others generously took time from busy schedules to search case files and offer information and expertise. W. J. Craig, Ph.D., in cooperation with the Kingston Psychiatric Hospital, sent a full summary on the twins presented in appendix A. Eiji Inouye, M.D., of the University of Tokyo sent pedigrees and summaries on the cases in appendices B and C. John Rainer, M.D., of the New York State Psychiatric Institute tracked down the original files on the twins presented in appendix D and, afterward, checked the accuracy of my summary. Einar Kringlen, M.D., sent the published case histories on all of the twins in his series when I was unable to locate them in libraries here. Drs. F. E. Stephens and J. C. Nunemaker tried to help me locate information on a set they had seen more than thirty years ago and it was through no fault of their own that I did not succeed. R. Cancro, M.D., R. Spitzer, M.D., S. Ashe, M.D., J. K. Wing, M.D., R. Murray, M.D., and A. Clare, M.D., did blind diagnostic ratings on case 180, and several offered extended and helpful criticisms after full information on the case was released. I. I. Gottesman, Ph. D., also offered useful criticism on the same case. Professor K. Fredga of the University of Lund generously provided the photograph in chapter 4.

Sol Cohen, M.D., Ilona Hertz, M.D., and Howard Rubinstein, M.D., read chapter 5 in rough draft and offered numerous, helpful criticisms. Nancy Zufall, Laura Brent, and Michael O'Kean helped organize raw data for the same chapter. Noel Dunivant, Ph.D., did the statistical analysis of IQ test scores, read through the full manuscript, authored appendix E, and is co-author of chapter 7. Anne Shapiro, Cleonie White, and Sherry Ross checked information for this and other chapters.

The search for obscure papers in an international literature could not have been done without the assistance of excellent librarians. Ms. Taylor of the New York Psychoanalytic Institute library was a magician in producing papers from sometimes incorrect or fragmentary citations. The leeway and atmosphere in which I pursued an unfunded study would not have been possible without the assistance of the New York University Department of Psychology, in particular, David Wolitzky, Ph.D., Leo Goldberger, Ph.D., Bettie Brewer, and Bill Francis.

The generosity of Dr. L. L. Cavalli-Sforza in reading the manuscript of a young, unknown author was exceptional. The perseverance of my friends, who know me well, was also.

Finally, the study would not have been possible at all had not Herb Reich, Jane Isay, Julie Strand and other staff at Basic Books decided to patiently cultivate what they thought was an interesting idea. Debra Manette taught me what a good copy editor can do.

Identical Twins
Reared Apart

Chapter 1

Introduction

I take it as given that each individual creates his own image of reality, actively painting it on his mind's eye much as an artist puts brush to canvas or a sculptor molds clay. Freud's revolution introduced the notion that this creative process is circumscribed by inborn parameters. His elaboration of the unconscious as a cluster of processes governed by a continuous interplay between soma and psyche and seeking expression in somatic gratification essentially placed man back within the evolutionary scheme of the animal kingdom. In effect, he described man as a particular form of primate, functioning according to laws bequeathed by his biological heritage and, in turn, shaping the world around him in ways congruent with or at least adapted to the multileveled constraints his inherited structure places on him.

Subsequent theorists have altered and turned away from the full impact of Freud's early work, particularly his emphasis on somatic linkages and the ubiquity of unconscious processes. In Great Britain and the United States, Freud's challenge to free will and adaptability has been met with the development of ego psychology, particularly with the concept of inborn, conflict-free autonomous functions. Though the idea that we are born with such capacities as sight, motility, and a blueprint for language tends, as one analyst put it, to leave the "dirty stuff" out of Freud's theory, it does fit both with empirical observation and common sense. Numerous capacities are present at birth or develop in all people and seem not to arise strongly, if at all, out of some conflict of the individual with internal or external pressures. When not used to avoid the issue of inherent constraints, ego psychology also returns to the fundamental concept of biological underpinnings in human psychology. For example, in what way are the capacities used for adaptation to reality limited by inborn parameters? Why are some individuals able to flourish despite the most deprived of environmental circumstances while others wither in even the most enriched? Within the range of normality, why do two uniquely different individuals develop and display dissimilar traits and symptom patterns despite a broad range of similar environmental circumstances? When not arguing from hindsight and counting minuscule environmental dissimilarities, the usual explanation is that the two individuals were born different. Because of differences in their inherent adaptational faculties, they perceived, processed, and integrated similar experiences in highly dissimilar ways.

This idea and the fundamental concept of Freud's early work—that we are members of the animal kingdom, operating on a continuous interplay between soma and psyche—are the starting-points of this study. The question is to what degree the psychic and somatic tools with which we interpret and shape reality, the brush and palette as it were, are predetermined by the genetic code. The study will not answer such questions; nor will it deal directly with unconscious processes or specific ego functions. However, in an oblique way it reflects on both, for if it is possible to begin estimating which traits are more influenced by environment and which less, a more parsimonious and specific investigation of psychological functioning may begin.

There are many routes for beginning what is essentially a nature-nurture study. Family pedigree and fostering and adoption studies are traditional means. However, the classical method has been the twin study, and within the twin literature there is a cluster of obscure, unsummarized cases on identical twins separated early in life and reared apart. These cases comprise the core of this work, partly because they offer a unique route to approach the heredity-environment question, more because of their intrinsic interest, and primarily because, quite simply, they are provocative. Though I emphasize the speculative nature of conclusions in all that follows as a means of avoiding the grievous errors offered the public in the past, a more refined and rigorous approach to this literature emerges as fruitful. Toward that end, let us begin.

The study of twins is based on the premise that they share an identical genotype, which makes them ideal subjects for investigating the degree to which various environmental conditions may instigate change. The identical-genotype hypothesis differentiates between two types of twins: *monozygotics,* often called identical twins (or MZ twins), which presumably are formed when a single egg, fertilized by a single sperm, splits into two parts, each of which develops into a separate embryo; and *dizygotics,* otherwise known as fraternals (or DZ twins), which develop when two eggs are released more or less simultaneously from one or both ovaries and are fertilized by two separate sperm. Dizygotics are thought to account for all opposite-sexed twins as well as a number of same-sexed sets. Their development from two separate eggs and sperm leave them no more genetically similar than two siblings, but their common pre- and postnatal environments make them useful in comparison groups with MZ twins.

Monozygotics often are considered to be nature's unique controlled laboratory experiment on the interplay between heredity and environment. In its most elemental form, the rationale for their study rests on two basic assumptions. First, monozygotic twins are thought to share an identical genotype, since they presumably have developed from the union of a single egg and sperm. From this flows the second assumption that, given the identical genetic fabric of the two individuals, similarities between them may be explored for hereditary factors while differences may be linked to environment. Although this formulation catches the thrust of much of the literature, it is not correct as stated. No trait is independent of hereditary or environmental agents. Certain environmental conditions are necessary before a genetic potential becomes expressed (or, conversely, inhibited), while the genetic endowment of any individual is certain to influence the way he perceives, experiences, or processes environmental stimuli. Just as important, genetic endowment influences an individual's ability to mold the environment and shape his surroundings and the responses he receives. Thus the correct question to ask of data is how much of the variability among individuals for any given trait is due to hereditary differences. In the literature, this variance due to genetic differences is known as "heritability in the broad sense."

When stated in this manner, the proposition immediately suggests the usefulness of MZ twins as subjects. Although their genetic endowment is not known, the fact that it can be assumed to be identical for both leaves environmental influences more clearly delineated. However, when twins are reared in the same family, the environmental input becomes markedly tangled. Although they share the same parents, socioeconomic class, nutrition, and, in short, almost identical environments, they also are subjected to exaggeratedly different responses as adults and peers attempt to differentiate between them. Often these responses focus on attributes that would be otherwise unremarkable in a singleton. A few ounces difference in birth weight, the name of one relative rather than another, or an imagined glint in one twin's eye may be exaggerated by onlookers to the degree that differences become blown out of proportion. Thus, though macroscopically the twins' environment may be the same, microscopically and in the potent nuances of interaction their environments may resemble each other quite minimally.

Added to this is a factor unique to twin studies: When partners are raised together they begin an exceedingly complex and idiosyncratic interaction known as *twinning*. Partners seesaw, both by observation and self-report, between close identification with and exaggerated independence of each other. If one does well in math, the other maps out territory elsewhere. If one achieves motor milestones earlier in infancy, he or she may be relegated to the role of "athlete" while the other becomes "intellectual." One may be "active," the other "passive," either in alternating episodes or consistently as a character pattern. There is question whether this asynchrony in development is due to psychological factors or to developmental rhythms. Whichever is the case, twins themselves report its power. It leads one to the question of whether the psychology of twins may be slightly different from the psychology of singletons. Particularly if one follows psychodynamic child development literature with its current emphasis on separation-individuation and the hypothesized major influence of this process on later development and symptom choice,[1] the question becomes one of whether twins have markedly atypical early developmental experiences. If, in fact, this is the case—and recall that we are talking only of the effect of the twins on each other and the slight parental differences in attitude—then the generalizability of twin studies is placed in question. To the degree that their psychology is different just because they are twins, findings cannot be expanded to singletons.

Thus, in theory at least, the clearest demarcation of heredity and environment may be found when twins have been separated early in life and reared apart in different homes, by different parents, and often in widely varying socioeconomic and geographic circumstances. Cases of this type minimize the unique input that develops when outsiders attempt to deal with two almost identical individuals and, presumably, eliminate completely the powerful relationship between the twins themselves. Put closer to home, one could say that cases of twins reared apart allow us to study their growth and development as nontwins—which, after all, is what all but a small fraction of the human race is—while retaining the unique research advantages of controlling for genotype.

The Development of MZ Twins

Frequency of Birth

The frequency of twin births varies in different populations. In studies of multiple births in the United States, results tend to cluster around rates of one twin birth for every eighty-nine white deliveries

1. See Mahler (1968) and Blank and Blank (1974) as examples.

and one for every seventy or seventy-one black births. The different frequencies are related primarily to differences in the frequencies of DZ births, which vary according to racial or ethnic population and which have a curvilinear relationship with age and parity of the mother. Thus, DZ births occur more often among Danes and Belgians than among Orientals. For all groups, the probability of a dizygotic birth increases as the mother approaches the age of thirty-nine, and decreases in the forty to forty-four age category. In the United States, it is estimated that about one monozygotic birth occurs for every three dizygotics, although the ratio alters somewhat if one views discrete racial or ethnic subgroups. There is debate over what factors contribute to the fluctuation, most hypotheses centering on the degree to which possible hereditary tendencies toward multiple ovulation interact with assorted variables such as age or nutrition. Studies in polygamous cultures indicate that DZ twinning tendencies may have a small polygenic component expressing itself by way of the mother and not the father (Novitski 1977).

The frequency of monozygotic births appears to be more stable throughout all populations, accounting for about 0.30 to 0.40 percent of the total number of births. It is disputed whether the probability of an MZ birth increases with the age of the mother. One factor that may contribute to the positive correlation is that a woman who has borne a number of children will have a better chance of carrying and delivering twins than will a less experienced woman, since multiple pregnancies carry with them an increased degree of risk. Indeed, most authorities agree that the number of twin conceptions, both mono- and dizygotic, probably is substantially higher than the number of births in which at least one twin is born alive, and it is possible that many early miscarriages involve multiple embryos. In a bizarre twist, it emerges that in certain rare instances, singletons are discovered years after birth to carry cells that have been incorporated into their bodies from a DZ twin who died prenatally. Such cases are known as *chimeras*.[2]

Frequency of Separation

No figures exist on the frequency with which monozygotic twins are separated after birth and placed in different homes. Factors such as war, poverty, and culturally related child-rearing attitudes[3] probably

2. Conversely, *teratomas*—cysts containing cells from bone, teeth, hair, connective and neural tissue, and so forth—have a normal complement of chromosomes and may arise from a form of parthenogenesis, or development of an egg without fertilization. Linder et al. (1975) speculate that it occurs by fusion of the second polar body with the oocyte or by suppression of the second meiotic division.

3. For example, in Japan twins are routinely separated far more often than in Europe or the United States.

play a part in making the frequency vary from population to population. The single best estimate would be one that stated the ratio of MZ
twins separated soon after birth to a given population figure. (Since, as
mentioned earlier, the frequency of MZ births is fairly stable across all
populations, it is a factor that need not be of concern.) The only study
that allows estimate is one done by Niels Juel-Nielsen (1965) in Den-
mark from 1954 to 1965. From various sources, including twin registries for births from 1870 to 1910, he was able to uncover forty sets,
though only twelve of these met his criteria of being monozygotic, separated early in life, and having both partners alive and available for
study. Twelve sets out of a population of about 5 million give a ratio of
approximately three per million who meet the basic criteria; more than
ten per million meet the ciriteria if dizygotics, poorly separated sets,
and those not available for study are included. If we assume some
roughly comparable ratio in the United States, we would estimate there
to be more than six hundred adult sets, more than twenty of them in
the New York metropolitan area alone.

A different estimate is derived from the work of James Shields (1962)
in Great Britain. Out of a population somewhat over 45 million, he
found forty-four sets. However, Shields's sample was elicited through
an appeal over television and included only those twins where at least
one partner knew of or suspected the other's existence. Thus, it is likely
that a substantial number of subjects were lost. Combining the estimates based on the two studies, and taking nothing else into account
(such as the proportion of twins who knew each other but did not vol-
unteer), the best estimate seems to be that there are roughly three sets
per million population who meet the basic criteria, and only about one
set per million population who know of each other's existence.

The figures, which are highly speculative, indicate how rare such
subjects are. On the other hand, if they are at all accurate, they also indicate that a large pool of subjects exists, much larger than has been indicated, much less tapped, by previous investigations. The last large-
scale published study of twins reared apart in the United States
(Newman et al. 1937) occurred more than forty years ago and has not
been followed up. This is surprising considering the otherwise rapid
increase in interest, sophistication, and investigative methods in the
biological and social sciences during this period.

The Identical-Genotype Hypothesis

Of all hypotheses in the study of twins, the one that has received the
least challenge is the assumption that monozygotic partners share an
identical genotype. It appears to be universally agreed that the process
by which one obtains MZ sibs is one in which a single egg, or zygote,

fertilized by a single sperm, splits into two separate though genetically identical embryos. Interestingly, the process of twinning has been observed in animal species such as the armadillo, but not in primates or man. Nonetheless, the process is assumed to be the same. Also, it has not been established at what point the cells divide into two separate groups, though the literature abounds with speculation that the stage at which the splitting takes place may be of profound importance for later development (see Mirror Imaging, especially p. 12).

The few questions raised about the identical-genotype hypothesis tend to fall into two categories. The first is the possibility of mutation or chromosomal damage to one twin that does not occur in the other. Heterochromia (eyes of two different colors) is an example of possible mutation that occurs in the sample studied here (see chapters 4 and 5). Chromosomal damage, not known to occur in this sample, could be illustrated by an MZ pair with XX zygote, where loss of one of the X chromosomes would lead to two females, one normal and one with Turner's syndrome. Mosaics may occur, and it is possible for MZ twins to be discordant for Down's syndrome, depending on the degree of mosaicism (Novitski 1977).

A second critique suggests that there may be types of twins other than mono- or dizygotic. The most frequent reference is to *oocytic* twins, which, according to some, may be formed when a single ovum and its polar body are fertilized by two separate sperm. The result would be twins who share an identical maternal inheritance but different paternal contributions. Technically, they would be uniovular like monozygotics but would have different genotypes. Gedda (1961) discussed the experimental literature on this topic but concluded that such twins, if they exist at all, would be mistaken for dizygotics. Others (Bulmer 1970; MacGillivray et al. 1975) consider oocytic twins extremely rare. Juel-Nielsen dismisses them as of no importance to studies of twins reared apart since the probability of such a pair being found in a sample of monozygotics is so small as to be meaningless.

Other variations in the twinning process have been described as well. *Superfecundation* refers to multiple ova produced simultaneously but fertilized by different males.[4] Instances of superfecundation have been observed in animals such as cows and dogs, and at least two possible cases are reported for humans (Gedda 1961; Bulmer 1970). However, such cases are presumed to be extremely rare. The second variation, *superfetation*, occurs when one fertilized ova is implanted and followed by a second ova, fertilized by the same or a different male. Again, this is generally dismissed in the literature, though some consider it worth further investigation (Gedda 1961). None of these variations is likely to

4. In some cultures, the birth of twins automatically indicated that the mother was an adultress.

challenge the identical-genotype hypothesis for MZ twins, since any instances, if they occur at all, would be within the fraternal or dizygotic class.

Mirror Imaging

Mirror imaging, also known as *asymmetry*, refers to those sets of monozygotics who show some degree of mirror reversal in various physical traits. For example, many sets have one right-handed and one left-handed partner. The degree of mirror imaging can be extensive, including handedness, footedness, hair whorl, facial features, and even aspects of the shape of internal organs. At other times, the asymmetry is only partial as, for example, in twins who have reversed hair whorls and facial characteristics but the same hand/foot dominance. Cases of situs inversus viscerum have been described, where the location of internal organs within the body is reversed. This occurs most frequently in conjoined, or Siamese, twins and is not frequent in monozygotics who are fully separated.

In this sample, mirror imaging is rated according to handedness. Though this is an imprecise method of estimating both mirroring and any correlaries with broader laterality preferences, it was the only consistent means possible and is used as a first step. Various explanations have been offered on the etiology of mixed-handedness in identical twins, none of them fully satisfactory and none universally accepted (Gedda 1961; Bulmer 1970; MacGillivray et al., 1975; Carter-Saltzman et al. 1976). Indeed, the etiology of handedness and/or cerebral dominance in nontwins is unknown (Levy 1976; Huhey, 1977; Annett 1978; Fuller and Thompson 1978), neither the hypothesis of genetic transmission or of pre- and postnatal events being sufficiently explanatory. The hypothesis of postnatal events seems immediately dismissible, requiring only the observation, easily made, that many newborn MZ twins show tendencies to laterality preference when they arc to opposite sides, kick, smile, or wave their arms in distinctively mirror-image patterns immediately after birth. Carter-Saltzman et al. (1976) summarizes other major hypotheses of mixed-handedness in MZ twins, questioning the genetic and convincingly dismissing ideas such as crowding and placement *in utero* or cerebral damage at birth.

In general, mirror imaging is broken into three, and sometimes four, classifications: anatomical, functional, pathological, and psychological (Gedda 1961). Anatomical asymmetry refers to situs inversus viscerum as well as asymmetry in other characteristics such as head shape, shape or location of facial and body characteristics, fingerprints, teeth, or the shape of internal organs (as for example, when an enlargement or indentation occurs in the right lobe of an organ in one twin and in the left lobe in the other. The side of the body in which the organ is located, however, is the same in both.). The usual analogy for anatomical mirror imaging is that the left side of one partner's body and the right side of the other partner's are more alike than are the two sides of either individual's body. Numerous instances of anatomical mirror imaging occur in the sample studied here.

Functional forms of mirror imaging refer chiefly to dominance in voluntary muscular activity such as handedness, footedness, preferred eye, and so forth. It is not uncommon to discover that only partial asymmetry occurs, as when one partner is fully right dominant while the other is either ambidextrous or has mixed hand and foot dominance. The literature abounds with speculation on the degree to which differences in functional asymmetry may influence later development, though, as yet, no consensus has been reached. For example, case studies sometimes offer evidence of dissimilar environmental reactions to differences in handedness: In one instance only one twin had her left hand tied behind her back in childhood in order to force her to become right dominant. More often, speculation centers on the ways in which functional asymmetry is associated with more germinal differences such as hemispheric dominance, with all the potential differences in intellectual functioning, ability, and styles of thinking to which this may contribute. Functional asymmetry scored via handedness is noted throughout the sample.

Pathological asymmetry refers to mirror imaging in pathological conditions for which twin partners are concordant. Gedda (1961) cites investigations in which a pathological condition, such as paralytic poliomyelitis or congenital malformations, occurs on opposite sides of the body in mirror-image sets. Such instances are recorded in this sample (see chapter 4, Dentition). Physicians and developmental biologists may be those primarily interested in pathological asymmetry, since it speaks to a remarkable specificity of cellular differentiation and may shed light on the degree to which individuals may be susceptible, or susceptible in only certain ways, to various types of disorders.

The last category, psychological asymmetry, was suggested by Bouterwek (1936) and is meant to suggest that partners may complement each other in psychological characteristics, as when one is viewed as more active, the other more passive, or when one is high in verbal skills, the other in motor tasks, and so forth. This category of mirror imaging seems inextricably bound to functional or anatomical asymmetry, but it has not yet been demonstrated with any degree of clarity. The concept refers to inherent predispositions and excludes the idea of "twinning" in pairs reared together, though, obviously, it may be strongly associated since some of what is labeled as psychodynamic "twinning" may, in fact, according to Bouterwek's hypothesis, stem from constitutional or congenital differences. Newman et al. (1937) suggested that the greatest psychological differences may be found in those sets who are only partially mirror image, with the underlying assumption that partial reversals may lead to more mixed and discordant interplays and experiencings with the environment than when sets are clearly identical or reverse images of each other. Their work could not demonstrate this, though they thought it might be because their sample was too small. Others have continued the investigation (Boklage 1974; Carter-Saltzman et al. 1976) but, as yet, no exhaustive study of asymmetric twins has been performed and, of the studies attempted, most are limited to examinations of only one or two variables.

In 1928, Newman offered an interesting speculation on the etiology of mirror imaging. His explanation focused on the point in embryonic development where the split into twins takes place. He suggested that splitting before bilateral symmetry would produce "identical identicals" and splitting after would produce mirror imaging. Bilateral symmetry refers to the symmetrical arrangement of anatomical features on either side of a midline (two eyes, two arms, two legs, two sides of the brain, and so forth). The concept can be illustrated if the reader places his hands, palms together, in an upright position. If we assume that the hands represent the cells that will develop into a fetus, bilateral symmetry can be represented by making an imaginary line down the length of the hand, using the fingertips to represent the anterior end (where the head will develop) and the heel of the hand as the posterior end (where feet will develop). If we assume that areas that later will develop into the two sides of the body have begun to be established, anatomical asymmetry can be illustrated by separating the hands into two "twins," noting that the side of the face that develops toward the "thumb" side of the lateral line is on the right in one individual and on the left in the other.

The example can be taken a step further by assuming that differentiation has reached a point where a dominant side of the cell mass has begun to be established or exists as a potential. Imagining the "thumb" side as the dominant one and separating the hands produces a dominant area on the right in one "twin" and on the left in the other. This was used as the explanation for functional asymmetry, where one twin was right-handed and the other left-handed. Partial asymmetries were explained by recourse to the proposition that development proceeds from anterior to posterior (top to bottom). If the splitting took place when the anterior or "head" region was more differentiated than the lower torso or legs, the result would be partial mirror-image pairs whose upper parts of the body were asymmetric while the lower parts were not.

It is interesting that neither the process of twinning nor asymmetry in humans has been solved by investigators. However, the result, mirror imaging, is potentially important in any analysis of data since it indicates an area in which "identical" twins may differ significantly. The question is whether there are broader associations with personality or intellectual functioning. In statistical studies, the effects would tend to be embedded in within-group variance.

The Intrauterine Environment

"Environment" begins as soon as the egg is fertilized. It is possible that the environment within the womb may have as decisive, and, in some instances, a more decisive influence than the world into which the neonate emerges at birth. The proposition stems from the common principle in embryology and developmental psychology that the earlier in development an intervention takes place, the more global and lasting its potential consequences. Though the twin-reared-apart literature contains little information on pregnancy and delivery, the issue is important conceptually, for it may contribute to differences within sets incorrectly attributed to postnatal environment or to large numbers of sets being differently susceptible to postnatal environment than singletons. Of the list of many variables that could be involved, two will be mentioned: fetal blood supply and birth complications.

Fetal Blood Supply. Though there are overriding similarities in the embryonic development of MZ twins, it generally is acknowledged that a marked "competition" exists between them for space, position, and, in particular, blood supply in the increasingly limited confines of the womb. Bulmer (1970) concluded that the most salient variable is inequalities in blood supply, and Newman et al.'s (1937) early comment summarizes the situation well:

That this imbalance in blood exchange does produce marked differences in surviving twins is evidenced by the extensive observations of Schatz, who found that, at about the middle period of pregnancy, size differences in monozygotic twins average much greater than in dizygotic twins. This is the opposite of what might be expected on a genetic basis. Identical twins that survive this period tend to be more nearly equal in size, but even at birth their size differences equal on the average those of dizygotic twins, many of the former showing more marked differences than the average of the latter. As has been said, such size differences produced by this prenatal factor extend beyond mere size and involve also differences in vigor and general health. How much of the observed size and weight differences in adult identical twins trace back to the factor under discussion we have no means of knowing, but it seems obvious that the effects of this factor are too important to be ignored. [pp. 36–38]

In the decades following Newman's observations, many studies have attempted to investigate whether, or how much, size differences at birth may continue throughout life. For example, adult height appears to be influenced somewhat, though the smaller or weaker partner tends to catch up slightly during childhood. Unfortunately, the literature is far from complete, much less in accord, on variables of more interest, such as IQ, personality, general vigor, or differential susceptibility to physical or mental disorder. However, as Newman et al. said, it is a factor "too important to be ignored" since virtually all infant studies, whether on twins or not, indicate that size, weight, and, most important, general vigor at birth may become significant factors coloring larger areas of later development.

Birth and Birth Trauma. Though most studies of twins reared apart give at least lip service to possible aftereffects of differences in fetal blood supply, almost none mention the event of birth itself as an area of concern. This is surprising considering the marked consequences attending difficulties at this period, such as, for example, the type of intellectual impairment that emerges years after some degree of anoxia at delivery. Two issues appear salient when considering the possible associations between delivery and later traits. The first centers on the possible difference within sets due to differing birth experiences. MacGillivray et al. (1975) offer a detailed discussion. Bulmer (1970) summarizes:

... the second twin probably suffers a greater risk of anoxia because of the increased length of labour and because of the possibility that the placenta may separate after the birth of the first twin. On the other side of the balance sheet is the fact that the first twin probably has a greater risk of birth injury since it must dilate the cervix whereas the second twin passes through an already dilated cervix. It is not possible to separate the effects of these different factors with the data at present available. [pp. 63–64]

A broader issue, potentially affecting entire samples of twins, is the high frequency of pregnancy complications and premature births in multiple deliveries. The two most common complications during pregnancy that occur with multiple births are toxemia and hydramnios. Both can have deleterious effects on the babies. Since both disorders result in high fetal mortality, it is not clear what proportion of twins born alive are affected (Bulmer 1970; MacGillivray et al. 1975). However, prematurity affects up to 50 percent or more of twins (Schienfeld 1967), and the tendency to low birth weight and short gestation period is even higher in same-sex as opposed to opposite-sexed pairs (Howard and Brown 1970; Fuller and Thompson 1978).

The literature is inconsistent in its findings on long-term consequences of prematurity.[5] However, conservatism and common sense dictate that an assumption of sequelae must be made. For example, does being premature make an individual so different from nonpremature

5. See Wiener 1962, 1968; Strang 1974; MacGillivray, 1975; and Tilford 1976 as examples.

infants as to undermine all comparisons? How does prematurity affect IQ, personality, or motor development? Does it lead to increased susceptibility to disease or certain disorders? What the question probably boils down to is whether being premature makes an individual somehow more or differently susceptible to the environment than a full-term individual is. The question cannot be answered at this point, but it is more than worthy of consideration since the entire assumption on which twin studies are based is the belief that the degree to which environment leaves an impact on a twin is similar to how it might affect a nontwin. If we are dealing with subjects who are differently susceptible to environmental influences than most of us, the value of twin studies becomes moot.

Biases in Data Collection

Embryonic development, prenatal environment, and birth differences may contribute to differences within sets and over groups of twins that have not been taken into account when results are reported in the literature. However, the most blatant bias results from the way the data were collected in the first place. Most studies of twins reared apart offer conclusions that cannot be supported or must be modified by taking into account the material being analyzed. Quite stunning omissions in elementary design requirements such as random sampling or assignment to groups exist in this sample, but they are rarely, if ever, mentioned in reports. Sometimes it seems that the material is so rich and intriguing that investigators become blinded to the biased nature of their samples. Several areas are of primary concern. These are random sampling, determination of zygosity, socioeconomic status, degree of separation, and awareness of twinship.

Random Sampling: Zygosity Determination

That there are different types of twins was not understood in the early days of twin research. The first compelling demonstrations of two types of twins, mono- and dizygotic, came from statistical investigations. Until fairly recently, zygosity was determined through a comparison of physical traits such as hair color and texture, eye shape and pigmentation, and fingerprints. As knowledge and techniques grew, so did the refinements in evaluation. A wide variety of methods for determining zygosity now exists, the best probably being tissue transplants, though the most common is a comparison of blood-group types, in which monozygotic twins are highly concordant. Since many studies, particularly the earliest ones, could not or did not establish zygosity in this manner, a look at some of the other methods and their validity is in order.

One of the oldest and most widely used methods is based on a tautological assumption. Since all monozygotic twins are assumed to be identical, then all twins who appear identical or nearly so in a variety of ways can be considered to be monozygotic. This is the basis of selection in most of the early studies. The method is a moderately good one for determining zygosity since later investigators (Cederlof et al. 1961; Cohen et al. 1975) have compared zygosity evaluations derived by these means with more modern methods and have estimated that correct evaluations were made in 90 to 95 percent of cases. A positive answer to the two questions "Were you and your twin ever confused by family members and other people?" and "When you were growing up, were you as alike as two peas in a pod?" (Cederlof et al. 1961) has been assumed to be a fairly accurate indicator of monozygosity. However, a recent and serious challenge to this long-held assumption has been raised by Carter-Saltzman and Scarr (1977), who found that twins themselves and outside raters incorrectly assigned zygosity in substantial numbers of cases, sometimes almost 40 percent of the time.

With Carter-Saltzman and Scarr's study in mind, the direction of error in the current sample becomes ambiguous. However, since other means of validation were used in substantial numbers of cases, my own impression is that the problem is not in the sets included for study, but the sets excluded. Many investigators first used a questionnaire about similarity before employing other methods. The "different" sets were assumed to be fraternal, and an unknown number of MZ twins who differed significantly probably were lost. Ironically, these are precisely the sets in whom investigators should be most interested since they presumably could give the greatest information on the differential effects of environment.

The same problem, but on a lesser scale, exists for studies that used palm and fingerprints as either a first- or second-level means of evaluation. MZ twins show about twice the rate of resemblance on dermatoglyphic characteristics as DZ twins of the same sex and an even higher proportion when compared with DZ twins of the opposite sex. Interestingly, they frequently show greater cross resemblance (between the two right hands or feet of twin partners) than internal resemblance (between the two hands or feet of one twin). The problem again is the loss of MZ twins who fall into the less similar category.

Dentition may turn out to be as reliable as, if not more reliable than fingerprints (see chapter 4), and, though it was not used specifically as a method of zygosity determination in the early studies, the extremely high rate of dental resemblance in this sample argues for homogeneous monozygosity.

Yet another criteria is based on an evaluation of the placenta, amnion, and chorion at birth. In the early years of twin research (indeed, until fairly recently), it was assumed that all MZ twins were born with a single placenta, double amnion, and single chorion. However, it now is known that all arrangements are possible, though many of the atypical cases die before birth. Physicians or midwives using the old criteria to determine zygosity at birth could have been misled or could have mistaken DZ twins with fused placentas as identicals. Fortunately, few of the MZ-reared-apart sets were evaluated solely by this means, so bias is minimal from this source.

Overall, everyone seems to agree that there are few sets in the reared-apart data that are not actually monozygotic. Only two sets were eliminated from the current sample on this basis, and my evaluation may have been overly conservative. As mentioned, the real problem is that an unknown number of identical subjects were overlooked or rejected because they were not identical enough phenotypically to be included using the methods of the time. This in itself biases the data in the direction of greater similarity throughout the sample than would be truly representative of all twins reared apart.

The net result is that close to 90 percent of the cases were chosen on a similarity basis before any other methods of determining zygosity were used. For example, the two studies that include the largest number of subjects, Shields (1962) and Newman et al. (1937), used similarity as the method by which sets were chosen in the first place. Only later were more discriminant methods used on the subjects thus selected. Newman sent out questionnaires asking about similarities in physical and psychological characteristics, and rejected those sets who showed noteworthy differences. As noted earlier, Shields acquired his sample by an appeal over television, thus limiting himself to those sets who knew of, or who suspected each other's existence. The same problem exists with almost all of the smaller twin studies, since often twins learned that they were twins only because they were so alike that they came to each other's and the investigator's attention. Only one series, the smallest in the literature, can be considered to be based on a truly representative sample since Juel-Nielsen (1965) discovered his subjects by tracing them through twin registries and other official listings, thus ensuring that their knowledge of each other was not the prerequisite for selection. Unfortunately, Juel-Nielsen's subjects account for less than one-tenth of the total sample, leaving the bias clear: *The MZ-reared-apart sample is not representative of MZ twins reared apart; it is representative of those sets who, despite environmental fluctuations, have remained very similar to each other.* The problems this raises for data interpretation are obvious.

Random Sampling: Assignment to Environments

In a truly representative sample, separated and reared-together sets would be randomly distributed throughout all socioeconomic classes and rearing conditions. A few would be rich, most middle-class, and a few poor. Placement via adoption or foster families would put children in homes generally different from those of their biological parents. Neither of these conditions is met even minimally in the data. Twins usually are separated because of poverty or death in the family. Though the different cultures and time spans make exact rating of socioeconomic status impossible, it is clear that most of the cases were born to poor families and reared in conditions not greatly different. Many were reared by relatives. The sample, thus, is highly biased in the direction of lower and lower-middle-class rearing conditions (see chapter 3).

The problem is compounded when one considers the reared-together samples with which the MZ twins reared apart are compared. Again, definitive information is lacking, but the impression is that the reared-together sets are more representative of middle-class groupings (Eysenck [1976] reports the same impression). No one has indicated, much less demonstrated, that reared-apart twins are representative of the society at large. Thus it seems that most generalizations have been made on the assumption of random distribution through environments, when, in fact, the comparison is between lower-class separated sets and middle-class reared-together partners. The nonrandom placement of adopted-out twins further assures a high similarity between rearing families and biological ones. Again, a marked bias is present that leaves suspect any unqualified generalizations from the data.[6]

Degree of Separation

The three basic criteria for a twin-reared-apart study are that the subjects be (1) MZ twins; (2) reared apart from early life; and (3) both available for investigation. Once having weeded out available from non-available subjects, the question arises of what constitutes being "reared apart." Though a few workers have attempted to define this quite loosely,[7] most agree that the criteria must be based on being raised in

6. The IQ literature has touched on this issue under the heading of G–E correlation. See C. Jencks et al. (1972) for a lucid discussion.

7. Studies of adolescent and adult sets who have lived apart for a few years (Hirsch 1930; Canter 1973) are not included in this reanalysis.

different families and in different locations. Anything short of this undermines the basic assumptions of the entire approach. These and related questions have been touched on in most large-sample studies, the
salient variable usually being age of separation.

However, two points are not even indicated in most studies. The first
is the degree to which partners in a set had some type of contact with
each other during their early years (childhood and adolescence), since
some subjects, though reared by different families in different towns,
did occasionally meet for periods ranging from a few hours to several
months. A number lived with each other for varying amounts of time.
The process of "twinning" can be assumed to have begun under such
circumstances, and it seems unavoidable that some significant impact
would be left from these meetings that would not be present in those
sets whose separation was more complete.[8] The problem seems to be
that no one knows if there is a lasting effect or, if there is, in what area
of functioning it would show.

The second point—the length of time the twins have spent together
after the separation but prior to study—is related to the first and appears never to have been analyzed in any study. Case histories are replete with illustrations of the repercussions the meetings may have on
partners, and there are scattered indications that personality shifts may
have taken place as a result. This sample is almost entirely affected by
mutual contact (only three cases being exceptions), and it is worth considering what residue has been left. Thus, the assumption that this is a
sample of reared-apart twins is incorrect. Most were reared apart only
partially, and almost all had contact with each other by the time they
were studied.

Awareness of Twinship

Related to the degree of physical separation is the degree of psychological separation between the partners. In many cases twins who met
the criteria of being reared in different families and sometimes widely
divergent environmental conditions always knew that they had a twin
living somewhere else. Psychodynamic theorists would postulate that
this in itself may be enough to allow a child to begin to formulate a
fantasy "twinning" with the absent partner, particularly if he has scattered bits and pieces of information about him. Such an occurrence
would be most likely to be significant when the environment in which
the child is raised is an unhappy one—which it was in many of these

---

8. Many authors have worked on the assumption that a brief meeting leaves insignificant impact. *Impact* in this sense is defined in quantitative rather than qualitative terms.
For those who ascribe to this belief, one may ask the standard question: Losing one's vir-
ginity took only a moment of time. Does this mean that the event is forgotten or had no
psychological "impact"?

cases—though many consider some degree of fantasy about imaginary families or sibs to be present throughout normal development, particularly for foster or adopted children. In cases of psychotic twins, there are instances where it seems reasonable to speculate that this fantasy may have contributed to onset and/or content of the disorder (see chapter 6); and one wonders if the effect is shown only in these extreme circumstances. Whether the knowledge of twinship becomes significant only when there is contact is unknown. Psychodynamic case studies on other variables could argue either way—for example, by using analogies to the differences between a child who idealizes a father killed in war and who constantly feels inferior because he cannot live up to his projected ideal versus a child whose mother remarries and gives him a new father, warts and all, with whom to more reasonably compare himself. Those who dispute the power of intrapsychic processes will dismiss the significance of this contamination. Those who believe in noteworthy intrapsychic influences will see it as a monkey wrench thrown in the works.

Factors Limiting the Expression of Genetic Variance

When discussing individual sets, it stands to reason to try to link differences between partners to variations in the environment, and similarities either to similar environments or to strong genetic potentials showing themselves despite environmental fluctuation. At certain points, however, data from many sets are pooled and the degree of similarity or difference of twins reared apart *as a group* becomes important. The prime example is when IQ scores are tabulated and their mean and variance computed. These figures, based on the twin-reared-apart population, can then be compared with other populations, such as nontwin siblings and unrelated individuals, in order to estimate how much of the genetic contribution is present.

Here a unique problem arises, and not the immediately obvious one of asking if the subjects were reared in a variety of circumstances. The important question, really, is whether some supraordinate environmental conditions automatically limit the expression of innate malleability of the organism, and whether these limiting factors are present in this sample. Several have been suggested: prematurity, atypical birth experiences, knowledge or contact with twin. Others potentially present are traumatic separation experiences, maternal deprivation, and/or malnutrition.

However, the factor most often mentioned in connection with limiting conditions is the issue of the low socioeconomic class of many of the subjects during their early years. As Dobzhansky (1973) notes, studies of aptitude and achievement test scores indicate that privileged children vary more than poor ones from the same population (as well as scoring higher on the average), thus suggesting that the limited variance in the lower classes is due not to a narrow range of endowment (since they are from the same population in genetic terms) but to an environmental limiting of expression. In other words, some characteristics of this sample may act to limit the amount of variance that would be shown otherwise, thus inflating the estimates of the contribution of the genetic coding.

One might use an example that by its very banality may serve to better highlight the point. Suppose a manufacturer in a southern climate produced mobiles which, when hung in the open-air rooms of his milieu, swing through an arc of up to ten inches. The mobiles are attractive and are sold to a northern distributor but, when hung in the sealed rooms of northern climates, they swing through a much smaller arc. The most meticulous and exacting of investigators, were he to sample primarily from the northern mobiles, would observe that the arc of the pendulums was rather limited, and he might conclude they were structured that way. His observation would be correct but the conclusion wrong because of the bias of his sample and the fact that the majority of his "subjects" were circumscribed in their expressivity because of the environmental conditions.

So also must one deal with caution when generalizing about statistics taken from the twin-reared-apart data. Not only is it biased in respect to the full twin-reared-apart population that potentially might be tapped, it also is biased from the population at large and cannot be used as directly representative of the full range of potentials open to individuals. Political arguments and ethical sensibilities have thus far centered this criticism around the IQ data. However, the limitation is true of all generalizations from this literature, and I suspect that once the faulty analyses and the nonsense about racial "strains" are relegated to the background they deserve, the truly challenging and, in indelicate hands, potentially dangerous topic will emerge as personality styles of individuals that have nothing whatsoever to do with group membership or race. It is the question with which the study opens, and it will be the question that lingers once the underbrush begins to be cleared away: Namely, what is inherent in the *individual* that leads him to formulate his unique mental representations of reality?

Notes on Statistics and Design

Genetics texts and, more specifically, behavior genetics texts, offer rigorous discussions of statistical procudure.[9] What follows is meant as an introduction and schematic representation of a few concepts, some of which have been discussed earlier. The reader versed in statistics and the reader genuinely dismayed by anything resembling numbers may skip it though terms will reemerge later, particularly in chapter 7 on IQ. There are many ways of lying with statistics,[10] but when the data are good and meet minimal design requirements, a statistical analysis is both invaluable and a safeguard. The problem with the data presented herein, as should already be evident, is that they are not good and do not meet even elementary design requirements. Thus it is surprising to learn of the extraordinary and complex approaches that have been devised to deal with these data and data like them. Fuller and Thompson are polite when they state that ". . . further developments in statistical methodology will not add appreciably at the time to our knowledge of the genetics of behavior traits. There still remains much to be done at a simpler and more basic level" (1978 p. 257). My own evaluation, particularly of the allegedly scientific analyses made of the IQ data, is more caustic. Suffice it to say that it seems that there has been a great deal of action with numbers but not much progress—or sometimes not even much common sense.

However, let us begin by assuming that any trait is a product of both hereditary and environmental factors. The aim is to learn the relative contributions of each. One way to go about it is to study groups of individuals with two assumptions in mind:

1. Some differences in the sample will be based on subjects acting in accord with different genetic blueprints.
2. Some differences will be due to subjects acting in accord with environmental fluctuations.

For the word "differences" above, let us substitute the term *variance*, a statistical concept that is a convenient shorthand for talking about fluctuations around a mean in a group. The question now can be phrased as "What proportion of the variance is attributable to the different genotypes in the group and what proportion to the different environmental backgrounds?"

Taking two groups, one of MZ twins and the other of DZ twins, the variance of the pairs around their respective group means can be computed, and the problem begins solution. In the MZ group, variance is

9. See Fuller and Thompson 1978 for a recent review.
10. See Jencks et al. 1972 for delightful examples.

attributable only to differences in environment (since genotype is held constant). In the DZ group, variance stems both from the different genotypes of the fraternal twins and from differences in environment. Schematically:

$$\text{Variance}_{\text{DZ}} = \text{Variance}_{\text{Environment}} + \text{Variance}_{\text{Genotype}}$$

$$\text{Variance}_{\text{MZ}} = \text{Variance}_{\text{Environment}}$$

Subtracting, we obtain:

$$\text{Variance}_{\text{DZ}} - \text{Variance}_{\text{MZ}} = \text{Variance}_{\text{Genotype}}$$
$$= \text{Heritability}_{\text{Broad}}$$

As an example, assume we examined the twins on trait X and discovered a variance in the DZ group of 20 and in the MZ of 5. Subtracting, we obtain 15, which, changed to a proportion (15/20) gives 75 percent as the proportion of the variance due to genetic contributions. In other words, 75 percent of the variance in the group of all twins for the trait X can be attributed to genetic factors and only 25 percent to environmental ones.[11] (See graph 1.1.)

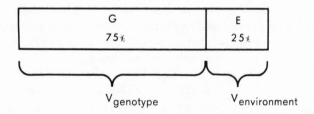

GRAPH 1.1
Initial heritability estimate for hypothetical trait X.

It would seem that this hypothetical trait X is not influenced very much by changes in the environment.

Suppose, however, that we consider further some of what was said about individual variation. Not only are there contributions from the genetic side and the environmental one, but also from the interaction of the two. The way a person perceives the world leads to his action upon it, which, in turn, alters the environment he next responds to. A

11. In the following bar graphs, G stands for genotype effects, E for the environment, G × E for the interaction between genotype and the environment, G - E for the genotype-environment correlation, and V for variance.

musically gifted person will utilize rhythm and sounds in a way that a
tone-deaf person in the same situation will not, while the tone-deaf
person, if he is athletically talented, may perceive and use motor cues
missed by others. We thus must add another element to the diagram. In
genetics it is known as the *genotype x environment interaction*, and, if we
continue with the hypothetical trait X, let us say that it accounts for 25
percent of the variance. (See graph 1.2.)

G	G×E	E
50%	25%	25%

GRAPH 1.2
Intermediate heritability estimate for hypothetical trait X.

The importance of direct genetic contributions now seems dramatically
less pronounced, and the plasticity of the organism is emphasized.

How do we compute this and from which side—genotype or environment—do we subtract the G × E component of variance? We cannot return to the original formula for broad heritability and simply
subtract MZ from DZ rates. If the MZ twins are reared in the same
home with, presumably, identical environments, we also must assume
the G × E interaction will be the same, leading the variance to look as if
it were stemming from genetic factors. If there are differences in the
same home environment stemming from more subtle nuances of interaction, it will show as differences *within* individual sets of twins, both
MZ and DZ, and may push heritability estimates in either direction in
ways not known without controlling for the exact environmental parameters. Thus some variance, not strictly gene-related, is hidden in
the simple heritability calculation. In practice, the variance from G × E
interaction usually is subtracted predominantly from the genotype
side. Using our bar graph as an example, the original estimate of 75
percent of the variance stemming from genetic factors can be superim-
posed on the new estimate to illustrate environmentally related sources
of variance that may be hidden in the simple heritability estimate. (See
graph 1.3.)

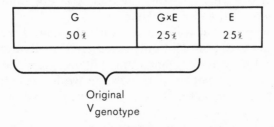

GRAPH 1.3
Intermediate heritability estimate for hypothetical trait X.

Similarly, other factors may limit the expression of full genetic potential in entire groups of subjects. For example, individuals raised in poverty may differ from each other, but *none* may show the full range of potential that they might under more enriched circumstances. If we examine only this group, or a sample taken substantially from this group, the limited variance will look as if it stemmed from limited genetic sources (since it affects *all* members of the group in question). Human societies automatically tend to introduce this source of bias because of the stratification embedded in even the most democratic ones. Children of poor people tend to have more limited ranges of enrichment and opportunity than children of the rich. Children of poor people who are adopted away still tend to be put in homes more like the homes of their biological parents than random placement would allow (Jencks et al. 1972). This causes the organism to appear less "plastic" because the full range of environments for the G × E interaction does not occur. The nonrandom distribution of genotypes is known as the *genotype-environment correlation*, and it too will tend to be obscured in the traditional heritability estimate. It is as if the previous bar graph had been split and one part was lying on top of the other. The full length of the bar (that is, the true degree of variance from all sources) is artificially lowered. (See graph 1.4.)

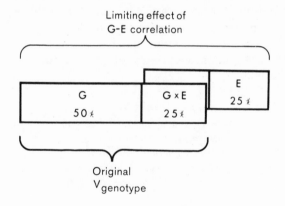

GRAPH 1.4
Intermediate heritability estimate for hypothetical trait X.

If we stretched the bar out to its full length, the proportions attributed to genotype, G × E, G - E, and environment would change. In the example, the original bar was four units long. Two units were attributed to genotype, and one each to environment and G × E interaction. The new bar might be five units long, with two units representing variance due to different genotypes, and one unit each representing G × E interaction, G - E correlation, and environment. Recalling the original heritability estimate of 75 percent, it emerges that substantial environmentally related effects were hidden, and the more accurate estimate of the direct effects of different genotypes in the population is reduced markedly. (See graph 1.5.)

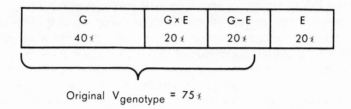

| G
40 % | G × E
20 % | G – E
20 % | E
20 % |

Original $V_{genotype}$ = 75 %

GRAPH 1.5
Final heritability estimate for hypothetical trait X.

In animal studies, some attempt to distinguish these sources of variance may be done by (1) controlling strictly for genotype and environment and (2) assuring random distribution (thus eliminating G - E correlation). This leaves the G × E interaction more clearly delineated. Bodmer and Cavalli-Sforza (1976) and Gottesman (1972) cite a well-known example. If two strains of rats, one bred for "brightness" in running mazes and one for "dullness," are distributed through three controlled environmental conditions, one can observe the interaction of each strain with the environment and begin to estimate the range of plasticity. Table 1.1 is an adaptation of the example in the Bodmer–Cavalli-Sforza text.

TABLE 1.1

Maze running for two strains of rats raised under three environmental conditions (adapted from Bodmer and Cavalli-Sforza 1976, Gottesman 1972, and Pettigrew 1964).

	Number of Errors	
Environment	Bright	Dull
Enriched	112	120
Normal	117	164
Deprived	170	170

Within the normal range the two strains appear quite different. The "bright" ones are bright and the "dull" ones, true to their label, do poorly.[12] However, the overall range of performances is similar for both strains (58 versus 50 errors), indicating that both have roughly comparable degrees of "plasticity" (sometimes called *reaction range*), if the full spectrum of environments is examined. It is the specific G × E interaction that accounts for their seeming disparity. Under normal rearing conditions, "bright" rats appear to have an inherent capacity to make use of environmental nutriments to a degree unavailable to the "dull" ones. For "dull" rats, it takes a superdose of stimuli before the innate capacities become mobilized.

Such studies are not possible with humans. But let us, for the moment, construct a "thought experiment." Assume a wealthy scientist-ancestor wished to learn how similar genotypes respond to different rearing environments. For subjects he took sets of MZ quadruplets, $A_1A_2A_3A_4 \ldots N_1N_2N_3N_4$, randomly chosen and thus representative of genotypes in the population. He took the first two partners in each set, separated them, and placed one in a deprived and one in a normal rearing environment. He defined the environments by macroscopic variables (SES), education, and so forth and assumed that the full range of microscopic variables (attitudes, child-rearing customs, and so forth) that correlate with the macroscopic variables were present. In a genuinely random sample, this is a fair assumption to make. In effect, he set up an experiment similar to the "bright rat" one cited earlier, using only one strain and two environmental conditions. Genetic variance and macro- and microscopic environmental variance are controlled, and there is no G - E correlation. These circumstances are depicted in table 1.2.

TABLE 1.2

Rearing Conditions	
.	.
.	.
.	.
C_1	D_2
D_1	C_2
B_1	A_2
A_1	B_2
Deprived	Normal

Family →

← Environment →

Alas, our ancestor, in addition to being wealthy and omniscient, was fond of English detective novels. He disappears, taking all notes delin-

12. Actually, the position may be reversed under other conditions, leading contemporary experimentalists to use the labels "maze bright" or "maze dull" (Fuller and Thompson, 1978).

eating environmental conditions with him, leaving us with a single typed list of which subjects match up in pairs. We know he eliminated genetic variance and varied only family and environmental conditions. Therefore, we know that all variance computed by comparing partners stems from within family or between environment sources (plus measurement error due to the imperfection of our tests). This is restated in table 1.3.

TABLE 1.3

Later Comparison	
$A_? - A_?$	—differences due to effect of
$B_? - B_?$	family on subject
$C_? - C_?$	—differences due to different
. .	environments
. .	
. .	

or:

$$V_{\text{MZ reared apart}} = V_{\text{Environment within group}} + V_{\text{Environment between group}}$$

If we restated this in terms of correlation, knowing each partner came from a different environmental condition, the degree of their similarity to each other would account for the genetic likeness they showed despite the different rearing conditions. The remaining differences (transformed back into variance terms) would be attributable to the effects of environment, broken into the same within-group and between-group terms described above. The similarity is known as an *intraclass correlation*, r', and when used with MZ twins reared apart is assumed to be one of the best indicators of heritability$_{\text{broad}}$.

Let us now redo the experiment using the last two members of our quadruplet sets, $A_3A_4 \ldots N_3N_4$. We shall keep everything the same, including the same families, except that we assume our ancestor placed the partners *together* in families to be reared as twins. The original conditions and the later comparisons are depicted in tables 1.4 and 1.5.

TABLE 1.4

	Rearing Conditions	
	.	.
	.	.
	.	.
	C_3C_4	D_3D_4
Family →	A_3A_4	B_3B_4
	Deprived	Normal
	← Environment →	

TABLE 1.5

	Later Comparison
$A_3 - A_4$	—differences due only to effect of
$B_3 - B_4$	family on subject (same environ-
$C_3 - C_4$	ment for both partners in each
• •	set)
• •	
• •	

Since our later computation is done for all subjects (we do not know which belonged to the deprived or normal groups), and since it is done pairwise, the environmental condition does not enter into the variance. *Both partners* in each set were subjected to the same environment, no matter which type, and they should not differ from each other on that account. The only source of variance, other than measurement error, will stem from family (within-group) effects. This usually leads to the following proposition:

$$
\begin{array}{ll}
V & -V \\
\text{MZ reared apart} & \text{MZ reared together} = \\
V & +V \\
\text{Environment} & \text{Environment} \\
\text{within group} & \text{between group} \\
-V & \\
\text{Environment} & \\
\text{within group} & \\
\end{array}
$$

$$
\begin{array}{c}
=V \\
\text{Environment} \\
\text{between group}
\end{array}
$$

This is the paradigm for studies of twins reared apart. They are assumed to give an estimate of broad heritability (via correlation) and an estimate of the effects of different environments (via differences in variance). Further, it is assumed that the "within-group" variance is about the same for reared-together and reared-apart sets, with any differences being based on slight anomalies between twins, slight random differences in family attitudes, and measurement error. "Slight anomalies" in this context refers to prenatal differences and the like, all of organic derivation.

A review through our thought experiment, however, indicates that this latter proposition and, hence, the paradigm, is slightly in error. Remember that the second experiment was an exact replication of the first, even to using the same families. Assuming the "slight anomalies" are randomly distributed (you're no more likely to have prenatal trouble and sequelae if you're a reared-apart twin than if you're a reared-together twin), it becomes evident that the sources of within-group variance were identical for both situations, except that in the second experiment the subjects were reared as twins. Thus, in comparable samples, the within-group variance between monozygotic twins reared apart and monozygotic twins reared together may give an estimate of the potency of one purely intrafamily and psychodynamic variable: twinning.[13]

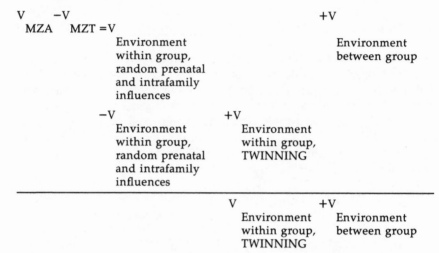

How close is the actual data to the "well-designed experiment"? Obviously we do not have MZ quadruplets, but with samples of MZ twins representative of the genotypes of the population at large, a close approximation could be obtained. In order to fulfill the experimental requirements, the following would be needed:

1. Genetically identical individuals (MZ twins).
2. Random selection, thus allowing the assumption that reared-apart and reared-together samples are representative of their respective populations and of the population at large.
3. Random assignment to rearing conditions (thus eliminating G - E correlation).
4. Reared-apart sets actually are reared as single individuals with no contamination from twinning.
5. No organic but nongenetic features within pairs (such as prematurity, birth trauma) to artificially inflate or deflate heritability estimates.

To the question of how close the actual data are to the ideal (or even minimal) requirements, the answer is that they approach them hardly at all. The only requirement that seems fulfilled is the assumption that MZ twins are genetically identical. Thus, *all results of this study or those*

13. See Jencks et al. 1972 and Fuller and Thompson 1978 for more rigorous discussions including numerous other sources of error not discussed here.

that have preceded it must be considered speculative. No conclusion from twin-reared-apart data as they now exist is generalizable, and until a reputable and rigorous study is done, anything discussed herein should be construed only as speculation about which areas of investigation might bear fruit and which might not.

Summary

What, then, are we dealing with? The following appears to be the general outline of the problem.

Within the larger twin literature there is a small, fragmented, and rather obscure literature on monozygotic twins reared apart. The value of these studies lies in the fact that they are the only studies on human subjects where the genetic component is constant while environmental components are variable. Some investigators have questioned the identical-genotype hypothesis, but it, of all assumptions, remains the most unshaken. Often those who deal with this literature liken it to a laboratory experiment. They assume that similarities stem from hereditary factors and differences from environmental agents. They also assume that each twin acts as a control for the other, so that discordance indicates an environmental factor influencing one that was not present for the second. However, this assumption can be shown to be overly simplistic for a number of reasons.

First, the analogy of the controlled experiment is useless in practical application since too much data is missing and, more important, since the most elementary design requirements have not been met. Second, although the twins may be identical genetically, this does not mean they are identical at birth or any time thereafter. Frequently they are not. Environment begins prenatally, and factors such as blood supply, birth trauma, or prematurity may combine to produce differences that last throughout the individual's lifetime. Even if sets have fairly equivalent prenatal and birth experiences, the assumption of complete physiological similarity is still not justified. Mirror imaging of one type or another may exist from the instant the cells divide into twins, and this can have lasting consequences, ranging from the mundane details of opposite-handedness, to what some believe may be far-reaching correlaries in hemispheric dominance and cognitive or general personality styles.

Finally, even if all of the preceding issues were eliminated or controlled, it still could not be assumed that differences in a twin set indicate purely environmental shaping with no hereditary components involved. Quite simply, there is no such thing. For the environment to assume valence, the predisposition must be present. To cite the axiom, everything is both 100 percent genetic and 100 percent environmental. Thus the question must be rephrased to ask how much of the variance within and among twin sets may be ascribed to environmental factors, not a simple counting of "this heredity" and "that environment." And the question of how much of the variance over all sets is limited by the factors of prematurity, knowledge of each other, and low socioeconomic status—factors that permeate the sample—must be raised.

Why then bother to study these cases if a multitude of complications present themselves? Because, quite simply, they are the best sources available on the nature-nurture question in human subjects. Also, despite all the cautions above and more, these MZ twins *are* genetically identical people—two of any one of us—who have lived in different worlds.

This leads to the last point. Are these twins really from different environments? The answer, even at this early stage, has to be a qualified "only sort of." Some twins studied were more separated than others, and many had either intellectual knowledge of the partner or noteworthy contact. The implications of these complications have to be acknowledged though in the broad view, the twins do come from different backgrounds, sometimes stunningly different ones.

Regarding the sampling procedures themselves, can we trust them? The best estimate, again, is only a qualified yes. Aside from questions of just how separated any set really was, the broader problem is that the vast majority of subjects were chosen precisely because they were so alike. In fact, only one study (on less than 10 percent of the sample) even approaches the criteria of having selected a representative group of MZ twins reared apart. All of the others are decidedly biased in the direction of the most similar pairs being the only ones studied. The more unalike sets, some of whom probably were MZ twins and who offered the richest information, were eliminated in the first go-round of sample selection. This, thus, raises a tautology. We wish to study variations in phenotype while geneotype is a constant, yet almost 90 percent of the time phenotypic similarity was the basis for assuming the genetic identicality.

So again, why bother? Basically, because nothing else like these cases exists in the literature or quite approximates them. They may answer questions. They must be analyzed before a better study can be designed. In the next chapter, individual studies will be summarized and, for those who remain skeptical, perhaps the fascination will become clearer. For those already hooked on the idea of what Juel-Nielsen once ruefully toasted as "monozygotic monomania," the maddening gaps, omissions, and inexplicable findings may begin to take focus.

Chapter 2

Prior Studies

TWINS: AFTER 40 YEARS, A "MIRROR"

CINCINNATI (UPI)—On Aug. 19, 1939, a 14-year-old unwed girl gave birth to identical twin boys in Piqua, Ohio. The twins were adopted by different families—the Ernest Springer family in Piqua, and the Jess Lewis family in Lima, Ohio, 45 miles away. They grew up in different homes, 45 miles away, and led separate adult lives. The Lewis twin, who learned from his adoptive family that he had a brother, kept searching for him. Nearly 40 years after birth, he found probate court records this year that led him to his brother, now living in Dayton, Ohio. When the twins got together, they discovered some amazing coincidences:

—Both had been named Jim.

—Both boys had named their pet dogs "Toy."

—Both took law enforcement training. Both enjoyed similar hobbies: blue-printing, drafting and carpentry.

—Jim Lewis had been married three times, Jim Springer twice. Both their first wives were named Linda. Both their second wives were named Betty. Both named their first sons James Allan.

"When I went to meet my brother for the first time," said Jim Lewis, "it was like looking in a mirror." Both are 6 feet, weigh 180 pounds, have dark hair and brown eyes, identical faces. University of Minnesota researchers recently examined the two for a week. "They found out that our brainwaves and heartbeat patterns are the same," Springer said. "Our handwriting is similar. We have virtually identical fingerprints. Our eye and ear structures are exactly the same. And," he added," all the tests we took looked like one person had taken them twice."

New York Post, May 9, 1979

CASE XV: EDWIN AND FRED

This is a remarkable case of identical twins, young men of twenty-six years, who were separated in very early infancy and . . . have led extremely parallel lives. Both have been electricians for telephone companies. Both married at about the same time, the wives being of similar types. Each has a four-year-old son, and they lay stress on the fact that each owns a fox terrier dog named Trixie. . . . According to their statements, both of them from early boyhood on were obsessed with the idea that they had a brother who died and often stated this to their playmates. . . . [It emerged] that when the twins were small boys they had attended school together for a short time and the other children had often noticed their close resemblance. The twins had even noticed the resemblance, but they were not close companions and never knew they were twin brothers. It occurs to us that this early association of the twins may have led to the above-mentioned mutual feeling about a brother who had died. [And I wonder what child in their mutual grade school owned a dog named Trixie—S.F.]

. . . Their visit with us at the time of the Chicago World Fair was made even more interesting . . . by reason of a confusion of dates which resulted in their coming to us at the same time as a pair of young female twins. The two pairs of twins became great friends . . . [and] visits to the Fair were made together, each young man taking one of the young women. When they walked about, people were startled to see one couple walking ahead and a duplicate couple following behind. Everywhere they went they attracted attention and enjoyed the sensation they created. On one occasion they attended a sideshow featuring a pair of Siamese twins and, according to their statement, stole the show, attracting more attention than the exhibits [adapted from Newman et al. 1937, pp. 147–148, 281]

Though cases crop up in newspapers or stroll into sideshows, causing a stir, few reports of separated twins have filtered into the scientific literature. There is no central registry of reared-apart sets or even an updated bibliographic reference file. The gap seems inexplicable in view of the ubiquitous citation of individual cases in medical and psychological texts and the ferocious debates that sometimes accompany use of the data. It is more understandable if one considers the multinational nature of the reports and the quite remarkable obscurity of many of them.

Overall, the literature[1] contains references to 121 sets of separated monozygotic twins scattered through more than thirty books and articles. The starred items in the bibliography contain the core citations. The compilation has been checked by twin investigators, and should be fairly exhaustive. Some error is possible where cases have been extracted from studies that reuse cases and give them new index numbers, but insofar as is known, this source of error has been eliminated in this study.

Table 2.1 lists the known studies in order of their appearance and also gives brief indications of the types of topics studied and the amount of detail available from the case histories.

Cyril Burt's publications are not listed since his cases appear to be fraudulent (Hearnshaw 1979). None of his alleged 53 sets is included in the data analysis (or in the listing of 121 sets), a loss that is not great in any event since no information has ever been offered on them other than purported IQ scores and minimal SES data. Should any of his cases prove authentic, they would overlap substantially with Shields's sample, an overlap Shields never mentioned.

1. Only literature from western nations was surveyed, including a few studies from Japan. I am unaware of Soviet or nonwestern sources.

TABLE 2.1
Studies of monozygotic twins reared apart.

Year	Author	No. Pairs	Ages	Case Topic	Case History	Detail	Source
1922	Popenoe (also Muller 1925, Saudek 1934a)	1	Adult	Nature-Nurture	Yes	✔✔✔	Chance
1931	Wagenseil	1	Adult	Race	Yes	✔	Chance
1931	Lange	1	Adult	Crime	Yes	✔	Convicts
1934	Saudek(b)	1	Adult	Nature-Nurture	Yes	✔✔	Chance
1935	Rosanoff et al. (also Farber, Shields, Craig 1979)	1	Adult	Psychosis	Yes	✔✔✔	Hospital
1936	Bouterwek	2	Adoles.	Nature-Nurture	Yes	✔	Chance
1937	Rosanoff et al.	1	Adult	Mental Deficiency	Yes	✔	Hospital
1937	Fukuoka	1					
1937	Newman et al.	19	Child Adoles. Adult	Nature-Nurture	Yes	✔✔✔	Public appeal
1938	Kallman	1	Adult	Psychosis	yes	✔✔	Hospital
1940	Gardner et al.	1	Adult	Nature-Nurture	Yes	✔✔✔	Chance
1941	Essen-Möller (also in Kaij 1960)	1	Adult	Psychosis	Yes	✔	Hospital
1941	Yates & Brash	1	Adoles.	Nature-Nurture	Yes	✔✔✔	Chance
1941	Yoshimasu	1	Adult	Crime	Yes	✔	Convicts
1942,49	Burks (and Roe)	5	Child Adoles. Adult	Nature-Nurture	Yes	✔✔✔✔	Chance
1943,50	Stephens (and Nunemaker) (and Thompson)	1	Adult	Nature-Nurture	Yes	✔✔✔	Chance
1945	Craike and Slater	1	Adult	Psychosis	Yes	✔✔✔	Hospital
1952	Schwesinger	1	Adoles.	Nature-Nurture	Yes	✔✔	Chance
1952	Stenstedt	1	Adult	Psychosis	Yes	✔	Hospital
1956	Kallman and Roth	1	Adoles.	Psychosis	No	✔ (from Rainer 1977)	Hospital and records
1958	Dencker	1	Adult	Head Injury	No	✔	Hospital
1960	Kaij	3 (+1 Essen-Möller)	Adult	Alcoholism	Yes	✔✔	Twin register
1961	Slater	2	Adult	Hysteria	Yes	✔✔	Hospital
1962	Shields (includes Slater 1961)	42 (+2 Slater)	Child Adoles. Adult	Nature-Nurture	Yes	✔✔✔✔	Public appeal
1963	Tienari	3	Adult	Psychiatric Illness	Yes	✔✔	Twin register
1965,80	Juel-Nielsen	12	Adult	Nature-Nurture	Yes	✔✔✔✔	Twin register
1964,67	Kringlen	4	Adult	Psychosis	Yes	✔✔✔	Hospital
1969	Lindeman	1	Adult	Nature-Nurture	Yes	✔✔✔✔	Chance
1972	Inouye (also in Mitsuda 1972)	9	Adult	Psychosis	No	✔✔ (from Inouye 1978)	Hospital
1973	Prokop and Druml	1	Adult	Psychosis	Yes	✔✔	Hospital

✔ Very low
✔✔ Moderate
✔✔✔ High
✔✔✔✔ High and includes tests and/or information on biological parents.

It is instructive to examine the "source" column in the table. It indicates the method of selecting the cases for study in the first place. In theory, the only type of study that could be considered to be broadly generalizable would be one that studied the topic of nature-nurture and that excluded no set by virtue of its being very much alike or very much different. There is only one such study, the one on twelve sets by the Danish investigator Juel-Nielsen (1965, 1980). In choosing his subjects from twin registries, Juel-Nielsen's only criteria were that they were MZ, separated early, and both alive at the time of study. All other studies using twin registries, with the exception of Tienari's, selected only those sets having specific disorders, thus potentially biasing the data on other variables and excluding anyone not having the disorder. Tienari also studied all separated MZ twins within a certain geographical area of Finland, but his three sets were separated so late or so poorly that they carry little weight in the overall reanalysis.

Bias also is present for the twelve studies (covering seventy-six sets) that recruited subjects on the basis of "public appeal" or "chance" information coming to the investigator's attention. Almost all of these sets knew of each other's existence, and often they learned of this because of their striking similarity to their absent twin. The similarity was not confined to physical appearance. It also included voice, mannerisms, and sometimes traits that would have to come under the broad rubric of "personality." The subjects chosen via hospital admissions are doubly biased, since not only were they twins who knew each other, but also were sets where at least one partner showed some striking psychiatric or social dysfunction far beyond the norm.[2] *Thus, approximately 90 percent of the known cases of separated MZ twins have been studied precisely because they were so alike. This circular reasoning undermines the generalizability of patterns in the sample to the population at large.*[3]

On the positive side, table 2.1 indicates that subjects of all ages and many nationalities are represented. In recent years, an increasing number of studies of psychosis in twins has appeared, in keeping with the trend toward looking for a genetic predisposition to mental illness in hope of discovering biochemical factors that might be involved. This places an overabundance of severely disturbed individuals in the sample; still, the majority are not classified as psychotic, alcoholic, mentally deficient, or socially deviant. It is doubtful that anyone would claim

2. One might compare Juel-Nielsen's data with the rest of the sample to estimate how definite the bias and in what direction. This is done to a degree, in later chapters, but an overall comparison is impossible because degree of separation, as discussed in chapter 3, reduces his twelve subjects to numbers too small for generalization.

3. In the long run this may turn out to be a tempest in a teapot, for it may be that physical appearance, voice, and mannerisms have such a high heritability across all sets that when confronted with each other, most twins would have an immediate flicker of recognition. However, until we know better, high concordance in physical traits in the sets who discover each other should be assumed to be potentially related to high concordance on other variables such as personality, IQ, or psychiatric status.

the sample to be representative of any society, but it does seem to have a core group of subjects from middle and lower-class backgrounds.

The amount of detail cited in the reports is highly variable. A scattering of reports contains no more than a mention that a separated set was studied, while others present data so uneven or sparse as to simultaneously whet the reader's curiosity and set his teeth on edge. The occasional article, usually from one of the Axis powers during World War II presents data filtered through political-psychological models baffling to the contemporary reader. Another small number—almost exclusively American—is written with a moralistic rhetoric that is almost prissy. By and large, however, a substantial body of case histories of moderate to good detail exists, the best being the British and Scandinavian work.

Since new information on a few of the sets has been uncovered and, equally as important, since many reports are difficult if not impossible for the average reader to obtain, a brief summary of some will be presented. All summaries on psychotic twins are reserved for chapter 6. Though the summaries fail to do justice to the originals, they may serve to introduce the questions one might ask and to suggest common findings that can be checked against results presented in later chapters of this work.

Individual Cases

P. Popenoe (1922). This brief three-page entry in the *Journal of Heredity* was one of the first scientific reports on a set of twins reared apart and remains of scientific as well as historical interest to this day. The twins, *Bessie* and *Jessie,* were separated at two weeks of age because of their mother's illness and were permanently separated at eight months, following her death. They met again for a few months at ages eighteen, twenty, and twenty-four, though they corresponded from at least the age of eighteen on. Both were raised on the American western frontier at the turn of the century. *Bessie's* family moved through many states, and she received only four years of formal education, while *Jessie* remained settled and finished courses beyond high school. Popenoe was struck with their physical similarity (a photograph accompanying the article well substantiates this claim) and seemed particularly intrigued with the similar onset and course of attacks of "weak lung," better known to us as tuberculosis. He quoted a letter from *Bessie*

... and [we] have been run down from that cause, and nearly always at the same time. I am very sorry that I cannot remember exact dates of illness, but many times our letters bearing word of enforced idleness have crossed, until we began to expect to hear of the other's illness as soon as one of us was indisposed.

Bessie continued with notes on mental similarities:

It is almost uncanny, the way we are always doing identical things at the same time. The latest instance is in having our hair cut, each without the other's knowledge. This really took courage, because the majority of our friends do not approve. We are both high strung and do not conserve our energy as we should, but I have been resting more gracefully this summer than I ever have before, and in her latest letter she [*Jessie*] expresses the same mood.

Popenoe's article leaves one with the impression of vast mental and physical similarities between the two women, similarities much, in Popenoe's mind, like the psychic similarities allegedly binding together Siamese twins.

The well-known geneticist H. J. Muller soon became interested in the case and in 1925 published a detailed study that established zygosity and, for the first time, utilized intelligence and personality tests as tools of evaluation. He noted that on IQ testing both women scored very high and received similar scores—*Bessie* 156 and *Jessie* 153 on the Army Alpha test. How could this be explained in view of the large difference in educational level (fourth grade versus college-level courses)? Muller noted that, despite the difference in years of formal schooling, both actually had approximately similar educations—one obtained in classrooms, the other by voracious reading in a home that encouraged it. Though he used this feature of the case histories to indicate that the twins' backgrounds were not, all in all, very different, nonetheless he concluded that a substantial portion of the Army Alpha test—"when applied to persons of a given social class and territory"—may tap a genetic or inherent capability little affected by moderate degrees of variation in environment.

And what of personality tests? Here Muller drew a blank. He found the twins essentially no more alike on many variables than unrelated individuals. He found this explicable on the basis of some environmental differences but baffling in the face of clear observational similarities. For example, the twins had similar interests, vocations (teaching), alertness, zest, and "stance," and behaved virtually identically in even minor details of many aspects of the examination. Regarding their medical history, one twin had a "nervous breakdown" (not fully explained in any report) and the other almost had one either prior to or at about the time of their first meeting. Both were considered quite alike by themselves and many who came in contact with them. Muller concluded that the personality tests did not tap whatever features of "personality" might have a genetic basis, though it strongly was indicated that there might be some, and he called for better tests, all the while cautioning against too rapid an assumption of genetic rather than environmental transmission. He added that the twin relationship itself seemed to have had some effect on the twins' concordances—the two became more like each other over time, yet, paradoxically, one twin married only when the other had an unhappy romantic loss.

In 1935 Robert Saudek of London reanalyzed the case, adding more historical information and essentially attempting to prove that the study of handwriting was a good tool for identifying personality differences. His findings based on graphological analysis agreed with Muller's on personality discrepancies between the two women; some differences were maintained over time and even became accentuated (one twin traveled to Europe, an experience that reportedly changed her moral code considerably compared to her married twin who remained home on the farm; it is not quite clear how Saudek viewed this early feminist budding). He believed the twins were far more different in personality than first impressions seemed to indicate, and he noted that the twins probably interacted with each other to try to accentuate similarities.

With these three articles, all on the same set of twins, the general outline of the debates and dilemmas of all later investigators seem established. There is the finding of similar IQ scores and the embryonic question of how much can be attributed to genes and how much to similar environment. The quandary of how to evaluate personality variables emerges. The question of a twinning interaction is raised, and finally there is the overall tenor of several methodological approaches to the material: descriptive, empirical, and a touch here and there of vaguely mystical awe.

A. J. Rosanoff, L. M. Handy, and I. R. Plesset (1937). As part of an extensive study of twins where one or both showed mental deficiency, the team of Rosanoff, Handy, and Plesset included one reared-apart pair. Though the set appears to be among the more separated of those in the literature, unfortunately, the degree of detail is low. Briefly, the case (#91) described twin girls, the illegitimate offspring of a mentally retarded woman, who were placed separately for adoption while still infants. "As they matured, each got into trouble repeatedly, mainly on account of sexual promiscuity with illegitimate pregnancy, etc." (1937, p. 25). At age twenty, exactly one month apart, each was committed to the same women's reformatory. They had different names, and neither they nor the institution staff knew they were twins. However, their close similarity in both appearance and behavior led to an investigation that unearthed their history. No mental tests were done, but they were recognized as mentally retarded and were observed in occasional epileptic seizures (type not stated). One twin was released from the reformatory at age twenty-two, but she was in and out of institutions until age twenty-four when she married and disappeared. The other also was released at age twenty-two, but within three months was reinstitutionalized and ended in an almshouse where she eventually was studied at age thirty-eight. From ages twenty-four to thirty-eight she was diagnosed as having mental deficiency without established epilepsy and without psychosis.

N. Yates and H. Brash (1941). Though the reference is obscure, the British pair of MZ twins studied by Yates and Brash emerges as one of the most separated sets mentioned in the literature. The boys were adopted at three months by different couples. Each child grew up not knowing he was adopted until age fourteen and without knowledge of being a twin until a series of "mistaken-identity" accidents led to the boys' meeting at age sixteen. They were studied only a few months after this initial meeting.

Both were named John. For convenience, one was called *JJ* and the other *JB.* Extensive physical examinations indicated great similarity (even to the shape of their teeth), but, remarkably, intellectual testing consistently produced a difference of about 19 points in IQ. Since the boys had almost identical educational experiences and since there were only minor differences in the observable milieu of each, the authors were at a loss to explain the large discrepancy. Other tests also produced differences that had been obscured by the initial impression of likeness. Two tests provided particularly interesting results. The first, a test of musical ability, produced no overall similarity of pattern in scores although both boys had shown a precocious musical talent, a talent all the more striking in view of their academic mediocrity. The second, a battery of tests on reaction times to auditory, tactile, and visual stimuli—the only one of its kind in the literature—produced responses that appeared to the authors to be more widely scattered than should have been expected from MZ twins. Though history is meager, all in all it is a detailed case on a highly separated set.

S. Yoshimasu (1941).[4] This early Japanese report tells of *Kazuo* and *Takau,* brothers who were separated at birth and studied at age thirty-two. The case is interesting because of an unusual twist—one brother went to prison for theft and embezzlement while the other became a Christian minister. Both had tuberculosis and a history of stammering. Despite the ostensible differences in occupation—prison versus pulpit—Yoshimasu estimated that both men shared a "weak-willed" nature that had been channeled differently.

B. Burks (and B. Burks and A. Roe) (1942, 1949). In the early 1940s Bar-

---

4. The case was not translated in time to be included in the index. However, all information from it has been footnoted in the relevant analyses.

bara Burks, well-known to American adoption workers, began publishing what she evidently intended to be a series of studies on separated MZ twins. Her work is notable for the detailed psychological testing and rating systems used and for the fine quality of her evaluations. Burks—and later workers can be grateful to her for this—not only drew her own conclusions but also published the raw data of the tests for others to investigate as they wished. The final four cases, published after her death with the assistance of Anne Roe, who organized the notes, are available in *Psychological Monographs* and do not warrant extensive summarizing here. The histories are sometimes detailed and sometimes only sketches. The one case where zygosity was questioned by Burks herself as well as later workers (see Shields 1962) has been omitted from the current analysis in the interest of conservatism.

Burks's first case, originally published in a book in honor of Lewis Terman, is more difficult to obtain, and is worth summarizing:

Adelaide and *Beatrice* were separated at nine days and placed in adoptive families of somewhat above-average socioeconomic status. *Adelaide's* family moved many times, and she and her mother often quarrelled. Discipline was strict, administered by the mother, and extreme enough that when *Adelaide* showed tendencies to use her left hand, her mother tied it behind her back until she used her right. *Adelaide* was enuretic two or three times a week until four and then less than once a week until nine. The mother punished and scolded her for this. The girl bit her nails continuously until twelve and then had relapses from twelve to eighteen, when she still was gnawing at the cuticles. Menarche was at ten years four months, but her second period did not occur until about eleven and one-half and the third at twelve and one-half. By eighteen she was regular.

Beatrice had a more comfortable life, was scolded less and accepted more. When she started to use her left hand, her mother also tied it behind her back but stopped on doctor's orders. Of her own accord, *Beatrice* learned to write with her right hand but used her left otherwise. She was bladder trained by two, but became enuretic from three and one-half to nine. She was not punished for this. She bit her nails until the age of sixteen. Menarche was at eleven and one-half and was irregular at first. By eighteen she was in a normal cycle.

Both girls weighed the same at one year and walked at about the same time (fourteen to fifteen months). *Adelaide* crept shortly before walking while Beatrice skipped creeping entirely. Both were emotionally labile as babies to a rather noteworthy degree. Both girls were bossy in their first contacts with playmates. *Adelaide's* mother called it "irritability" and talked of her "demandingness." *Beatrice's* mother called it "excitability." Overall, one gains the impression that the girls were quite alike as babies; it was the mothers' descriptions that varied considerably.

How would such differential child-rearing attitudes affect the girls in later development? At twelve and one-half *Adelaide* and *Beatrice* met the examiner. "Each child shook hands without perceptible pressure, smiled fleetingly and turned her head away." Both had similar hobbies and similar disinterests. However, differences emerged. *Adelaide*, from the more hostile mother-child relationship, rarely had friends over and seemed isolated. *Beatrice's* house was filled with her friends.

The difference in sociability continued into adolescence, and by eighteen, *Beatrice* was far more popular and engaged with friends than *Adelaide*. *Beatrice* looked forward to planning for her future and thought of helping others. She had found a teacher in high school toward whom she felt warmly and who influenced her considerably. *Adelaide* remained as before, telling of no adolescent role-model, seeming somewhat withdrawn and irritable, and not persevering in tasks. She began "blossoming" somewhat shortly before eighteen, but the impression is that she did not match her sister. Burks wrote that the major differences seemed to be in the happier mood and tone of *Beatrice* and her firmer belief in the pleasures of social interaction. *Adelaide* was only beginning to catch up.

Both continued to show an underlying lability, and psychological tests suggested even deeper concordance. Rorschachs were more similar than were those of twins reared together, and both girls were rigid and subservient to authority. Both had suggestions of hidden rebellion and defiance, which they studiously tried to control.

All in all, it seems that the twins remained identical in developmental milestones, symptoms, and underlying temperament. The major difference was in mood and pleasure in people. *Adelaide*, from the harsher home, trusted less and showed less warmth than *Beatrice*. Their earliest memories reflect this—*Adelaide's* memories were of the birth of a sib, of damaging a car, of the new baby being hurt, and of wetting her father while he held her in his lap; while *Beatrice's* included trips to a grandmother who gave her gifts, singing and playing in the sandbox, and fighting with a male cousin.

The problem with the similarities between the girls is that the twins knew each other throughout development. They spent much time together up to the age of two and one-half, summers together in childhood, and maintained contact through adolescence. Hence, conclusions are difficult to evaluate.

F. E. Stephens and R. B. Thompson (and F. E. Stephens and J. C. Nunemaker) (1943,1950).[5] The problem of the twins knowing each other does not exist in the case of *George* and *Millan*, first published by the

5. Further information on this case could not be obtained despite the cooperation of both Drs. Stephens and Nunemaker. Case records may be stored in the Veterans Administration, but they could not be located in time to be utilized in this reanalysis.

American investigators Stephens and Thompson in 1943. Again, this is an instance of one of the more obscure references producing one of the most clearly separated sets.

George and *Millan* were separated at birth and adopted into different families who ended by living more than two thousand miles apart. Neither knew he was a twin until the age of eighteen; until this time *George* did not even know that he had been adopted. At the age of nineteen the boys managed to make contact and met for the first time. They were studied at the time of this first meeting. They were so similar in physical appearance that neighbors mistook them for each other. Contrary to some other cases, their intellectual and psychological tests were strikingly similar even to the underlying pattern by which they achieved overall scores. One was slightly more robust physically (surprisingly, the "city boy"), and the authors thought they could verify slight differences in "social attitudes" such as "freedom from antisocial tendencies" or in school relationships, but the overall similarities were so strong that the tests were rechecked because it was thought an error had been made.

In 1950, a second report on this set appeared, this time by Dr. Stephens in conjunction with John C. Nunemaker, then with a Veterans Administration Hospital in Salt Lake City, Utah. It emerged that the twins had spent a few weeks together at age nineteen when they were first studied and then had gone their separate ways without further meetings. During World War II both entered the armed forces, *George* becoming a glider pilot and *Millan* joining the Coast Guard. In 1943, at almost exactly the same time and without knowledge of each other's illness, the twins developed symptoms of spondylitis (a progressive, crippling disease of the spine). The authors investigated the onset and course of the disease, noting the marked similarity even of the X rays and response to treatment, and were struck with what appeared to be a high degree of genetic susceptibility not only to the disorder but also to the form of its expression. A family pedigree is included in the report, showing no instances of spondylitis and only a few instances of the related disorders of rheumatism and arthritis.

The reports, in particular the second one, clearly demonstrate the sometimes exceptional concordance in physical traits and disturbances one encounters in the literature on separated twins, but they are not as rich in investigating the history or psychological makeup of the two men.

E. Slater (1961).   Eliot Slater, well-known to twin investigators, included one set of separated monozygotics as part of the series in his November 1960 Maudsley lecture. The case, MZ8, was reported in greater detail by Shields (1962) in his comprehensive survey (case SmP9: Harry and Alfred).

Briefly, the boys were separated at three weeks and, although they claimed separateness, they attended the same schools with *Harry* discovering he was a twin only at age ten. After school their lives took different courses, and they lived without contact for twenty-two years until they met at the time of investigation at age thirty-nine. They were so different in appearance at this time that only blood groupings convinced the investigators of their monozygosity. *Harry* was three and one-quarter inches taller and sixty-two pounds heavier than *Alfred*. Slater noted the twins to be somewhat discordant for hysterical symptoms at the time of his investigation. *Alfred*, the twin from the poorer environment, exhibited anxiety, fainting spells, and a psychogenic symptom of pain in his heel so severe it required medical and psychiatric treatment. *Harry* showed no similar symptomatology.

Interestingly, Shields followed this set past the initial reunion and learned that *Harry* had been in an accident at age thirty-nine and had been unable to walk because of "shock." The symptom was so similar to his twin's "heel pain" of six years earlier that some mutual identification process was suggested.

B. Lindeman (1969).   This entry is one of the more unusual ones, for it stems from a popular book published in the United States in the late 1960s. The story is told of *Tony* and *Roger*, MZ twins separated at two weeks and reared apart with no contact until age twenty-four. The two came from quite different backgrounds. Tony grew up as an indulged child in an Italian Catholic family. Roger was raised in the Jewish faith and spent his childhood bouncing from institution to foster care to contact with his somewhat untrustworthy father. Their meeting occurred partly through a search instigated by one twin and partly through a series of mistaken-identity incidents crossing several state lines on the eastern seaboard.

When they reunited, each felt he had found something important. They lived and worked together for six years prior to the time Lindeman wrote of them. In many ways they tried to become alike; their searching for sameness reached such proportions that those who loved them began to despair. Lindeman felt they were almost merging into one person.

IQ and psychological testing was done, though detailed results were not given. The book is not a scientific study, nor does it pretend to be. Though it suffers at times from dramatic digressions into the vaguely mystical link Lindeman thinks exists between the two men, it nonetheless is an interesting book and the material presented is both rich enough to warrant reanalysis and not so different from similar cases published under more rigorous guidelines.

Series of Cases

Excluding Cyril Burt's work, three large series of twins reared apart have been published: Newman et al. (1937), Shields (1962), and Juel-Nielsen (1965).

H. H. Newman, F. N. Freeman, and K. Holzinger (1937). This is the first of the large-scale studies on twins reared apart and probably is the best known. Since it remains in publication and is easily obtained, the summary here will be brief. In the late 1920s, Newman, a biologist, Freeman, a psychologist, and Holzinger, a statistician, joined together at the University of Chicago to study the nature-nurture issue via large twin samples. In the course of the work, and with the inducement of a free trip to the Chicago World's Fair, they managed to gather nineteen sets of separated monozygotics. The first nine cases were published by Newman in different issues of the *Journal of Heredity* but were revised and updated for the 1937 book.[6] In this latter work, the reared-apart sets were compared with fifty identical and fifty fraternal sets who had been reared together.

The separated twins (twelve female and seven male sets) ranged in age from eleven to fifty-nine, the majority of them being young adults. Interviews, physical examinations, and IQ and personality tests comprised the inventories.

In some areas the results were expected. For example, the IQs of the reared-apart sets, while highly similar, were less alike than those of the monozygotics reared together, but were more similar than the fraternals reared in the same home. Roughly expressed, the rank order went as follows:

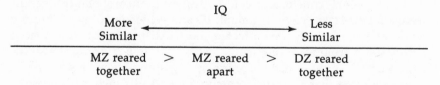

Physical characteristics such as height, weight, and appearance were highly concordant, though since the twins were chosen by a similarity method in the first place, this reasoning is tautological. (The analysis of blood groupings had not yet been developed as a method of determining zygosity.)

The paradoxical finding was in the area of personality structure. Analysis of personality tests and observer ratings indicated that the

6. The 1937 book incorporates and corrects the earlier work. Therefore, only it will be referred to here.

reared-apart twins often seemed more alike than the reared-together sets, a result that has threaded its way through later studies and that might indicate that when the potent twinning interaction is avoided, the inherent genetic predisposition shows itself more forcefully. Again, roughly expressed, the rank order of the personality evaluation was:

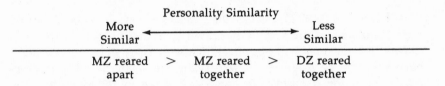

Personality Similarity

More Similar					Less Similar
MZ reared apart	>	MZ reared together	>	DZ reared together	

The results were perplexing to the authors, and despite the alleged similarity on tests, they noted differences in "personality" that, though they sometimes sensed them strongly in interviews, they could not quite articulate. When they tried to correlate variations in personality or IQ with similarities or differences in the twins' backgrounds, they failed. None of their environmental ratings seemed sufficiently explanatory. However, as later workers have indicated, the grounds of Newman et al. for rating environment were singularly narrow, usually revolving around socioeconomic factors and excluding almost entirely any in-depth thought about psychodynamic interactions in the foster family. Also, despite the exceptional detail unearthed in the study, massive gaps remained in information on the functioning of the twins and the environments from which they came.[7] The omissions were confounded by the writing style that was dictated by the mores of the day, which required an exceptional delicacy in describing symptoms and, when mentioned at all, sexual functioning.

In the end, the overall results were so paradoxical and ambiguous that only general conclusions could be offered: Anthropomorphic traits were affected least by environment; IQ and achievement were affected more; and personality was affected most. All in all, the conclusions hardly differ from what one would expect before beginning the study. However, the authors had some intriguing speculations. For example, they suggested that there may be components of functioning close to the physiological level that are unique to each individual but which never, or rarely, show in what we usually term personality. If we were to translate this into terms of "temperament" or "arousal patterns," the suggestion has a surprisingly contemporary ring.

In a later paper (Gardner and Newman 1940), Newman noted that

7. While writing this book, I attempted to track down the original data, ambiguously said to be stored "in the archives." Despite the help of the University of Chicago library, the Library of Congress, and examination of the stored files of correspondence between Newman and Holzinger, the data could not be found. As a result, all information rests solely on the published case reports as they emerged in the 1930s.

the authors were split in their opinions on the 1937 book. The biologist (Newman) and statistician (Holzinger) were struck by similarities and gave less weight to environment. The psychologist (Freeman) was struck by differences and gave less weight to heredity. This split in opinions also has a thoroughly contemporary flavor.

In total, one may say that *Twins: A Study of Heredity and Environment* (1937) is remarkable and is to be respected for including raw data for others to use. It developed statistical methods used to this day. However, it also is flawed by the delicacy of description and lack of clinical evaluation. Perhaps one of the major flaws is that the control groups were not adequate controls at all. The reared-apart sets were predominantly adult, the controls predominantly children. The tests used often were suitable only for adults but were given to children and analyzed anyway. Still, the book is enjoyably readable, thoroughly reputable, and decidedly thought provoking. It is unfortunate that it remained the only easily available resource on the subject for so long, since later works by Shields and Juel-Nielsen are more detailed. (Shield's 1962 book has been out-of-print for a decade, and Juel-Nielsen was published in the United States only as this manuscript went to press.)

J. Shields (1962). The wide-ranging and exceptional investigation on forty-four sets of separated twins by the British worker James Shields was the first major study after a twenty-five-year hiatus. It includes far and away the largest sample of twins and, to quote Juel-Nielsen, ". . . entailed enormous labour . . . meticulous care and . . . critical treatment and interpretation of the collected data" (1965, p. 35). Subsequent to this work on reared-apart twins, Shields, in conjunction with I. Gottesman, became a major figure in behavioral genetics for his work on predisposition to schizophrenia.

During the early 1950s Shields appealed on a BBC television program for separated twins to step forward in the interest of research. The resultant outpouring produced forty-one sets of separated MZ twins and a smaller number of dizygotics. Shields added three sets known from other sources (cf. Slater 1961), and detailed his findings in his 1962 work.

Overall, the subjects consisted of fifteen male and twenty-nine female sets ranging in age from eight to fifty-nine years. Most were interviewed by Shields himself, others by his colleagues. In addition to psychiatric evaluations, the twins filled in booklets and took IQ and personality tests. Where possible, details of physical examination were included. Control groups of forty-four MZ and thirty-two DZ twins reared together and matched for sex were used to balance the interpretation of results.

The material is so rich as to defy condensation. Perhaps the most tantalizing data are the complete case histories of all of the sets. In general, however, the patterns found by Shields were in moderate to close agreement with those of Newman et al.

For example, IQ scores tended in the same direction as the Newman findings, with reared-together sets being most similar and separated sets second. The differences between the two groups were smaller in the Shields study than in the American work, but the tests were not the same (Shields used the Mill Hill Vocabulary Scale in conjunction with the Dominoes Intelligence Test, while Newman used the Otis and Stanford Binet). Unlike the Newman study, Shields's study indicated a slight tendency for discrepancies in IQ scores to correlate with discrepancies in early environment and degree of separation. Females who menstruated first tended to have higher IQs than their partners.

The evaluations of personality variables produced a problem similar to that found in earlier works. For example, paper-and-pencil tests of personality characteristics such as "neuroticism" or "extroversion" indicated that reared-apart sets tended to be more alike than their reared-together controls. As earlier researchers had done, Shields raised the possibility that being reared as a twin may overshadow genetically based tendencies toward identical functioning. Nonetheless, the impression of differences in personality that were not shown on the objective tests remained, and to deal with this Shields utilized a rating system based on impressions from interviews. Here he found slightly more indications of differences in the parted sets than in the reared-together ones. None of these tendencies was statistically significant, but it did seem significant in another sense, the same as reported by numerous other workers: namely, that standardized tests found separated sets quite similar while human interaction somehow picked up on nuances of unique individuality that were hard to articulate. Shields also noted the often striking similarity in the description and expression of physical and psychological symptoms.

It is rather remarkable that this work has not obtained higher circulation in the United States. It is almost always quoted in articles on the heritability of IQ, a fairly minor investigation, yet often is bypassed in articles on personality development or structure. Perhaps this is due to the American belief in being able to shape both individual and environment, though an equally plausible explanation lies in the data and results themselves, which puzzle and provoke rather than conforming to clear patterns allowing easy categorization.

N. Juel-Nielsen (1965). While Shields investigated the largest sample of twins reared apart, it could be said that that the Danish psychiatrist Juel-Nielsen has produced, overwhelmingly, the most in-depth work. His study was of twelve sets of Danish pairs (three male, nine female), ranging in age from twenty-two to seventy-seven. The selection procedure leaves them representative of Danish reared-apart twins and the extensive case histories include not only interviews with the twins and their mates and siblings, but also information on the biological and foster families. Extensive medical work-ups were included. In many instances, the twins themselves did not know the information Juel-Nielsen unearthed. Compared to most other studies, the data provide an embarrassment of riches. Both Juel-Nielsen and the reader are left with the problem of digesting and sorting out such quantities of information.

Statistical treatment was limited because of small sample size. However, the analysis of IQ produced results similar to those in the larger studies. Twins reared apart were similar in overall IQ scores (using the Wechsler-Bellevue Form I and the Ravens progressive matrices), with their average difference in the same range as in the Newman's and Shields's studies. Interestingly, as did Shields, Juel-Nielsen found the tendency for the IQ score to be influenced by differences in education and separation, though statistical significance was reached only in the analysis of verbal scores. The more separated sets had more divergent scores, and those with greater differences in education showed greater differences in verbal abilities.

Differences in personality functioning were more difficult to evaluate because the test used was the Rorschach (its first usage since the Burks's study years before), an instrument notoriously difficult to quantify for research purposes yet thought by many to be better designed to pick up subtleties than less subjectively scored tests. Juel-Nielsen was struck with how similar the Rorschach reports were to his own clinical evaluations. Overall, he estimated that two of the sets were very much different in personality, four were about equally alike and different, and six were very much alike. His summary is one of the clearest yet published:

In all 12 pairs there were marked intra-pair *differences* in that part of the personality governing immediate psychological interaction and ordinary human intercourse.

In their attitude to the investigator, and to others, the twins behaved, on the whole, very differently, especially in their cooperation, and in their form of and need for contact.

Corresponding with these observations, the twins gave, as a rule, expression to very different attitudes to life, and very divergent views on general culture, religion and social problems. Their fields of interest, too, were very different.

These personality differences found concrete expression in their references to, and attitudes towards, their early environments, to their present situations in life and to their families. In this connection, it was remarkable that their spouses presented no similarities whatsoever, neither in personality nor in outward appearance; on the contrary, in every case they appeared quite different and accorded with the twins' own different attitudes as to how family, marital, and, particularly, sexual problems were to be treated. Those twins who had children treated, on the whole, their children differently, and their ideas on upbringing were, as often as not, diametrically opposed.

Characterologically, the twins presented differences in their ambitions and in their employment of aggressive behavior. Emotionally, there was a deep-going dissimilarity with regard to the appearance of spontaneous emotional reactions or to the control of affective outbursts. Various traits of personality found their expression in differences in taste, mode of dress, hair style, use of cosmetics, the wearing of a beard or of glasses. Finally, it must be noted that their handwriting seemed strikingly different.

The most striking intra-pair personality *similarities* were found in the twins' general appearance, especially in their motility pace, their carriage, their gait, their movements, their gestures and in small involuntary movements such as a turn of the head or the hands, their facial expression, especially their smile or their laughter, to say nothing of their voices which, both in tone and pitch, were strikingly alike in spite of the various differences of dialect, vocabulary and linguistic proficiency.

Striking, too, were the similarities between the descriptions of their symptoms, which often tallied remarkably, and must be expressions of similarly experienced physical and psychical phenomena.... Similarities [such as these] must be taken to be a clear expression of hereditary behavior. Shields (1962) makes the same point. [emphasis added; Juel-Nielsen, 1965, pp. 75–76]

It is interesting that Juel-Nielsen, a clinically trained psychiatrist, concluded that, while early experiences undeniably have profound impact in at least some areas, the middle years of life and the serendipitous events that happen during them may have more effect than many had previously thought. Eventually he concluded that the question of what is hereditarily determined and what is environmentally determined is misleading. The more pertinent issue may be how a particular genotype is affected by various environmental conditions—each genotype assimilating experience in its own way. Hence the title of his work is not *Heredity and Environment* but *Individual and Environment,* a direct statement of the uniqueness, including genetic uniqueness, of the person.

Other Reports

The remaining eleven case reports on nonpsychotic twins all are of poor quality. A twelfth case, Fukuoka's, was unobtainable.

Wagenseil's Micronesian-American sisters are of dubious separation, their parting probably coming only in late childhood or possibly as late as when one decided to become a steamship hostess on the Yokohama run.[8]

8. I am grateful to Dr. N. Gedda of Rome, Italy, for sending this article after repeated library searches in this country failed to unearth it.

Easen-Moller's set separated only after age seven, and the same problem exists for *Lange's* study of criminal twins.

Kaij and *Dencker* gave compact reports in which the degree of contact is unclear and history is minimal. At least one set is of doubtful zygosity.

Bouterwek's paper gave minimal detail, enough to eliminate one pair for late separation (seven years) and to raise a question about the other pair, who were reared together past the age of nine. *Saudek's* brothers also were reunited at nine and their history is minimal, though testing is reported.

This leaves *Schwesinger's* report, which is an interesting anecdotal case, but, again, of dubious separation. *Esther* and *Elvira* were Mexican-American sisters, reared in homes next door to each other. Despite this, one of the girls claimed she did not know she was a twin until adolescence, when the discovery supposedly came as a shock. Both girls became delinquent, and one was found dead of a morphine overdose.

Chapter 3

The Combined Sample

> We have never had a disagreement between ourselves, and while I am fond of my older sister and two brothers, yet they have never seemed as close to me as Bess.
> —*Jessie* about *Bessie* in a letter to Popenoe, 1922, p. 144

> He is the most unpleasant person I have ever come across.
> —*Kaj* about *Robert* to Juel-Nielsen, 1965, p. 132

Not every twin likes meeting his partner. Though not as succinct as *Kaj*, many meet, experience emotions ranging from awe to disgust, and leave to go their own ways with little if any further contact.[1] More, it seems, meet and find themselves pulled into a strange, boundary-blurring union that they find hard to articulate but that they struggle to label as profound. Psychoanalysts might speak of narcissism, and of the ebb and flow of cross-currents toward fusion with a person seen as a carbon of oneself and toward panic as one runs from a merging that threatens to dissolve the boundaries of uniqueness. Less analytically oriented observers write of the frequent pattern that, on meeting for the first time, partners exchange clothes and exceptional intimacies as if belatedly trying to form twin bonds, and how, "accidentally on purpose," partners sometimes become involved in events that mirror those

---

1. *Kaj's* distaste for his brother did not abate with time. At the followup, he remembered only in passing to tell Juel-Nielsen (1980) that *Robert* had dropped dead of a heart attack a few years earlier.

experienced by their twin. With a novelist's license, Lindeman describes it:

In the five years during which I have watched them grow close as brothers, I
have also witnessed a blurring of their personalities until Roger Brooks becomes, if only temporarily, a mirror twin to Tony Milasi. He is then a reflection
of his monozygotic partner, subordinating his will and life-style in order to
share his brother's attention and love. [1969, p. 223]

One probably could learn a great deal about identity by studying
reared-apart twins at their first meeting and in the later vicissitudes of
their relationship. What seems more important for our purposes is that
"twinning"—that psychic phenomena of shuffling similarities and differences—seems not limited to childhood. The case histories and the
twins' own voices state that there is, for them at least, the *experienced*
impression that a potent interactional effect is occurring after meetings
in adulthood. One is reminded of Juel-Nielsen's observation that the
middle years of life may allow for more malleability than has previously been thought. To whatever degree there is a belated twinning effect
for those partners who meet after separation, that response must be
considered to be an environmental pressure, and research must seek to
determine in what way, in what areas, and to what degree this interactional effect colors the fundamental similarities and differences between partners.

It is interesting that although age of separation and global impressions of overall degreee of separation have been studied, no one has
systematically included degree of contact and potential twinning prior
to interviews. The omission is understandable given the eagerness to
analyze any case that presents itself—as Shields said, subjects are so
rare that it is best to spread one's net wide—but overlooking this
source of bias seems a disservice to the data and to the importance of
the questions being asked. In the material that follows, the degree of
separation between partners and the amount of contact after reunion
but prior to study has been kept in mind.

Table 3.1 gives the reclassification of all 121 sets of twins reared apart
mentioned in the literature. They are grouped into six broad categories.
Since the last three eliminate sets on the basis of doubtful zygosity,
minimal information, and/or late separation, the first three groups are
the only ones important for reanalysis. Reclassified, the core sample
(groups I, II, and III) contains 95 sets, three-fourths of the total mentioned in the literature. The other one-fourth must be eliminated by
even the roughest evaluation.

Of these 95 sets (hereafter referred to as "the sample"), a number of
features are of interest. If we assume three broad classes as possible di-
visions—I. Highly Separated, II. Mixed Separation (little or no contact
during separation, much contact thereafter), and III. Little Separation

TABLE 3.1
Index of monozygotic twins reared apart.

Case #	Name	Sex	Hand: R,L, Amb.	Birthweight in grams	Birth order	Age of separation	Knew was twin prior to reunion?	Age learned
GROUP I. HIGHLY SEPARATED								
Ia. No knowledge of twin; interviewed soon after reunion								
102	George/Millan	M	L/LR			Birth	no	19
104	Olga/Ingrid	F	R/R			2 mo	no / yes	35/22
106	JJ/JB	M	R/R			3 mo	no	16
108	Palle/Peter	M	R/R			10 mo	no	22
110	Madeline/Lillian	F	R/L		1/2	16 mo	yes/no	23/36
112	Olive/Madge	F	R/R			Birth	yes	child/9
Ib. No knowledge of twin; little or no contact after reunion and prior to study								
114	Kamma/Ella	F	A/A-L	{more {less		Birth	no	12
116	Bessie/Jessie	F	L/L			Birth(8 mo?)	no	18
118	Paul C/Paul O	M	R/R			2 mo	no	21
120	Esther/Ethel	F	L/R			6 mo	no	30
122	Mary/Gertrude	F				infancy	no	20
124	Gladys/Helen	F	R/R			18 mo	no	28
126	Tristram/Russell	M	L/L	{2608 {2041	1/2	20 mo	no	7
128	Marjorie/Norah	F	L/R		1/2	22 mo	no	19
Ic. Learned was a twin prior to reunion; met in adulthood; little or no contact prior to study								
130	Signe/Hanne	F	R/R			3 wks	yes	14
132	Amy/Teresa	F	R/R		1/2	6 mo	yes	5 or 6
134	Florence/Edith	F				9 mo	yes	child
136	Berta/Herta	F	R/R		2/1	4 yrs	yes	child
Id. Learned was a twin prior to reunion; met but had little or no contact prior to study								
138	Lois/Louise	F	R/R	{2722 {2268		Birth	yes	child
140	A/B	F	R/R		1/2	Birth	?	?
142	Kenneth/Jerry	M	R/R			1 mo	yes	12(3?)
144	Raymond/Richard	M	R/R			1 mo	yes	child
146	Maren/Jensine	F	R/R	{less {more	1/2	6 wk	yes	child
148	Millicent/Edith	F	L/R		2/1	3 mo	yes	child
150	Mildred/Ruth	F	L/R	{2722 {1588		3 mo	yes	child
152	Betty/Ruth	F	R/A			11 mo	yes	child
154	James/Reese	M	L/R			"1st yr"	yes	child
156	A/B	F				12 mo	yes	child?
158	Edith/Fay	F	R/R			14 mo	no	16
160	Thelma/Zelma	F	R/A			18 mo	yes	child
162	Gene/James	M	L/R			25 mo	yes	child
164	Maxine/Virginia	F				30 mo	yes	child
166	A/B	M		{3600 {3800		36 mo	yes	child
168	Martha/Marie	F	R/R	"tiny"		42 mo	yes/no	child/?
170	Astrid/Edith	F	R/R	{2500 {2000	1/2	42 mo	yes	child

Age met	Age seen	Degree of contact over lifespan (0=none, L=little, M=much); ages 0–6; 6–10; 10–20; 20+	Years apart and degree of contact: None, Little, Much	Comment	Reared by: Parent, Relative, Other	Original ID
19	19	0/0/0	19N		O/O	Stephens, G&M
35	35	0/0/0/0	35N		O/O	Juel-Nielsen II
16	16	0/0/0	16N		O/O	Yates & Brash
22	22	0/0/0/0	22N		O/O	Juel-Nielsen I
36	36	M-0/0/0/0	1M,35N		O/O	Shields sf9
39	35	M-0/0/0/0	3M,32N	1/week until age 3; no contact until after study.	P/R	Shields sf8
12	50	0/0/0-L/0-L	12N,38L		O/P	Juel-Nielsen VII
18	30	0/0/0-L/0-L	18N,12L		O/O	Popenoe (Muller, Saudek)
21	23	0/0/0/0-L	21N,2L		O/O	Newman III
30	39	0/0/0/0-L	30N,9L		O/O	Newman XIV
20	38	0/0/0/L?-0	20N,18L-N		O/O	Rosanoff '37,91
28	35	M-0/0/0/0-L	1½M,27N,7L		O/O	Newman XI
7	18	M-0/0-L/L	1½M,6N,11L		P/O	Shields sm3
9	36	M-0/0/0-L/0-L	2M,17N,17L		O/O	Shields sf10
20	54	0/0/0/L	20N,34L		R/O	Juel-Nielsen VIII
17	55	0/0/0-L/L	17N,38L		R/P	Shields sf26
24	52	0/0/0/0-L	24N,18L		O/O	Craike & Slater
49	43	M-0/0/0/0-L	4M,32N,9L	Different continents; letters ages 36–49; seen age 43; met age 49.	O/P	Shields sf19
child	18	L/L/L	18L		O/R	Gardner L&L
?	33	L/L/L/L(?)	33L	Sparse information.	R/R	Shields sf6
? & 12	19	0-L/0/0-L	12N,7L	Met once at age 3.	O/O	Newman XIII
child	13	L/L/L	13L		O/O	Newman VII
child	37	L/L/L/L	37L		R/R	Juel-Nielsen III
child	40	L/L/L/L	40L		R/P	Shields sf14
child	15	L/L/L	15L		R/R	Newman VIII
5	12	M-L/L/L	1M,4N,7L		O/O	Newman X
child	27	0-L/0-L/0-L/0-L	26LN		R/R	Newman XVIII
child?	58	M-L/L/L/L	1M,57L		P/R	Stenstedt 106
16	38	0/0/0/M-L	2M,15N,21L	Lived together 1 yr; some contact thereafter.	O/O	Newman V
child	29	M-L/L/L/L	1½M,28L		O/O	Newman XII
child	14	M-L/L/L	2M,12L		O/O	Newman XVII
child	11	M-L/L/L	2½M,9L		O/O	Newman XVI
child	33	M-L/L-0/L-0/L-0	3M,3ML,27LN		O/PO	Tienari 1080
?	49	?	3½M,46L	Case reports "little contact."	O/R	Juel-Nielsen VI
child	72	M-L/L/L/L	3½M,69L		P/O	Juel-Nielsen XI

TABLE 3.1 *(continued)*
Index of monozygotic twins reared apart.

Case #	Name	Sex	Hand: R,L, Amb.	Birthweight in grams	Birth order	Age of separation	Knew was twin prior to reunion?	Age learned
	Ie. Highly separated but with intervals of more intensive information or contact							
172	Megan/Polly	F	R/R		2/1	Birth	no	17
174	Alfred/Harry	M	R/R		2/1	Birth	yes/no	10/39
176	Herbert/Nicholas	M	R/R	{less more	2/1	Birth	?	5
178	Karin/Kristine	F	R/R	{more less	1/2	3 wks	?	6
180	A/B	M				2 mo	yes	child
182	Edwin/Fred	M	R/R			6 mo	no	25
184	Petrine/Dorthe	F	R/L	{2500 less	1/2	12 mo	no	12
186	Gertrude/Helen	F	R/R	{1360 1360		12 mo	no/?	13/?
188	Ingegerd/Monica	F	R/R	{1375 1125	1/2	12 mo	yes	child
190	Keith/Edward	M	R/R		2/1	24 mo	yes	child
GROUP II. MIXED SEPARATION								
	IIa. No knowledge of twinship; much contact after reunion in adulthood							
202	Tony/Roger	M	R/R	{less 2835		2 wks	no	24/7
204	Earl/Frank	M	R/R			6 mo	no	23
206	Kaj/Robert	M	R/R			9 mo	no	40
208	Eleanore/Georgiana	F	R/R			18 mo	no	21
210	Alice/Olive	F	R/L			18 mo	no(?)	18(?)
212	Clara/Doris	F	R/A			24 mo	?	?
214	Olwen/Gwladys	F	R/R		1/2	30 mo	no	21/24
	IIb. Knowledge of twinship; little or no contact during separation; much contact after reunion in childhood							
216	Joanna/Isobel	F	R/R		1/2	Birth	yes	child
218	Mary/Nancy	F	L/R			Birth	yes	child
220	Rodney/Barry	M	R/R		1/2	Birth	yes	child
222	A/B	M		{2000 2200	1/2	Birth	yes	?
224	June/Clara	F	R/R	{2722 1134	1/2	Birth	no	8/14
226	Kaete/Lisa	F				Birth	yes	child
228	James/Robert	M	R/R		1/2	3 wks	yes/no	child/10
230	Jacqueline/Beryl	F	R/R	"very tiny"	1/2	3 wks	yes	child
232	Ronald/Dennis	M	R/R		1/2	1 mo	yes	child
234	A/B	F		{3000 2800		1 mo	?	child
236	Richard/Kenneth	M	R/R	{1361 1134	1/2	3 mo	yes	5-6
238	Jessie/Winifred	F	R/R	{less more	1/2	3 mo	yes	5
240	A/B	M		{1500 1700	2/1	20 mo	yes	?
242	Adelaide/Beatrice	F	AR/A			9 days & 30 mo	no(?)	8
244	Ada/Ida	F	R/R			36 mo	yes	child
246	William/Stanley	M	R/R		2/1	48 mo	yes	child

Age met	Age seen	Degree of contact over lifespan (0=none, L=little, M=much); ages 0-6; 6-10; 10-20; 20+	Years apart and degree of contact: None, Little, Much	Comment	Reared by: Parent, Relative, Other	Original ID
17	32	0/0/0-L/L-M-L	17N,2M,13L	20-22 wrote weekly.	P/O	Shields sf5
39	39	M-0/L/L/0	3M,12L,24N	Contact till 3; same school 6-18; "not close."	P/R	Shields sm9 (Slater mz8)
5	22	0-M/0-M/L/L	5N,1M,16L	Lived together at 5 & 7½ for less than 1 yr periods.	R/O	Shields sm4 (Slater mzll & Gottesman MZ 17)
6	64	0/0-L/L/0-L	6N,58L	Met once per yr in late childhood.	O/R	Juel-Nielsen IX
child?	23	0-?/0-?/0-?/M-?	20LN,1M?		R/P	Rosanoff '35 (Farber et. al)
25	26	0/0?0/0/0-L	23N,2?,1L	Same school ages 6-8 but "did not know."	O/O	Newman XV
16	70	0/0/0ML/L	1½M,15N,54L	Lived together age 18 for 6 mo.	O/P	Juel-Nielsen X
13	52	M-0/0/0-M/M-L	1M,12N,39L	Visited twice/yr past 13; apart as adults.	O/P	Burks & Roe G&H
child	42	M-L/M/M-L/L-0	8M,34L	Lived together for 7 yrs.	PR/RP	Juel-Nielsen IV
11	38	M-L/L/LM0/0	2M,36LN	Same orphanage but met only at 11, 13, & 20.	O/O	Shields sm8
24	30	0/0/0/0-M	21N,23M		O/OP	Lindeman
15	37	0/0/0M0/0-M	23NL,14M	"Cousins"; met age 15; families wrote often.	O/R	Burks & Roe E&F
40	45	0/0/0/0-M	40N,5M		O/O	Juel-Nielsen V
21	27	M-0/0/0/0-M	7½M,19N		O/O	Newman II
18	19	M-0/0/0/0-M	2½M,16½N		O/O	Newman I
30	39	M-0/0/0/0-M	11M,28N		O/O	Burks & Roe C&D
24	48	M-0/0/0/0-M	26½M,21½N		O/O	Shields sf22
5	50	L-M/M/M/M	5L,45M	Same family since 5.	R/P	Shields sf24
8	47	0/0-M/M/M	8N,39M	Same family since 12.	R/P	Shields sf21
9	34	0/0-M/M/M	9N,25M	Same family since 9.	R/P	Shields sm7
8	36	0/0-M/M/M	8N,26M	Same family since 8.	P/RP	Tienari 173
8	41	0/0-M/M/M	8N,33M		O/O	Shields sf16
child	<22	0-L/0LM/L-M	10NL,12LM		R/R	Kallmann 1938
10-11	49	0/0-M/M/M-L	10N,14M,15L	Much contact 10-24.	P/R	Shields sm12
16	41	0/0/0-M/M	16N,25M		R/R	Shields sf17
9	20	L/LM/M	9L,11M		P/R	Saudek 1934
9	15	0/0-M/M	9N,6M	Same family since 9.	R/R	Bouterwek E115
9	14	0/0-M/M	9N,5M	Once per wk since 9.	P/R	Shields sm1
2 & 5	8 & 16	0LM/L-M	2N,6M	Same school since 5.	O/O	Shields sf1
16(?)	38	?/?/?-M/M	18M,14L	A in mental hosp. 29-36 yr.	O/R	Kringlen #22
8	12 & 18	M-0/0LM/M	6N,6L,6M	Much contact to 2½; summers together 6½-12½; wrote 12½-18.	O/R	Burks '42 A&B
16	59	M-0/0/0-M/M	13N,46M		R/R	Newman VI
child	39	M/0/0-M/M	10N,29M	Same family since 14.	O/O	Shields sm10

TABLE 3.1 (continued)
Index of monozygotic twins reared apart.

Case #	Name	Sex	Hand: R,L, Amb.	Birthweight in grams	Birth order	Age of separation	Knew was twin prior to reunion?	Age learned
GROUP III. LITTLE SEPARATION								
302	Bertram/Christopher	M	R/R		1/2	Birth	yes	child
304	Kathleen/Jenny	F	R/R	{2948 / 1588}	1/2	Birth	yes	child
306	Laura/Charlotte	F	R/R	{stronger / weaker}	1/2	Birth	yes	child
308	Timothy/Kevin	M	R/R	{weaker / stronger}	2/1	Birth	yes	child
310	A/B	F		{less / more}	1/2	7 days	no	7/10
312	Nina/Christine	F	R/R		1/2	3 wk	yes	child
314	Annie/Trixie	F	R/R	{more / less}	1/2	1 mo	yes	child
316	A/B	F		{more / less}	1/2	3 mo	yes	child
318	Mabel/Mary	F	R/R			5 mo	yes	child
320	Harold/Holden	M	L/R			6 mo	yes	child
322	Frederick/Peter	M	R/R		2/1	6 mo	yes	child
324	Foster/Francis	M	R/R		1/2	6 mo	yes	child
326	A/B	F	R/L		1/2	6 mo	yes	child
328	Benjamin/Ronald	M	R/R		2/1	9 mo	yes	child
330	Esther/Elvira	F				9 mo	yes	child
332	Alois/Oskar	M		{2250 / more}	1/2	9 mo	yes	child
334	Victor/Patrick	M	R/R		2/1	12 mo	yes	child
336	Brian/Hubert	M	R/R		2/1	12 mo	yes	child
338	Valerie/Joyce	F	R/L		2/1	13 mo	yes	child
340	A/B	F		{1500 / 1300}	1/2	32 mo	?/no	?/17
342	Fanny/Odette	F	R/R	{tiny-weaker / tiny-stronger}	1/2	0–12yr	yes	child
344	Viola/Olga	F	R/R	{weaker / stronger}	2/1	0–11yr	yes	child
346	Maisie/Vera	F	R/R		2/1	3mo–12yr	no/yes	11/child
348	Peter/Bert	M				6mo–17yr	yes	child
350	Dora/Brenda	F	R/R		1/2	9mo–12yr	yes	child
352	Joan/Dinah	F	R/R		2/1	0–5yr	yes	child
354	A/B	M	R/L	{4000 / 3500}	1/2	12–30mo 6–11yr	yes	child
GROUP IV. SEPARATED AFTER 4 YEARS								
402	A/B	F	R/R		2/1	5 yr	yes	child
404	A/B	F				5 or 13yr	yes	child
406	Viggo/Oluf	M				6 yr	yes	child
408	Augusta/Helen	F	L,A/R			6–17yr	yes	child
410	Pauline/Sally	F	R/R	{1588 / 2041}	1/2	7 yr	yes	child
412	A/B	M		{1350 / 1250}		7 yr	yes	child
414	Alfred/August	M				7 yr	yes	child
416	Molly/Dorothy	F	R/R		1/2	8 yr	yes	child
418	Ferdinand/Luitpold	M				8 yr	yes	child
420	A/B	F			1/2	8 yr	yes	child
422	Adeline/Gwendolen	F	R/R		1/2	9 yr	yes	child
GROUP V. INSUFFICIENT INFORMATION								
GROUP VI. DOUBTFUL ZYGOSITY								

*Specific degree of contact unknown; placed in Group III as a conservative estimate.

Age met	Age seen	Degree of contact over lifespan (0=none, L=little, M=much); ages 0–6; 6–10; 10–20; 20+	Years apart and degree of contact: None, Little, Much	Comment	Reared by: Parent, Relative, Other	Original ID
child	17	M/M/M	17M		R/R	Shields sm2
child	33	M/M/M/M	33M		R/R	Shields sf7
child	45	M/L/M/M	3L,42M	{ Long distance apart ages 6–9.	P/R	Shields sf20
child	45	M/M/M/M	45M		P/R	Shields sm11
child	30	M/L/?M/?M	30?	{ 1 per mo as child; later contact unknown.	O/P	Inouye 4138*
child	42	M/M/M/M	42M		R/P	Shields sf18
child	48	M/M/M/M	48M		R/P	Shields sf23
child	50	M/M/M/M–0	26M	Met weekly; A died at 26.	R/R	Kringlen 48
child	29	M/M/M/M	29M		R/R	Newman IV
child	19	M/M/M	19M		R/R	Newman IX
child	30	M/M/M/L–M	30M	{ Diff. schools; apart in WWII; now work together.	R/O	Shields sm5
child	32	M/M/M/M	32M		R/P	Shields sm6
child	23	?/M/?/M	23M(?)	{ Reunited 5–7; much contact now; minimal history.	P/R	Shields sf2
child	52	M/M/M/M	52M		P/R	Shields sm15
child	18	M/M/M	18M		R/P	Schwesinger
child	16	M/M/M	16M	Same school until 14.	O/P	Prokop & Drum1
child	51	M/M/M/M	51M		P/R	Shields sm13
child	51	M/M/M/M	51M		R/P	Shields sm14
child	30	M/M/M/M	30M		O/P	Shields sf3
child	19	M/M/?	19M(?)	{ Visited yearly when young; now?	O/O	Inouye 4192*
child	51	M/M/M/M	51M	Same family since 12.	P/R	Shields sf25
child	39	M/M/M/M	39M	Same family since 11.	R/P	Shields sf13
child	59	M/M/M–L/L–0	17M,32LN	{ Same family since 12; A emigrated at 17.	P/R	Shields sf28
child	26	?	?		R/R	Kaij 17*
child	56	M/M/M/M	56M	Same family since 12.	R/P	Shields sf27
child	40	M/M/M/M	40M	Usually w/aunt 5–15.	P/R	Shields sf15
child	33	M/L/M/M	27M,6L		PR/PO	Tienari 466
child	32	M/M/M/L–M	28M,4L	Different countries 22–26.	PR/P	Shields sf4
child	15–18	M/M/M	18M		PO/PO	Kallmann 1956
child	77	M/L/L/L	6M,71L		PO/PO	Juel-Nielsen XII
child	41	M/L/L–M/M	30M,11L		PO/PO	Newman XIX
child	38	M/M/M/M	38M		P/PR	Shields sf12
child	19	M/M–L/L		{ Estimated contact, sparse data.	O/O	Bouterwek E81
child	21 & 43	M/M–L/?		Sparse data.	?/?/	Kaij 19 (Essen-Moller #3)
child	38	M/M/M/M	38M		R/P	Shields sf11
child	33	M/M/M/M	33M		PO/PO	Lange F&L
child	45	M/M–0/M–0/?	8M,35?		PR/PR	Kringlen #55
child	59	M/M/L/L–0	9M,12L,38LN		P/PR	Shields sf29
				1 set; may not have been separated.		Wagenseil
				5–7 sets.		Inouye, Mitsuda
				1 set.		Kringlen '67, #66
				1 set.		Kaij #18
				1 set.		Denker MZ Pr 18
				Marked difference in finger-ridge count.		Burks & Roe, J&K
				Original author questions zygosity.		Kaij #31

(much contact throughout life)—it emerges that about half the sample were well separated (45 sets), a quarter had mixed separations (23 sets), and a quarter were hardly separated at all (27 sets). The first group could be expected to show the least contamination from twinning, the second somewhat more, and the last to be cases greatly confounded by interactional effects.

Within groups I and II, further subdivisions rank the twins according to when they learned of each other and met.[2, 3] Ranking within groups was done by age of separation, which allows one to include or discard pairs separated past ages two, three, or four. There are only two cases of separation past four, and four is a liberal cutoff point. At first glance the subclassifications may seem overly detailed, but the distinctions seem warranted in view of questions to be discussed later. Nonetheless, for the time being the sample may be viewed simply as three groups—much, mixed, and little separation.

It must be noted that only six sets (group Ia) fall into the classic paradigm of being separated early, reared completely apart, and investigated before or at the time of reunion. Of these, only three are pure cases who were separated in the first year, reared with no knowledge of twinship, and seen at the period of first meeting. In other words, *of the 121 cases reported in the last fifty years, only three are "twins reared apart" in the classic sense.* The difference between the assumptions underlying most usage of twin-reared-apart data and reality is striking.

Other parameters of the sample are worthy of note. Insofar as the case histories report, almost all subjects are Caucasian, usually of European or North American extraction. A few Japanese sets are found in group III. Some pairs were born before the turn of the century; others have birthdates in the 1950s. The twins have been reared in a variety of cultures, a few sets even being reared on different continents without a primary language in common. However, as noted earlier, most are American, British, or Scandinavian.

There are almost twice as many females as males in the core sample (I, II, and III), with the ratio of two female sets for every male pair in the most separated group. The mixed and low separation categories come closer to a 50–50 distribution.

2. "Contact" was rated from the case histories with "no contact" meaning, literally, no contact. "Little" contact referred to letters, a brief meeting, or a statement by the investigator of little contact. "Much" referred to living together, neighboring houses, vacationing, lengthy stays with each other, or some analogous situation. In instances where degree of contact was unclear, the most conservative estimate (of greater contact) was used. It is possible, even likely, that more detailed case histories might move sets from one category to another, but the overall grouping appears to be the most accurate possible at the present time. The extremes probably would not change, even with more complete histories.

3. All sets have been given code numbers at two-digit intervals. Should future researchers wish to indicate where their cases fit in the overall literature, they may give them an index number and insert them in the appropriate space.

Age is more normally distributed. Using the age at which the twins were seen as the criterion, the average age is thirty-five years, with a range from eight to seventy-two years. The largest number of sets are in the thirty-to-thirty-nine-year age group; about a third of the sample is in the two decades younger than thirty and about a third in the two decades older than forty. Only one set is younger than nine years and only three are older than sixty. Also, the age at separation tends to be quite young, with fully 77 percent of the core sample being separated within the first year and an additional 13 percent between the first and second birthday. Only ten cases, or about 10 percent of the sample, were separated past the age of two. Within subgroups, the majority of pairs in each group tend to be parted early in life.

Asymmetry, judged by same- or opposite-handedness, seems randomly distributed throughout. Information is available on 79 of the 95 sets (39 in group I, 19 in II, and 21 in III), and indicates three-fourths to be "identical identicals" and one-fourth mirror-image twins. (Group I: 69 percent same, 31 percent mirror; II: 79 and 21 percent respectively; III: 81 percent, 19 percent; Total sample: 75 percent same, 25 percent mirror).

Rearing environment is not randomly distributed. About two-thirds of the sample consists of sets where one or both partners were reared by parents or relatives. Only one-third went to nonfamily environments. The resulting genotype-environment correlation is high. To a degree the classification into group II or III parallels whether twins were reared with relatives, since those who were poorly separated most often came from different branches of the same family, a fact that led to their continuing contact. However, as table 3.2 indicates, these cases are not isolated to mixed or low separation.

TABLE 3.2
Rearing Status of Monozygotic Twins Reared Apart.

	Group I	Group II	Group III	Total Sample (N=95)
Both to relative/parent	11 (24%)	11 (48%)	21 (78%)	43 (45%)
One to family/ one outside family	13 (29%)	3 (13%)	5 (18%)	21 (22%)
Both outside family	21 (47%)	9 (39%)	1 (4%)	31 (33%)

Social class is more difficult to evaluate, with the very diversity of the sample in time, location, and culture leading to confusion as to how to rate social standing. Several methods of evaluating SES were attempted with this sample; none worked. Nonetheless, although fine discriminations are hard to make, it is clear that the sample is heavily biased in the direction of the twins having been born and reared in lower- and lower-middle-class families.[4] Poverty or parental death in a poor family often was the reason for the twins being separated in the first place, and, although the families that raised the children had somewhat more resources, one is struck when reading the case histories by the high numbers of farm families living a marginal existence or urban dwellers struggling in cramped quarters. A small number of the twins, but a noteworthy group, could by most criteria be said to have suffered significant emotional and situational deprivation in their early years. Very few were raised in wealth; a moderate number were comfortable; in adult life, none were rich. Although as adults many twins raised their status above the class in which they were reared, again one is struck by the vast majority of sets who remain lower to lower-middle class throughout life. Subjectively, I would estimate about 90 percent of the twins to have been born to poor or situationally deprived parents, and anywhere from 50 to 75 percent of the twins were reared in clearly deprived homes or in homes in which the resources and options were more limited than those we would associate with the middle class today. It would be satisfying if someone could return to the data and give a more discriminating evaluation. Until this is done, I offer a subjective estimation that approximately two-thirds of the twins came from homes that would be judged lower or lower-middle class by today's standards, the remaining third being middle-class. Only two or three individuals were adopted into professional families.

Due to the absence of data, prematurity and possible birth trauma cannot be estimated. The birth weights that are mentioned tend to be in the premature range, and they seem to have been included or excluded in case histories for no discernible reason. Some investigators asked about birth, most did not. Estimates of prematurity among MZ twins range around 50 percent (Schienfeld 1967), and I see no reason to dispute the figure for this sample. The poverty and desperation of the biological parents might argue an even higher figure, but the fact that these twins survived past birth, often without medical treatment, counters this. Any analysis of the data, particularly any statistical analysis, should take into account the certainty that this sample contains a high proportion of individuals with "at risk" birth factors. It is probable that the vast majority of subjects belongs in this group.

---

4. Shields did SES ratings on his sets and stated that even those sets who fell in a grade III class (out of a five-point scale) were actually less-well-off than grade III reared-together sets.

Summary

Of the total sample of 121 sets of MZ twins reared apart mentioned in the literature, 95 are suitable for varying degrees of reanalysis. Forty-five sets were highly separated, 23 had mixed separations, and 27 had substantial contact with each other. There are more females than males in the group, particularly in the most separated pairs. Ages tend to cluster around the mid-thirties. Almost three-fourths of the sample were separated in the first year, less than 10 percent parting past the age of two. About one-fourth are asymmetric or mirror-image pairs, the remainder being "identical identicals." In two-thirds of the sample one or both twins were reared by parents or relatives. Only one-third of the pairs were placed beyond the boundaries of the biological milieu. Subjective evaluations estimate that almost all of the twins were born to biological parents of lower-class standing or rather desperate circumstances, and probably about two-thirds were reared in environments that would be considered lower to lower-middle class by today's standards. Many of the twins probably had premature or difficult births, more of them, certainly, than in a sample of nontwin subjects.

Of the 121 cases reported in the last half-century, only three sets are monozygotic twins reared apart in the conservative meaning of the term.

Chapter 4

Appearance and Other Normative Traits

Given identical genotypes, it is not surprising that MZ twins of whatever rearing status remain alike in height, skeletal structure, or even electroencephalogram patterns (EEG). However, remarkable similarity in traits such as weight, gestures, speech patterns, or even menstrual symptoms even when the twins have been reared under a variety of environmental circumstances gives rise to serious thought.

This chapter reports concordance-discordance rates for a wide variety of attributes and symptoms generally falling under the rubric of "normal" functioning. Concordance is scored in a simple pairwise manner (of those sets offering data on a variable, how many were alike and how many different), and intraclass correlations are given. The intraclass correlation, r', often is used as an estimate of heritability in the broad sense, but it should not be used in this manner for this sample. The lack of random samples or distribution through rearing environments probably makes r' overly high. Where possible, rates are compared with Juel-Nielsen's more representative sample, but this is only a rough correction and should not be accepted at face value.

For the sake of convenience, mean differences will be reported in pounds, inches, and so forth. Metric conversions are easily made and are included in the charts in the appendix.

Height

In almost all instances, twins reared apart differ very little from each other in height and are virtually indistinguishable as a group from MZ twins reared in the same family. Tall twins tend to have equally tall partners, and short twins, equally short ones, so much so that correlations in most studies tend to be above .90, often exceeding .95. From the pooled and reanalyzed data, the average difference is about two-thirds of an inch, and the corresponding r' is very high. Table 4.1 summarizes results.[1]

TABLE 4.1
Height—MZ Twins Reared Apart.

Source	N Sets	Mean Difference	r'
Shields	39	.81 inch	.82 (.82 male) (.82 female)
All others	31 (10) (21)	.57 inch (.54 inch) (.58 inch)	.98 (.99 male) (.96 female)

The difference in height between Shields's twins and those from other studies is minimal and may be due either to measurement error or some idiosyncracy of his sample. For example, 12 percent of his sample differed by more than 1.5 inches, while this amount of difference was seen only once in the rest of the cases and, in that instance, the discrepancy is easily explained. Two girls (case 164) were seen at age eleven. One had passed through her adolescent growth spurt; the other, 3.3 inches shorter, had not. All studies concur that the difference in height is less than an inch (Newman, 0.71 inch; r'=.97); and Juel-Nielsen's twins actually were more identical in height than any subgroup (0.39 inch, r'=.97).

When comparing MZ twins reared apart with MZ and DZ twins reared together, zygosity seems more important than rearing status. Table 4.2 summarizes results from various studies[2] and indicates no noteworthy difference between identicals from any source.

No association between differences in height in a pair and sex, degree of separation, or degree of deprivation in childhood emerged

1. Shields's figures are reported separately, since he gives only overall difference scores and correlations but does not give height and weight for each twin studied.
2. Only same-sex DZ are compared.

TABLE 4.2

Height—MZ twins reared together, MZ twins reared apart,
and DZ twins reared together. *

MZ Together		MZ Separated		DZ Together	
Mean Difference	r′	Mean Difference	r′	Mean Difference	r′
.5[s]–.6[n]inch	.93[n]–.98[s]	.6[f]–.8[s]inch	.82[s]–.98[f]	1.7[n,s]inch	.44[s]–.65[n]

*n=Newman, s=Shields, f=Farber.

from the data. The lack of support for the deprivation hypothesis probably should not be taken seriously, as inspection was the only method of analysis and the numbers were small and confounded by other variables. Since Shields reported one significant finding of the heavier birth-weight twin ending as the taller adult, histories were examined with this in mind. It emerged that Shields's report was based on a faulty analysis,[3] and while twins reporting different birth weights also reported different adult heights (observed ratio = 20:8; chi square = 5.14), it did not mean that the heavier twin ended as the taller adult. In almost half the sample the heavier baby ended as equal or shorter in height than his partner (observed ratio = 20:17).

In sum, the twin-reared-apart literature supports the hypothesis of a high heritability for adult height. Rearing status, sex, or degree of separation affect it slightly if at all. Differences in birth weight may be a possible, but not an exclusive, precondition for later differences in adult height.

Weight

Weight usually is considered to be somewhat more labile than height, though it too has a high degree of heritability. Studies of reared-together twins find larger differences in weight and lower correlations than are found in evaluations of adult stature (Osborne and De George 1959). Still, when translated into everyday terms, the differences in weight for MZ twins reared apart are small. Partners tended to differ from each other, on the average, by only about 10 pounds, with fat

3. On page 112 of Shields's (1962) book it is noted that he compared only partners who differed in height. Including those sets who were the same height produces results that do not differ from chance.

ones being equally as fat and thin ones equally as thin. In one set studied, partners were well over 200 pounds; in others, partners both were tiny. Table 4.3 presents the results of the reanalysis.

TABLE 4.3
Weight—MZ twins reared apart.

Source	N Sets	Mean Difference	r'
Shields	37	10.5 pounds	(.87 male)
			(.37 female)
All others	30	10.2 pounds	.91
	(9)	(6.9 pounds)	(.96 male)
	(21)	(11.6 pounds)	(.89 female)

In comparison to Juel-Nielsen's sample, a safer estimate might be that differences are in the 10- to 14-pound range, with correlations closer to .67. The figures suggest that, to a substantial degree, adult weight is predetermined, with gains and losses in a fairly narrow range.

A look at MZ and DZ rates for adult weight[4] supports the hypothesis that genotype has a significant influence.

TABLE 4.4
Weight—MZ twins reared together, MZ twins reared apart,
and DZ twins reared together.*

MZ Together		MZ Separated		DZ Together	
Mean Difference	r'	Mean Difference	r'	Mean Difference	r'
10.4[s] pounds	.79[s]–.81[s]	10[f]–14[j] pounds	.37[s]–.91[f]	17.3[s] pounds	.56[s]

*s=Shields, j=Juel-Nielsen, f=Farber.

The low correlation of .37 for reared-apart females leads to an interesting issue. In the very few studies that reported rates by sex, females tended to have lower correlations for weight than males. Although Shields's extremely low figure may be an anomaly of his sample (height differed more than usual as well), it may not be incorrect in pointing to different "plasticities" for the sexes. For the group of twins reared apart minus Shields's sets, the differences in weight were greater for females than males (6.9 versus 11.6 pounds; $p < .13$). Similarly, samples composed primarily of female sets, such as Juel-Nielsen's, re-

---

4. Only same-sex DZ twins are compared. Newman's control group was excluded because it consisted primarily of children.

ported larger differences and lower correlations. Studies on reared-together sets also sometimes emerge with widely varying correlations for female weight.[5]

While genetically determined factors may differ between the sexes (females having higher ratios of fat cells, for example) environmental variables seem implicated as well. For example, a simple explanation would be that women diet more, in keeping with a socially syntonic emphasis on ideal weight and beauty. A subjective analysis of the case histories suggests that this might be the case, since the women generally were more fashion-conscious than the men, although neither sex was very style-conscious. Another possibility is that the degree of separation is important since it is reported occasionally that partners adjusted their weights up or down to be more like their twin after meeting (see case 174). However, this does not often seem to be the case for either sex.

The most frequently mentioned hypothesis for the differences in the female sets is a linkage between weight gain and number of pregnancies. A study on twins unrelated to this sample (Cederlof and Kaij, 1970) indicated that when genotype is controlled, each pregnancy after the second accounts for an increase of about 2 kilograms (4.8 pounds) of body weight. Increases are presumed to be related to endocrinological shifts associated with pregnancy. In this sample, in fifteen of the twenty-two female sets on whom there was data, one or both partners was scorable for completed pregnancies. The females with the largest differences in weight (2 standard deviations above the mean or more) also included the only sets where partners differed by three or more children. However, chance seems the best explanation, partly because of the limited sample size but more because while about half the time the woman with more children was the heavier, about half the time she also was the lighter. Although the relationship between pregnancy and weight gain could not be seen in this data, so many of the twins' interviewers thought there was a relationship that it seems safest to say only that the influence may be masked by other factors and poor data collection, and testing of the hypothesis will have to come from other sources.

Data on birth weight and deprivation were also reexamined for the total sample. Again, inspection revealed nothing in the few cases where unequivocal deprivation could be inferred, but data were so sparse that no firm conclusion is warranted. Birth weight and adult weight could be obtained in only eight cases. In six the heavier child was the lighter adult, in two the heavier child was lighter or equal to his partner. Possibly the heavier infant remains better able throughout life to regulate homeostasis while the lighter, more vulnerable as a

5. See Fuller and Thompson 1978.

neonate, remains more labile from then on. With so few cases, however, the result might best be ignored.

In sum, it appears that differences in weight are relatively small in identical twins reared apart, the average difference being in the 10 to 14 pound range. Females differ more in weight (12 pounds) than males (7 pounds), though no clear explanation for the discrepancy is discernible in the limited data. The results are enough to give one pause when considering the emphasis on "ideal weight" for stature emphasized by actuarial methods. Instead, the data suggest that hypotheses of patterning of proportions of fat to muscle cells for each individual are more fruitful and accurate lines of investigation.

Other Anthropomorphic Traits

The twins in this sample were so similar down to the most minute details of physical appearance that, in general, it seems that the effects of environment showed only in hairstyle, dress, and makeup. Shape of eyes, nose, ears, and even the distribution of hair or freckles, the rosiness of cheeks, or pigmentation seemed unaffected by rearing conditions. Many of the early studies gave detailed rundowns of traits that varied hardly at all, and later studies took the likeness for granted. Like the twin-reared-together literature, it is the exception that deserves a photograph and caption to remind the reader that differences occasionally emerge.

For example, seventeen of the early studies included detailed measurements on head length and width. The mean differences are minuscule: 0.11 inch for both length and width. Translated into everyday terms, this means that the shape of the skull varied by little more than the width of a pencil lead. Since most of these cases were chosen on a similarity basis, the actual differences between reared-apart MZ twins could be presumed to be slightly larger, but this, rather concretely, is like saying they are a mere hairsbreadth apart.

Of the few differences reported, some can be linked to prenatal or birth injury. *James* and *Reese* (case 154) both had hand tremors, probably from birth trauma. *Reese* also had a deformed arm, two inches shorter than his twin's. Less explicable was the case of *Harry* and *Alfred* (case 174) who differed by more than 3 inches in height and 60 pounds in weight. Shields, who examined the pair, suspected early deprivation to be the cause. However, because other cases with extreme deprivation do not always differ as adults, some factor other than, or in addition to, deprivation is implicated. For example, *Kamma* and *Ella* (case 114) had vastly different home lives in their early years. *Kamma* was comfortable, even coddled, while *Ella* was neglected to the point of early retardation and was left in an unheated room to die. In adult life they were identical in weight and build and differed by only 2 centimeters (0.78 inch) in height. The easiest speculation is that certain genotypes, such as theirs, have a greater capacity to recover from trauma. It also might be that *Harry* and *Alfred* were discordant for an unknown endocrinological disorder (see "Musculoskeletal System" in chapter 5).

The remainder of differences cited were not really differences but rather the effects of mirror imaging. These mirror-image twins were concordant for abnormalities but showed them in asymmetric fashion. For example, *Herta* and *Berta* (case 136) grew up on different continents. One had a deformity of the right foot, the other a similar deformity of the left. *Esther* and *Ethel* (case 120) had identically deformed little fingers, one on the left and one on the right hand. The literature is replete with such instances, the material on dental structure, presented later in this chapter, being perhaps the most thought-provoking.

Electroencephalogram Patterns

An extensive literature on the EEG patterns of MZ and DZ twins exists,[6] most of it indicating marked similarity between MZ partners. The patterns are identical enough in MZ partners to offer another method of zygosity determination (Lennox et al. 1945), though one less exact than those now used. Some have suggested that there may be a tendency for bilateral EEG asymmetry in MZ twins, (Raney 1938; Inouye 1970) though more recent work has not demonstrated it. In the last few years, investigations have begun to suggest that functioning in different parts of the brain may have varying degrees of genetic determination, and the door has been opened to study of which modes of functioning are more susceptible to environmental influence and which less (Dustman and Beck 1965; Osborne 1970; Lewis et al. 1972; Fuller and Thompson 1978). Interestingly, in the midst of all this similarity, two studies (Young and Fenton 1971; Hume 1973) that examined shifts in EEG related to altering and attentional responses did not find differences between MZ and DZ pairs, a result particularly surprising when one considers not only the degrees of genetic similarity but also the fact that

6. See Fuller and Thompson 1978 for a recent review.

pairs were raised in the same homes with constant contact with each other.

In 1958 Juel-Nielsen and Harvald published a report on the electro-encephalogram of eight sets of MZ twins reared apart. The larger literature yields five other cases. The additional sets alter neither the analysis nor the conclusions of the Juel-Nielsen and Harvald paper. No matter what their rearing status, the twins were, for all practical purposes, almost completely alike in EEG patterns, often even to the subclinical level. In most instances, the recording of one twin was interchangeable with the other's and, in case 330, reported by Schwesinger, the neurologist saved himself time by sending only one report.

Two of the thirteen cases were discordant for symptoms that might be expected to show on EEG. *Russell* (case 126) had severe idiopathic epilepsy from infancy and was reared for many years in an epileptic colony. His brother, *Tristram*, had no history of seizures of any type. However, on examination, *Tristram's* EEG showed typical epileptic spikes and waves at flicker-lamp provocation, and the two brothers had what was called remarkably similar records. The neurologist concluded that both boys had a genetic tendency toward epilepsy, but only one developed seizures, possibly because of birth injury. The EEG records for *Alois* and *Oskar* (case 332), also discordant for seizures, were reported in identical terms.[7]

Mirror imaging was investigated, though data was limited since only two of twelve sets were asymmetric, using the criteria of handedness. (*Alois* and *Oskar*, the thirteenth set in the series, do not include information on asymmetry.) The records as reported by Juel-Nielsen do not demonstrate any definitive difference. The two right-handed partners had amplitudes slightly higher over the right hemisphere, while the ambidextrous, originally left-handed, partners were split. One had amplitudes slightly higher on the left hemisphere. The other had equal amplitudes over both hemispheres. Further series of asymmetric sets would be needed to form a conclusion.

Overall, the results strongly support those of studies of MZ twins reared together, almost all of which indicate EEG patterns to be strongly influenced by heredity. A brief anecdote reported in Juel-Nielsen and Harvald's paper illustrates the point. The authors were approached by two twenty-eight-year-old women who were convinced they were monozygotic twins. EEG investigation showed entirely normal conditions in one and a definite pathological curve in the other. Later blood-group examination demonstrated that the women could not possibly be identical.

A table of EEG results for each set in the series is included in the ap-

7. While seven cases in the total sample reported epilepsy, only the two discordant cases that also reported EEGs are included here. For a full summary on epilepsy see chapter 5.

pendices (table A2). Dencker's set, studied specifically because of discordance in closed-head injury, has not been included in the reanalysis because of the paucity of information.

Electrocardiogram Patterns and Blood Pressure

Though data are limited, the twin-reared-apart results suggest that ECG patterns are strongly influenced by genetic factors. Juel-Nielsen reported seven sets where ECGs were performed and all were concordant, even to subclinical abnormalities. Only one other report included ECG data (case 106) and, again, the pattern was identical although the subclinical features differed slightly. Twin *JJ* had a splintering of the QRS complex while his brother, *JB*, had a sinus arrhythmia.[8] All data is listed in table A3 in the appendices with the discussion on heart disease and death rates reserved for chapter 5.

Routine cardiac examination other than ECG was reported for thirteen sets. All were normal and concordant, including one case where minor subclinical abnormalities were discovered (case 108).

Blood pressure was reported for both partners in fifteen sets and for only one partner in an additional two cases. The quality of data varies; some authors gave specific results, others noted only if readings were in the normal or hypertensive range. Stern (1973), Bodmer and Cavalli-Sforza (1976), and Cavalli-Sforza and Bodmer (1978) offer discussions on heritability of blood pressure and on the difficulties of scoring a continuous trait. Harvald and Hauge (1965) found MZ twins significantly more concordant than DZ twins for arterial hypertension, though they, too, noted the necessity of further evaluating information according to age levels and distribution. Based on their data, heritability has been estimated as between 53 to 62 percent (Cavalli-Sforza and Bodmer 1978) and though estimates of monogenic inheritance have been put forth, most authors appear to favor the hypothesis of polygenic contributions (Riccardi 1977; Fraser, Roberts and Pembry 1978).

Depending on age, cutoff points, and how one construes the data, the concordance rates may vary somewhat.[9] However, the overall similarity is clear. If one takes the data at face value and uses a cutoff of

8. This set, interestingly, is one of the three most separated in the literature and consistently is one of the most different on numerous variables.

9. Interested readers may refer to table A3 in the appendices to make their own evaluations of concordance for the reared-apart data.

140/90, irrespective of age, approximately fourteen sets are concordant, and one discordant. Table 4.5 summarizes the results.

TABLE 4.5
Blood pressure—MZ twins reared apart.

Both in normal range	Borderline, elevated, or labile range	
	Concordant	Discordant
7 sets	7 sets	1 set

The concordance is in the range of 7:1 for hypertension (7:3 if two cases with missing information not included here are discordant, as they appear). Though case histories do not allow for detailed examination of factors contributing to elevated readings, the results suggest a noteworthy genetic contribution. Obscured in the concordance rates, however, are the somewhat different ages at which the twins develop hypertension. Though most are similar in developing it at specific eras in life (middle age, old age, one set only in pregnancy, and so forth), a number of years may intervene, and sets discordant at one age may become concordant many years later. *Karin* and *Kristine*, (case 178), for example, differed in middle age, with only *Kristine* having an episode of hypertension. Two decades later *Karin* died of heart disease, while *Kristine* remained asymptomatic and died of cancer. It would be interesting to discover if the sets discordant in age of onset also were discordant in diet, exercise, smoking, stress, or other variables considered to be contributors to hypertension, but too much information is lacking.

In sum, it appears that the ECG pattern and the characteristics of cardiac functioning discernible from clinical examination are highly similar in MZ twins reared apart. A strong genetic component, even to the presence of minor subclinical abnormalities, is suggested. Blood pressure also appears strongly influenced by heredity, but environmental factors, at least for periods of time, may remove even genetically susceptible individuals from the hypertensive range.

Vision

Sorsby's remarkable book on ophthalmic genetics (1970) offers convincing evidence of the strong genetic contributions to errors of refraction. In his study, he found MZ twins to be highly concordant down to fine criteria of ophthalmic exam including refraction, depth of anterior chamber, thickness of the lens, powers of anterior and posterior surfaces of the lens, and axial length. Only slight concordance showed for DZ twins or unrelated control pairs. Though Sorsby concluded that the data were sufficient to establish the paramount significance of heredity in refraction, precise modes of transmission remain to be evaluated.

In contrast to Sorsby's work, the information on vision among twins reared apart is crude and highly variable. However, data of one form or another were included in thirty-five cases, approximately one-third of the sample (see table A4 in the appendices). Specific details of ophthalmic examination were offered for a few sets, a general statement about type of disorder was given for more, and statements such as that "glasses were worn" or "glasses were needed for eyestrain" were given for others. The information was used in two ways: to score for presence or absence of visual disturbance and, to a minimal degree, to score for type.

Even taking the variable quality of the information into account, the concordance still is striking. Scoring only for presence or absence of disturbance (both normal or both report symptoms), twenty-seven out of thirty-four cases were concordant. Scoring for type of disturbance, the similarity remains high. Of the thirty-two cases reporting visual symptoms of one type or another (some cases reported multiple symptoms), twenty were entirely alike and the others were predominantly similar. Figure 4.1 lists symptom concordance. The high degree of similarity suggested for this sample is obscured by the figure since the discordant symptoms stem from only a small proportion of the sample. However, within the sample, concordance was highest for nearsightedness (myopia), farsightedness (hypermetropia), and strabismus (mild in most cases), while it was lowest for disorders due to infection and cataract. The results should come as no surprise. One case included an interesting discordance for heterochromia, which Juel-Nielsen speculated may be due to mutation.

Mirror imaging showed in some of the asymmetric sets, though not all, and was mentioned for one set otherwise considered symmetric (probably an example of partial mirror imaging, though it is possible that one partner was ambidextrous and did not report it). In cases 150 and 160, the left-handed partners had strabismus in the right eye and the right-handed partners had strabismus in the left. In some asymmetric sets, opposite eyes were dominant. *Kathleen* and *Jenny* (case 304), two right-handed partners, each had squint severe enough to require correction, one in the left, the other in the right eye.

Overall, it appears safe to speculate that ophthalmic features are highly concordant in MZ twins reared apart, though data do not allow for comparison with reared-together sets as a means of estimating environmental contributions. Concordance is highest for errors of refrac-

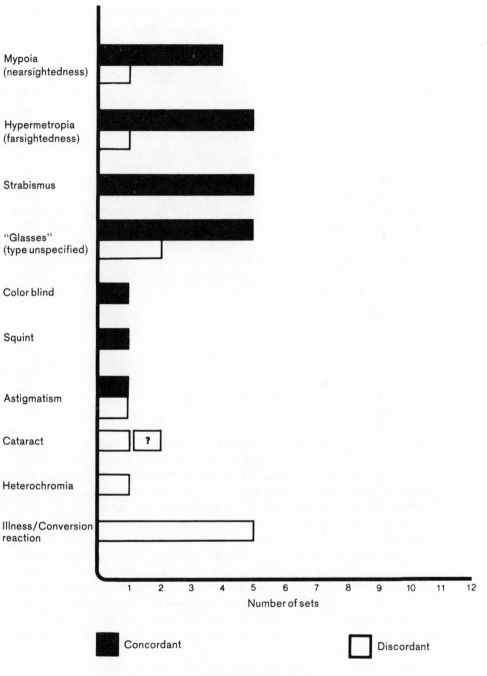

FIGURE 4.1
Ophthalmic symptoms—MZ twins reared apart.

tion and lowest for infections, cataract, and heterochromia. The data, rough as they are, could be construed as in accord with Sorsby's conclusion of the largely genetic basis of refractive errors.[10]

Hearing

Little information is available on auditory examination, as only eight cases reported even minimal data. In five cases hearing exams were part of the work-up, and in three others auditory disturbances of some type were mentioned. Of the eight cases, seven were concordant, the one discordant set reporting a partner who had deafness for three hours and aphonia for a week following a vascular disturbance of some type. The data are poor and are included in table A5 in the appendices only as a curiosity. Information on musical aptitude is discussed in chapter 8.

Dental Examination

The quantity of moderately detailed information on dental traits came as a surprise. For some peculiar reason, not many investigators tested hearing or vision, but quite a few looked into people's mouths. The twins appeared to be extremely alike in the structure of the mouth and teeth, a fact that might be expected since dentition now is known as a satisfactory method of zygosity determination (Kraus et al. 1959, 1969; Osborne et al. 1958; Lundstrom 1963). However, that the twins were similar and often identical even to the number and location of cavities within specific teeth was surprising when one considers that these sets lived in different homes, often in different locations, with most probably not having the best of diets and hygiene. Mirror imaging occurred and can be seen when one twin reported cavities in certain teeth and his asymmetric partner reported them in the same teeth on the opposite side.

Information on dental structure and pathology was available in thir-

10. One case not reported here because of poor separation is particularly intriguing for its suggestion of similar susceptibility. A and B, Kallmann's "schizophrenic" pair (case 404, see appendix), both developed crossed eyes as sequelae of pneumonia.

ty-six sets. Of these, twenty-six offered information on the structure of the mouth and teeth. Only one set out of the twenty-six was discordant, and it probably was an example of only temporary discordance. *Maxine* and *Virginia* (case 164), the same eleven-year-olds mentioned for a difference in height, were reported to have notable differences in the shape of the dental arch and spacing of teeth. In all other particulars their teeth were identical, including the size and shape and the fact that each girl had two cavities filled. Since one had gone into her adolescent growth spurt while the other had not, it seems possible the differences would decrease at maturity.

The high concordance for dental structure (26:1) is parallel to the almost equally high concordance for presence or absence of disorder. Asking only the simple question of whether both twins had dental problems or not, the concordance was 28:3. Of the three discordant sets, only one is worthy of note. *Edith* and *Fay* (case 188) differed considerably: One had marked decay in more than half her teeth while her partner had none. The twin with the severe problem had suffered through the 1918 influenza epidemic and subsequently had borne several children under what appears to be near-starvation conditions. It seems possible that the difference might be attributed to her malnourished state and the pregnancies. Interestingly, this seems to be almost the only case in which true discordance showed in this sample, since other discordant pairs were discordant only for one twin having a few fillings and the other none. Overenthusiastic dentistry could be implicated as easily as anything else.

Since a large proportion of the population at large has dental problems, one might try to put the high concordance in this sample into perspective by saying that perhaps these twins are not so much similar to each other as they are similar to people of their eras and SES who did not have the time or inclination to pay close attention to themselves. While their background and life style undoubtedly played a part, the specificity of concordance even to the type, degree, and location of disorder makes the genetic hypothesis more plausible. Of the thirty-one cases with pathology, only five instances of minor discordance were noted, including the sets cited above, and a few additional instances of the degree of tooth decay differing minimally. In other words, if any reader were to discover an identical twin somewhere, he or she could assume with a high degree of certainty that the twin would have identical teeth, close to identical amounts of decay or other anomaly, and even assume that cavities would be in the same teeth—unless, of course, the twin was a mirror, in which case cavities would be in the same teeth on the opposite side.

The similarity in structure will not come as a surprise to most, but the indications that the potential for decay is so minutely specified are worthy of note and might be worth investigating in future studies.

Pubertal Development, Menstruation, and Menopause

Males. Only two references exist to pubertal development in males, and the larger literature on MZ twins reared together is equally unrevealing. Case 106, one of the best-separated sets in the literature, reported that *JB* began developing pubic and axillary hair at about thirteen to fourteen, while *JJ* was substantially delayed in comparison, developing pubic hair at fifteen years two months and axillary hair a few months later. Information on birth order or birth weight is absent, but this symmetric set differed greatly on a number of other variables, including IQ and physical symptoms.

It appears that *Bertram* and *Christopher* (case 302) differed somewhat less. *Bertram*, the firstborn, reported that his voice broke six months earlier than *Christopher's*. Information on birth weight and other pubertal development is missing. The set, again, was symmetric.

A vague but possible reference to similar delays in sexual development occurs in Prokop and Druml's set (case 332), where it is noted that both partners, seen at age sixteen and one-half, were about two years behind norms. Overall, no conclusions can be drawn.

Females. Information for females differs dramatically. A large amount of information exists, though it is of variable quality. Interestingly, information on menarche and menstrual symptoms was not systematically requested in various studies, and some investigators, particularly Newman et al., avoid it as indelicate. It was the female twins themselves, in their persistence in reporting, who made menstruation and associated symptoms one of the more extensively documented variables in the literature.

Age of menarche, either exactly or approximately, was reported for twenty-eight sets. The mean difference was 9.3 months,[11] with a range from 0 to 48 months. However, only six sets reported differences greater than one year, and of these, only two differed by more than two years. Tisserant-Perrier (1953) reported differences of 2.2 and 8.2 months respectively for MZ and DZ twins reared in the same homes. However, the reared-apart results are compared here with Petri's 1934 study, a fairer comparison, it is thought, since most of these twins reached sexual maturity in roughly the decades covered in Petri's sample.

The distribution of scores fits well with expectations. Monozygotics of whatever rearing status are more like each other than are pairs of dizygotics or women of other degrees of consanguinity. The interaction

11. This figure is a lower estimate since those sets reporting similar age of onset without giving exact differences were scored as 0 in computing difference scores. The real difference may be even closer to the DZ rate.

TABLE 4.6

*Mean difference of first menstruation for women
of varying degrees of consanguinity.*

No. of Pairs	Relationship	Difference (months)
51	MZ twins reared together	2.8
28	MZ twins reared apart	9.3
47	DZ twins reared together	12.0
145	Siblings	12.9
120	Mother-daughter	18.4
120	Unrelated women	18.6

SOURCE: All figures except for twins reared apart are taken from E. Petri (1934) as cited in C. Stern, *Principles of Human Genetics* (San Francisco: W. H. Freeman, 1973) p. 666.

of genotype with environment may be seen in the ranking of MZ twins reared apart between MZ and DZ twins reared in the same home. However, considering the inexact nature of this data and the slightly different results obtained by Petri and Tisserant-Perrier, it is possible that MZ twins reared apart may be most similar to DZ twins who have shared the same environments.

Degree of blood loss during menstruation is not reported. Since Rybo and Hallberg (1966) have demonstrated that blood loss for MZ twins is significantly more similar than for DZ twins (intraclass correlations of .64 and .07 respectively), this would be an interesting question for future studies.

Other questions may be put to the data. For example, some studies on nontwins indicate that unrelated young women in college dormitories tend to begin menstruating in synchrony after prolonged contact with each other (Frieze et al. 1978). Is it possible that these reared-apart twins are synchronous? Unfortunately, no information exists in the case histories. However, it is possible to ask whether contact with one's twin might lead to closer ages in onset of menarche. A comparison of the twenty-one sets who met before puberty with the seven sets who met after indicated a tendency in this direction (8.7 months versus 11.1) but at a nonsignificant level. Similarly, inspection indicates no relationship between earlier or later menarche in a set and birth order, birth weight, or handedness. Inconsistent and missing information probably obscures any underlying patterns that are present, and it is hoped that future researchers will investigate with more rigor.

Despite the inconsistent information in the reporting of menstrual symptoms, striking patterns emerged. The twins were almost universally alike, no matter what rearing status, what degree of separateness, or what other illnesses or symptoms afflicted them. Table 4.7 lists the major symptoms. The table obscures the even more striking similarity observed in the case histories. *Not only did the twins have the same men-*

strual symptoms, but they also tended to describe them in identical ways, and they tended to have them at about the same ages or periods of life. Knowledge of the other twin, personality differences, or psychiatric status seemed minimally important.

TABLE 4.7
Menstrual symptoms—MZ twins reared apart.

Symptom	Sets concordant	Sets discordant	Comment
Irregular menstruation	5	0	A sixth set reports for only one partner.
Dysmenorrhea* (difficult/painful)	6	1	Two additional sets report for only one partner.
Menostasis (suppression of flow)	1	0	Two additional sets report for only one partner.
Headache, including migraine, associated with flow	6	0	Two additional sets report for only one partner.
Emotionality/ mood swings specifically linked to menses	2	0	
Vomiting, fainting	2	0	
Mittelschmerz (pain at ovulation)	1	0	

*Juel-Nielsen's description of molimina (personal communication) appears closer to dysmenorrhea than to emotionality and is scored in the former category.

One of the best examples comes from *Olga* and *Ingrid* (case 104), the most highly separated female set in the literature. They were separated at two months and raised with no knowledge of each other, one not even knowing she was adopted. *Ingrid* learned she had a twin at age twenty-two; *Olga* did not learn until they met at thirty-five. At the ages of eighteen to nineteen, within a year of each other and with neither twin aware of the other, each had a prolonged cessation of menstruation. Each concluded she was pregnant, and each made arrangements with the man involved to get married. One twin resumed menstruating prior to the wedding ceremony, the other after. Neither was pregnant, and one wonders if other symptoms of pseudocyesis (false pregnancy) were present.

A psychodynamically oriented clinician confronted with either woman might reasonably be led to interpret the woman's inner life and question whether her wish to be pregnant led to the cessation of her periods. While this is possible, the more parsimonious conclusion is that both twins, for reasons evidently related to the blueprint of their development, ceased menstruating and came to the most appropriate conclusion. The fantasy life, in such a situation, would have to be considered a secondary elaboration.

Similarly, the almost uniform concordance in menstrual symptoms leads to a conclusion that many, perhaps most, of the anomalies and discomforts women associate with their cycle have more of a somatic than psychic base. The concordances cannot be explained away by the fact that such symptoms are widespread in the population and may have happened by chance, nor can mutual identification suffice. Sets reported a wide variety of symptoms, giving opportunity for discordance to show itself, which it rarely did; and reporting of symptoms, at least on the level scorable here, was unaffected by degree of separation or contact. Hence, parsimony suggests that many, if not most, menstrual symptoms might better be described as somatopsychic rather than psychosomatic, if psychic factors are involved to a significant degree at all. Psychoanalytically derived explanations of etiology of menstrual discomfort or disturbance find no support in these data at any point. Instead, explanation points in the direction of organically based etiology, and the results suggest that the psychiatric community and those physicians who advocate psychiatric explanations should suspend judgment and take a more rigorous approach to investigations of menstrual symptomatology.

Menopause and menopausal symptoms were mentioned briefly in twelve cases (see table A7 in the appendices). Only nine are scorable, since two were eliminated for absent information and one for menopause brought on by a surgical procedure. Of these nine sets, all but one pair reported menopause or associated symptoms within two years of each other. The average difference was 2.4 years. However, if one excludes the one large difference (ten years or more, *Dora* and *Brenda*, case 350), the mean difference drops to 1.43 years. The best estimate, at the moment, appears to be that the average difference in menopause is about one and one-half to two years for nine out of ten MZ twins reared apart. Of the five cases reporting symptoms, three were concordant. However, only *Signe* and *Hanne* (case 130) offered details (reporting identical symptoms except for degree). Since their case is clouded by possible thyroid disorder (see chapter 5), evaluation must await a better series.

Marriage and Fertility

Seventy-eight adult pairs included information on both partner's marital status. Of these, fifty-one were sets where both partners were married, seventeen were sets where neither partner was married, and ten were sets in which only one partner was married. The ratio, 68:78, translates into a concordance estimate of 87 percent. Cultural factors undoubtedly play a noteworthy role in the high similarity. However, a reading of the case histories suggests that some sets may have had similar personality features that kept them single (see chapter 8).

Age of first marriage was scorable for forty-nine pairs. The mean difference was 4.24 years, but enough sets were widely discrepant to give an intraclass correlation so low (.17) that environmental factors appear to be almost exclusively involved.

Fertility was calculated by scoring the number of completed pregnancies in those female sets where both partners were married. However, once a set was in the scorable pool, illegitimate children were counted as well as legitimate ones, and stillbirths were counted the same as live deliveries. Twin births counted as one completed pregnancy. Forty-nine female pairs met the criteria and offered a heritability estimate of .52. The mean difference was 1.54 completed pregnancies. Interestingly, the correlation between the difference in age of marriage and the difference in number of completed pregnancies was not significant. What this means in everyday terms is that once partners were married, even if at widely differing ages, they tended to have a similar number of children. Though cultural mores and mutual identification probably are involved here, some degree of similar fertility seems a plausible hypothesis as well.

Sleep Patterns and Sleep Disorders

Information on sleep patterns was given in thirty cases, though it was not solicited by most interviewers. No sleep EEGs were done. Sleep disturbances tended to fall into four groups: (1) nightmares, usually in childhood but severe enough to be remembered by adults; (2) sleepwalking and sleeptalking; (3) insomnia; and (4) very light or disturbed sleep. The instances are summarized below; full information is included in table A8 in the appendices.

TABLE 4.8
Sleep disorders—MZ twins reared apart.

Disorder	Concordant	Discordant	Comment
Nightmares	3	6	A tenth set reports childhood nightmares for one partner, no information on other.
Sleepwalking/ Sleeptalking	3	3	
Insomnia	5 (3)	1	Two of the concordant sets had insomnia associated with schizophrenia. Six additional sets give information for only one partner.
Disturbed or very light sleep	8 (7)	1	One concordant set had epilepsy.

Overall, the figures are not particularly revealing, especially considering the small numbers of reporting pairs in each category. However, the type of severe childhood nightmares remembered into adulthood are primarily discordant, suggesting environmental or psychodynamic etiology, while tendencies to very light or easily disturbed sleep as adults tend to be concordant. Sleep disturbance of any type did not appear to be affected by degree of separation, birth order, or birth weight, though, on inspection, there is a slight tendency for concordance to rise the more contact the twins have with each other. A more rigorous study would be required to demonstrate if meeting one's identical twin leads to increased internal stress that shows itself in restless or disturbed sleep.

The numbers, though small, are interesting when compared with results of studies on MZ twins reared together. For example, EEG and patterns in the stages of sleep are similar for MZ twins and tend toward discordance in DZ twins (Zung and Wilson 1966; Kohler 1969). The pattern of restlessness, 7 or 8 to 1 in this sample, may be related. However, results of studies on sleep disturbance in MZ and DZ children vary widely, making the hypothesis a tenuous none. Brown et al. (1967) found MZs significantly more concordant than DZs, while Wilson et al. (1971) found no appreciable difference.

More specific symptoms, such as sleepwalking, seem congruent between the reared-apart and reared-together sets reported in the literature. Interestingly, though concordance is low, it may eventually emerge that heritability is fairly high. For example, Bakwin (1970) found a concordance rate of 47 percent for sleepwalking for his nineteen sets of MZ twins reared together. This compares well with the 50 percent (3 out of 6) reported here. Though concordance in Bakwin's study was less than half, it still translates to MZ twins being concordant about six times as often as DZ twins. Malkoff and Mick (1970) suggested that sleepwalking may be even more specifically linked to undiagnosed cases of mild temporal lobe epilepsy.

In sum, the data on sleep and sleep patterns are minimal and open to a variety of interpretations. Nightmares are primarily discordant, a fact suggesting that future work may support the concept of significant psychodynamic etiology in their occurrence. Sleepwalking, though concordant in less than half the cases, still compares favorably with the literature on reared-together sets, suggesting some genetic etiology.

Insomnia and very light sleep were largely concordant, and though numbers are low, the rates may support the findings of the larger literature that sleep EEG and stage patterns are similar in identical twins. The slight, statistically nonsignificant tendency for twins who knew each other to report disturbed sleep more often might be more rigorously investigated in future work in order to see if internal stress due to contact with an image of oneself might be inflating heritability estimates. Finally, the similarity of age of occurrence of sleep symptoms was high enough in this sample (see table A8 in the appendices) to suggest that future workers may wish to investigate common developmental patterns in MZ twins. It would be fruitful if future cases of reared-apart twins were investigated for both nocturnal and diurnal rhythms, since this may have important implications for broader personality functioning.

Enuresis and Encopresis

Enuresis is discussed since it is a common childhood developmental symptom occurring predominantly during the sleep cycle. Eleven sets reported enuretic episodes, consisting almost entirely of nocturnal episodes during childhood. Four were concordant and seven discordant. Correlation with birth order, birth weight, or asymmetry could not be made.

Though the concordance, at face value, suggests a strong environmental influence, as with other sleep disorders the rates may be misleading. Bakwin (1971) and Badalyan et al. (1971) studied MZ and DZ twins reared together and, though differing in concordance rates, both unequivocally supported the hypothesis of significant genetic transmission of a tendency toward enuresis, since even moderate MZ concordance is significantly higher than DZ or sibling rates. Further, a pattern of enuresis often could be related to the symptom occurring in the family pedigree.

The current concordance rate of 36 percent approximates the fraternal rate of 36 percent in Bakwin's study, and, though it is much higher than the 8 percent fraternal rate in the Badalyan work, it is notably lower than the 50 to 68 percent MZ rates in the two works. Despite this, the problem may lie in inconsistent reporting. Only nine percent of the sample reported histories of enuresis, while the incidence rate in various populations ranges around 12.5 to 22 percent. Probably about half the sets having enuresis did not report it; thus these results should be held in abeyance until future studies can be done. The cases studied in childhood and giving detailed listing of symptoms tend to show a higher concordance.[12]

Two mentions are made of encopretic histories. Both are discordant. One set (case 240) reported enuresis and encopresis for the one partner who later became psychotic; neither symptom was reported for the partner who remained stable. The second case (206) also reported a childhood history of enuresis and encopresis for one partner and not for the other, though neither showed decompensation as adults. *Robert*, the symptomatic twin, was reared in a severely militaristic and punitive household and became notably obsessional as an adult. *Kaj*, his twin, was the overindulged and rarely punished child of an older couple. He became psychopathic, but settled down in late middle age.

Voice and Speech Patterns

The pitch, tone, and overall characteristics of the twins' voices were so stunningly alike that almost all investigators made mention of the similarity. Forty cases mention vocal traits. Of the twenty-one cases in which tone and pitch were mentioned, only one set was discordant, and the type of difference was not mentioned. It is likely that the rate of concordance is even higher since many investigators took the similarity in voice so much for granted that they mention it only in their summaries, not including it in each case. The most frequent comment in many cases is that husbands, wives, children, friends, and the interviewers themselves had difficulty and often found it impossible to tell

12. See Adelaide and Beatrice, case 242, as a prime example.

the twins apart. Even the laughs are alike—for Juel-Nielsen they were the most tellingly similar feature, more similar than even the impact of the speaking voice, which could be affected by dialect or tension.[13]

Table 4.9 lists the concordance rates. Overall, it seems reasonable to suggest, even from highly variable data, that a lifetime of exposure to different environments and opportunity to identify with foster and adoptive parents had minimal impact. Only stuttering seems environmentally related. If you happen to sound like your mother or father, particularly on the telephone, or if you laugh like your sisters, brothers, or grandparents, identification seems not the explanation of choice.

TABLE 4.9

Voice quality and speech patterns of MZ twins reared apart.

Characteristic	Concordant	Discordant
Voice: tone, and pitch	20	1
"Talkative" or "taciturn"	15 (16)	9 (8)
Hoarse	2	0
Stammer/lisp*	0	6

*Yoshimasu's set, not included in the core sample, was concordant for stammering.

Stuttering, the one notably discordant variable, remains ambiguous. There is insufficient information to link it to asymmetry, birth weight, or birth order; nor, by inspection, can family patterns or pressures be discerned.

There is no information on language development, one of the most widely studied variables in examinations of twins reared together.

Gestures, Mannerisms, and "Body Language"

As with voice, the way the twins held themselves, walked, turned their heads, or flicked their wrists was more alike than any quantifiable trait the observers were able to measure. Again, the uniformity of re-

13. No one analyzed tapes of the twins' voices. However, the widespread impressions of similarity, uniform over decades and geographic boundaries, seem convincing. It would be interesting if future workers could document the similarity with more rigor.

porting crosses decades and geographic boundaries. If one twin had a limp, moist handshake, so did the other. If one had a spirited prance, so did the partner. If one turned her head just so, the twin did no different. In the small, involuntary movements that comprise so much of the impression given to the world and so much of the feedback one gives to oneself, the twins were virtually indistinguishable, according to almost all of the reports given. The data usually are reported only in summary form, but for those who have met twins reared together or apart evidently no convincing is needed. Though this section is the briefest in the chapter, the overwhelming similarity of gestures and mannerisms is one of the most pronounced observations of almost all studies. On the assumption that a picture tells more than words, the following photograph of twins, albeit twins reared together, is included. The photo and caption may do more to explain the uncanny similarity imparted in the case histories than all the tables and charts that have gone before.

FIGURE 4.2.
Concordance in identical twins. The physical similarity of the twins, being genetic, is expected, and so is the similarity of dress, which is environmental. The striking feature to this photograph, however, is something else—without having been given any instructions about how to hold their hands, each twin pair has unconsciously put them in a characteristic position. (Courtesy of K. Fredga, University of Lund.)
SOURCE: From E. Novitski, *Human Genetics* (New York: Macmillan, 1977), page 293.

Longevity

Using the Danish Twin Registry, Harvald and Hauge (1965), gave the average intrapair differences of age at death as 14.5 years (±.94) for monozygotics and 18.6 years (±.84) for dizygotics of the same sex. Opposite-sexed DZ twins rise to an average intrapair difference of about twenty years. The differences between MZ and DZ twins are statistically significant, and heritability is calculated as .29.

Juel-Nielsen (1980) commented that longevity in his sample appeared to be strongly influenced by heredity. On follow-up twenty years after his original study began, if one twin lived to be eighty or ninety, there was a good chance that the other twin did also; similarly, if one twin became seriously ill or died earlier in life, often the other twin did too. Too few sets were followed to the death of both partners to offer responsible heritability estimates. However, table 4.10 may give a flavor of the influences of heredity, barring accidental death, on longevity in this sample.

TABLE 4.10

*Influence of heredity on
longevity in MZ twins
reared apart.*

Set	Twin A	Twin B
104	expected to die at 60	alive 60
114	died 69	alive 73
168	alive 71	died 68
170	died 83	died 80
178	died 77	died 79
184	alive 93	died 75
186	alive 52	died 52
206	alive 68	died 65
406	died 92	died 96

Summary

Similarities between monozygotic twins reared apart are noteworthy enough to suggest substantial genetic determination over many anthropomorphic traits. Reunited partners tend to be within an inch of each other in height and within 10 to 14 pounds in weight, although, on the average, female sets differ more in weight than male. Skeletal structure, the fine details of freckles, hair, and pigmentation are alike. The twins' electroencephalograms are similar—even if only one twin has epilepsy—as are their electrocardiograms. Blood pressure readings suggest that if one twin has hypertension, both will be at risk. However, the onset of hypertensive episodes may occur at different ages.

MZ twins have highly concordant ophthalmic traits. Nearsightedness, farsightedness, and strabismus are frequently the same, and mirror-image sets sometimes exhibit the same error in opposite eyes. All aspects of dentition are also highly concordant, even to the degree that many twins report cavities either in the same teeth or in mirror-image patterns.

Female sets, on the average, begin menstruating within about nine months of each other. The difference is probably somewhat greater than between twins reared together, but less than between dizygotic twins reared in the same home. Menstrual symptoms of MZ twins are often identical, or differ only in degree, and sometimes they occur at about the same time in life even when twins have had no contact. Menopause is documented only infrequently. The best estimate is that partners have onset within about one and one-half years of each other, though there is a substantial chance that the difference in onset may be considerably greater.

The little information available on sleep patterns suggests that there is a less-than-even chance that both partners will report sleepwalking or sleeptalking. Reports of severe nightmares are also predominantly discordant, but reports of insomnia and light sleep patterns are more similar. Enuretic histories were reported with less than 50 percent concordance. However, since MZ twins reared in the same homes have higher rates than DZ twins reared under the same circumstances, a familial transmission of the tendency to enuresis still may be present.

One of the most striking similarities—and one of the most poorly documented—is the repeated statement by various investigators that sets spoke and moved in a remarkably similar manner. Evidently the tone of the voice, the phrasing of speech, and the degree of talkativeness remained highly alike in many sets, despite sometimes widely divergent rearing conditions. When partners laughed, they sometimes could not be told apart. Only stuttering or lisping was notably discordant. Possibly the most interesting observation over the years was that many sets had identical "body languages"—that is, they unconsciously moved and gestured in the same way, even when they had not had an opportunity for mutual identification. Though neither speech patterns nor physical mannerisms were operationally recorded and scored, the frequent reports by a disparate group of investigators over the last half century suggest that these similarities are likely to be found even when a well-designed and rigorous study finally is done.[14]

14. Many of the similarities described in this chapter may be confirmed in a new study of twins reared apart now being conducted at the University of Minnesota. In an article published after this manuscript was completed (Chen 1979), the Minnesota investigators report preliminary results that indicate marked similarities in gestures, mannerisms, weight gains, speech patterns, and temperament.

Chapter 5

Physical Symptoms and Disorders

In reading the case histories, one obtains an impression of remarkable similarity within sets, not only for appearance but also for physical disorders. If one twin has a tendency to respiratory, gastrointestinal, or cardiac disease, often the other does too. In the literature, symptoms frequently are described in identical terms, and ages of onset are close. Though none of the larger studies systematically classifies diseases, the rhetoric and style of presentation leave an impression of numerous, almost uncanny likenesses. Juel-Nielsen was the only investigator to specifically hypothesize that the twins, because of innate susceptibility, tended to have either the same disorders or disorders within the same body system. Since his sample included only twelve sets, rigorous hypothesis testing could not be done.

With Juel-Nielsen's propositions in mind—concordance rates for specific disorders and concordance rates for disorders within systems—data from all case histories were pooled and analyzed. The results, not surprisingly, turned out to be more complex than the pan-similarity suggested by a subjective reading of the case histories. Areas of noteworthy discordance emerged and equivocal results were obtained in others. The concept of system vulnerability was difficult to clarify. At times, concordance rates for particular disorders agreed strongly with rates reported in the larger literature on those disorders, while at other times, rates were surprisingly divergent. Most fell into some middle ground where they were not firm enough for hypothesis testing but were too thought-provoking to be easily disregarded.

For those unfamiliar with medical genetics, a few issues may be noted.[1] Heritability can be calculated by comparison of MZ and DZ twins. Even if MZ twins have a low concordance rate, it is possible to obtain a high heritability estimate, *if* that rate is substantially higher than in the DZ group (see chapter 1). Heritability can be a useful concept even when discussing diseases known to be infectious. The issue in these instances is susceptibility to the agent. The classic example is tuberculosis, where MZ twins are more frequently concordant even when both types of twins are equally exposed.[2] Given problems with studies of twins reared together—shared environment is one of the main ones—the best information is that which pulls together rates for twins and other individuals of varying degrees of consanguinity. Family studies do this. However, they too are problematic since high incidence still may be related to shared genes or to shared transmission of an environmental determinant such as a virus. Thus, in theory at least, a sample of separated MZ twins randomly scattered through rearing environments might be viewed as a sample that most unequivocally eliminates shared environment as an explanatory hypothesis. Were the sample large enough and the rearing environments diverse enough, information might be obtained not only on heritability but also on whether transmission was mono- or polygenic.[3]

In this sample, seventy-six sets offered some degree of information on medical history. The method of analysis was to code all disorders and physical symptoms mentioned in the case histories according to the nosology of the *International Classification of Diseases, U.S. Adaptation* (ICDA).[4] Concordance and discordance were scored in a simple pairwise manner, with information in the histories accepted at face value. Each was scored only when information on both partners was given for a particular variable. Sets with no information for one or both partners were not counted. However, when it seemed that a medical history had been taken on both partners of a set but a disorder was mentioned for only one twin, the set was scored discordant. (This occurred most frequently in Shields's work.) Rates were compared with information from the larger literature and, in particular, with information from McKusick's (1978) standard reference. The latter was used so frequently that it is referred to in this chapter only as "McKusick."

Though classification according to the "systems" of the ICDA provided structure, a few areas of ambiguity arose. For example, hernia is listed in the ICDA under the digestive system rather than the muscu-

1. There are several excellent introductory texts; see Fraser Roberts and Pembry 1978 as one example.
2. See Stern 1973 for discussion.
3. Stern (1973), for example, notes that discordance above 27 percent is evidence against simple dominant determination of a trait.
4. The eighth revision was used in the original scoring. Classifications were rechecked against the ICD-9-CM (1979). The sequence of presentation in this chapter does not follow the ICD sequence.

loskeletal. Similarly, disorders of the reproductive system were included under the genitourinary system in the ICDA-8 while disorders of pregnancy were moved to a separate listing in the most recent revision (ICD-9-CM). My solution was to retain the original system heading while separating disorders under the main heading so that they may be viewed separately or in clusters. Other problems occurred when only a single set reported incidence of a disorder or when only a single symptom was recorded. In the interest of providing a comprehensive survey, I have included almost all information, even these minimal references. I also chose to use the term "cancer" rather than malignant neoplasm.

As a preliminary attempt to evaluate the hypothesis that concordance might occur within systems if not for specific disorders, the two following methods of scoring are reported. First, all sets reporting even a single incidence of disorder in a system were scanned. If both partners scored positive at least once, the set was scored positive for the system. The set did not have to be concordant for specific disorders, as table 5.1 indicates.

TABLE 5.1
Physical disorders: scoring system 1.

ID		Disorder X	Disorder Y	Score
Set 1	A	+	−	positive in system
	B	+	−	
Set 2	A	+	−	positive in system
	B	−	+	
Set 3	A	+	+	negative in system
	B	−	−	
Set 4	A	+	−	negative in system
	B	−	−	

Given the inconsistent quality of most data, the second method of scoring was designed as an attempt to be more discriminant. Again, all sets reporting incidence of disorder within a given system were scanned. However, all sets reporting only one incidence in the system were eliminated, irrespective of concordance. The remainder—those sets who reported two or more incidences within the system—were then scored positive or negative. The criterion for a positive "system" score was that the set not only reported two or more incidences, but also that both partners scored positive at least once. Table 5.2, though not exhaustive of the possibilities, illustrates the scoring.

The limits on generalization of results are considerable. Although cases from the entire literature were pooled, the sample still is small, leading to incidence rates that are minuscule. The lack of random sam-

TABLE 5.2
Physical disorders: scoring system 2.

ID		Disorder X	Disorder Y	Score
Set 1	A	+	+	positive in system
	B	+	−	
Set 2	A	+	−	positive in system
	B	−	+	
Set 3	A	+	+	negative in system
	B	−	−	
Set 4	A	+	−	eliminated
	B	+	−	

pling and the bias toward greater within-pair similarity has been mentioned repeatedly in earlier chapters. An equal if not greater problem is the fluctuation in the quantity and quality of information. Some sets had extensive work-ups that included both specific laboratory results and diagnostic labels. Others were only interviewed, and there is ample reason to question the accuracy of the twins' memories and reports, as well as the tenacity of the interviewers' questioning. Diagnosis also may be suspect in many instances, not only because of variability in reporting and questions of diagnostic acumen, but also because of the widely disparate geographic locations and decades in which the twins were found. Finally, there is the question of the appropriateness of combining genetic subpopulations (British versus Scandinavian versus American), an issue particularly important if one wishes to study incidence rates.

Indeed, since the data are very poor in many instances, the tables and rates presented herein undoubtedly will undergo major revision as more discriminating work is done in the future. Other investigators of twins reared together (Harvald and Hauge 1965) found that both incidence and concordance increased for some disorders when samples were studied more rigorously. I suspect the same would be true for a sample such as this. However, at the present time, these cases provide the only extant information on twins reared apart, and their patterns may at least offer possibilities of hypothesis formation. With this in mind, all material that follows includes complete listings of case IDs so that other investigators may go to original sources or reclassify as they wish.

Cancer

Six cases of cancer were reported, all of them in women.[5] Four were reports of malignant breast tumors, two of stomach cancer. All cases are discordant.

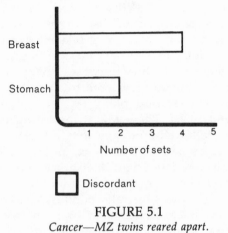

FIGURE 5.1
Cancer—MZ twins reared apart.

Due to the young average age at interview (mid-thirties), most of the sample was not followed through the risk period for malignancy, and the incidence (6/76) undoubtedly is lower than the true rate might be.

Breast Cancer

Breast cancer accounts for 22 per cent of cancer in women in the United States and, among malignancies in women, is the greatest killer. Lynch (1976) noted the pattern of some families having high aggregations of breast cancer, though he and others question whether this necessarily indicates genetic transmission, as viral etiology also is possible. Women who do not have a full-term pregnancy by the age of thirty have a risk that exceeds that of nulliparous women, and nulliparous women in turn have a rate that exceeds that of women who have their first child before the age of twenty. Risk appears to increase with early menarche and also with later natural (nonsurgical) menopause. The risk is two times greater for women who have menopause past fifty-five years than for women who have a natural menopause earlier than forty-five. All texts reviewed indicated that twins have very low concordance rates. Cavalli-Sforza and Bodmer (1978), using figures from Harvald and Hauge (1965), give MZ-DZ rates for cancer at the same site as 6.8 percent versus 2.6 percent respectively, and for cancer

5. Cases 104, 114, 170, 178, 184, and 218.

at any site as 15.9 percent versus 12.9 percent. Fraumeni (1975), after reviewing the literature, estimated MZ concordance to be about double the DZ rate for breast cancer, gastric cancer, intestinal cancer, and leukemia. McKusick notes that any genetic basis may be multifactorial.

Lynch suggested that the following parameters should be included in any twin citations to breast cancer: (1) geographic area; (2) socioeconomic status, religious, racial, and ethnic factors plus parity; (3) family background, including relative age of onset of cancer (pre- or postmenopausal), plus the presence of unilateral or bilateral disease; and (4) the presence of other histologic varieties of cancer in the family. These are covered, where possible, in the brief synopses below. The information in the original histories can be considered trustworthy for at least the three cases from Juel-Nielsen's sample.

Case 104, *Olga* and *Ingrid*. These MZ twins were first seen at age thirty-five and were followed-up to age sixty. Throughout their lives they remained the best separated female set, having almost no contact with each other. Both were Caucasian, Danish, with no strong religious belief in adulthood. *Olga* had, by far, the harder life and was of lower SES throughout life. *Ingrid* was basically middle class. Both menstruated at twelve and were described as premature in their sexual development. Their biological mother menstruated at thirteen. *Olga* had her only child at age nineteen. *Ingrid* had four normal pregnancies between the ages of twenty-three and thirty-four. Both breast-fed their first child. *Ingrid* had hypogalactia after that. Both were overweight, as had been their biological mother. Both had a slight masculinity in hair growth. Information on menopause is not available. At the age of fifty-eight, a left-sided cancer of the breast was diagnosed in *Olga* and was treated by mastectomy. Between ages fifty-eight and sixty, widespread metastases were found, and, at follow-up at age sixty, she was expected to die soon. *Ingrid* exhibited good physical and mental health up to the follow-up at age sixty. *Pedigree:* Their maternal grandmother died at age 42 from uterine cancer, and an aunt on the mother's side may have died at forty-four or forty-five from abdominal cancer. No other instances are noted, although, interestingly, their mother, unbeknownst to them, was a street prostitute nicknamed "Fatty" with a long record of uterine fibroid tumors and a pronounced fear of cancer.

Case 114, *Kamma* and *Ella*. These twins were first seen at age fifty, and were followed up to age seventy-three. Both were Caucasian, Danish, with no strong religious belief as adults. SES was estimated as lower class for both in childhood, with *Kamma* somewhat more middle class than her twin as an adult. *Ella* had severe developmental retardation as a child. Both developed severe migraines at eleven. *Kamma* also began menstruating at that time. *Ella* menstruated at thirteen. *Kamma* had six full-term pregnancies beginning in early adolescence, with an abortion between the second and third. *Ella* had seven pregnancies beginning at age seventeen, with two abortions. *Kamma* never was able to breast-feed; *Ella* could not breast-feed her first three children but the rest were suckled for a year or more. Age of menopause was not stated.

At age of sixty-eight a right-sided malignant breast tumor was discovered in *Kamma* and was treated with mastectomy and radiation. No metastases were found. At sixty-nine she died of a massive pancreatic hemorrhage. The autopsy found no metastases of the earlier breast cancer, but a small tumor was discovered in the right lobe of the thyroid. At seventy-three, *Ella* was still alive and in good health aside from slight cardiac symptoms. *Pedigree:* An aunt on the maternal side may have died of uterine cancer at age seventy-five.

Case 170, *Astrid* and *Edith*. These women were first seen at age seventy-two and were followed up to age eighty-three. The twins maintained close contact. Both were Caucasian, Danish, with no other noteworthy affiliations. *Edith's* SES was estimated as more middle class in childhood but more lower to lower-middle class in adulthood than *Astrid*, who had more middle-class standing. Both menstruated at fourteen. *Astrid's* menopause was at fifty-four with no symptoms; *Edith's* was at fifty-two with a few relatively mild symptoms. *Astrid* had three children, bearing the first when she was thirty-two. *Edith* had two children, the first born when she was twenty-six.

Astrid died at age eighty-three from what was recorded as cerebral apoplexy. No autopsy was performed. *Edith* died at age eighty of congestive heart failure with pulmonary edema. The autopsy showed a right-sided breast cancer without known metastases. *Pedigree:* Their father died at age fifty-four from rectal cancer; one sister died of uterine cancer at seventy-three; and another was diagnosed as having uterine cancer at sixty-nine. There are mentions of fibroid adenoma of the breast in the family pedigree. (Interestingly, one of the twins' nephews became a surgeon specializing in cancer of the rectum.)

Case 218, *Mary* and *Nancy*. These twins were seen at age forty-seven as part of Shields's study. At age forty-seven, *Nancy* had a mastectomy for breast cancer (no further details) followed by radiation treatment. *Mary*, seen nine months after her sister's surgery, was symptom-free except for a reactive depression to her sister's hospitalization. There was no history of cancer in the meager family pedigree. Both were poor in childhood, *Mary* slightly more middle class in adulthood. Both married at twenty-five. The dates of pregnancies are not given. Both menstruated at fourteen; *Nancy* had premature menopause at thirty-six.

Stomach Cancer

McKusick includes no references specifically to stomach cancer. Brandborg (1975) and Fraumeni (1975) cited higher MZ than DZ rates, though the rate of concordance was low for both types of twins. Familial constellations are known, with the most famous being the family of Napoleon Bonaparte. He died in 1821 of stomach cancer, as allegedly did his grandfather, father, brother, and three of his sisters (Lynch 1976). For a number of years an association has been suspected between blood group A, pernicious anemia, and stomach cancer (Aire et al. 1953; Fraumeni, 1975; Lynch 1976), and Brandborg lists other potentially significant contributory factors. Of those he mentions, dyspepsia and ulcer disease are the only two found in one of the twin sets with cancer, and they are present only in the twin who reported malignancy. However, both sets scored for stomach cancer mentioned abdominal or biliary colics, although the family pedigrees did not mention gastric or abdominal disturbance. Both of the cases below come from Juel-Nielsen's trustworthy sample.

Case 178, *Karin* and *Kristine*. These women were first seen at age sixty-four and were followed-up to age seventy-nine. They maintained some contact with each other. Their blood group was O. *Karin* died of heart disease at age seventy-seven. An autopsy was performed. Throughout life she exhibited good health apart from a history of pneumonia and intermittent biliary colics, which ceased at age seventy. *Kristine* died at age seventy-nine of schirrous carcinoma of the stomach. No autopsy was performed. No history of gastric disturbance was mentioned in the case report. *Pedigree:* Family data is sparse. No predisposition to somatic illnesses was noted in the information that was gathered.

Case 184, *Petrine* and *Dorthe*. Seen at age seventy, these twins were followed-up to ninety-three. Their blood group was O. *Petrine* was in good mental and physical health at age ninety-three. *Dorthe* died at age seventy-five of carcinoma of the stomach with metastases to the lungs. No further information is available. Both twins had a history of identical abdominal colic, *Petrine's* beginning at age forty, *Dorthe's* at age thirty. *Dorthe* also had a history of dyspepsia and, in middle age, a diagnosis was made of two small stomach ulcers. *Pedigree:* The family pedigree includes cardiovascular disorder, obesity, cancer, and tuberculosis, but no history of gastric complaints. The paternal grandfather died of "cancer" (type unspecified), one of their sisters died at age forty-five of breast cancer, and another at age sixty-eight of "cancer coeci perforata."

The uniform disordance for breast and stomach cancer was a striking feature of the sample. The only other disorders scored in two or more sets in which there was uniform discordance were those of an infectious nature. Though the family pedigrees of the twins included references to cancer in almost all cases, in no case was it the same type of cancer, and there was no history of breast or gastric disorder in the information available on the appropriate family trees. It should be noted that other family pedigrees included reference to cancer with no incidence in the twins; although this may be due to the fact that the twins had not yet had time to develop and display symptoms. Of the six sets, three were symmetric and three asymmetric, a higher proportion than in the general sample. For the time being, this result is probably best viewed as occurring by chance.

The meager evidence offered by this sample supports environmental agents as being etiologically more significant than genetic factors. This is in accord with evidence from the Danish Twin Registry and the conclusions of Harvald and Hauge (1965).

Benign Neoplasms

Benign neoplasms were difficult to score due to the inconsistent quality of the data; some undoubtedly were obscured in reports of other disorders, particularly of the genitourinary system. Five instances will be discussed. Only one was a case where both twins had neoplasms, and, in that set, tumors were reported in different locations.

Angioma

Case 108, *Peter* and *Palle*. At birth, *Peter* was diagnosed as having telangiectatic nevi dispersed over the left side of his chest. Radiation treatment was suggested. Reference to "Tumor angiomatosus thoracis" was entered into his records at age ten months, and when examined at age twenty-two he had a reddish nevus roughly the size of a shilling on his left breast and a *café-au-lait*-colored one of the same size on his right calf. *Palle* had none, one of the few differences between the twins.

Case 146, *Jensine* and *Maren*. *Jensine* had a small *café-au-lait* nevus hemangioma on her right leg. *Maren* had none.[6]

Myoma

Case 136, *Herta* and *Berta*. At age thirty-one, *Herta* had surgery for a myoma. Further information was not given. Her twin, *Berta*, offered no similar report up to the time of follow-up at age forty-nine. Both women were troubled by numerous cysts and polyps for which they fre-

6. In Yoshimasu's (1941) set, *Kazuo* had hemangioma telangiectatica on the right side of his face; *Takao* did not.

quently had surgery and other forms of treatment. They were reared apart and continued throughout adulthood to live on different continents.

Lipoma

Case 306, *Laura* and *Charlotte*. At approximately age forty-five, *Laura* had a lipoma removed from under her arm. No further information was available. Prior to that she had a hysterectomy for an unspecified type of "uterine growth." Though both twins had a history of subfertility related to a retroverted uterus, *Charlotte* was not mentioned as having a tumor or fibroids of any type. Both twins were seen close to the time of *Laura*'s surgery, so tendencies in *Charlotte* may not have had time to be expressed. McKusick mentions cases of multiple lipomas running in families, but this set, with so little information, exists only as a curiosity.

Unspecified

Case 212, *Clara* and *Doris*. Burks and Roe reported that at age thirty-nine, *Clara* had a nerve tumor removed and, at age twenty-five, *Doris* had surgical intervention for a uterine tumor. Both had a history of intestinal adhesions, and both had hysterectomies at a young age.

Circulatory System

Figure 5.2 lists concordance rates for circulatory disorder. Excluding rheumatic fever and sequelae, the concordance was high, which should come as no surprise, considering the substantial literature demonstrating familial transmission for hypertension and arteriosclerotic heart disease (Cavalli-Sforza and Bodmer 1978; Bodmer and Cavalli-Sforza 1976; Riccardi 1977; Fraser Roberts and Pembry 1978). Those who wish to examine the cases for environmental factors accelerating or delaying onset may use the index numbers. No pattern worthy of comment was evident.

Varicose Veins

McKusick cites evidence of genetic predisposition to varicose veins. One study in his review suggested dominant inheritance with reduced

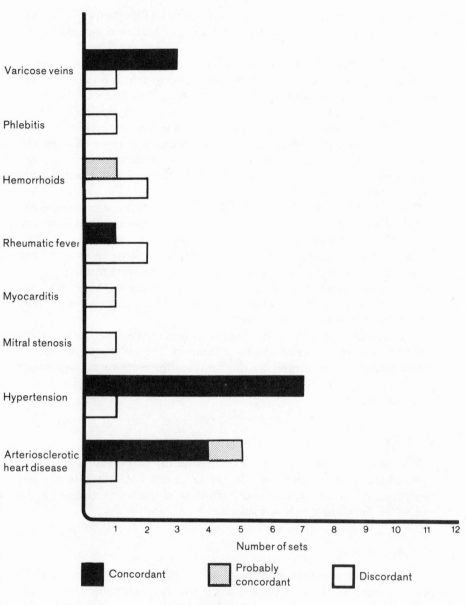

FIGURE 5.2
Circulatory system—MZ twins reared apart.

penetrance, while others implicated multifactorial transmission with about 50 percent heritability. The incidence is much higher among women, raising the possibility of X-linked dominance. Arnoldi (cited in McKusick) speculated on a relationship between late menarche and varicosity.

Three out of four sets scored for varicosity in this sample were concordant. All were female. Relationship to age of menarche could not be calculated.

Case 132, *Amy* and *Teresa*. This was the only discordant set. It is suspected that the women might have been concordant if Shields had included full medical work-up. At age fifty-five, *Amy* had varicose veins severe enough to impair her gait. *Teresa's* gait was unimpaired, with no report of varicosities. *Amy* had seven children; *Teresa*, three deliveries. Their histories included suggestions of chorea and chest trouble, but there was no mention of circulatory disease. *Amy* smoked about ten cigarettes a day and drank heavily. *Teresa* smoked about thirty cigarettes a day but rarely drank.

Case 170, *Astrid* and *Edith*. *Astrid* developed varicose veins at the age of thirty-two, *Edith* at twenty-six. Both began menstruating at fourteen. No family history of circulatory disorder was mentioned.

Case 178, *Karin* and *Kristine*. *Karin* developed varicose veins at the age of twenty, *Kristine* at eighteen. *Kristine's* symptoms were mild. She menstruated two years earlier than her twin (eleven versus thirteen years), one of the largest differences in the sample. There was no noteworthy family history of circulatory disease.

Case 344, *Olga* and *Viola*. When seen at age thirty-nine, both women had varicose veins. Age of onset is unknown. The difference in onset of menstruation is the largest in the sample (thirteen versus seventeen years). *Pedigree:* Family history is meager, with no tendency to circulatory disorder noted.

Phlebitis

The one instance of phlebitis is discordant. *Karin* (case 178) developed phlebitis at age forty, while her sister did not. When in her late seventies, *Karin* developed severe arteriosclerotic heart disease, while her sister developed only a mild case.

Hemorrhoids

Of the three sets that mentioned hemorrhoids, only one case (172) may be concordant, and concordance was questionable. Two of the three sets (130, 168) were concordant for hypertension and other circulatory disorders later in life, despite discordance on this variable.

Rheumatic Fever and Sequelae

Harvald and Hauge (1965) found MZ twins to have a significantly higher concordance rate for rheumatic fever than DZ twins. Using the Harvald and Hauge data, Cavalli-Sforza and Bodmer (1978) calculated heritability estimates of 47 to 55 percent. Heritability here referred to innate susceptibility being higher in some individuals than in others exposed to the same external agents. Despite the statistically significant difference in concordance rates, Harvald and Hauge speculated that susceptibility was not necessarily implicated if one assumed that MZ twins had more intimate contact with each other than DZ twins.

In the reared-apart data, where one could probably safely assume that intimate contact between MZ twins is reduced (though not eliminated), three cases of rheumatic fever were mentioned. Two of them were discordant.

Case 170, *Astrid* and *Edith*. Both twins had rheumatic fever, *Astrid* at age twenty-seven, *Edith* at fourteen and sixteen. *Astrid* developed endocarditis as a sequela.

Case 246, *William* and *Stanley*. *William* never had rheumatic fever, though *Stanley* reported repeated episodes.

Case 334, *Victor* and *Patrick*. *Victor* had rheumatic fever as a child with subsequent endocarditis. His twin had neither.

Myocarditis

Myocarditis was suspected in one partner of pair 112, but the diagnosis was not confirmed.

Mitral Stenosis

Mitral stenosis occurred in only one partner of pair 148. There was a question of whether both twins may have had rheumatic fever earlier in life.

Hypertension

Hypertension was scored for eight pairs, concordance showing in seven of the cases. Two additional sets reported for only one partner. The variable was scored if at any point in their lives the twins reported either a diagnosis of hypertension or, lacking that, a blood pressure reading greater than 140/90. The flaws in such an approach are obvious, but exist in most other studies as well. (See chapter 4 and table A3 for further information.) Though there were problems in scoring and in interpretation (for example, which of the sets could be said to have essential benign hypertension versus other forms), the results were in accord with the larger literature, which uniformly suggests hereditary prediposition of a fairly substantial degree. Cavalli-Sforza and Bodmer (1978) gave heritability estimates between 53 and 62 percent using Harvald and Hauge's data (1965). Riccardi (1977) and Fraser Roberts and Pembry (1978) estimated polygenic inheritance, though McKusick notes the debate in the literature over possible monogenic transmission as well. The data presented here add little clarification.

However, although the data were troublesome, the variable age of onset in some sets suggested that environmental factors removed even susceptible individuals from the hypertensive range. Contributory factors were unknown. Interested readers should go to the original material.[7]

Arteriosclerotic Heart Disease

Though only six cases of arteriosclerotic heart disease were scored, concordance was high.[8] Four were definitely concordant, a fifth probably was, and the discordant set was not examined in enough detail to be certain. Conservatism dictated that it be scored discordant. What seemed more interesting than hereditary tendencies to hypertension or arteriosclerotic heart disease was the discordance for heart attack and stroke. Harvald and Hauge (1965) found no difference in concordance rates of MZ and DZ twins for coronary occlusion, though their category of cerebral apoplexy was significantly more concordant in MZ twins. Results from these reared-apart twins also suggest discordance for death by coronary occlusion.

Case 114, *Kamma* and *Ella*. At about age fifty, *Kamma* developed hypertension with increasing symptoms of angina (substernal discomfort, functional dyspnea, and ankle edema.) At fifty-nine and sixty coronary occlusions occurred, from which she recovered. Breast cancer was diagnosed at sixty-eight, and she died at sixty-nine of pancreatic hemorrhage. The autopsy showed massive arteriosclerosis. *Ella* had no signs of hypertension until late in life and then exhibited only mild symptoms. Still alive and in good health at seventy-three, she was diagnosed as having mild hypertension and symptoms of angina (substernal discomfort and functional dyspnea.) *Pedigree:* A strong history of thrombosis existed in the family.

Case 168, *Martha* and *Marie*. *Martha*, still alive at seventy-one, had no symptoms despite a diagnosis of mild hypertension. *Marie* had noteworthy hypertension in her sixties and, at age sixty-five, entered a nursing home where she repeatedly fell out of bed. At age sixty-seven, a costal fracture plus a fissure in the left occipital region were found, accompanied by changes in EEG. She died at age sixty-eight. Her autopsy listed the cause of death as an intracerebral bleed. *Pedigree:* Apart from a pronounced tendency to migraine shared by the twins, information is sparse.

Case 170, *Astrid* and *Edith*. *Astrid* began to have what was described as

---

7. Cases 114, 130, 168, 170, 172, 178, 184, and 218.
8. The infrequent instances, such as case 314, where is is stated only vaguely that "heart trouble" of an unspecified nature was present, were not scored here.

stenocardiac attacks at age seventy-five and, at seventy-six, was hospitalized for severe angina. Coronary occlusion was diagnosed and treated with anticoagulants. She died at eight-three of a stroke. *Edith* died at eighty of pulmonary edema. Her autopsy showed hypertrophy and degeneration of the left ventricular myocardium, widespread artheromatosis of the coronary arteries and the aorta, and advanced pulmonary edema. The malignant breast tumor, noted earlier, also was found. Both twins had rheumatic fever as young women and varicose veins. *Astrid*, the twin who died three years after her sister, also had endocarditis. *Pedigree:* The family history was unremarkable for circulatory disease, though numerous cases of cancer are reported.

Case 178, *Karin* and *Kristine*. As young women, both had varicose veins. *Karin's* were more severe and were followed by phlebitis at age forty. Only *Kristine* reported transient mild hypertension in middle age. At the age of seventy-seven, *Karin* showed signs of cardiac disease. She died within three weeks, her autopsy placing cause of death as arteriosclerotic heart disease. *Kristine*, with no report of hypertension or symptoms past the transient episode in middle age, died at age seventy-nine of cancer. No autopsy was performed. *Pedigree:* Family history was not noteworthy.

Case 186, *Gertrude* and *Helen*. When seen at age fifty-two, both women were obese (236 and 222 pounds). Both developed rheumatism and, at the ages of forty-seven and fifty-one, respectively, each was hospitalized with severe ankle edema. At fifty-two, a few months after the study, *Helen* was hospitalized with a "heart disturbance" and died of pulmonary edema. There was no follow-up on *Gertrude*.

Case 206, *Kaj* and *Robert*. Neither twin had a history of hypertension. At age fifty-two, *Kaj* developed acute episodes of angina, and at fifty-four a coronary arteriogram showed marked arteriosclerotic changes in the left coronary artery. He received treatment and remained alive at age sixty-eight. *Robert* died at age sixty-five of a sudden coronary infarct. His mild attacks of angina had not led him to seek hospital admission. Each drank and smoked only moderately. *Robert*, however, had always been markedly obsessional and a worrier, while *Kaj* was overtly psychopathic in his youth.

The data on heart attack and stroke fit the results of the Swedish twin survey (Liljefors and Rahe 1970). Some genetic background for heart disease was suggested, but concordance for death by heart disease was low. Serum cholesterol was not reported for the reared-apart group, but obesity, smoking, or drinking could not explain discordance in the few cases cited. As in the Swedish reared-together group, however, the twin with fatal heart disorder in reared-apart sets tended to be the one in the pair with the unhappier life and in general the more nervous, neurotic, or stressed of the two.

Summary

Seventeen sets reported circulatory disorder of one type or another, most reporting multiple symptoms. Hypertension, varicose veins, and arteriosclerotic heart disease were largely concordant in the relatively few sets reporting. However, death from heart disease was concordant in only one of six sets. All other circulatory diseases reviewed (phlebitis, hemorrhoids, rheumatic fever, endocarditis, myocarditis, and mitral stenosis) had minuscule incidence and almost uniform discordance. If one twin had a circulatory disturbance of any type, in twelve cases the other twin also was scored in the system. Discordance showed in five cases. However, if more than one symptom or disorder was scored in the system, both twins were positive in seven out of eight cases.

Musculoskeletal System

Disorders of the musculoskeletal system frequently were highly concordant. This perhaps comes as no surprise, considering the very high physical concordance, down to the most minute details of skeletal structure, reported in chapter 4. (There also may be an interesting parallel between this and the high concordance suggested for movement and gestures. See chapters 4 and 8.) Figure 5.3 lists concordance rates in this sample. Figure 5.4 is taken from *Copeman's Textbook of the Rheumatic Diseases* (Scott 1978) and offers educated guesses, based on the larger literature, of the relative heritability of various disorders in the musculoskeletal system. It may be useful in quick comparison with the twin-reared-apart results.

Arthridites

This term was chosen as an umbrella to cover the variable reports of arthritis or "rheumatism" in cases that span half a century of (usually poor) medical reporting. Twelve cases were scored.[9] Seven were concordant and five discordant.

Estimates of incidence of rheumatoid arthritis in the general population range from 1 to 3 percent in European and North American groups, with women affected two to three times more frequently than men. Excluding juvenile forms, onset usually is in the fourth to fifth decades (Christian 1975). Given even the young average age of the

9. Cases 128, 130, 168, 170, 178, 184, 186, 210, 214, 218, 336, and 350.

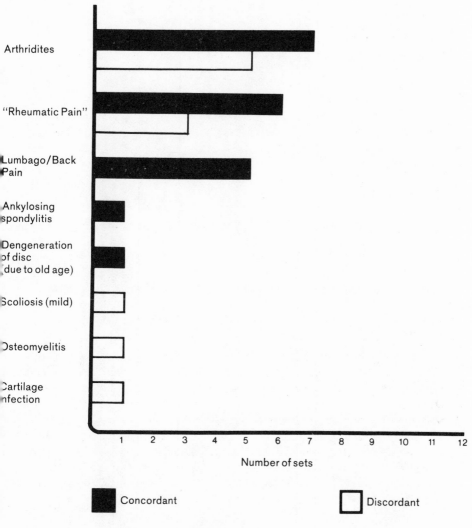

FIGURE 5.3

Musculoskeletal system—MZ twins reared apart.

twins at interview and the variable quality of reporting, the incidence of 16 percent (12/76) indicated considerable departure from the general population. Men accounted for only one case. Onset followed the expected pattern. The exact ages of onset tended to be similar in the twins (when ages were given) and appeared similar in other less precisely delineated instances.

Location also tended to be similar when indicated. Family pedigrees were too sparse to be useful.

McKusick reports cases of familial aggregation of rheumatoid arthri-

FIGURE 5.4

Spectrum of various rheumatic disorders showing the approximate relative contributions of genetic and environmental factors.*

Nature (genetic factors)   (environmental factors) Nurture

1. Diseases

Marfan's syndrome

Ankylosing spondylitis   Psoriasis   Rheumatoid arthritis   Lupus erythematosus   Rheumatic fever   (Back pain)   Septic arthritis

Congenital dislocation of hip   Osteoarthrosis of hip   Osteoarthrosis of other joints

Ehlers-Danlos syndrome   Gout   (Chondrocalcinosis)   Serum sickness   (Enthesu-pathies)   (Occupational synovitis of wrist)

Hurler's syndrome

2. Associated attributes

Sacroiliitis   Serum uric acid levels   Rheumatoid factor

*The scale of magnitude of inherited factors corresponds to estimates for the heritability of liability, the maximum extent to which genetic factors could account for the observed occurrence of disease in families. The figure is based on assessments of all available data, which were often poor, rather than on precise numerical estimates; conditions shown in parentheses are only guesstimates.
SOURCE: Reprinted by permission of the publisher from Copeman's Textbook of the Rheumatic Diseases, 5th ed., ed. J. T. Scott (New York: Churchill Livingstone, 1978), p. 32.

TABLE 5.3
*Onset of arthritic
disorders in MZ twins
reared apart.*

Case	Age of Onset
178	50 years
186	47 and 51 years
336	51 years
350	42 and 52 years

tis as well as cases in which no aggregation was found. He lists rheumatoid arthritis in his dominant catalogue, indicating that a simple Mendelian mechanism cannot be proved. Katz (1977), in addition to noting that the cause is unknown, estimated that a genetic basis has not been demonstrated despite family aggregation, an evaluation that is echoed by Riccardi (1977). Scott (1978) left open the possibility of a genetic contribution (see figure 5.4) and additionally noted the increased likelihood that a patient suffering from rheumatoid arthritis would have tuberculosis, peptic ulcer, or psoriasis.

Twin-reared-together data were only minimally informative. Though MZ concordance was higher than DZ concordance at a statistically significant level, the overall concordance was very low (Harvald and Hauge 1965). Cavalli-Sforza and Bodmer (1978) used the Danish data to make heritability estimates ranging from 63 to 74 percent. However, Harvald and Hauge evaluated their own data as questionable in demonstrating a genetic contribution, speculating that the more intimate and similar environments of MZ twins might be the significant factor. Given the poverty of information and the small numbers, the twin-reared-apart data support either hypothesis. However, at face value and with knowledge that the twins were from environments less similar than those of reared-together sets, the hypothesis of some degree of heritability appears viable.

Rheumatic Pains

The vague category of rheumatic pains referred primarily to pronounced "growing pains" in childhood or adolescence. Of the nine cases[10] reporting, six were concordant, all of them stating that the discomfort occurred during the same period of development. Of the discordant cases, one may have been due to infection, one is unexplained, and the last is the twins *Harry* and *Alfred*, who had the largest difference in height and weight in the sample (see chapter 4). *Alfred*, the shorter by more than three inches, reported rheumatic pains through-

10. Cases 174, 212, 224, 228, 246, 302, 304, 306, and 334.

out childhood. *Harry* had none. Shields (1962) speculated that a deprivation effect might explain the difference, a hypothesis not supported by other sets in the sample. Somatic disorder or endocrinological dysfunction might be a better explanation.

"Lumbago, Back Pain"

Lumbago or back pain of unspecified etiology was scored in five cases,[11] all of them concordant. Three of the five sets were male, two female. The sparse information seemed to indicate onset at the same stages of life.

Ankylosing Spondylitis

The single pair of twins with ankylosing spondylitis (though some of the cases of lumbago might in fact be spondylitis) exhibited such stunning concordance down to the most minute details that one is immediately led to suspect genetic susceptibility. *George* and *Millan* (case 102) were the most separated set in the literature. They were parted at birth and adopted into separate families. Raised in New York and Salt Lake City, they knew nothing of each other, one not even knowing he was adopted, until the age of nineteen, when they met and were studied. As mentioned earlier, after this initial meeting they parted and went into different branches of the armed services in World War II. At almost the same time, with no knowledge of each other and while in different theaters of war, each developed acute symptoms of ankylosing spondylitis. The report on their condition, by Stephens and Nunemaker (1950), two respected names in medicine, demonstrated the almost identical X rays, course of disease, and response to treatment. Family history included some instances of arthritis. The twins were not followed past this time.

McKusick lists ankylosing spondylitis in his dominant catalogue. Others (Beeson and McDermott 1975; Riccardi, 1977; Fraser Roberts and Pembry 1978) noted that infectious agents are suspected, although the incidence of ankylosing spondylitis is thirty times greater among relatives of spondylitic patients than in the general population. In recent years an association has been demonstrated between disorders in specific genetic immunologic markers (HLA-B27) and ankylosing spondylitis. McKusick estimates that the HLA findings have established autosomal dominant inheritance with reduced penetrance.

11. Cases 108, 112, 184, 206, and 328.

"Other" Musculoskeletal Problems

Ingegerd and *Monica* (case 188) both had similar forms of back trouble from the age of fifty on. Examination indicated some degeneration of discs. Mild scoliosis in old age was noted only for *Signe* (case 130), who also had arthritis while her twin did not. An unspecified cartilege infection in childhood in another set (case 144) left one partner with a leg several inches shorter than his brother's, and osteomyelitis, also considered infectious, was discordant in one set (case 348). This last pair was almost uniformly discordant in all somatic variables coded in other systems as well.

Summary

Twenty-nine sets reported musculoskeletal disorder of one type or another. Seven of the twelve sets reporting arthritic complaints were concordant. Information was poor, for the most part, and the incidence seems much higher in the sample than in the general population. Ages at onset were similar in those cases offering information, but it is unclear whether this should be construed as due to chance, as a reflection of the fact that most arthritic patients have onset in the fourth and fifth decades, or as some more specific similarity in these sets. Lumbago and ankylosing spondylitis all were concordant in the six sets reporting. Infections such as osteomyelitis had only single mentions, always discordant and probably not worthy of interpretation. Rheumatic pains of unspecified etiology were concordant in six of the nine cases scored. They occurred at the same period of life for concordant sets, irrespective of the discordance for rheumatic fever scored elsewhere for two pairs.

The ratio of both partners scoring positive within the system was nineteen positive, ten negative. Only two sets reported multiple incidences; one set positive in the system, the other negative.

Digestive System

Thirty-three sets reported disorders within the digestive system. In most instances, information was of poor quality and should be viewed with even more caution than already indicated for this sample.

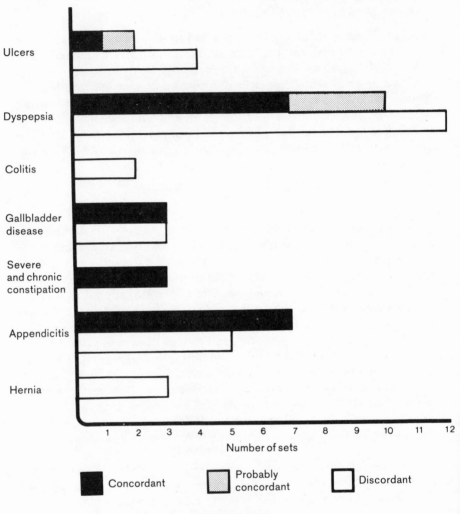

FIGURE 5.5

Digestive system—MZ twins reared apart.

Ulcers

Levitan (1977) states that heritability for ulcers has not been established unequivocally, though most other texts surveyed indicate that genetic factors of a polygenic type are implicated.[12] Predispositions to gastric or duodenal ulcer are presumed to be independent of each other. Relatives of gastric ulcer probands have a higher incidence of gastric ulcer, and close relatives of duodenal ulcer probands have about three times the expected number of duodenal ulcers. The more specific

12. See Beeson and McDermott 1975 as an example.

relationship between duodenal ulcers, blood group O, and secretor-nonsecretors is discussed at length in the literature (Fraser Roberts and Pembry 1978; Cavalli-Sforza and Bodmer 1978). Harvald and Hauge (1965) found no appreciable difference in the rates of peptic ulcer for MZ and DZ twins. They speculated that mutual ulcerogenic environments rather than mutual genes may be important in the concordance that does exist. Assuming polygenic inheritance, the statement still could explain the data. With a diathesis-stressor model, the predisposition (diathesis) would require environmental agents (stressors) to result in symptom formation. Differences between twins may indeed indicate different levels of environmental stress, but they do not necessarily indicate lack of an essential genetic base.

Of the six cases[13] reporting ulcers in the reared-apart data, only one set was concordant; a second was possibly concordant. In the concordant set (case 308), both were diagnosed as having gastric ulcer: *Timothy* had surgery at thirty-six; *Kevin* at thirty-nine. Both had a history of severe stomach trouble from the age of eighteen on. The set possibly concordant is *James* and *Robert* (case 228), both of whom had a long history of acidity and gastric pain severe enough to cause them to miss work. *James*, the more severely afflicted twin, was diagnosed as having duodenal ulcer. *Robert*'s pains increased when he underwent stress. His doctor diagnosed gastric catarrh.

The four discordant sets offered no information to indicate why one twin developed ulcers while the other did not. In three out of four cases, however, even discordant sets stated that both partners were troubled by high acidity. The problem with this data overlaps with the one confronted by Harvald and Hauge (1965) in their Danish study. When clinical examination and X ray were given to every set in one Danish subgroup, concordance went up. Symptom report and statement of diagnosis proved to be insufficient. In these data, too, one partner in a discordant set was discovered to have gastric ulcers only when X ray turned them up. Probably the most interesting set is *JJ* and *JB* (case 106). Though they were discordant for ulcer disease at age sixteen, the X ray and clinical work-ups suggested striking similarities. Interested readers should refer to the original paper for full information.

Dyspepsia/"Stomach Trouble"

This heterogeneous category was formed to cover the majority of reports that consisted of statements of "dyspepsia," "indigestion," "stomach trouble," and so forth. Only one set (case 188, discordant) reported gastritis while twenty-one others reported dyspepsia or tendencies to vaguely defined gastric complaints. Even those sets with ulcers or his-

13. Cases 106, 184, 228, 308, 324, and 328.

tories of heavy drinking did not give specific diagnosis of gastritis, though it would be considered probable. Thus with data on twins reared apart one may ask only if gastric discomfort reported for one twin is reported for the other too. Interviewing techniques and reporting styles must be considered to influence the rates considerably, though it is not known in which direction.

Of the twenty-two sets reporting, seven[14] were concordant, three[15] probably were concordant (symptoms present in both with specific statement of diagnosis for only one), and twelve[16] were discordant. Concordance and discordance, by inspection, seemed unrelated to birth order, handedness, or degree of contact.

Colitis

The larger literature implicates genetic factors as significant in predisposition to ulcerative colitis and suggests a possible association with ankylosing spondylitis. The disease tends to run in families, and although one summary (Janowitz 1975) stated that five of eight MZ sets in one series were concordant, another (Lynch 1976) stated that seven concordant sets of MZ twins have been reported in the literature with no case reports of discordance. The small samples make slight differences in reports insignificant.

In the reared-apart sample, two cases of colitis were reported. Detail was not given, and it is equivocal whether the disease was ulcerative colitis or not. Both cases (136 and 350) were female and discordant. Family pedigree could not be evaluated. However, it appeared that the twin who developed colitis had more illnesses than her partner through the life span, though it was unclear whether she also was the more psychologically stressed or disturbed. Neither set had partners with noteworthy obsessional features. However, in both instances the twin who developed colitis was the twin separated from her childhood rearing environment at a late age (four years and twelve years respectively), and in case 350, *Dora*, the twin with colitis, also reported "osteoarthritis of the spine."

Gallbladder Disease (Cholemia)

Six sets[17] reported gallbladder disease. Three were concordant, two discordant, and one set probably discordant. Two additional sets (cases 188 and 184) reported abdominal colics that may have been related to gallbladder disorder, though specific statements to that effect were not

14. Cases 106, 184, 214, 228, 308, 314, and 324.
15. Cases 128, 134, and 354.
16. Cases 108, 112, 114, 116, 130, 188, 190, 224, 332, 344, 348, and 350.
17. Cases 104, 114, 130, 170, 178, and 350.

made. One was concordant, one discordant. Information was so poor that further evaluation was unwarranted other than to note that all but one of the sets were female, in keeping with the approximately 3 to 1 ratio of women to men with gallbladder disease in the population.

Constipation

Chronic, severe constipation was reported for three sets,[18] all of them concordant and all of them reporting occurrence during the same time of life. The underlying disorder of which this was a symptom is unknown. However, in the histories the similarity of the chronic complaints is interesting.

Appendicitis

Twelve sets reported appendicitis. Seven[19] were concordant and five[20] discordant. Age of onset or surgery in the concordant sets was strikingly similar, though this may be a reflection of the finding that most episodes of acute appendicitis occur in the general population in the second and third decades of life (Beeson and McDermott 1975).

TABLE 5.4

Occurrence of appendicitis in twins reared apart.

Set	Ages of Surgery or Illness	
128	20	16
136	26	24
176	18	18
188	22	17
214	46	24
242	17	12
316	13	13

Six of the seven concordant sets were female, with a representative mixture of symmetric and asymmetric partners. All but one set had had contact by the time of onset or surgery. Three of the five discordant sets were female, with no association suggested between discordance and symmetry or degree of contact.

McKusick reports a 1937 study suggesting familial predisposition to appendicitis with a pattern consistent with dominant inheritance with irregular penetrance. Though more recent twin studies could not be lo-

18. Cases 106, 130, and 168.
19. Cases 128, 136, 188, 176, 214, 242, and 316.
20. Cases 142, 168, 174, 184, and 350.

cated for contrast, the current data could be considered tangential support of the thesis that a genetic component for appendicitis is worth investigation.

Hernia

Only three cases[21] of hernia were reported, all of them discordant. Onset was in the late forties and mid-fifties. McKusick lists inguinal and hiatus hernia in his dominant catalogue. He cites six studies, most reporting increased family incidences, some suggesting sex-linked patterns. Information sufficient for discussion of the reared-apart cases is lacking.

Summary

Of the thirty-three sets reporting symptoms or disorders within the digestive system, in twenty both partners reported disturbance and in thirteen only one partner scored. However, of those sets reporting more than one symptom or disorder, *all* were positive within the system (14:0). It is implied that there may be a tendency for some individuals to be particularly susceptible within the digestive system.

Though concordance is high when two or more disorders are scored, only appendicitis (which tended to occur at similar ages), chronic constipation, and possibly gallbladder disease were of even 50 percent concordance as specific similarities. Ulcers were surprisingly discordant despite evidence from the larger literature indicating predisposition. This may be an artifact of the sample, particularly since twins were not followed through the risk period, or it may be an indication of the differential effects of early environment on the equally susceptible pairs. The overall ratio for dyspepsia and other complaints of gastric discomfort (ten concordant, twelve discordant) is unenlightening since it is unknown whether it is due to real differences between partners or slipshod interview techniques.

Nervous System and Sense Organs

Thirty sets reported disorder in the nervous system and sense organs. The tally excludes the incidence of nearsightedness, farsightedness, and astigmatism reported in chapter 4 but includes infections and oth-

21. Cases 114, 130, and 348.

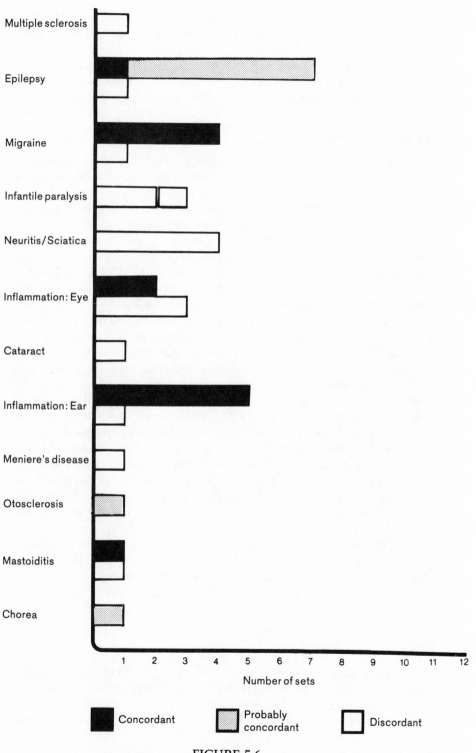

FIGURE 5.6
Nervous system and sense organs—MZ twins reared apart.

er eye disorders. The majority of symptoms and disorders in this category were of an infectious nature and, as such, tended to fall toward the "environmental" end of the spectrum. The issue, again, was susceptibility. Did both partners tend to have the same type of infections, infections in the same sense organs (eye, ear, and so forth), or proneness to disorder in the nervous system and sense organs in general?

Multiple Sclerosis

McKusick and others (Beeson and McDermott, 1975) note that genetic factors may be implicated in multiple sclerosis, though currently they do not appear to be of great importance. MZ twins have higher concordance than DZ twins, but concordance rates are very low for both groups. McKusick's data indicate that multiple sclerosis is about twenty times more frequent among relatives of probands than in the general population, this incidence declining as consanguinity becomes more remote. Though one study interpreted the family data as congruent with autosomal recessive inheritance with reduced penetrance, exogenous factors also were thought to be very strong.

Case 314, *Annie* and *Trixie.* These twins were discordant for multiple sclerosis. Seen at age forty-eight, *Trixie* had been diagnosed the year before, and the disease reportedly worsened after the interview. The onset may have been at age twenty-five, when *Trixie* suffered from an undiagnosed disease with symptoms of double vision and loss of power in the arms. *Trixie* was much the smaller at birth, "so small you could put her in a pint pot" (Shields 1962), and she remained the smaller of the two throughout life. Apart from overacidity (reported also for her twin), her history reported only scarlet fever and an operation for "swollen glands in the neck" during childhood. She menstruated a few months after her twin and was menopausal at the time of the interview while her twin was not. *Annie,* who had close and intimate contact with her twin throughout life (the two even attended the same school) was asymptomatic at the time of interview. However, at thirty-one, six years after *Trixie*'s undiagnosed illness, *Annie* had a bad attack of influenza that left her weak and prone to feelings of anxiety. Her history otherwise included only mention of tonsillitis at twenty-one followed by some form of heart trouble. *Pedigree:* Family history is meager and unremarkable.

Epilepsy

Various studies implicate genetic factors in the development of epilepsy. MZ twins are concordant at a rate significantly higher than DZ twins, and some forms of epilepsy are known to run in families. However, the concordance rates are so low even in MZ twins (only about a third of the sets concordant) that environmental factors appear critical in the majority of cases (Bodmer and Cavalli-Sforza 1976; Cavalli-Sforza and Bodmer 1978; McKusick 1978; Harvald and Hauge 1965).

The reared-apart cases match the larger literature.[22] Of the eight cases reporting epilepsy, only one pair was concordant for diagnosis and seizures. However, of the seven remaining cases, either EEG or symptoms such as blackouts and fainting suggested an underlying concordance in six (see chapter 4). This again raises the question of at what level concordance should be scored. If it should be scored at the level of overt symptomatology clear enough to be diagnosed, concordance is very low in MZ twins reared apart. However, if it should be scored at underlying prediposition, concordance may be very high. Presumably, environmental effects, including different birth experiences, are deciding influences in determining which twin will display seizures. However, in this sample, no association was suggested between discordant sets and symmetry, birth weight, or birth order. Given the quality of data, the lack of association may be spurious. Specific type of epilepsy was not stated in the cases, though most twins gave histories suggestive of grand or petit mal seizures.

Migraine

Concordance for migraine was high in the few cases reporting. Four out of five sets were concordant.[23] Ages at onset were similar in the three cases reporting (eleven years for both; fifteen and sixteen years; and eighteen and twenty years respectively). Family history, when available, indicated migraine in the biological pedigree but not in the foster or adoptive families. In at least one instance, the pattern of headache was strikingly alike.

Case 114, *Kamma* and *Ella*. For *Kamma*:

Menarche occurred at the age of 11. At about this time she started to have attacks of migraine and they continued up to the time of our investigation. She described them as attacks of headache localized to the back of the head, but to some extent also to the forehead, diffused over the skull and never restricted to one side. The headache "pressed and throbbed," was accompanied by nausea and usually also vomiting, which, however, failed to ease the headache. There were no visual symptoms, but a tendency for the area around the eyes to swell and itch prior to the attacks. Normally she had to go to bed when the attacks came; they remitted after 3–4 days, and during this time she was incapable of any form of work. She believed that the attacks were to some extent provoked by "nervousness," they could be brought on by work and often occurred premenstrually; she had also noted that she always had attacks during thunderstorms.

22. Cases 108, 122, 126, 134, 214, 332, 334, and 340.
23. Cases 114, 168, 214, and 344, concordant; 312, discordant.

For *Ella*:

Menstruation commenced when she was 13. She had begun to have attacks of migraine two years previously. Her headache, localized to the back of her head, and less pronounced in her forehead, was experienced as a "throbbing pressing" pain, diffuse and never unilateral. The attacks lasted 2–3 days; usually she was forced to go to bed and the headaches did not stop spontaneously until she had slept. There did not appear to be external provocation, although her attacks were related in some degree to menstruation, and had improved somewhat during later years since menstruation had become more irregular, but had not been affected by pregnancy.... She had also suffered from "car-sickness" since childhood and described it in exactly the same way as *Kamma*, although *Ella*'s case seemed to be more severe. [Juel-Nielsen 1965, pp. 170, 174–175]

Since these twins had little contact with each other, mutual identification is insufficiently explanatory.

McKusick and all medical texts reviewed were unambiguous in citing familial tendency to migraine. Only the pattern of inheritance is unclear. According to figures cited in McKusick, when two affected people mate, estimates of incidence in their children range from 69 to 83 percent in various studies. When one parent is affected, incidence estimates are from 44 to 61 percent. When neither parent is affected, incidence in the offspring drops down to a low of 3 to 29 percent. That even MZ twins reared apart are highly concordant is perhaps less striking in view of these data. What does seem interesting is the highly similar ages of onset despite different rearing environments and seemingly irrespective of contact.

Infantile Paralysis (Polio)

All instances[24] of infantile paralysis were discordant. The illness in case 112 was not clearly differentiated from chorea (see below).

Neuritis and Sciatica

Neuritis, a nerve inflammation, and sciatica, pain specifically along the sciatic nerve, were discordant in the four cases[25] reporting.

Inflammations of the Eye

Five sets[26] reported eye inflammations of one type or another. Only two were concordant, and, even then, not for type. *Marjorie* and *Norah* (case 128), both of whom possibly had congenital syphilis, reported

24. Cases 112, 128, and 150.
25. Cases 136, 190, 206, and 308.
26. Cases 128, 130, 212, 242, and 352.

keratitis for one at age twenty and blepharatis for the other at age twenty-eight. The other cases are uninformative, giving no reason to speculate on particular susceptibility in this sample.

Cataract

The one report of cataract occurred in case 168, which also reported heterochromia. Their biological mother was mildly diabetic with some opacity of the lens but no definite cataract. *Marie* reported that she had not noticed that the iris of her right eye had a brownish-yellow area until age thirty-six to thirty-seven when the sight in that eye deteriorated badly. Surgery for cataract occurred at thirty-eight, leaving her almost blind in the eye. *Martha* was discordant for both cataract and heterochromia.[27]

Inflammations of the Ear

Reports of noteworthy or chronic ear infections occurred in six cases,[28] concordance scored for five. Specific diagnosis was almost never given. The rate (5:1) was noteworthy, but it was unclear why infections of the ear should be more often concordant than infections of other sense organs. Inconsistent reporting might be the best explanation, or possibly the high incidence of otitis in the population at large (Ballenger 1977).

Ménière's Disease

Case 136, the single report of Ménière's disease, was discordant. *Berta* reported episodes over a ten-year span from approximately age thirty to forty, while *Herta* reported none. *Berta* reported numerous diseases discordantly from her twin and was suspected of emotional disorder and possible thyroid disease. McKusick reports that although genetic factors probably are involved, it is unusual to find high incidence of episodic vertigo and hearing loss in family lines. He lists Ménière's disease in his dominant catalogue.

Otosclerosis

Otosclerosis was diagnosed in one set—case 134—positive for one twin, probable for the other. McKusick lists a number of studies indicating dominant transmission with less than 50 percent penetrance.

27. Case 336 reports that "a film of skin" grew over one twin's eye and was successfully treated. No further information is given.
28. Cases 108, 112, 190, 330, 340, and 346.

One study in his review estimated a 25 percent risk to the child of an affected person.

Mastoiditis

Mastoiditis was listed for two sets, concordant in one (case 152), discordant in the other (case 348).

Chorea

Chorea of unknown etiology was listed as possible for both partners in set 132. A second case—112—may be discordant. It was not clearly differentiated from infantile paralysis and is mentioned here though scored in the section on polio.

Summary

Of the disorders of the nervous system and sense organs cited in this section, only epilepsy, migraine, and ear infections had noteworthy concordance rates. The ratio of both twins scoring positively within the system (not necessarily for the same disorder) versus only one scoring in the system was 19 to 11. When the tally was limited only to those cases scoring two or more symptoms in the system, both twins were positive in seven, possibly eight cases, to only one discordant.

Respiratory System

Forty-one sets reported incidence of disorder in the respiratory system. Concordance for tuberculosis is reported separately. Again, most of the symptoms and disorders in this system are infectious and would be expected to fall toward the "environmental" end of the spectrum. As figure 5.7 indicates, the reared-apart data do not give strong, immediate evidence of overall susceptibility. Also, aside from the poverty of data, the broader literature contains little information on reared-together MZ-DZ rates that would be needed for comparison.

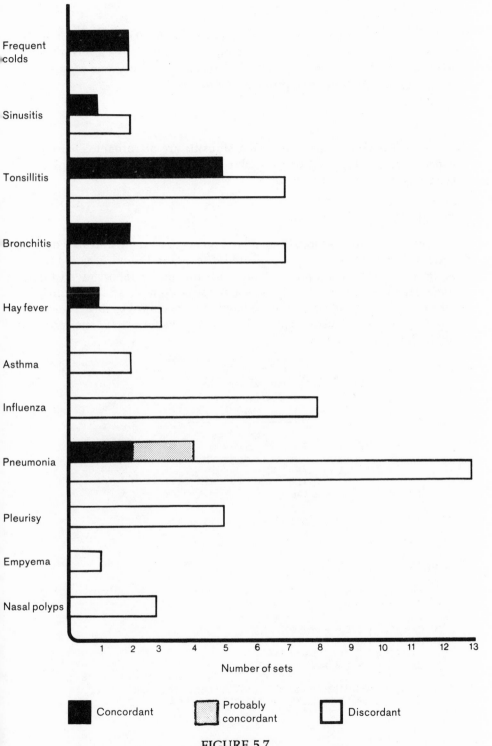

FIGURE 5.7
Respiratory system—MZ twins reared apart.

Frequent Colds

A history of frequent colds, almost always in childhood, is reported for four sets.[29] Interestingly, the two most separated cases are concordant while the two least separated are discordant. Only one of these sets (242) reported other respiratory symptoms.

Sinusitis

Two of the three cases[30] reporting sinusitis are discordant. The one concordant set (168) had onset at about the same time in mid-adolescence (ages fifteen and sixteen).

Tonsillitis

Twelve sets reported tonsillitis. Five[31] were concordant, and six[32] discordant. An additional set[33] was scored discordant, though it was puzzling. *June* had tonsillitis at sixteen, with no similar report given for *Clara*. However, as an adult *Clara* was reported to have an unspecified "throat abscess." Concordant sets tended to be twins with more contact, which mitigates against speculation about reasons for overall similarity or similarity in ages of onset.[34]

TABLE 5.5
*Onset of tonsillitis
in MZ twins reared
apart.*

Set	Age of Surgery	or Illness
210	child	9
212	23	4
236	2	2
242	2	7
332	child	child and adult

Bronchitis

Bronchitis was reported in nine sets,[35] concordant in only two.

29. Cases 112, 138, 220, and 242.
30. Cases 104, 146, and 168.
31. Cases 210, 212, 236, 242, and 332.
32. Cases 108, 118, 136, 146, 168, and 314.
33. Case 224.
34. Yoshimasu's (1941) set reported tonsillar hypertrophy for both twins.
35. Cases 108, 128, 146, 162, 170, 204, 210, 212, and 242.

Hay Fever.

Hay fever is reported for four sets,[36] concordant in one, *Megan* and *Polly*, (172) both of whom had onset at age twenty-four. McKusick lists it in his recessive catalogue, noting that the genetics are not simple. He suggests that the demonstration of immune-response genes may support dominant inheritance. Harvald and Hauge (1965) found MZ twins significantly more concordant than DZ ones, and Cavalli-Sforza and Bodmer (1978) gave heritability estimates of .58 to .71.

Asthma

Harvald and Hauge (1965) found MZ twins significantly more concordant for asthma than DZ twins. Using the Danish data, Cavalli-Sforza and Bodmer (1978) gave heritability estimates of .58 to .71. McKusick notes the possibily strong association between HLA-W6 and intrinsic asthma. The two reports in this sample—cases 128 and 312—were both discordant.

Influenza

Reports of influenza in this sample were predominantly severe cases; at least one case occurred during the 1918 epidemic. The eight sets[37] reporting all were discordant.

Pneumonia

Pneumonia was reported in seventeen cases. Two—184 and 228—were concordant, two more possibly concordant (190 and 224), and the rest discordant.[38]

Pleurisy

Pleurisy was reported in five cases,[39] all of them discordant.

Empyema

Empyema was reported in one discordant set, case 328.

---

36. Cases 136, 140, 172, and 246.
37. Cases 130, 158, 168, 184, 212, 314, 318, and 340.
38. Cases 106, 108, 128, 146, 162, 178, 204, 212, 238, 302, 304, 340, and 348.
39. Cases 136, 190, 206, 212, and 318.

Nasal Polyp

Nasal polyp or adenoids were reported in three sets,[40] all discordant. Two of the sets also had tonsillitis. In the set discordant for tonsillitis (136), the twin with tonsillitis also had nasal polyps. In the set concordant for tonsillitis (332), only one twin reported nasal polyps.

Summary

The results support the hypothesis of predominantly "environmental" (infectious) influence on the disorders listed. Without twin data from elsewhere, and probably even with it, the reared-apart data are not illuminating. Tonsillitis might bear more investigation. Of sets reporting respiratory illness, eighteen were pairs where both partners scored positive in the system and slightly more (twenty-two) were sets reporting only one partner positive. If scoring is done only for sets reporting two or more respiratory disorders, thirteen have both partners positive in the system while four have only one partner positive. The ratio (13:4), though more suggestive of underlying susceptibility in some individuals, is based on such a small number of cases with questionable data that it would not bear the weight of close scrutiny. Greater concordance in MZ twins for bronchitis, nasal polyps, sinusitis, frequent colds as well as asthma and hay fever might be expected since all may be related to allergic diathesis. This is explored in the section on allergies.

If scores for pulmonary tuberculosis and/or whooping cough are scored in the respiratory system, the results are not changed in any appreciable way.

Skin and Subcutaneous Tissue

Information on disorders of skin and subcutaneous tissue usually was given only if the disorder was severe or if it was present at the time of interview. It is safe to assume that most cases were missed and, in the thirteen sets reporting, information was almost uniformly poor. Grouping according to possible atopic hypersensitivity is given in the next section.

40. Cases 126, 136, and 332.

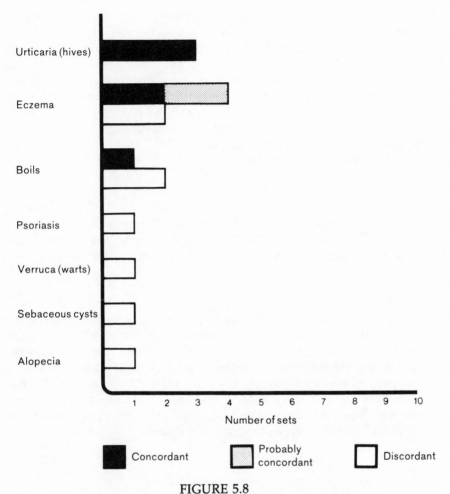

FIGURE 5.8
Skin and subcutaneous tissue—MZ twins reared apart.

Urticaria

Urticaria, commonly known as hives, occurs in response to a variety of agents. The three sets[41] reporting urticaria all were concordant. Two reported incidence during adulthood, the third reported the symptom only for childhood.

Eczema

Eczema was reported in six sets:[42] It was concordant in two, possibly concordant in two others, and discordant in the remaining two pairs.

41. Cases 104, 136, and 216.
42. Cases 104, 130, 168, 184, 206, and 212.

Without contact or knowledge of each other, from the age of ten on *Olga* and *Ingrid* (case 104) developed a severe tendency to "boils" localized predominantly on the face and back with occasionally severe squamation. *Olga* once was diagnosed by a dermatologist as having purigo. Both twins reported almost constant disturbance from the age of onset to when they were seen at age thirty-five. Symptoms increased during times of mental stress. At sixteen, *Ingrid* had a localized eczema-like disease on the palm of her hand. Years later, *Olga*'s daughter had the same symptoms in the same location.

The other cases are unremarkable.

Boils

Apart from *Olga* and *Ingrid,* all other cases[43] reported discordance for boils. Case 138 reported discordance for an unexplained abscess in one twin. Though mentioned here, it was not scored in this category.

Psoriasis

McKusick lists a substantial number of studies, all supporting the hypothesis of noteworthy genetic determinants for psoriasis. As with spondylitis and atopic allergies, abnormal immune responses associated with the HLA system are implicated (HLA-BW17 and HLA-BW13). The single case in this sample was discordant. *Christine* (case 312) had psoriasis from ages forty to forty-two and also suffered from asthma. She was thought to have thyroid disease. *Nina* was asymptomatic for psoriasis, asthma, allergies, and thyroid disorder.

Other

The few other references all were discordant. Case 148 reported warts[44] and sebaceous cysts. Case 106 reported alopecia and hinted strongly of neurotic contributions.

Summary

Of the thirteen sets scored, only five, possibly six, were concordant within the system and, except for set 104, there were no noteworthy instances of multiple symptoms. The data are extremely poor.

43. Cases 104, 212, and 242.
44. Verruca is listed under "infectious diseases" in the ICD but seemed appropriate to include here.

Allergies

Some forms of allergic susceptibility are considered to be inherited. Disorders falling into this class are grouped in varying ways under the heading allergies or hypersensitivity (see Ballenger 1977). McKusick notes that the genetics are not simple, and Riccardi (1977) lists them as probably polygenic. Data on eczema, urticaria, heat spots, asthma, and hay fever, in addition to bronchitis, nasal polyps, sinusitis, and frequent colds, were considered to be possible sources of information in this sample. They have been combined in table 5.6 with four additional cases of allergy with unknown manifestations. About half the cases are concordant. Sets reporting incidence of two or more disorders have both partners positive in six out of eight cases.

Genitourinary and Reproductive System

Thirty-eight sets offered information on genitourinary and reproductive functioning. Twenty-one of them offered data beyond those on menstruation and/or menopause. All cases were female. Figure 5.9 presents concordance rates broken down into menstrual and genitourinary symptoms versus those associated specifically with pregnancy and delivery. The count excludes instances of infections such as salpingitis, endometritis, and gonorrhea, which were reported in a haphazard manner and which, in this sample at least, probably reflect more on the sexual functioning of the twins and their partners (and their openness in reporting) than on susceptibility. (The minimum count was two sets concordant, three discordant.) Data specifically on menstrual functioning is discussed in chapter 4 and is listed in table A7 in the appendices.

Menstrual Symptoms

Twenty sets offered information beyond age of onset of menses (see chapter 4 and table A7). Four sets reporting headache have been tallied along with instances of migraine cited earlier in this chapter. Though numbers were small in individual categories, the overall concordance for menstrual symptoms was strikingly high. It might be even higher than suggested by the figure since, in accord with the methods used herein, sets reporting for only one partner have been scored discordant

TABLE 5.6
Allergies—MZ twins reared apart.

Case	Eczema	Urticaria	Allergy: unspecified	Heat Spots	Asthma	Hay Fever	Allergic Diathesis-Respiratory			
							Bronchitis	Nasal Polyps	Sinusitis	Frequent Colds
104	+ +								− +	
108		+ +					− +			
112										+ +
126					+ −			+ −		
128	− +						− +			
130										
136		+ +				+ −				
138								+ −		
140						+ −				+ +
146							+ +			
162							+ +		+ −	
168	− +									
170							− +		+ +	
172						+ +				
184	+ (+)		+ +							
204							+ −			
206	− +									
210							+ +			
212	+ +						+ −			
216		+ +								
220										
222			+ −							− +
238				+ +						
242							+ −			+ −
246						+ −				
312					− +			+ −		
332										
348			+ +							
352			+ −							

or eliminated. Though degrees of severity sometimes varied within sets, the fundamental similarity was one of the more interesting results to emerge from the twin-reared-apart data. The suggestion is strong that, should MZ-DZ and consanguinity studies be made, the heritability on menstrual symptomatology may be quite high. Information on the relationship between prostaglandin metabolism and dysmenorrhea may shed light on some of the high concordance.

Pyelonephritis

The one set reporting pyelonephritis, (case 188) was discordant.

Cystitis

Cystitis or bladder infections were reported for three sets, one concordant (136) and two discordant (130 and 188).

Mastitis

Mastitis was reported for three sets[45] and was concordant in one (case 136).

Fibroids/Cysts

The seven cases reporting fibroids or cysts are combined in the figure but will be discussed separately. Cases 214, 224, 350, and 352 reported cysts. (Three reported ovarian cysts, one a vaginal cyst.) All were discordant. Cases 128, 148, and 212 reported fibroids. Two were concordant and one discordant. *Marjorie* and *Norah* (case 128) both had hysterectomies at age thirty-four. *Marjorie* reported fibroids as the reason, *Norah* left it unexplained. *Clara* and *Doris* (case 212) had at least partial hysterectomies at ages thirty-two and twenty-nine respectively. Data on them are poor in this respect and since *Doris* reported a "cervical tumor," fibroids were presumed, possibly incorrectly. *Millicent* and *Edith* (case 148) were discordant, *Millicent* reporting a total hysterectomy for fibroids shortly before she was seen, while her sister reported no similar disorder.

For the purposes of scoring, *Marjorie* and *Norah* were presumed concordant, *Clara* and *Doris* probably concordant, and the rest discordant.

45. Cases 132, 136, and 344.

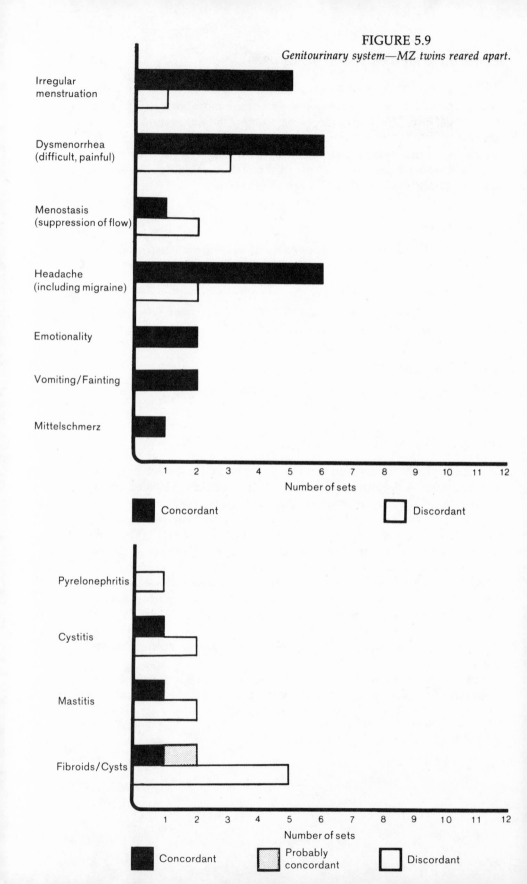

FIGURE 5.9
Genitourinary system—MZ twins reared apart.

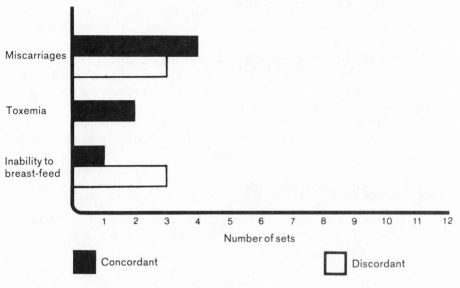

FIGURE 5.9
Genitourinary system—MZ twins reared apart.

Miscarriages[46]

Miscarriages were reported in nine sets. Only seven[47] were scored, on the assumption that both partners had to report at least one conception for concordance-discordance to have meaning. In the two sets not scored—cases 316 and 338—one was a pair where a partner died early and the other was a pair where one of the partners had been married only a year and reported no pregnancies.

Four of the sets scored were concordant and three discordant, a proportion that, though based on small numbers, is suggestive of susceptibility. As with menstrual symptoms, it would not be surprising to learn from future MZ-DZ and consanguinity studies that the tendency toward miscarriages had a respectable degree of heritability.

Toxemia/Eclampsia

McKusick lists toxemia in his dominant catalogue and cites studies that indicate a much higher incidence of toxemia in daughters of women who had toxemia in pregnancy than in a comparison group. Both sets reporting toxemia in this sample were concordant. *Megan* and *Polly* (case 172) and *Laura* and *Charlotte* (case 306) had major difficulties with

46. Cases reporting abortions were scored only if it was stated that the abortions were spontaneous.
47. Cases 112, 188, 160, 172, 214, 306, and 352.

pregnancy. At age thirty *Polly* delivered one child by caesarean that died seven weeks later from spina bifida. *Megan* had five miscarriages between ages twenty-four and thirty before delivering MZ daughters. *Laura* and *Charlotte* both miscarried their first pregnancies and had toxemia at five months in their second. *Laura* miscarried the second pregnancy, but *Charlotte* was able to carry to delivery. *Charlotte* also had a third successful pregnancy while *Laura* had a hysterectomy. Both of *Charlotte*'s sons were born in transverse positions.

Both *Laura* and *Charlotte* reported having a retroverted uterus and both had been treated for subfertility.

Hypogalactica

Hypogalactica or difficulty in breast-feeding was scored for four sets.[48] Only one pair appeared possibly concordant (case 114).

Other

Ingegerd and *Monika* (case 188) reported discordance for perimetritis, and *Monika* alone had instances of postpartum fever and disturbance. They are not scored in the figure.

Summary

Although rates are low, menstrual symptoms, toxemia, and miscarriages were concordant enough to suggest that future workers may find some significant genetic base. Difficulty in breast-feeding was almost never concordant. Cystitis, mastitis, fibroids, and cysts were reported at such low rates and with such mixed concordance that no conclusion is offered.

If one includes menstrual symptoms, the rate of both twins scoring positive in the system is extremely high. For reports with at least one symptom, the ratio is twenty-two sets having both partners positive in the system to only five with one partner positive. If one includes menstrual symptoms but scores only when two or more genitourinary disorders are reported, the ratio remains high (16:1).

If one excludes menstrual symptoms, the rates drop considerably. Both twins are positive in the system in only half the cases (10:10). However, for those sets reporting two or more disorders (but excluding menstrual complaints), the ratio again moves up (6:1).

It is possible that some degree of generalized susceptibility within the genitourinary and reproductive system may be found in future

48. Cases 104, 114, 188, and 178.

studies, particularly for those individuals who have multiple symptoms or disorders.

Endocrine, Metabolic, and Nutritional Systems

Only eleven sets reported in this category, and information for the most part is poor.

Thyroid Disorder

McKusick discusses Hashimotos thyroiditis (struma) and myxedema. Hashimotos struma is listed in the dominant catalogue, with several studies listing impressive familial aggregations, and one suggesting autosomal dominant inheritance of the tendency to autoimmunity. Myxedema also occurs in familial aggregations, though frequently it does not. McKusick lists it in the recessive catalogue, and reports a study that found results consistent with suggestions of a genetic relationship between myxedema, hyperthyroidism, and nontoxic goiter.

Seven sets reported thyroid disorder or the suspicion of thyroid disorder, but further information, except in one case, was sparse. *Ada* and *Ida* (case 244) both had goiter. *Alois* and *Oskar* (case 332) had struma when seen at age sixteen, though with no other findings. (*Alois*, it may be worth recalling, was psychotic.) *Viola* (case 344) also was reported to have an enlarged thyroid at age thirty, but her twin appears discordant. Hyperthyroidism was discordantly reported for case 136, and an unspecified thyroid disorder was suspected in case 338 when one twin began putting on weight between ages twenty-eight and thirty.

Two noteworthy cases are summarized below:

Case 312, *Nina* and *Christine*. These twins had one of the largest differences in height and weight in the sample, with *Christine* much the smaller throughout life. *Christine* was, for many years, the more irritable and jumpy twin and, from the ages of fifteen to thirty-nine, suffered from migraine. Between thirty-two and forty-one she had asthma with positive reactions on allergy tests. At age forty-one, swelling in her legs and neck and almost continuous asthma led to hospital tests that showed "thyroid trouble." She was treated with iodine, and the swelling and asthma were relieved. Childless, she and her husband believed the husband was infertile. *Nina*, her twin, had two children and none of the above-mentioned symptoms.

Case 130, *Signe* and *Hanne*. This was perhaps the most interesting case, not only for the detailed description but also for the questions raised. They are scored as possibly concordant in figure 5.10. According to Juel-Nielsen (personal communication, 1979), those who have had contact with the twins still have questions about the degree of somatic involvement in their symptoms. At issue is the close similarity in symptomatology between the twins. One was diagnosed as having Graves disease; treatment lessened the symptoms. The other also was worked up for thyroid disorder but, with results at a subclinical level, was not treated; the symptoms persisted and were assumed to be linked to psychiatric disturbance. While the description in Juel-Nielsen is lengthy and detailed, the following summaries can provide an overall sketch.

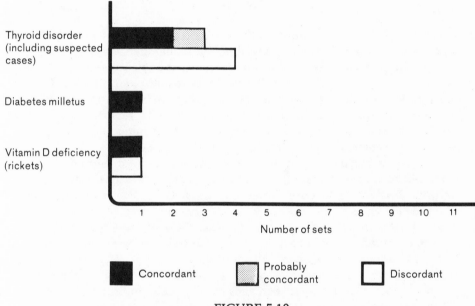

FIGURE 5.10

Endocrine, metabolic, and nutritional systems—MZ twins reared apart.

Signe menstruated at fourteen with considerable premenstrual discomfort. She suffered chronic, severe constipation all her life. Menses became sparse and irregular from twenty-five to forty-nine, after which menopause intervened. At thirty-eight symptoms were pronounced enough that a diagnosis of climacterium was given. She was nervous for many years and slept poorly. In her adult life she reported a mass of somatic complaints, including pains in all parts of the body, particularly in the arms, legs, knees, and joints of the feet, as well as in the back, neck, and head; a feeling of pricking pressure in her abdomen; constant headache; dizziness; "black stripes before eyes"; poor appetite; a feeling of "a lump in the throat"; weight loss; frequent urination; palpitations. At age thirty-nine, her basal metabolism was 103 to 104 percent. At forty-five, there were no definite alterations in the size of the thyroid and no clinical signs of thyrotoxicosis or Graves disease. Neurological studies disclosed universal analgesia; the plantar and pharyngeal reflexes could not be stimulated.

At fifty-four, *Signe* was evaluated again. She now complained additionally of being easily frightened, irritable, and anxious. She perspired easily and then chilled. Pricking paresthesias were reported in her fingers and toes, some symptoms on the left side of the body but not the tongue. Fatigue, dyspepsia, and loss of appetite remained, as did visual complaints. She was postmenopausal, and clinical examination still revealed no thyroid disorder. Weight at age fifty-four: 60 kilograms (132.3 pounds).

She was referred for outpatient psychiatric treatment with a diagnosis of severe depressive neurosis, probably psychogenic though including endogenous elements. Eight ECTs produced some subjective improvement but no change in the basic alterations in mood.

Hanne menstruated from the age of fourteen with considerable premenstrual discomfort. She suffered chronic, severe constipation all her life and menostasis, but her symptoms were not reported to be as severe or chronic as her twin's. At age thirty-six her symptom list included: pains in the right fossa iliaca spreading down the right leg; frequent urination; poor appetite and sleeplessness; slight paresthesias in her fingers; and the feeling of "a lump in the throat." She complained additionally of headache, exhaustion, nervousness, and mood fluctuation. At age thirty-eight, she reported severe epistaxis during one menstruation, perspiration, and all the earlier symptoms. Basal metabolism was measured as 127 percent. Her weight was 66.8 kilograms (147.3 pounds). No definite ocular symptoms of Graves disease were present though the thyroid gland was somewhat enlarged. She was diagnosed as having Graves disease, was given iodine and X ray treatment, and the symptoms abated. At around the age of forty-nine, she discontinued iodine on the advice of her physician. She underwent menopause at age fifty-one with some increase again in symptomatology. *Hanne* was considered to have a depressive neurosis, but one not as severe as her sister's.

Pedigree: Their biological mother had many of the same symptoms and was diagnosed and treated as hyperthyroid. Numerous instances of nervousness and other of their symptoms were reported in their relatives. A maternal aunt was diagnosed and treated as having Graves disease. "Nervousness," mood shifts—particularly toward depression—and "psychosomatic" complaints abound in the relatives with whom the twins had little or no contact. *The twins did not know of each other's illness.* [Condensed from Juel-Nielsen 1965, pp. 185-207. Emphasis my own.]

Diabetes Mellitus

Riccardi (1977) suggested genetic contributions to diabetes and offered more than one pattern of inheritance. Neel et al. (1965) described it as a "geneticist's nightmare . . . presenting almost every impediment to a proper genetic study which can be recognized." Though they noted familial constellations and MZ twin rates that were higher than DZ rates, a genetic hypothesis was implicated only because it was the most parsimonious explanation, not because it had been demonstrated.

Two instances of diabetes mellitus were reported in this sample, though only one was scored. Twins *A* and *B* in case 316 had severe diabetes from age thirteen on. One twin died. *Kamma* and *Ella* (case 114) reported that *Ella* developed mild diabetes in late life (age 73) but since *Kamma* died at age sixty-nine, comparison could not be made.

Vitamin D Deficiency

Two reports of rickets emerged from the sample (cases 184 and 240). *Petrine* and *Dorthe* (case 184) were concordant during infancy; the other set reported for only one partner. Discussion on the genetic transmission of vitamin D-resistant rickets exists in the literature (see McKusick 1978), but these two cases gave insufficient information for evaluation or discussion.

Summary

By concordance rates, nothing can be said about disorders in the endocrine, metabolic, or nutritional system for twins reared apart. The data were extremely limited and poor in detail. *Signe* and *Hanne*'s case was interesting for the questions it raised about possible underlying subclinical thyroid dysfunction in two women who were diagnosed as neurotic.

Infective and Parasitic Diseases

Infective and parasitic diseases fell toward the "environmental" end of the spectrum, with many, such as measles and mumps, so pandemic that even issues of susceptibility are moot. The data in this sample were

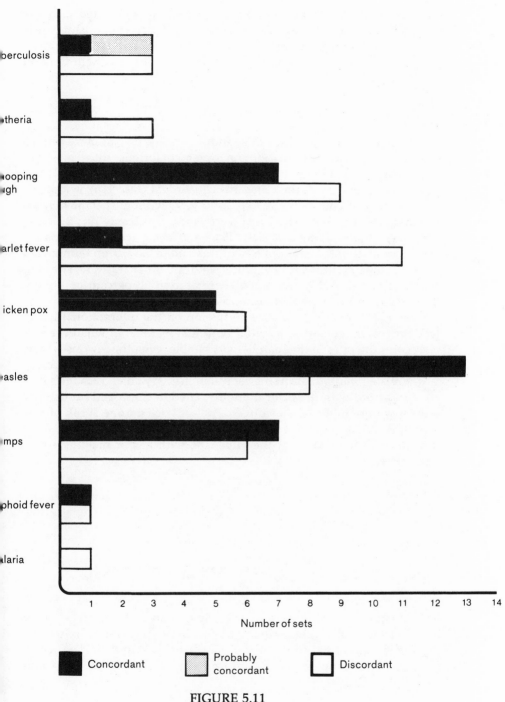

FIGURE 5.11
Infectious diseases—MZ twins reared apart.

variable. Some cases could not be scored because they listed only the statement of "usual childhood diseases" (usually concordantly), while others gave listings, the exhaustive nature of which could be questioned. Because of this, figure 5.11 is presented with comment only on tuberculosis.

Tuberculosis

The data on tuberculosis in this sample were worthy of more serious consideration than information on other conditions since most instances of TB were likely to have been reported.

Of the six sets[49] reporting, one was concordant (case 116), symptoms were present in both twins of two other pairs without specific diagnosis (cases 160 and 164), and three were discordant (cases 108, 238, and 354). One of the discordant sets, *Palle* and *Peter*, (case 108) possibly should be discounted, since one twin was said to have been immunized at twenty-one months (BCG vaccine?) and the other was not. The concordance rate probably was somewhere around 50 percent or higher, depending on how one scored imprecise reports.

Stern (1973) offered a concise discussion on the international literature suggesting genetic susceptibility to tuberculosis. In whatever way one scores the rates in the reared-apart sample, even the few cases were more like the rates of MZ twins reared together than of DZ or more distantly related individuals in his compilation. Harvald and Hauge's data were in accord with the prior literature, cited by Stern and heritability estimates were high. As Stern noted, not only could one speak of susceptibility but also even of specific localization. MZ twins tend to show the effects of the disease at the same site, with mirror imaging sometimes present (Gedda 1961).

Summary

By and large, information on physical symptoms and disorders was of questionable quality. Only about one-fourth of the seventy-six sets reporting here included substantial clinical work-ups in their data. Thus, the data in this chapter were meant primarily as a spur to curiosity and

---

49. An additional case from Yoshimasu (*Kazuo* and *Takao*) was concordant for pulmonary TB.

cannot be taken as hard or conclusive. Rates for specific disorders may be found in the appropriate sections.

The question of system vulnerability, proposed for this literature by Juel-Nielsen, was approached in two ways. First, it was asked whether both twins in sets reporting incidence scored in the same system, even if not for the same disorder. Second, sets reporting only a single incidence of disorder in a system (no matter how they scored on it) were eliminated and pairs with two or more citations were examined. To be scored positive in the system, the disorders did not have to be the same; rather two or more disorders in any given system had to have been mentioned and each twin had to be scored positive at least once. The results are presented in table 5.7. They suggest that the hypothesis of system vulnerability may be worth testing in a better sample and with more rigorous evaluation. Also, better definitions of "systems" are needed. For example, should pleurisy be scored under musculoskeletal or respiratory; hernia under musculoskeletal or digestive; mastitis under reproductive or subcutaneous? At least two other systems, both along embryologic and developmental lines, may be suggested. One would be to score according to degree of ectodermal, endodermal, or mesodermal structure involved. Another method would be to map which structures are developing at specific embryologic and fetal ages (six weeks, seven weeks, and so forth) and score for susceptibility in structures that develop at the same time.

The issues are interesting and potentially useful. Control groups of dizygotic twins and unrelated individuals would be necessary for adequate evaluation.

TABLE 5.7

Physical symptoms and disorders: Concordance within systems for MZ twins reared apart.

	All sets reporting incidence in system		Sets reporting two or more incidences in system	
	Positive*	Negative*	Positive*	Negative*
Cancer	0	6		
Circulatory	12	5	7	1
Musculoskeletal	19	10	1	1
Digestive	20	13	14	0
Nervous system and sense organs	19	11	7	1
Respiratory	18	22	13	4
Skin and subcutaneous	5	8		
Genitourinary and reproductive	22†(10‡)	5†(10‡)	16†(6‡)	1†(1‡)

*Positive=Both partners had one or more incidences in the system. Negative=Only one partner had one or more incidences in the system.
†Including menstrual symptoms.
‡Excluding menstrual symptoms.

Chapter 6

Psychosis

Studies on the heritability of psychosis increasingly indicate significant genetic contributions both for the schizophrenias (Gottesman and Shields 1976; Rome 1979) and the affective disorders (Allen 1976; Perris 1973; Perris and d'Elia 1966; Winokur et al. 1969; Bertelsen et al. 1977). Though the largest number of subjects in various studies come from kinship, adoption, and foster-child samples, twin series comprise a respectable contribution. However, twins reared apart have not been central in the literature, giving little information on the schizophrenias and even less on affective disorders. What minimal information twin-reared-apart studies offer consistently emphasizes high concordance and support for the genetic hypothesis.

In the material that follows, all cases were reanalyzed, whenever possible from original records. The result was a narrowing of the number of cases appropriate for inclusion and adjustments to concordance rates. Though the reanalysis did not provide a major challenge to the hypothesis of genetic predisposition, the findings did raise question about possibly potent environmental influences on onset and content of psychotic episodes.

Affective Disorders

Affective disorders of psychotic proportions include depressions severe enough to impair reality testing and cyclical mood shifts from mania to depression. The latter often goes under the label of manic-depressive psychosis. In recent years, new nomenclature has been introduced to better classify syndromes and to allow more discriminating investigations into etiology. Episodes of only depressive or manic components are labeled "unipolar," with patients showing only manic phases being very rare. Mood swings including both components are called "bipolar." The spectrum is further broken down according to the patient's hospitalization status. Within the bipolar class, BPI refers to hospitalization for mania, BPII to hospitalization for depression, and BPO (bipolar other) to outpatient treatment with no hospitalization. Schizoaffective, a diagnosis not universally accepted, refers to cases where the disturbance seems a mixture of mood shift and thought disorder.

The sketch of nomenclature is included to introduce the fundamental problem of diagnostic confusion that permeates this literature. For years British-trained psychiatrists gave greater weight to evidence of mood shifts, with their American counterparts focusing more on thought disorder. The same case would thus be diagnosed in two different ways. The system now is shifting toward an acceptance of the British model, but cases already in the literature remain potentially ambiguous. One can clarify the ambiguity by obtaining descriptive case material and submitting it to blind diagnosis by a team of raters.

In the twin-reared-apart literature, only three dated references exist to affective disorders severe enough to be considered psychotic. One is a brief undocumented mention by Burks and Roe in 1949 (case 212), another is a 1952 study by Stenstedt (case 156), and the third is a 1935 report by Rosanoff, Handy, and Plesset (case 180). Juel-Nielsen reported one pair (case 188) who had depressions and suicide attempts, but his final diagnosis was neurosis rather than psychosis. Their case is reported in chapter 7.

Of the three cases potentially scorable as psychotic, none was satisfying in its original description. Burks and Roe wrote only that one of their twins once was called "manic-depressive" along with various other labels. Stenstedt offered a two-paragraph description of sisters, one of whom fell ill at age forty-seven with depressive and hypomanic phases. The co-twin (not seen by Stenstedt) was thought to have been depressed at age twenty-five but never was hospitalized and was not known to have had hypomanic phases. The Rosanoff et al. study offered a one-page description of MZ brothers who were hospitalized for mania within a few weeks of each other and who had an older brother, also hospitalized, who was given a diagnosis of dementia praecox (schizophrenia), hebephrenic type. The pair have been summarized repeatedly (Slater 1953; Price 1968) with the comment that since follow-up was short, the final diagnosis might be schizophrenia.

Reanalysis

Of the three cases, only the one studied by Rosanoff et al. emerged as worthy of further consideration. Through the courtesy of William Craig, Ph.D., and the hospital in Canada where the twins spent most of their adult lives, a summary of more than four decades of hospital records was obtained. The records allow for a reexamination of the manic-depressive diagnosis given in the 1930s. Although the notations made over the years are not up to current standards, the summary is the only detailed and comprehensive study of psychotic affective disorder in separated twins now available to the literature. The complete text of the summary is included in appendix A. The following outline will serve to introduce the case and the diagnostic and theoretical issues it raised.

Rosanoff Twins A and B

The twins were born in rural Ontario, Canada, in March 1909. They and a brother three years their elder (sibling C) were the only children to survive infancy from at least five births in the family. They were separated when two months old due to poverty in the home. B remained with his family while A was sent to live with an uncle and aunt on a farm more than one hundred miles away. The boys are reported to have had little if any contact during childhood and may have met for the first time only around 1929 when both were twenty, within approximately a year of their first hospitalization in 1930 at age twenty-one. The twins were "identical in colouring, measurements and features" and were "practically indistinguishable" (Rosanoff et al. 1935, p. 730). Photographs recently found in the files indicate them to look very similar to each other and quite different from their older brother.

A, who was sent to the uncle and aunt, was brought up in relative comfort and was said to have completed one year of high school. He was described as clever in school and was said by the uncle to be hard-working, truthful, fond of social activities, with many friends in the community and without tendencies to drink or get into trouble. Rosanoff described A as having been "the life of the party." A left the farm at age twenty to move to a town closer to his biological mother so he could be of financial assistance to her, and the uncle heard no more of him until the next year when he was hospitalized.

B remained at home with his father, mother, and elder brother. It was not known whether the two children who died in infancy preceded or followed him. The father was a poor provider and, after a three- to five-year illness, died when B was thirteen. C, the older brother, became mentally ill when B was fourteen. The mother was said by Rosanoff et al. to have been hospitalized in Toronto with involutional melancholia and to have died there probably in 1932 or earlier. However, an exhaustive search of the records indicated that Rosanoff was in error on this point. The mother died in 1942, ten years later, and she corresponded with her sons at least annually until then. Additionally, there was no indication that she suffered from involutional melancholia. Rather, it probably was the mother's sister-in-law (with no genetic line to the twins) who was so diagnosed. Hence, it appears that although the father and older brother were deteriorating or absent, the mother probably was present in the home at least until the time the twins were hospitalized.

B, who grew up with his biological family, contrasts with A in several areas. He was said to have disliked school and left after seven years to work in lumbering. Additionally, Rosanoff reported that in his premorbid state, he was "somewhat unstable and never seems to have held any position for very long."

Brother C, three years older than the twins (not younger as Rosanoff reports), was said to have had an uneventful early life, beginning school at age eleven but not learning well. At age sixteen he had influenza and, at age seventeen, sunstroke. Following this, he became excited, confused, restless, and suffered from impaired memory. For the next two years he did not work, instead rambling around the country in an excited, twitching, deteriorating state until he was hospitalized in 1925 at the age of nineteen. (This was five years prior to his twin brothers' hospitalization.)

Outline of Hospital Admissions

Twin A.   He was admitted May 1930, at age twenty-one years two months five days. His illness was of recent onset. He was assaultative and had placed obstructions on the railway track of a firm that would not hire him. He believed he was to be hanged for this. Diagnosis: manic-depressive, manic. A went home on probation to his uncle in October, after five months' hospitalization, and was formally discharged as recovered on January 29, 1931. He was readmitted in a manic state in 1933 (age 24:3:23), seven weeks prior to his twin's readmission. He had been living with his uncle, so the degree of contact with his twin, if any, is unknown for this period. Following his readmission, he remained in the hospital with varying periods of excitement alternating with depressive episodes and periods of more affective equilibrium. In 1942 (age 33:7; also the same year his mother and twin died) he was rediagnosed as schizophrenic. He believed he was a priest, hallucinated, and smiled inappropriately. In 1962 (age 53) diagnosis was changed back to manic-depressive. During these years, he was treated with the usual methods of the day, including continuous baths, sedatives, and, in 1954, ECT. In 1968, after thirty-five years of hospitalization, he was transferred to a community home where he remained in stable condition on Mellaril for the nine years preceding this case summary.

Twin B. He was admitted June 1930, at age twenty-one years four months twenty-six days. In early 1930, *B* gradually developed ideas that the town where he lived had a connection with Noah's Ark. He left his job to search for its landing place and the site of the Garden of Eden, and assaulted those who contradicted his ideas. *B* was upset when his twin was admitted to the mental hospital in May after a more recent acute onset. In June *B* was arrested and transferred from a jail to the same mental hospital his twin had entered ten weeks earlier. Diagnosis: manic-depressive, manic. He spent six months in the hospital and was discharged from probation in August 1931. (Note: His twin's stay was five months.) He was readmitted in a manic state in 1933 (age 24:5:14), seven weeks after his twin was readmitted. Like his twin, *B* had subsequent manic episodes interspersed with depressive and euthymic phases. He was treated with the usual methods of the time, including continuous baths and sedatives (no ECT). In 1942, after nine years in the hospital (age 33), he ran away and was found dead, probably due to exposure.

Elder Brother C. He was admitted in 1925, at age nineteen. The onset of mental illness was at seventeen. According to Rosanoff et al. the official diagnosis was dementia praecox, hebephrenic type. Records indicate that *C* was regarded as a disturbed defective. *C* deteriorated, ate rubbish and paper, developed subacute peritonitis, and died at age thirty after eleven years in the mental hospital.

Since, as noted earlier, diagnosis often is a problem in this literature and, in particular, has been at issue for this case, the summary was submitted for blind ratings to three British and three U.S. judges. In the United States, the psychiatrists were completely blind, having been told only that the case histories were on each of "three brothers born in the early 1900s." All reference to twinship was eliminated, and Rosanoff's name and summary were excluded. In Great Britain, the psychiatrists were given the case histories plus a few of Rosanoff's comments on the content of the delusional material on first admission. Two psychiatrist received separate write-ups on each of the brothers with all references to twinship omitted, but with birth dates left intact. A third knew of the twin status. Thus, the British raters were only partially blind since a close reading could infer twinship from birth dates.[1] Table 6.1 gives the results of the diagnostic evaluations.

Manic-depressive psychosis was scored as the diagnosis for twin *A* by five out of six judges prior to disclosure of full information and by six out of six after "unblindfolding." Twin *B* had an identical differen-

1. James Shields organized the British ratings before his death in 1978. The raters, in alphabetical order not corresponding to their listing in the text, were Stuart Asch, M.D., Robert Cancro, M.D., Anthony Clare, M.D., Robin Murray, M.D., R. Spitzer, M.D., and J. K. Wing, M.D.

TABLE 6.1

Diagnostic ratings of twins A and B and their elder brother C.

Rater (Great Britain) C (Elder brother)	A (Twin)	B (Twin)
1. ? Mental retardation with manic episodes and possible global verbal disorder (Earl's "catatonia of idiocy"). Schizophrenia cannot entirely be excluded.	Manic-depressive psychosis	Manic-depressive psychosis
2. Manic-depressive illness superimposed or acting in concert with postencephalitic dementia. (The "sunstroke" and precipitation of mania by influenza are reminiscent of Bonhoeffer's "exogenous psychoses," though there is the suggestion here of a connection with manic-depression.) Alternatively, mental subnormality.	Manic-depressive illness	Manic-depressive illness
3. ? Chronic mania. (The sleep reversal, irritability and grandiosity following the "sunstroke" episode favour this.) Second choice, schizo-affective disorder.	Bipolar affective disorder	Bipolar affective disorder
Rater (USA)		
1. Mental retardation and manic excitement, at first episodic and then continuous. The hallucinations are not typical. Progressive CNS disease—the onset with sunstroke—would have to be ruled out in a more complete differential.	Bipolar affective disorder (Perhaps schizoaffective because of potentially more autism than one would expect in simple affective disorder.)	Bipolar affective disorder
2. Organic brain syndrome of unknown etiology, although possibly related to his influenza.	Manic-depressive psychosis	Catatonic schizophrenia. Minimal confidence in this diagnosis. (A probability estimate based on the sparse information and early death of B. The differential is between manic-depressive and catatonic-schizophrenia.)
3. Initial impression of manic-depressive. Probability suggests schizophrenia and/or organic brain syndrome, particularly some type of familial degenerative brain disease such as porphyria. (Later changed to manic-depressive.)	Schizophrenia (A probability estimate; later changed to manic-depressive.)	Schizophrenia (A probability estimate; later changed to manic-depressive.)

tial but in a forced-choice situation, only four out of six judges scored him as manic-depressive, with two-thirds of the U.S. raters scoring schizophrenia. The American judges who scored schizophrenia spontaneously wrote lengthy letters stating minimal confidence in the diagnosis and their tendency to vote for manic-depressive if further information indicated grandiosity of thought as more typical than disorganization. After receiving the Rosanoff material, which contains more information on delusional ideation, plus the ratings of the other judges, both wrote back: one to change his diagnosis, the other to question if the knowledge that the subjects were twins had affected the British consistency.

It emerged that the differences in diagnosis stemmed only slightly from the reported behavior and ideation of twins themselves, since even totally blind judges gave them identical differentials. The major problem was the lack of information on twin B and the current transitional state of diagnosis. In the absence of firm evidence for schizophrenia, the cyclical mood swings pushed the British toward ratings of bipolar illness. The Americans used the same process but in reverse. In the absence of firm evidence of bipolar illness, evidence of thought disorder tilted the scales to schizophrenia. In the end, all raters expressed the belief that the case should be discussed as an example of manic-depressive psychosis (BPI) in separated twins, even if it was not a certain one.

Sibling C, as the table indicates, was problematic for all judges, though a majority included mania as a component in the primary diagnosis.

What is most impressive about the case is the concordance for manic-depressive psychosis (BPI) and the stunning similarity in age of onset. Both twins moved into their first manic episode at about twenty-one years two months and were hospitalized for five to six months. A's episode differed from B's only in being slightly more acute (A was reared under better circumstances, it might be noted). Rehospitalization occurred within seven weeks of each other, and both twins showed some decrease in excitement at about the same time (August–September 1933), with excitement then flaring up again. Figure 6.1 gives a rough approximation of synchronicity of cycle.

The figure was constructed from the original hospital notes, which are uneven in reporting (exact dates have been omitted in the summary in appendix A at the request of the hospital). Even with this unevenness, however, a remarkable similarity between the twins can be seen. A's manic episodes at first occurred about every six weeks (duration is unknown, as is mention of depression), while B's manic episodes at first lasted ten days and then increased to about three weeks' duration. His were followed by depressions. For B, the cycle occurred quite frequently during 1933 to 1936, reducing to only six flareups in 1937. Following this, the intervals between episodes and within the manic, depressive, and euthymic phases increased for both twins.

Since this is the only case of its kind in the literature, chance might be the best explanation for the similarity. However, the larger literature is convincing in demonstrating genetic transmission of bipolar illness, noting that concordance rates for bipolar are higher in MZ twins than unipolar rates, and suggesting even that unipolar and bipolar are

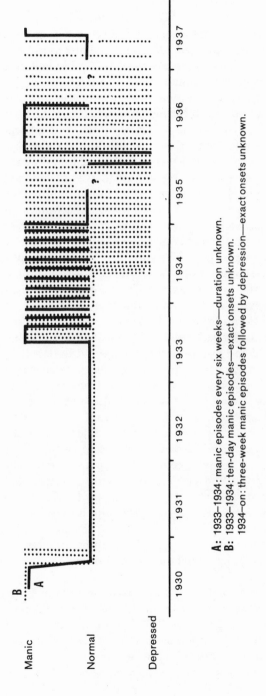

FIGURE 6.1

Mood swings of twins A and B (case 180).

A: 1933–1934: manic episodes every six weeks—duration unknown.
B: 1933–1934: ten-day manic episodes—exact onsets unknown.
1934—on: three-week manic episodes followed by depression—exact onsets unknown.

of different genetic etiology (Perris 1973). In this context, the case has a better probability of being worthy of note.

Assuming the twins to be MZ, which their close physical similarity makes probable (see chapter 1), and assuming this to be an example of bipolar I illness in separated MZ twins, what might be inferred from the case? First, it is somewhat atypical. Several judges commented that both twins showed more autism than might be expected, and B's early death did not allow as complete a picture of the unfolding process as might be expected. Countering this were comments from several judges that both twins probably were depleted by a social breakdown syndrome resulting from prolonged years of unrelenting hospitalization. Also, A was reclassified as schizophrenic for two decades in which the diagnosis was much in vogue, and he was reclassified in the same year that he suffered the deaths of his mother and twin brother. The possibility exists of a pathological mourning reaction in an already psychotic individual, coloring the picture considerably. Nonetheless, all the dilemmas cannot be explained away, and it seems wisest to say that the case, to the degree it may be classified as BPI, is atypical. The possibility of familial transmission is suggested slightly: One uncle (genetically related to the twins) was thought to be a suicide, the elder brother was rated as having some manic elements intermixed with other features, and question might be raised about the stability of the father.

Since studies of twins reared together are criticized for overlooking similar perinatal and environmental factors in their estimates of heritability, this case may shed further light. For example, common environmental factors—at least on the gross level observable here—seem unimportant. The twins were rated as quite different in premorbid personality. From the minimal information, it seems that it was only, or primarily, B who experienced serious object loss and stress (illness and death of father, breakdown of brother, possible exposure to infant deaths of two sibs, knowledge of twin in better circumstances). The divergence supports Allen's (1976) comment that studies of environmental variables, such as early loss of parents or disturbed childhood, have not provided consistent data regarding the importance of these variables in the etiology of affective disorder. Although Allen was referring to investigations of unipolar depressive illness, the conclusion appears to hold for the bipolar variety as well, and, from what little is known, applies to this case.

Somewhat more weight might be given to the possibility of a constitutional but nongenetic determinant for affective disorder. The very fact of twinship raises the possibility of prematurity and pregnancy or birth complications. Further support for this hypothesis derives from knowledge that the mother had at least two children who died in infancy, and her eldest son may have been retarded. However, studies of the relationships between perinatal hazards and later psychotic status are, themselves, still in their infancy. The results are inconsistent, and subjects are almost exclusively schizophrenic (Hanson et al. 1976; Rieder et al. 1977), so the question must remain open.

The question remaining thus becomes one of whether there might be a substantial degree of genetic determination not only over the vulnerability for bipolar affective disorder, but also even for onset or duration of cycle. Other studies usually do not confront this issue, and an inspection of Bertelson et al.'s (1977) data does not support the point. However, this case raises the interesting possibility of subdivisions within the bipolar spectrum, with some cases, perhaps atypical ones with more schizoaffective components such as this, having such a potent genetic load as to be relatively impervious to the power of the environment to modify or undo vulnerability.

Ironically, the marked similarity between the twins might be used for precisely the opposite argument, and, past the concordance, this may be one of the more interesting features of the reanalysis. There are suggestions of an unusual and extremely potent environmental influence on onset and content of episodes—the twin relationship itself. The twins had met and had contact for about a year prior to hospitalization, and B was reported to have been disturbed when he heard A had been admitted to the hospital. It does not stretch the imagination to wonder if A found his twin's giving up his job to look for the Garden of Eden upsetting, and conversely, if B's learning of A's admission to the hospital finally exacerbated his disturbance to the point of manic violence.

In this context, the content of B's Noah's Ark delusion becomes curious. The idea of Noah's ark and the Garden of Eden might be viewed by many as being rooted in the experience of manic patients that an episode is like a rebirth—a time of being born again or saved. However, of the many rebirth metaphors one might use, Noah's Ark is interesting if only for the fact that it is where the animals were saved "two by two." Similarly, the Garden of Eden is where the pair of original humans were expelled then to produce two brothers, Cain who smote Abel. Some Biblical commentary even describes them as DZ twins. In more commonplace terms, perhaps B, at least, was upset not only at his brother's state but also by jealousy and fantasies over his identical sib who had been expelled from the parental home into much pleasanter circumstances.

At this point, many might protest at wild analysis. However, the fact remains that studies of twins reared together stumble over the twinning issue, and the twinship issue remains even in a case of moderately well-separated MZ twins such as these. Also, just as the literature increasingly supports the idea of innate vulnerabilities, so also are there examples of one twin influencing the onset of breakdown of the other.[2]

The best estimate, thus, might be that case 180 supports the growing literature that indicates a significant genetic influence on the presence of bipolar affective disturbance, and it may offer support for the idea of some genetic etiology in the onset or duration of at least the initial episodes. Until a series of BPI separated cases can be presented, this case should be viewed with caution since it may have occurred by chance. However, to the degree it is representative, note should be taken of the possibly potent environmental influences on onset and content of episodes from the interpersonal and psychodynamic features of the twin relationship itself.

Schizophrenia

Gottesman and Shields (1972) summarized the twin-reared-apart literature on schizophrenia up to 1972. Table 6.2 follows their presentation, adding the more recent case by Prokop and Druml (1973). The overlap between Mitsuda's and Inouye's cases remains ambiguous.

TABLE 6.2

Reports of schizophrenia in MZ twins reared apart uncorrected for degree of separation.

Source	Age at Separation	Number of Pairs	
		Concordant	Discordant
Kallmann 1938	soon after birth	1	–
Essen-Möller 1941	7 years	1	–
Craike and Slater 1945	9 months	1	–
Kallmann and Roth 1956	?	1	–
Shields 1962	birth	1	–
Tienari 1963	3 years and 8 years	–	2
Kringlen 1964, 1967	3 months and 22 months	1	1
Mitsuda 1967*	infancy	5	3
Prokop and Druml 1973	9 months	–	1

*Inouye (1972) reports ten pairs, many of which overlap with those reported by Mitsuda. All sets were separated before the age of five but reunions occurred after two or more years apart. Of the ten, four sets were concordant, three were discordant, and three discordant but with a co-twin who had a schizophrenic-like illness.

SOURCE: I. I. Gottesman and J. Shields, *Schizophrenia and Genetics: A Twin Study Vantage Point* (New York: Academic Press, 1972), pp. 36–37.

2. See MZ 17 in Gottesman and Shields's 1972 study as an instance.

The figures in table 6.2 yield a pairwise concordance of 11:18 or 61 percent, slightly higher than the approximately 25 to 50 percent pairwise rate reported in various studies of MZ twins reared together (Gottesman and Shields 1976). The figures have not been corrected for age of separation or degree of contact (which would tend to lower the number of cases), nor is there an age correction (which probably would tend to raise concordance).[3]

Table 6.3 presents the cases adjusted for degree of separation and eliminates those cases with serious diagnostic ambiguity. No age cor-

TABLE 6.3
Schizophrenia in MZ twins reared apart
corrected for age of separation and
degree of contact over lifetime.

Case		Number of Pairs	
#	Source	Concordant	Discordant
Group I. High Separation			
134	Craike and Slater	1	–
166	Tienari*	–	1
176	Slater/Shields	1	–
Group II. Mixed Separation			
226	Kallmann	1	–
240	Kringlen	–	1
Group III. Low Separation			
310	Inouye/Mitsuda	1	–
316	Kringlen	1	–
332	Prokop and Druml	–	1
340	Inouye/Mitsuda	1	–
Group IV. Seperated After Age 4 plus "Questionable Diagnosis"†			
404	Kallmann and Roth	(1)	–
414	Kaij/Essen-Möller	(1)	–
420	Kringlen	–	1
Group V. Insufficient Information			
	Inouye/Mitsuda	–	2
	two sets separated		
	after age 4‡		

*Reference by Gottesman and Shields (1972) to a second Tienari case could not be verified. Possibly it stems from an erroneous reading of Tienari case 466 (case 354 in this study) where psychopathy was present but schizophrenia not diagnosed, or to Kringlen case 420.
†Pairs whose diagnosis remains questionable appear in parentheses.
‡Inouye (1972) and Mitsuda (1971) refer to five, possibly six, cases in addition to the four cited above. The cases had separations lasting only about two years.

3. "Age correction" refers to the long risk period for schizophrenia. A cross-sectional approach is likely to produce concordance rates lower than the actual values since a pair discordant at age twenty may become concordant at age fifty.

rection is included. The original sample of eighteen is reduced to nine by even the most cursory evaluation. Concordance remains approximately the same, 6/9, or 67 percent, and, taken in the context of the larger literature, can be viewed as minor support for the genetic hypothesis. By inspection of the gross parameters of degree of separation, it seems that quantitative measures of contact do not affect concordance. However, this leaves open the question of qualitative factors and/or common environmental stress that may have affected both partners in concordant sets, despite different rearing backgrounds.

Since some well-known cases are eliminated in the revised listing, a case review is included which gives reasons for exclusion and summarizes environmental influences on those cases retained. The disputed cases are listed first, and the remainder are grouped according to degree of separation. At the end, what information can be gleaned is summarized in terms of type of schizophrenia, age of onset, and whatever speculation might be offered about associated variables. No conclusions are warranted, only educated guesses to be checked against other work.

Review of Cases

Cases Eliminated for Late Separation or Questionable Diagnosis

E. Inouye, H. Mitsuda (7–8 cases.)   It is difficult to tell the exact overlap in subjects reported in Mitsuda's and Inouye's publications. Using Inouye's 1972 listing and code numbers, five cases out of his nine would be eliminated for being reared apart for only two to five years in childhood (cases 4317F, 4155M, 4143M, 4218M, and 490M). An additional two cases (4223F and 4145M) were separated after age four, the cutoff for this study.[4]

Two remaining cases were separated earlier in infancy and, through the generosity of Dr. Inouye, were made available to this study. They are summarized in the next few pages and in appendices B and C.

E. Kringlen (1 case).   The twins in case 420 (Kringlen case 55) were separated at eight years, too late for inclusion here.

---

4. The cutoff assumes a developmental proposition that significant twinning effects occur in early childhood. Those who dispute the idea may include the sets. They are not listed in chapter 3 (Group IV) since little information is given.

L. Kaij, E. Essen-Moller (1 case).   Case 414, reported by Kaij and, earlier, by Essen-Moller, told of *Alfred* and *August*, twins concordant for schizophrenia. The case is well known in the literature, but since separation occurred after age eight, it probably should not be claimed as a reared-apart set.

F. Kallmann and B. Roth (1 case).   For more than two decades, the reference in the 1956 Kallmann and Roth paper to a set of separated MZ twins discordant for childhood schizophrenia has been repeated in all major studies of genetic predisposition to schizophrenia. The original citation is as follows:

Only 5 pairs have been reared apart, 1 one-egg and 4 two-egg pairs. All of them have been discordant as to childhood schizophrenia, but in the one-egg pair the co-twin developed schizophrenia after adolescence, at the age of 18 years. [1956, p. 599]

Through the generosity of Dr. John Rainer of the New York State Psychiatric Institute, the notes on this case were retrieved and a case summary written. The full summary, checked for accuracy by Dr. Rainer, appears as appendix D.

Briefly, what emerged was that at the time of Kallmann's investigations, a period of five years apart was used as the criterion of separation, not separation in childhood. With the larger number of case histories now available, more rigor can be imposed, and this set, which was separated only at age five or possibly at age thirteen or fourteen, seems best withdrawn. Diagnosis might be questioned as well. Briefly summarized:

A and *B*, female twins, were the fourth and fifth children out of eight born from a mating between first cousins. The father was drunken and abusive, deserting the family when the twins were five. They were placed in a series of foster homes, though whether together or separately is unknown.

Information on definite separation at age thirteen or fourteen exists, when *A* was placed in a residential home. She had only two friends there, a social worker and a four-year-old blind girl. About six weeks prior to *A's* hospitalization around the time of her fifteenth birthday, the social worker was married and *A* became depressed, anorexic, fearful, restless, and subject to nightmares. She began to hear voices when alone and was hospitalized under certification. She was violently resistive, six ECT producing no change. After six weeks she was transferred to a state hospital where she quieted rapidly. No specific diagnosis of schizophrenia was made. Two years later she was placed in a family-care home where she did well up to the follow-up at age eighteen and one-half. She was, she said, "happy to be away from her twin."

When A was hospitalized, investigators attempted to see B. Her social worker refused, adamantly insisting on the "dissimilar" personalities of the twins. B was never hospitalized, but on follow-up three years later, when A had made a good adjustment to her foster home, B was said to have begun deteriorating. Again, permission to see her was refused and her social worker insisted it was only "imitation" of A's behavior of three and one-half years earlier.

Identical zygosity was assumed by all who came in contact with the twins, except B's social worker, who zealously guarded her differentness. Both girls were subjected to brutal conditions throughout childhood, including lack of food and beatings. A had somewhat more illnesses as an infant and was said to be the weaker baby and the passive twin. Both girls had pneumonia at age two and developed crossed eyes as a sequela.

Cases Included in Reanalysis[5]

Case 134. The best-separated set in the literature, reported by Cráike and Slater (1945) still is so poorly separated that the original paper speaks specifically to the issue of whether the twins' knowledge of each other, which they interwove in their delusional systems, was significant in the onset, course, and content of their paranoid states. The case is widely known, and only a brief summary is indicated.

Edith and *Florence* were separated at nine months and reared in entirely different environments prior to their first meeting at age twenty-four. Each knew she had a twin, and their face-to-face contact was exceedingly minimal—partly, if not wholly, because of their vast dislike of each other. *Florence* had a stable home with an affectionate maternal aunt while *Edith* lived with a drunken, violent father until eight and one-half and subsequently in an orphanage. Both were "nervous" as children (though with different symptoms) and had a history of theft. Some form of gastric disturbance with neurotic components is noted for each twin, one at age eighteen and one at age nineteen, which the authors note may have been precursors of an unfolding schizophrenic process. The chronic development of their paranoid ideation seemed somewhat similar, though it was *Edith*, the twin with the more disturbed family history, who seemed more severely afflicted in a chronic sense, while *Florence* maintained her equilibrium better overall but had

5. Nine sets have been included.

flare-ups, including hallucinations and severe depression that required hospitalization.[6]

Since the twins' paranoid symptoms seemed to have begun with their first meeting and since the content involved suspicions of each about the other, it is impossible to rule out mutual identifications.[7] The original diagnosis was of an endogenously determined chronic paranoid state, probably of a schizophrenic type.

Case 166. Tienari's (1963) case (1080 in his listing) can be summarized as follows.

A and B were born into a large family riddled with pathology. The father was drunken and violent. The mother was "simpleminded" and, from the time the twin boys were eight, she was in mental wards with confusional states, hallucinations, and inability to cope with the outside world. Of the five siblings in addition to the twins, two died in infancy, one had a normal adjustment, one was schizophrenic, and the last was reported to have "debility and psychogenic reaction" from wartime stress.

The twins were parted at age three, A going to foster homes, B staying with his parents. At age six (when the mother was deteriorating?) B also was placed in a foster home.

A, the stronger twin in childhood and the more "active," always was healthy. In adulthood he became a farmer, continuing to live with his aged foster parents. He never married. He was considered a "normal introverted person ... rather spontaneous and affiliative."

B was well-behaved in childhood, though he did poorly in school and felt uneasy with the other children in his foster home. At age eighteen he became withdrawn and soon was hospitalized. Over the years he deteriorated severely, becoming one of the "extinguished" patients common to all hospitals. Diagnosis: schizophrenia, hebephrenic type.

Case 176. The case of *Herbert* and *Nicholas,* illegitimate sons of a half-Chinese woman, has been widely summarized over the years (Slater 1961, case MZ11; Shields 1962, case SmP4; Gottesman and Shields 1972, case MZ17). Gottesman and Shields offered a moderately detailed fam-

---

6. Note the interesting similarity to the case described under "affective disorders"— the twin from the better home having more acute and florid decompensations, the other a more chronic deteriorating course.

7. Craike and Slater originally called it "folie à deux," though that term now is reserved for nonrelatives (see Shields and Gottesman 1971).

ily pedigree, indicating one case of schizophrenia in a maternal aunt (who was adopted away from the family, interestingly) and widespread antisocial or atypical behavior. Gottesman and Shields also offered a consensual diagnosis, (the only one in the reared-apart literature), where all raters agreed on schizophrenia, with hebephrenic and chronic undifferentiated mentioned as subtypes. Both twins were disturbed children, enuretic until early adolescence with histories of firesetting and rowdiness. The onset of fulminate psychosis is set at age twenty-two. *Nicholas* was rated as having the better home, but both twins had contact, and *Nicholas* decompensated after hearing of *Herbert's* hospitalization. Gottesman and Shields estimated that the close onset was related to a visit by the biological mother, which upset both twins. Their subsequent course, despite quite different environments, was as identical as any seen in a twin series.

Case 226. Kallmann's early (1938) classic case also involved twins whose knowledge of each other may have had an influence on onset of psychosis. Briefly:

> *Kaete* and *Lisa*, twenty-two-year-old sisters, were born out of wedlock to a mother "of limited mental endowment" with a history of hospitalization for catatonic stupor. She had a major catatonic episode at the birth of the twins. The father was unknown and untraceable.
>
> The girls were adopted soon after birth by different maternal uncles and grew up seeing each other during their first ten years "only a few times and then for very brief periods." Kallmann noted that they later met more often but "without developing the close affection which is characteristic of twins."
>
> They seemed to develop similarly in childhood and were described as "problem children ... stubborn, callous and indifferent." Physical characteristics were identical and menstruation began in the same month of their twelfth year. At the age of fifteen, *Kaete* gave birth to an illegitimate child and "lapsed very quickly into a profound catatonic stupor," much as her mother had done fifteen years earlier after the birth of the twins.
>
> *Lisa*, still a virgin, remained functional until slightly less than two years later when she too developed a "catatonic state of repression and anxiety" severe enough to require hospitalization. Kallmann noted that the twins' periods of excitement over the next few years followed the same course, though the cycles were slightly different with the less disturbed twin (*Lisa*) having shorter periods of excitement and longer intervals of relative equilibrium between episodes.

Kallmann concluded that the case indicated a genetic predisposition to schizophrenic illness and that the childbirth of one may have excited the underlying defect to emerge earlier, but it did not condition or cause the disturbance. He did not discuss any potential effect on onset or form of psychosis stemming from the twins' knowledge of each other and of *Lisa's* knowledge that *Kaete* had become gravely ill with a disturbance identical to that which removed their biological mother from their lives.

The diagnosis of schizophrenia may be questioned in this case. While a true catatonic stupor probably would not be misdiagnosed, one wonders if the initial episodes may not have been psychotic depressions followed by manic episodes rather than catatonic states of withdrawal and agitation. Though the case is listed as schizophrenic in table 6.2, some reservation seems indicated.

Case 240. Kringlen's (1964) description of brothers *A* and *B* (case 22 in his listing) is one of the few where the twin relationship seems not implicated. Briefly:

A and *B* were born out-of-wedlock to parents with no family history of mental disorder. Both babies were tiny (1.5 and 1.7 kilograms respectively; 3.3 and 3.7 pounds). *A* required resuscitation as the second child and was born in a breech presentation. He may have had convulsions, though a later EEG was normal.

The boys were separated at about twenty-two to twenty-four months, *A* going to a pious widow with a son of her own and *B* going to an uncle with three older daughters. The twins had contact in summers and were reunited, "for the love of adventure," with their mother at age sixteen.

Neither appeared disturbed in childhood. Both had friends and got along with their families. *A* had enuresis to age eight or nine and may have had encopresis to age seven.

Following reunion, the relationship was unremarkable. Both worked well and *B* married at age twenty-two.

At age twenty-eight, the mother's husband (the twins' stepfather) died and her legitimate son went to sea. *A* was left alone with the mother, the first time he had been alone with mother or foster mother with no brother of any degree of consanguinity present. Within a few months he decompensated and had a brief hospitalization. Diagnosis: acute amentic schizophreniform disorder. A few weeks after his release he was rehospitalized and deteriorated steadily over the next eight years of follow-up. Diagnosis in 1962 and 1965: schizophrenia, catatonic type (paranoid ideation present).

B remained well-adjusted and did well in his work. At first he was troubled by thoughts he too might fall ill but, over the years, he lost his concern.

Though Kringlen noted the possible symbolic significance of A finally being alone with his mother, the absent brother was a half-sib, just as in the foster home the brother had been a foster brother, not his twin. It is possible, but requires far more extrapolation than in other cases, to say that the "brothers" symbolically stood for his MZ partner, and the twin relationship thus may be insignificant in onset or content of disorder.

Case 310   Dr. E. Inouye has provided a summary on twins A and B, (MZ4138 in his table; case 10 in Mitsuda's 1967 report). The full text is in appendix B. Briefly:

> A and B, female twins, were born into a family riddled with schizophrenic pathology. Both were forceps deliveries, A born first and weighing less than B. They were separated at seven days and placed in adoptive families. A's family was economically poor and, though the adoptive father loved A, he is said to have felt "constraint." B's family was well-off and she was overprotected.
> The twins may have met about once a month in their early years. They thought they were cousins and did not learn of twinship until ages seven and ten. In their premorbid state, both were asocial, nervous, and obsessive, with A more introverted than B.
> At age twenty-seven, A was hospitalized because she was autistic, depressed, and had ideas of reference. Homosexual tendencies were noted. She was diagnosed as depressed, but seventeen ECT failed to stop the deterioration. By age forty she was diagnosed as hebephrenic with catatonic features.
> B showed similar symptoms at similar ages, but without systematic deterioration and, evidently, without hospitalization to the age of thirty-nine, when the reports end.
> The set is considered partially discordant: A with chronic progressive schizophrenia; B with chronic mild or transient type.

Information on the twin relationship is lacking.

Case 316.   A and B, Kringlen set 48 (1967), were sisters with substantial contact, though no information on how the contact may have influenced onset or content of psychotic ideation is available.

These female twins were born into a family where one aunt probably was catatonic schizophrenic. Their siblings all were disturbed as adults. The twins were separated at about three months and reared by different aunts and uncles. *A*, the firstborn and heavier twin, was slightly more shy and aloof as a child and slightly slower in development, though both were in the normal range. They met about once a week in childhood and were substantially together past the age of fifteen, working together in adulthood.

A was raised in a family with extremely precarious financial status and with a foster mother who later may have become psychotic. *B* was better off financially and seems to have had the more stable and accepting family.

At the age of thirteen, both developed diabetes mellitus subsequent to appendectomies. *A* was admitted to a medical ward at age twenty-six with elevated temperature. Within days she became emotionally changed and was transferred to a mental hospital with a diagnosis of reactive psychosis, probably of a catatonic type. She died in a diabetic coma and with worsened psychotic symptoms a few days later.

In the fifteen years following her sister's death, *B* had numerous hospitalizations for diabetes and mild depressions. She was first admitted to a mental hospital at age forty-two, following her foster mother's death. Diagnosis: reactive psychosis. She was hospitalized again at age forty-six though without florid psychotic symptomatology. Social functioning in subsequent years was marginal. Kringlen's diagnosis is of schizophreniform disorder, catatonic for *A*, paranoid-depressive for *B*.

Case 332. Prokop and Druml's German paper (1973) reported on brothers discordant for catatonic schizophrenia with very early onset, though the authors admitted the possibility that the disorder may have been a severe endogenous depression. Briefly:

Alois and *Oskar* were born into a family with a history of psychosis, type not stated. The biological father was assumed to have committed suicide after having been evaluated for a brain tumor. *Alois* was born first and was the smaller, weighing 2.25 kilograms (5 pounds) and measuring 49 centimeters (19.3 inches). Labor was induced and forceps were used. Both boys remained small and were developmentally retarded.

They lived with the maternal grandmother to the age of nine months. After this, *Alois* was sent to stay with elderly farmers who lived fairly secluded in the mountains near his village. *Oskar* returned to his mother in the village. The mother remarried when the twins were seven. Prokop and Druml rated *Alois* as having the poorer environment, both for the age of his foster parents as well as their severely religious attitudes. The boys had some, possibly a great deal of, contact since they went to the same village school.

However, *Alois* left quickly after attempting visits with his mother and twin.

From the age of twelve and one-half, *Alois* became increasingly shy and withdrawn. He complained of stomachaches and headaches and became religiously troubled. Tofranil had no noticeable effect. At the age of fourteen he was hospitalized in an extremely depressed, stuporous state, without hallucinations but with extreme self-reproaches. He was treated with Tofranil, Mellaril, and group activity therapies. After a stay of what seems to have been a few months, he was discharged, though a schizoid stance was believed still present. He returned to the farm and was treated by a quack with electrical collars and only slowly returned to health. A hypomanic state was not reported. When seen at age sixteen he was not psychotic, though he was still shy and had difficulty in forming contacts.

Throughout this time, *Oskar* is reported to have remained healthy, without inclination to depressions or other symptoms. He was described as having courage and being lively and active.

Both boys had struma and were small and about two years retarded in development. Both had dysrhythmical EEGs with photoconvulsive reactions, though only *Alois* appears to have a grand mal seizure at age six and only he was enuretic. Both boys were of normal intelligence, though, interestingly, *Alois* was the better in school. *Oskar* failed fifth grade and was the dominant twin.

The questionable diagnosis plus the presumably high degree of contact and possible organic components leave little room for generalization from the case.

Case 340.   Dr. Inouye's summary on case 340 is included in appendix C (Inouye's 1972 listing MZ4192; Mitsuda's 1967 case 9).

A and *B*, female twins, were born into a family without noteworthy pedigree of endogenous psychosis, though the father was alchoholic and two relatives may have had psychosis associated with general paresis.

Both were tiny (1.5 and 1.3 kilograms, or 3.3 and 2.9 pounds, respectively). *A*, the firstborn twin, was heavier and developed better than *B*, who may have had convulsions several times a year to age twelve. The girls were separated at thirty-two months into adoptive families. *B's* adoptive mother "hated her," and, following her adoptive father's death when *B* was twelve, the family was poverty-stricken. No information is available on *A's* family. The twins visited once or twice a year when they were young, though *B* claims knowledge of adoption only at age fifteen and of twinship at seventeen. Both were reserved and shy; *A* was more stubborn and hot-tempered, *B* was cranky, selfish, and cynical.

After the age of sixteen, *A* became fatigued and anxious. At age nineteen she visited a psychiatric clinic and was diagnosed catatonic. She received ECT 8 times and was slightly deteriorated when seen later that year.

After the age of fourteen, *B* became occasionally excited and hypochondriacal. She may have had a sexual trauma. At eighteen she became excited during menstruation and at one point stayed with *A* for a week. A month later she had ideas of reference. Two months later she visited a psychiatric clinic and was diagnosed hebephrenic. She underwent one ECT. *A* visited with *B* following *B's* release and the girls quarrelled. By age nineteen, *B* was still autistic with slight deterioration. Both girls were diagnosed as schizophrenic, relapsing type, by Inouye. Mitsuda listed the girls as concordant for atypical schizophrenia.

Table 6.4 summarizes the case material. So many facts are missing that it is unwarranted to weight the cases with detailed speculation. Overall, it appears that six of the nine cases were concordant. Of these, 4/6 were substantially concordant in type. Since antiquated nomenclature was used and only one case (176) was cross-checked by other diagnosticians, only minimal confidence in the results is suggested. However, the case histories impart a flavor of more similarity, leaving it possible to speculate that schizophrenic symptomatology in MZ twins reared apart may have similar features. Similar environments seem ruled out as explanatory, and mutual identification, while possible in every case, seems not as parsimonious an explanation as genetic predisposition.

Age of onset also was similar in five out of six concordant cases. While implications of twin interaction were present in two cases and cannot be ruled out in the others, interaction would not be sufficiently explanatory until demonstrated by a more rigorous series of cases. Rearing environment, from the rough evaluations possible, tended very slightly in the direction of the more gravely ill twin coming from the more problematic background. Genetic background also was implicated, most of the sets reporting schizophrenia in the family pedigree. Interestingly, no mention was made of severe affective disorders in the limited pedigrees available.

Laterality could not be evaluated, and associations with birth order and birth weight were ambiguous because of limited information. No ready explanation presented itself for the discordant cases.

From a broader viewpoint, no environmental factors etiologically significant for schizophrenia were suggested. Almost all of these sets came from poor, even poverty-stricken, backgrounds, and many twins

TABLE 6.4

Schizophrenia: Type, onset, family history of psychosis, and environmental ratings for MZ twins reared apart.

Case		Diagnosis	Severity	Age of Onset	Family History?	Birth Weight	Birth Order	Sex	Hand	Environmental rating	Twin Implicated?	Concordance
134	Edith	paranoid	more	24	?	?	?	F	?	worse	yes	++
	Florence	paranoid	less	24		?				better		
166	B	hebephrenic	more	18	yes	more?	?	M	?	worse	?	+−
	A	normal	−	−		less?				better		
176	Nicholas	chronic undifferentiated /hebephrenic	more?	22	yes	more	1	M	R	better?	yes	++
	Herbert	true/hebephrenic	less?	22		less	2		R	worse?		
226	Kaete	catatonic	more	15	yes	more	?	F	?	worse?	?	++
	Lisa	catatonic	less	17		?				better?		
240	A	catatonic/paranoid	more	28	no	more	2	M	?	same?	no	+−
	B	normal	−	−		less	1					
310	A	chronic progressive	more	27	yes	less	1	F	?	worse	?	(++)
	B	chronic transient	less	similar		more	2			better		
316	A	atypical/catatonic	more?	26	yes	more	1	F	?	worse	?	(++)
	B	atypical/paranoid-depressive	less?	42		less	2			better		
332	Alois	catatonic	more	12½–14	yes	less	1	M	?	worse?	?	+−
	Oskar	normal	−	−		more	2			better?		
340	A	atypical/catatonic	?	19	no(?)	more	1	F	?	?	?	++
	B	atypical/hebephrenic		18–19		less	2					

reported gross pathology and brutality in their childhood. However, the same pattern presents in numerous cases of reared-apart sets who did not become schizophrenic.[8] Similarly, most of these sets had traumatic separations, if only by virtue of being reared apart past the early stages of infancy. Again, the same is true of the vast majority of the nonpsychotic sample. However, as Kety et al. (1976) noted, this does not rule out environmental determination we do not yet know how to delineate.

Thus, the data may be viewed as being in accord with a diathesis-stressor model where a vulnerability must be present before environmental stressors such as neglect, brutality, poverty, or twin interaction take hold. A subjective impression of the data, unencumbered by empirical proof, is that the twin with the better background (fewer childhood stressors) tends to show more acute, even florid episodes, but recovers better than the other twin whose course is more chronic and insidious.

Summary

Of three references to severe affective disorder in the sample, only one offers evidence of bipolar I status (manic-depressive, hospitalized for mania). Diagnosis and onset of the initial manic episodes were strikingly similar. Content and course of the illness may have been influenced by the twins' knowledge of each other. While further case studies are necessary before conclusions can be drawn, the case supports the hypothesis of genetic predisposition to bipolar disorder and may offer support for the hypothesis of genetic contributions to onset and duration of cycles.

Of the eighteen references to schizophrenic disorders, using even lenient criteria, only nine belong to the class of twins reared apart. All twins had met and had contact, so interactional influences are possible. Similarly, the pairwise concordance of 67 percent may be artificially high due to sampling procedures. However, despite methodological problems, the concordance *in conjunction with* the similarity in the descriptions of symptomatology could be construed to be in accord with the hypothesis of genetic contributions to liability for schizophrenic disorders. Schizophrenia was present in the pedigree of almost all sets (with no severe affective disorders noted), and given the poor back-

8. See case 114 as an example.

grounds of the majority of all twins reared apart, environmental factors such as poverty, neglect, or traumatic separation cannot be judged fully explanatory. Evaluations of the influence of laterality or perinatal factors are impossible, given the poor quality of the data. However, there were slight indications of the more disturbed twin coming from the more disturbed rearing family, a pattern congruent with the diathesis-stressor model. Given even brutal rearing conditions and a partner who was known to be psychotic, some twins did not become ill, but the data were insufficiently detailed to allow speculation about what factors protected them.

Chapter 7

IQ[1]

A false notion that is clear and precise will have more power than a true principle which is obscure and involved.

Alexis de Tocqueville

Of all areas in twin studies, evaluations of the heritability of IQ have been the most controversial. The controversy stems partly from questions about the validity of IQ tests, partly from disputes over the rigor of analysis of various samples, and predominantly from the way IQ data have been analyzed and interpreted by Arthur Jensen of the University of California. The controversy is well known both within the field and to the public at large, and an extensive literature exists on it (Jensen 1970, 1973; Gottesman 1965, 1968, 1972; Deutsch et al. 1968; Cancro 1971; Jencks et al. 1972; Kamin 1974; Loehlin et al. 1975; Block and Dworkin 1976).

Briefly, the controversy centers on Jensen's analysis of IQ scores from racial and ethnic subpopulations within the United States and his hypothesis that genetic differences are predominantly explanatory for IQ test score differences between black and white subpopulations. Though he analyzes an extensive body of data, an important element of his hypothesis of a genetic basis for race differences is his analysis of data on twins reared apart and his estimate that they vary on average less than one standard deviation from each other and have intraclass correlations approaching .80 (1970, 1973). Since he assumes that twins reared apart are genetically identical but are randomly assigned to different environments, and since his data indicates that blacks and whites vary on the average much more than twins reared apart, he sug-

1. The plural "we" in this chapter refers to myself and Noel Dunivant, Ph.D., who performed the statistical analyses presented herein.

gests that the differences between the ethnic and racial groups must be presumed to stem substantially from differences in genetic potential (Wolff 1979).

The charges and countercharges that have arisen from this argument have ranged from dryly scientific to political and acrimonious. The scientific questions put to the analysis are so numerous that an exhaustive listing cannot be attempted here. However, among them are issues of how race can be defined in a genetic sense (Dobzhansky 1973), whether IQ measures only one aspect of cognitive style and is essentially a self-fulfilling prophecy, whether factors influencing IQ are not so numerous as to make specific estimates of heritability questionable (Gottesman 1972), and whether "heritability" is a useful concept at all in this context. Issues raised specifically around the data from twins reared apart include questions of the bias of the sample toward low SES, high genotype-environment (G-E) correlation, outdated tests, systematic testing error, and possible interactions between age and test score (Jencks et al. 1972; Kamin 1974; Fuller and Thompson 1978). In chapter 1, additional issues of prematurity, selection on the basis of phenotypic similarity, and mutual contact also were mentioned. Issues of the appropriate statistical methodology also have been raised over the years (McNemar 1938; Jensen 1973; Loehlin et al. 1975).

Since the controversy is an excellent example of the use and sometimes abuse of twin data (Shields 1978), the aim of this chapter is to present the data in as comprehensive a manner as possible. All information is included so conclusions may be checked and other analyses run. The chapter focuses exclusively on the twin-reared-apart data and, except for the commentary at the end, makes the assumption that IQ scores validly measure a cognitive capacity of the individual. This assumption, which is open to debate, is made only for the sake of argument and to speed the transition to the analysis of the data per se. The following section, "Heritability," is meant to remind the reader of issues surrounding the concept. The chapter is then broken into three parts. "Issues of Pooling Data" deals with the twins sample by sample; "Pooled Data: Heritability Estimates" reanalyzes the combined data from all sources; and "IQ Versus Cognition" suggests alternative questions that might be put to the issue of the genetic influence on cognition.

Heritability

Heritability is a construct originally designed for animal breeding purposes. It refers to the proportion of variance in a sample that can be attributed to the different genotypes in the sample. The remaining proportion of variance can be used to express the effects of environment. High heritability of a trait such as milk production in cattle might indicate that the milk production was determined primarily by the genotypes of the cattle in the sample with relatively little environmental influence. Conversely, low heritability might indicate that environment was important in determining differences in milk production in the group. Most significantly in this context, heritability (in the broad sense) provides a numerical index of the degree to which the trait in question, such as milk production, can be altered by selective breeding. By analogous reasoning, some have concluded that high heritability of IQ test scores can be construed as an indication that differences among individuals in a group are due substantially to the differences in their genotypes, while low heritability indicates that differences are more related to the differences in their environments.

In studies of twins reared apart, the intraclass correlation, r', frequently is used as a heritability coefficient. However, components of variance related to environmental interactions may be obscured in the intraclass correlation (see chapter 1, also Jencks et al. 1972), although methods exist to estimate their degree of contribution (Jensen 1970; Jinks and Fulker 1970; Loehlin 1975). An intraclass correlation or heritability coefficient (frequently designated h^2) may be computed by several methods (Jensen 1973; Loehlin 1975). In this chapter, heritability coefficients were constructed as ratios of components of variance that were estimated by standard analysis of variance techniques. Where more complex analyses of variance are done, the designs are noted.

It is important to remember that not only can the heritability coefficient be derived by several routes, each sometimes giving different results, but, more important, that it is an estimate based on a limited sample. As such it can be generalized to the population *only* if the sample is randomly selected from the population and, thus, is representative of it. With these data one may ask whether it is appropriate to generalize to the population of twins reared apart, to the population of all twins, or to the general population of children and adults. To the degree that this sample has not been randomly selected from any of these populations, it is not generalizable and any bias in either the environments of the sample or the genotypes represented in it will distort heritability estimates. Additionally, if deviations atypical of the larger population(s) are present (such as an exceptionally high number of mentally or physically ill individuals), the heritability estimate will be correspondingly distorted. Congenital disturbances or limitations on genetic expression will appear to stem from genetic sources. The lack of random sampling, which makes it questionable whether this sample of twins reared apart is representative of even the full population of twins reared apart, much less the normal adult population, has already been noted. A few additional issues will be discussed later in this chapter.

Another limitation on generalizability is mentioned less frequently but is equally as important. Heritability estimates are almost always based on a cross-sectional, nondevelopmental approach. While acknowledging that the estimates may be altered by introducing new environmental conditions, many people treat them as if the fundamental genetic blueprint were a fixed, immutable, and essentially static component. However, the action of genes is not fixed and unchanging. Genes are activated and suppressed by environmental conditions *and also are activated and inactivated as part of the developmental process* (Davidson 1976; McClearn 1970; Gottesman 1974). The portion of the genome operating at any one time or at different developmental levels may be different. Thus, repeated heritability estimates on a trait such as height may shift over time, and there are hints that the same may be true of IQ (Wilson 1978). When one considers as complex and probably as polygenic a trait as cognition, the implications of this variability are enormous and easily lead to issues of sensitive periods in development and intervention strategies. These will be touched on later. For the time being, we merely caution that heritability estimates from any sample are limited by numerous parameters including time, place, and developmental level.

Thus, generalization from this sample of twins reared apart is open to debate. Most sets were chosen because they were highly similar in the first place, a fact that immediately eliminates them as a random sample of twins reared apart. Additionally, generalization to the population of nontwins is limited by the bias in the sample toward low SES, prematurity, mental and physical illness, predominantly British and European rearing environments (most dating back to the turn of the century), war (all but a small fraction lived in countries occupied or under bombardment during world wars), fluctuating degrees of separation, and outdated and questionable tests. Almost all are adult and Caucasian, and only *three* are genuinely reared-apart in the true meaning of the term.

Issues of Pooling Data

This section deals with two interrelated issues: (1) can data from various studies be pooled into one large sample? and (2) is data generalizable to the population at large? In order to answer the questions, data were analyzed separately for each sample according to the type of IQ test used. We asked if it is legitimate[2] to take the average IQ from test-retest data, if it is legitimate to combine test scores (taking a verbal and

2. We use the term in the colloquial sense.

performance test to obtain a full-scale score), and if it is legitimate to combine the sexes into one sample. The questions were raised in order to avoid falsely assuming that IQ is a single, homogeneous construct and that data from the subsamples come from a single, homogeneous population. Such assumptions, if incorrect, can lead to greater errors in analysis and interpretation if the IQ scores are combined and analyzed by standard methods (Kirk 1968).

Table 7.1 lists all IQ scores and other data from various sources. For the time being, the shaded areas may be ignored. The following descriptions explain the entries and touch on test and sampling problems in each study.

Juel-Nielsen. Juel-Nielsen's 1965 sample accounts for twelve sets.[3] They are the only group not contaminated by a similarity method of ascertainment. The Danish version of the Wechsler Adult Intelligence Scale (WAIS) was used and almost all cases have test-retest scores. Juel-Nielsen also included all subtest scores in his published data. The WAIS is a widely known, reputable, contemporary IQ test and, though question has been raised about the Danish standardization (Kamin 1974; Jensen 1976), it is the best test on the best-selected sample in all the literature. However, the sample was drawn primarily from economically deprived environments, and has other limitations. The test scores have been entered directly from Juel-Nielsen's summary into table 7.1. His data from the Ravens test were not analyzed since we wished to examine tests using both verbal and performance components and considered the WAIS a superior measure of IQ. Juel-Nielsen reported a mean absolute difference of 6.5 points in full-scale IQ score between twins and an intraclass correlation of .68. He suggested that differences in education may influence differences in test score, particularly in the direction of twins with higher education tending toward higher verbal scores (1965, pp. 110–111). He used an impression of degree of separation (not the same type of measure of separation used in this study) and estimated that for both the WAIS and Ravens, the more separated the twins, the more divergent the absolute pair difference scores. Such a result would suggest that the lack of complete separation has inflated the estimation of h^2 by counting some environmental influences as genetic. However, the effects of separation were not statistically significant for his small sample.

Newman, Freeman, and Holzinger. Newman et al.'s (1937) data account for nineteen sets.[4] As previously mentioned, these sets were ob-

3. Cases 104, 108, 114, 130, 146, 168, 170, 178, 184, 188, 206, and 406; three male pairs and nine female pairs.
4. Cases 118, 120, 124, 142, 144, 150, 152, 154, 158, 160, 162, 164, 182, 208, 210, 244, 318, 320, and 408. Seven were male sets, the remaining twelve were female.

TABLE 7.1
IQ scores—MZ twins reared apart.

Group	ID	Name	Age	Sex	Hand	Birthweight	Birth order	Reared with	WAIS (verbal)	WAIS (performance)	WAIS full-scale	Stanford Binet
Ia	102	George	19	M	L			O				
		Millan			LR			O				
	104	Olga	35	F	R			O	94	103	99	
									96	102	99	
		Ingrid			R			O	99	105	103	
									105	105	106	
	106	JJ	17	M	R			O				124
												126
		JB			R			O				107
												105
	108	Palle	22	M	R			O	114	121	119	
									112	125	120	
		Peter			R			O	120	117	121	
									133	129	135	
	110	Madeline	36	F	R		1	O				
		Lillian			L		2	O				
	112	Olive	35	F	R			P				
		Madge			R			R				
Ib	114	Kamma	50	F	A	more		O	94	109	100	
									98	120	110	
		Ella			A/L	less		P	93	98	94	
									99	100	104 .	
	116	Bessie	30	F	L			O				
		Jessie			L			O				
	118	Paul C.	23	M	R			O				99
		Paul O.			R			O				101
	120	Esther	39	F	L			O				85
		Ethel			R			O				84
	122	Mary										
		Gertrude										
	124	Gladys	35	F	R			O				92
		Helen			R			O				116
	126	Tristram	18	M	L	2608	1	P				
		Russell			L	2041	2	O				
	128	Marjorie	36	F	L		1	O				
		Norah			R		2	O				
Ic	130	Signe	54	F	R			R	86	100	91	
									92	102	96	
		Hanne			R			O	93	105	98	
									94	110	101	
	132	Amy	55	F	R		1	R				
		Teresa			R		2	P				
	134	Florence										
		Edith										
	136	Berta	43	F	R		2	O				
		Herta			R		1	P				

Mill Hill	Dominoes	Other	MH I*	MH II†	Dominoes‡	F-D IQ§	Jensen IQ‖	Comment
		97						Otis test
		104						
								Form L then form M revised
14	27		74	89	98	94	93	
13	24		72	88	93	91	89	
25	35		91	114	112	113	113	
26	30		93	115	103	109	111	
		64/75						1922 Otis A and
		156/212						1918 Army Alpha
		62/75						
		153/212						
								"feebleminded"
14	30		77	95	103	99	95	
6	23		66	81	91	86	79	Epileptic
24	32		89	110	107	109	110	Possible congenital
16	18		78	93	83	88	88	syphilis for both
9	12		74	88	72	80	74	Chorea? No posi-
7	9		70	87	67	77	69	tive diagnosis
								Psychosis
14	28		74	89	100	95	94	Spanish and Danish
8	16		66	82	79	81	76	as first languages

TABLE 7.1 *(continued)*
IQ scores—MZ twins reared apart.

Group	ID	Name	Age	Sex	Hand	Birthweight	Birth order	Reared with	WAIS (verbal)	WAIS (performance)	WAIS full-scale	Stanford-Binet
Id	138	Lois	18	F	R	2722		O				107
		Louise			R	2268		R				110
	140	A										
		B										
	142	Kenneth	19	M	R			O				94
		Jerry			R			O				95
	144	Raymond	13	M	R			O				105
		Richard			R			O				106
	146	Maren	37	F	R	less	1	R	104	110	108	
		Jensine			R	more	2	R	96	98	97	
									98	103	101	
	148	Millicent	40	F	L		2	R				
		Edith			R		1	P				
	150	Mildred	15	F	L	2722		R				92
		Ruth			R	1588		R				77
	152	Betty	12	F	R			O				122
		Ruth			A			O				127
	154	James	27	M	L			R				96
		Reese			R			R				77
	156	A										
		B										
	158	Edith	38	F	R			O				89
		Fay			R			O				93
	160	Thelma	29	F	R			O				116
		Zelma			A			O				109
	162	Gene	14	M	L			O				115
		James			R			O				105
	164	Maxine	11	F				O				90
		Virginia						O				88
	166	A										
		B										
	168	Martha	49	F	R			O	95	116	105	
		Marie			R			R	85	113	97	
	170	Astrid	72	F	R	2500	1	P	109	115	111	
									113	117	115	
		Edith			R	2000	2	O	111	124	117	
									107	120	111	
Ie	172	Megan	32	F	R		2	P				
		Polly			R		1	O				
	174	Alfred	39	M	R		2	P				
		Harry			R		1	R				
	176	Herbert	22	M	R	less	2	R			75	
		Nicholas			R	more	1	O			76	
	178	Karin	64	F	R	more	1	O	101	108	104	
									96	112	102	
		Kristine			R	less	2	R	101	106	103	
									101	112	105	
	180	A	23?	M				R				(84)
		B		M				P				(66)
	182	Edwin	26	M	R			O				91
		Fred			R			O				90

Mill Hill	Dominoes	Other	MH I*	MH II†	Dominoes‡	F-D IQ§	Jensen IQ‖	Comment
								No tests
21	33		86	102	109	106	107	
14	24		74	89	93	91	90	
								Psychosis
								T:TB
								Psychosis
20	33		85	99	109	104	105	
22	32		88	106	107	107	107	
10	1		67	85		85		A tried Dominoes
10	16		67	85		85		twice. Unreliable?
11	10		71	90	69	80	75	Psychosis
6	13		76	81	74	78	71	
								Psychosis and ancient test

TABLE 7.1 *(continued)*
IQ scores—MZ twins reared apart.

Group	ID	Name	Age	Sex	Hand	Birthweight	Birth order	Reared with	WAIS (verbal)	WAIS (performance)	WAIS full-scale	Stanford-Binet
	184	Petrine	70	F	R	2500	1	O	119	127	125	
									112	129	122	
		Dorthe			L	less	2	P	109	115	111	
									109	124	116	
	186	Gertrude	52	F	R	1360		O				
		Helen			R	1360		P				
	188	Ingegerd	42	F	R	1375	1	PR	88	97	91	
									88	110	98	
		Monica			R	1125	2	RP	96	105	100	
									92	111	101	
	190	Keith	38	M	R		2	O				
		Edward			R		1	O				
IIa	202	Tony	29	M	R	less		O			108	
		Roger			R	2835		OP			109	
	204	Earl	37	M	R			O				
		Frank			R			R				
	206	Kaj	45	M	R			O	110	111	111	
		Robert			R			O	118	114	117	
									115	114	115	
	208	Eleanore	27	F	R			O				66
		Georgiana			R			O				78
	210	Alice	19	F	R			O				85
		Olive			L			O				97
	212	Clara	39	F	R			O				
		Doris			A			O				
	214	Olwen	48	F	R		1	O				
		Gwladys			R		2	O				
IIb	216	Joanna	50	F	R		1	R				
		Isobel			R		2	P				
	218	Mary	47	F	L			R				
		Nancy			R			P				
	220	Rodney	34	M	R		1	R				
		Barry			R		2	P				
	222	A										
		B										
	224	June	41	F	R	2722	1	O				
		Clara			R	1134	2	O				
	226	Kaete										
		Lisa										
	228	James	49	M	R		1	P				
		Robert			R		2	R				
	230	Jacqueline	41	F	R		1	R				
		Beryl			R		2	R				
	232	Ronald	20	M	R		1	P				100
		Dennis			R		2	R				104
	234	A										
		B										
	236	Richard	14	M	R	1361	1	P				
		Kenneth			R	1134	2	R				
	238	Jessie	8	F	R	less	1	O				
		Winnifred			R	more	2	O				
	240	A										
		B										
	242	Adelaide	12	F	AR			O				103
			18									108
		Beatrice			A			O				102
												111
	244	Ada	59	F	R			R				102
		Ida			R			R				94
	246	William	39	M	R		2	O				
		Stanley			R		1	O				

Mill Hill	Dominoes	Other	MH I*	MH II†	Dominoes‡	F-D IQ§	Jensen IQ‖	Comment
		66						Kuhlmann Stanford
		51						G: Helen ill
13	24		72	88	93	91	89	
11	20		67	86	86	86	83	
		96						1916 Stanford
		83						Binet, Form E
		70						Kuhlmann Stanford:
		61						also Psychosis?
13	4		77	89	58	74	73	Both Welsh
7	2		66	84	55	70	63	
27	41		95	118	123	121	121	
28	40		97	122	121	122	121	
13	32		77	89	107	98	96	
17	28		66	94	100	97	97	
15	26		76	91	97	94	93	
7	17		66	82	81	82	76	
								No tests
15	23		76	91	91	91	91	
11	21		67	86	88	87	84	
								Psychosis
21	26		87	103	97	100	101	
14	20		79	90	86	88	87	
25	38		91	114	117	116	116	
22	27		88	106	98	102	103	
								No tests
19	22		96	96	90	93	95	Mill Hill Junior
19	12		96	96	72	84	87	Scale
11	23		100	100	91	96	86	Mill Hill Junior
12	21		103	103	88	96	85	Scale
								Psychosis
								First test: age 12; second: age 18
22	26		88	106	97	102	102	
25	30		91	114	103	109	109	

TABLE 7.1 (continued)
IQ scores—MZ twins reared apart.

Group	ID	Name	Age	Sex	Hand	Birthweight	Birth order	Reared with	WAIS (verbal)	WAIS (performance)	WAIS full-scale	Stanford-Binet
III	302	Bertram	17	M	R		1	R				
		Christopher			R		2	R				
	304	Kathleen	33	F	R	2948	1	R				
		Jenny			R	1588	2	R				
	306	Laura	45	F	R	stronger	1	P				
		Charlotte			R	weaker	2	R				
	308	Timothy	45	M	R	weaker	2	P				
		Kevin			R	stronger	1	R				
	310	A										
		B										
	312	Nina	42	F	R		1	R				
		Christine			R		2	P				
	314	Annie	48	F	R	more	1	R				
		Trixie			R	less	2	P				
	316	A										
		B										
	318	Mabel	29	F	R			R				89
		Mary			R			R				106
	320	Harold	19	M	L			R				102
		Holden			R			R				96
	322	Frederick	30	M	R		2	R				
		Peter			R		1	O				
	324	Foster	32	M	R		1	R				
		Francis			R		2	P				
	326	A										
		B										
	328	Benjamin	52	M	R		2	P				
		Ronald			R		1	R				
	330	Esther	18	F				R	94	103	99	
		Elvira						P	83	96	88	
	332	Alois	16	M		2250	1	O	(114)	(100)	(108)	
		Oskar				more	2	P			(104)	
	334	Victor	51	M	R		2	P				
		Patrick			R		1	R				
	336	Brian	51	M	R		2	R				
		Hubert			R		1	P				
	338	Valerie	30	F	R		2	O			111	
		Joyce			L		1	P			92	
	340	A										
		B										
	342	Fanny	48	F	R	weaker	1	P				
		Odette			R	stronger	2	R				
	344	Viola	39	F	R	weaker	2	R				
		Olga			R	stronger	1	P				
	346	Maisie										
		Vera										
	348	Peter										
		Bert										
	350	Dora	56	F	R		1	R				
		Brenda			R		2	P				
	352	Joan	40	F	R		2	P				
		Dinah			R		1	R				
	354	A										
		B										
IV	406	Viggo	77	M				PO	102	103	99	
									102	109	102	
		Oluf						PO	110	116	112	
									105	121	112	
	408	Augusta	41	F	L			PO				88
		Helen			AR			PO				79
	410	Pauline	38	F	R	1588	1	P				
		Sally			R	2041	2	PR				
	416	Molly	38	F	R		1	R				
		Dorothy			R		2	P				
	422	Adeline	59	F	R		1	P				
		Gwendolen			R		2	PR				

*Calculated directly from Shields's scores, using MH manual.
†Calculated from MH manual using Shields's scores plus 10 points for adults.
‡Calculated from distribution on Dominoes instruction sheet used by Shields.
§Farber-Dunivant IQ (MH II IQ plus Dominoes IQ divided by 2).
‖Jensen IQ (1970) calculated by transforming Shields's stated means and sample standard deviation to IQ 100, sd 15.

Mill Hill	Dominoes	Other	MH I*	MH II†	Dominoes‡	F-D IQ§	Jensen IQ‖	Comment
11	36		71	95	114	105	96	
15	34		79	104	110	107	100	
19	30		84	98	103	101	102	
21	34		86	102	110	106	108	
20	27		85	99	98	99	101	
17	25		82	94	95	95	95	
22	35		88	106	112	109	110	
17	29		82	94	102	98	98	
								Psychosis
14	33		74	89	109	99	98	
16	26		78	93	97	95	94	
12	19		75	88	84	86	84	T: Multiple
6	9		66	82	67	75	68	sclerosis
								Psychosis
10	25		67	85	95	90	86	
5	30		66	76	103	90	84	
20	32		85	99	107	103	105	
23	28		88	107	100	104	105	
								No tests
10	4		67	87	58	73	69	
6	13		66	82	74	78	71	
								Both Spanish as first language
								Psychosis (WAIS?)
22	22		88	106	90	98	99	
25	28		93	114	100	107	108	
19	27		86	99	98	99	99	
21	21		87	103	88	96	97	
17	27		82	94	—	—	—	WAIS at age 52
11	1		66	86				
								Psychosis
17	40		84	95	121	108	107	
21	38		87	103	117	110	111	
19	9		84	98	67	83	84	
19	15		84	98	77	88	89	
								No tests
								No tests
12	13		79	90	74	82	79	
10	22		76	89	90	90	84	
14	10		74	89	69	79	79	
14	6		74	89	62	76	76	
								A: "Average"
								B: "Above average"
								Separated age 6
								Separated ages 6-17
11	22		66	86	90	88	85	Separated age 7
10	23		71	85	91	88	84	
19	27		84	98	98	98	99	Separated age 8
16	28		78	93	100	97	96	
23	29		93	110	102	106	106	Separated age 9
23	30		93	110	103	107	107	

tained through public appeal, which limited the responders to those who knew each other or suspected each other's existence. Sets were further preselected by a similarity questionnaire, and zygosity was ascertained by a similarity method, including fingerprints. Since sets usually meet because they are reared near each other in the same extended family or because they are so uncannily alike that chance encounters bring them together, the Newman sample must be expected to be more phenotypically similar than the total population of all MZ twins reared apart. To the degree that manifestations of intelligence are part of phenotype (and they evidently play an important role, see "Pooled Data," pp. 199–201, and chapter 9), the Newman sample is biased toward greater similarity.

The 1916 Stanford-Binet and the Otis test were used in the Newman Study. The Stanford-Binet is the more widely known of the two, and the scores from it are entered directly into table 7.1. The Newman study was published in 1937, with data collection evidently beginning in the mid- to late 1920s. The Stanford-Binet in use at that time did not use the method of obtaining IQs now considered appropriate. Corrections have been suggested to make the Newman scores conform more to population values (McNemar 1938), but since the purpose here is to estimate how similar or deviant subsamples are *before* generalizing to the population at large, the correction is not made at this stage of the analysis. Though the test scores were problematic, they are the second-best source of information in the literature. Newman et al. estimated that differences in IQ were related to differences in education, and their mean difference, 8.2 points, and intraclass correlation, .67, are similar to Juel-Nielsen's findings. It is interesting and perhaps noteworthy that the two best samples have larger intrapair differences and lower heritabilities than the Shields's sample, which is open to serious methodological criticisms (see pp. 180–185). However, though the Newman sample has a somewhat larger range of social classes and rearing environments than other studies—which some have linked to the larger variance in IQ scores (Bane and Jencks 1976)—it remains a sample biased toward low to lower-middle-class conditions and, compared with environments in contemporary life, must be considered unrepresentative.

Shields. Shields's 1962 study covered forty-four sets,[5] but four of them (cases 140, 326, 346, and 402) do not have test data and two others (174 and 338) require elimination of scores from the Dominoes portion of the tests. Of the forty pairs for whom test scores were available, fif-

5. Cases 110, 112, 126, 128, 132, 136, 140, 148, 172, 174, 176, 190, 214, 216, 218, 220, 224, 228, 230, 236, 238, 246, 302, 304, 306, 308, 312, 314, 322, 324, 326, 328, 334, 336, 338, 342, 344, 346, 350, 352, 402, 410, 416, and 422.

teen were male and twenty-five female. The sample was obtained through an appeal over television and respondents went through a preliminary similarity screening. As a result, the sample has the same bias toward phenotypic similarity as the Newman sample. Shields himself additionally noted that the sample is biased toward lower- to lower-middle-class living and rearing conditions. However, the major problems with the data stem from how the tests were administered from the nature of the tests themselves. One problem was that the tests were not administered individually. Instead, written forms were given—usually when the twins were together. Though there is no question of Shields's reputability or accuracy of reporting, some have questioned whether the form of administration may have tilted scores toward greater similarity. For example, Kamin (1974) found that the few sets not tested by Shields had within-pair differences in IQ more than twice as large as the sets where both partners were tested by Shields. Loehlin et al. (1975) pointed out that these differences may merely be related to two markedly atypical pairs in the sets not tested by Shields. Whichever is the case, Shields's short-form, self-administered, written tests differed from the type of testing used in almost all other studies.

The fundamental problem, however, may lie within the tests themselves. Shields used a synonyms portion of the Mill Hill Vocabulary Scale as his verbal test and the Dominoes Test (now known as the D48) as his performance scale. He reported the results as raw scores. Two problems emerge from this: (1) whether the tests can be construed as valid and reliable IQ tests, and (2) how to convert the raw scores into IQs.

The Mill HIll Vocabulary Scale is widely used in Great Britain and is associated with the use of Ravens Progressive Matrices in the United States. The test manuals over the years all indicate that, while the full vocabulary scale may be used as an *estimate* of verbal abilities, the scores should not be construed as precise indicators of verbal intelligence. The 1962 manual, in addition to indicating that the full test is only an estimate, is explicit about the limits of the synonyms subtest:

For some purposes the Synonyms Section half of the test can be used by itself. *This is suitable when an accurate estimate of a person's attainments is not necessary* or when the Definitions half of the test, with its fund of qualitative information and more accurate differential scoring, can be given afterwards, either as an individual or self-administered test. [Ravens 1962, p. 1; emphasis added]

The test manual, furthermore, gives norms based only on male samples, while the Shields's sample of twins reared apart was predominantly female. Thus, from a test that—as a whole—is questionable as a precise indicator of verbal intelligence, Shields, under pressure of time constraints, used only a single subsection and a completely pencil-and-paper one at that. This problem was compounded by the fact that the test was administered when twins were together and, probably more seriously, by the fact that it was compared with norms based predominantly on the opposite sex. It is questionable to treat such results as verbal IQ indices and, in a strongly worded paper, the last he wrote before he died, Shields (1978) argued against such use.

The Dominoes test is virtually unknown in the United States, though it has some currency in Europe. It is listed in the *Sixth Mental Measurements Yearbook* (Buros 1965) but has been dropped from the latest edition and is listed only in *Tests in Print II* (Buros 1974) under the title "D48 test." It is clearly labeled an "experimental" test (Buros 1965; Gough and Domino 1963). The test was used by the British Armed Forces during World War II, and the instruction sheet used by Shields[6] indicates that this test too was meant for males, and presumably was normed only for males, while the twin sample is predominantly female. Nor does the test have age norms. These omissions are potentially significant, since an examination of means in various British, European, and American samples (Gough and Domino 1963) indicates that means differ from each other and increase with age and education. Shields, using the percentile ranking previously cited, gave a mean of 28 for Dominoes. This is roughly similar to the mean for various other adult samples that were administered the test. However, the standard deviations in other samples range from about 4.7 to 8.5 raw score points, indicating differences in variance worthy of note.

Again, compared to other measures of nonverbal or performance IQ, one may question the trustworthiness of a test whose test-retest reliability is known to be on the low side (.69, Buros 1965). If obscurity is any indication of lack of trustworthiness, the test remains extremely obscure decades after its development. Again, Shields (1978) argued against using Dominoes scores as directly convertible into IQ.

Since, given the elimination of cases reported by Burt (see chapter 3), a substantial portion of the IQ data stems precisely from these two questionable tests, the Mill Hill and the Dominoes, it could be argued that IQ conversion should be attempted as estimates if not definitive

6. A copy of the instruction sheet used by Shields in his administration of the Dominoes was made available to the author (Gurling 1979; private correspondence). The percentile groups are as follows:

	Percentile	Dominoes Score
Top	0–10	40–48
	11–25	33–39
	26–50	28–32
	26–50	23–27
	11–25	14–22
Bottom	0–10	0–13

scores. If so, the question of how to convert raw scores into IQ arises. One method was used by Jensen (1970). The raw scores and *sample* standard deviations were transformed using a Mill Hill mean 19 and Dominoes mean 28 as equivalent to IQ 100, standard deviation 15. These means were given by Shields (1962, p. 59).[7] The transformed Mill Hill and Dominoes scores obtained by this method were then averaged to give a full-scale score. Such scores are listed in table 7.1 under the heading "Jensen IQ."[8]

Several serious problems arise from such a conversion. For example, it does not take into account the different scores expected at different ages, and it lumps together children's scores with those of adults. Using the Jensen conversion, a score of 19 always gives IQ at the fiftieth percentile, while taking age into account would place the person near the ninetieth percentile at age sixteen or closer to the fiftieth percentile past the age of forty-five. Equally as serious is the problem that, by setting the sample standard deviation equal to 15 (the standard deviation of the IQ distribution), one begs the question of whether the sample standard deviation departs significantly from the hypothesized norm of the general population. The effect of this problem when combining Shields's data with those from other studies is that one mixes scores obtained by different methods of standardization and, in practice, obtains an overly large standard deviation for the Mill Hill or Dominoes taken separately. Yet, as will be explained, the opposite effect obtains when dealing with the full-scale IQ computed as the average of the Mill Hill and Dominoes IQ. In effect, one mixes apples and oranges, and this affects estimates of components of variance obtained in all subsequent analyses.

Our approach, chosen because it seemed most precise and the one that would approximate conversion to IQ under normal testing conditions, was to take each raw score and convert it into an IQ, using norms, particularly age norms whenever possible, as given in the manuals for the tests. For the Mill Hill scores, the method was as follows. The raw score of each individual was located in Table IV of the Mill Hill manual

7. Shields derived these means by the following method: The Dominoes mean was taken directly from the percentile rankings on the instruction sheet. The Mill Hill mean was estimated by using the tables published in the Mill Hill manual (1938, 1950). Shields looked to the figures for the median age group of his sample and judged that a total score of 57 or 58 was equivalent to IQ 100. To achieve a 57 or 58, a synonyms score of about 30 would be needed. Subtracting 11 for automatically credited items leaves a mean of 19. (Shields 1974; private correspondence; communicated to the author in private correspondence by Gurling 1979).

8. The Mill Hill manual in use at the time of Shields's testing says that 10, not 11, points are to be credited. The mean therefore should be 20, not 19, using Shields's method of reporting and assuming that he gave the test according to instructions. This correction has not been made in the "Jensen" conversion. If Shields unwittingly did not credit the first worked item, his estimate of 19 would be understandable, though, to be accurate, all adult raw scores would require addition of the point.

(Table III if a junior scale) under the heading "Set B. Synonyms." From this, an expected score—the score that the individual presumably would have received had the whole test been given—can be obtained. This expected score was then compared with the percentile rankings according to age group given in Peck's (1970) paper, and the percentile was converted to an IQ using the conversion chart in the same paper. In table 7.1, the IQs under the heading MH I are those obtained when 10 points were not added to the raw score. The correct conversions, judging from the method of reporting stated in the manual over the years, were obtained by adding 10 points to all but the junior scales, and are listed in the column marked "MH II." These are the scores used in all subsequent analyses.[9, 10]

Dominoes was converted using the percentile rankings given in the instruction sheet used by Shields. Using these percentiles and assuming a normal distribution, the population standard deviation of the Dominoes can be estimated as 8.62, In the sample of Shields's twins reared apart, the male standard deviation is 7.4 points while the female standard deviation is 10.1. Though we cannot reject the hypothesis that the standard deviation equals 8.26 for either sex at alpha level .05, there is some indication against assuming normality for the female twins. The indication might be underscored by noting that the Dominoes appears to have been normed only for males and that the female sample standard deviation is atypical of other samples, including females, reported by Gough and Domino (1963). Also—needless to add—is the reminder that the lack of age norms is a critical omission for any precise estimates.

Full-scale IQ scores are reported in table 7.1 under the heading "F-D IQ" (Farber-Dunivant conversion). They were obtained by adding the Mill Hill and Dominoes IQs and dividing by two.[11, 12] The results of our conversions may be compared in table 7.1 with those obtained by the "Jensen" method. The individual IQs and sample means (Jensen mean

9. The listing of conversions based on not adding the 10 points to adult raw scores is included because references in the literature suggest that some authors may have attempted such conversions. Shields (1978) referred to conversions that place too many twins in the retarded range. More important, we wished to examine whether Gottesman's unpublished conversions (1968, 1972)—where he reports finding 14 points difference in verbal IQ and 10 points difference in performance IQ—could be approximated using either method. We were unable to replicate the results.

10. It is worth reiterating the fact that even the normative data on the Mill Hill is open to question since it is based on an entirely male sample, while the sample of twins reared apart is predominantly female.

11. Although averaging the Mill Hill plus Dominoes IQs is the most straightforward conversion, it emerges that the standard deviation of the Mill Hill plus Dominoes is artifactually low. For example, males have a Mill Hill standard deviation of 12 and a Dominoes standard deviation of 10, but the standard deviation of the averaged Mill Hill plus Dominoes is only 9. In separate analyses, we tried to take this into account by setting the

96.1, sd 13.7, versus F-D mean 96.8, sd 12.8) are not much different for the most part, but the distribution is affected by the more precise conversion.[13]

All in all, the problems in conversion and test validity cited should indicate that the Shields scores should be dropped or viewed as extremely tentative. However, for the purpose of presenting as broad and even-handed an analysis as possible, they are viewed as valid. At the end of "Pooled Data," we examine the effect on heritability estimates when Shields's and other questionable data are eliminated.

Other. The "other" category in table 7.1 covers all IQ data from individual case histories and small series. It accounts for thirteen cases with recorded data.[14] The type of test and the mental/physical status of the twins is given in the column entitled Comment. *Bessie and Jessie* (case 116) cannot be scored for IQ since only raw data from outdated tests was included.[15] Case 186 is excluded since, by numerous statistical tests, they were rated as outliers. The others are of variable degrees of reliability and will be included in various analyses in the pooled data section according to the criteria set for each analysis. Overall, seven male and four female sets from this category are included in the large-sample analysis later in this chapter.

---

full-scale sd for males and females separately and making it equal to the average standard deviation of the Mill Hill IQ and Dominoes IQ. Thus, males were given a standard deviation of 11 for full-scale IQ and females a standard deviation of 14. Appropriate transformations were then made. Choosing the standard deviation in this way was yet another attempt to make the Shields's sample comparable to the others which used full-scale IQ scores which had been set to a standard deviation of 15. Results were entirely congruent with those reported throughout this chapter.

12. For those unclear about the technical details in the preceding footnote, one may state the issue in another way: Test developers now standardize verbal, performance, and full-scale IQ scales separately. Thus, WAIS full-scale IQ scores are not obtained by averaging verbal and performance IQs but are obtained from a separate scale. Were they averaged, their standard deviation would be less than 15. The same problem exists when trying to combine Shields's data with other tests giving full-scale IQs with mean 100, sd 15. When we state that, at one point, we analyzed all of this data with Shields's full-scale IQ standard deviations set separately from the verbal and performance components, and separately for males and females, we are saying that data in this chapter have been analyzed by trying to give every position—whether hereditarian or environmentalist—every benefit of a doubt. No matter how we transform the Shields's tests, results turn out essentially the same.

13. The distribution is affected because Jensen did not consider the issues discussed earlier in constructing his composite IQ scores for the Shields's sample. As long as the correlation between the Mill Hill and Dominoes IQ scores is less than perfect, then the variance of the mean IQ scores will be less than 15^2 even when the variance of each component IQ score equals 15^2.

14. Cases 102, 106, 116, 138, 180, 186, 202, 204, 212, 232, 242, 330, and 332.

15. Vandenberg and Johnson (1968) gave a difference of 4 IQ points for this set. Since neither the source nor IQ conversions were included in their citation, we did not include the set.

Issues

Are test-retest scores comparable? In Jensen's original paper (1970) and in most analyses that followed, the sets with repeated testings were given an average score. This is standard procedure in most testing studies and would be acceptable if all sets had test-retest data. However, all sets do not, and the method of averaging tends to obscure differences. We wondered if it was legitimate to take averages in the twin-reared-apart sample. Our analysis indicated that it was not. Verbal, performance, and full-scale IQ on first and second testings were compared for Juel-Nielsen's data and, again, for all sets with test-retest scores. The means of the second test scores were significantly higher than the means of the first (appendix E).

If one cannot average, the issue then is to decide whether to use the first or second test scores as IQ indices. We opted to use the scores from the first testing since this makes the data comparable to all other sets who were only tested once. Thus, in table 7.1, the first scores were the ones used in all subsequent analyses.

Is it legitimate to combine verbal and performance IQ in order to obtain a full-scale IQ in this sample? This question has to be answered separately for the Shields and Juel-Nielsen samples. The issue is particularly relevant to Shields's twins since both the verbal and performance tests were short forms and are neither widely known nor usually combined into one overall IQ score. The issue is relevant for the Juel-Nielsen sample because the Danish version of the WAIS was used. The results for the Shields sample were as follows:

TABLE 7.2
*Correlations between Mill Hill
and Dominoes tests.*

	r Raw Score	r IQ
Males (N=13 pairs)	.32	.41*
Females (N=25 pairs)	.72***	.66***
Both Sexes	.56***	.59***

* p. <.04
*** p <.0001

As noted, the difference between the male and female raw score correlations was statistically significant. Thus it appears that the verbal and performance tests are more highly correlated for females than for males and, as such, may not measure the same thing in each sex and/or are more reliable for females. Thus it appears ill-advised to combine verbal and performance tests, particularly since correlations remain low even when corrected for attenuation.

Similarly, in the Juel-Nielsen sample, the correlation of .56 did not give evidence of the advisability of combining verbal and performance scores and, though there are only three male sets, there is question of whether they should be pooled with the females (see Juel-Nielsen 1965, 1980; also appendix E).

Overall, then, to the question of combining scores for verbal and performance tests in order to obtain and analyze full–scale IQ, the answer appears to be that it is questionable to do so in the samples of twins reared apart as they now stand.

Is it legitimate to combine scores from males and females, whether of verbal, performance, or full-scale IQ? Do the subsamples appear to be drawn from normal populations? In the preceding section, we suggested that the tests may be tapping abilities differently between the sexes or tapping different abilities. Thus we questioned whether it was legitimate to combine data from both sexes for any test in the entire sample. We further examined how closely each subgroup within the full sample approximated a normal distribution. The latter question refers to what is known in statistics as a mixture problem. While the full sample may appear to be normally distributed, that distribution may occur because each individual subsample contributes primarily to the high, middle, or low points rather than being scattered throughout.

The results of the various analyses are presented in table 7.3. The nonstatistician may read the table by noting each time there is an entry. Each entry indicates that the sample in question deviates from the expectations necessary to view the IQ data as normal or acceptable for pooling and further analysis.[16] Full information on the analyses can be found in appendix E. The following summaries may serve as a guide.

σ^2, *Variance.* An entry of $<15^2$ ($>15^2$) in the table indicates that the variance of the IQ scores for the test and sample in question was significantly less (or greater than) the variance of the IQ distribution in the general population. An entry of $\wedge(\vee)$ indicates, additionally, that the difference between the sexes was statistically significant. Almost all of the subsamples have restricted variance, and there are indications that *every* major study also has differences between male and female variances.

μ, *Mean.* Each subsample was tested to see if the mean IQ was significantly different from the population mean of 100. Tests additionally were done on raw scores of Mill Hill and Dominoes to see if they

---

16. Alpha level = .25.

TABLE 7.3
IQ: Analysis of subsamples of MZ twins reared apart.

		NEWMAN	SHIELDS					JUEL-NIELSEN			MISC.
		Newman Stanford Binet	Shields Raw Mill Hill	Shields FD Mill Hill IQ	Shields Raw Dominoes	Shields FD Dominoes IQ	Shields FD Full-scale IQ	J-N WAIS Verbal IQ	J-N WAIS Performance IQ	J-N WAIS Full-scale IQ	Other IQ
σ^2	Males	<15²	<7.8²	<15²	<	<	<15²**	<15²	<15²	<15²	
	Females	<	<7.8²	<15²	>8.6²	>15²	<15²	<15²	<15²	<15²	
μ	Males		<19	<100	<28	<100	<100	>100	>100	>100	
	Females	<100	<19	<100	<28	<100	<100	>	> >100	> >100	
$\sqrt{\beta_1}$	Males				<0	<0			<0*	<0	<0
	Females	>0		>0	<0				>0	>0	<0
β_2	Males		<3	<3	>3	>3	<3	<3*	<3*	<3	>3
	Females		<3	<3	<3	<3	<3			<3	<3
N	Males		non		non	non					non
	Females	non	non	non	non	non					non
Mdn	Males	>	<19	<100			<100	>100	>100	>100	>100
	Females	<100	<19	<100				>	>	> >100	>100

*Not tested because small n, but almost certain to be significant

**A population sd of 15 would not be expected in light of the finding that the Mill Hill and Dominoes correlate .41 for males and .66 for females.

differed from the stated means of 19 and 28 respectively.[17] Almost all of the subsamples have mean IQs significantly lower than 100, except, interestingly, Juel-Nielsen's twins, who are above population norms. Kamin (1974) and Jensen (1976) suggested that the high Juel-Nielsen scores were due to poor standardization of Danish WAIS norms. While possible, there is no evidence one way or the other, and if the WAIS is to be criticized, the criticism of standardization is equally, if not more, valid for the more dated and problematic tests used in other samples. The results, again, suggest that the subsamples are not drawn from the general population, but are on the average less intelligent and more restricted in variance. As such, it is questionable to pool subjects and generalize to the population at large. Schwartz and Schwartz (1976) made the same point in an analysis that used the original Jensen IQ conversions that, in turn, averaged Juel-Nielsen data and used the erroneous conversion method for Shields cited earlier.[18]

$\sqrt{\beta_1}$, *Skew.* The normal distribution, or bell-shaped curve, is symmetrical, with most scores occurring near the mean and two tails tapering off equally to the right and left.[19] The skew in a normal distribution is 0. In table 7.3, skew refers to whether the scores in any given subsample are distributed asymmetrically, no matter what the mean. The greater the departure the skewness coefficient from 0, the greater the asymmetry. An entry of > 0 indicates that the IQs cluster toward the low end with extreme scores trailing off to the right. An entry of < 0 indicates the opposite. The entries in the table offer evidence that a number of the subsamples are skewed from normality. The atypical distributions may be a function of geography, age, test construction, or some combination of these and other unknown factors. Whatever the cause, again, there appears to be reason to suggest that the subsamples not be pooled.

β_2, *Kurtosis.* Kurtosis is another way of describing the shape of a curve. A normal distribution has 3 as its kurtosis. An entry of >3 indi-

17. If the mean of the Mill Hill actually should be 20 (see earlier footnote regarding Shields's method of approximation), the differences would be even more noteworthy.
18. Jensen (1976) offered a short communication in response to the Schwartz and Schwartz's comments. His five points may be summarized under two main headings: (1) the combined studies appear to have a normal distribution even though the subsamples differ significantly in mean IQ; and (2) the important issue is differences within sets and correlations, not actual IQ level. The first point refers again to the mixture problem cited earlier. The distribution appears normal, but this may be related to different contributions at various levels from the various studies. As such, it does not meet the criteria necessary for a sample from which one can draw generalizable results. The second point, of difference scores and correlations, is discussed in the "pooled data" section of this chapter.
19. The IQ distribution in the total population has a small "hump" at the lower end, caused by a clustering of individuals with mental retardation.

cates that the curve in question is more leptokurtic, or peaked, than a normal distribution, while an entry of <3 means the curve is more platykurtic, or flattened. Most IQ test curves are peaked, while almost all of the curves in subsamples of this data are flattened. The evidence, again, suggests that the IQ scores, particularly of the males, are atypical of those generally found in the population.

N, *Normality.* All subsamples were tested for normality of distribution using the Anderson-Darling Goodness of Fit test. An entry of "non" in the table indicates the subsample was significantly deviant from normality. In the data from every major investigation including the combined "other" category, either the male or female subsamples differed significantly from normality. Again, the evidence leads to concern about pooling data and raises questions about significance tests and estimates of variance components from either pooled data or subsamples.

Mdn, Median. Throughout the samples, the mean IQ differs significantly from the population mean of 100. In atypical samples, which these appear to be, the mean may be a misleading indicator. The median may be used in such cases as a robust estimator of central tendency. Yet the entries in table 7.3 indicate that even tests of the median point to the same distortion in the subsamples that were suggested by tests of the mean.

Summary

Overall, there appears to be serious question of appropriateness of taking the IQ data at face value or of pooling data from various samples into one large sample from which estimates of the heritability of IQ and variance components might be derived. All of the tests used in the various studies are problematic, either because they are outdated and/or because they have questionable reliability and validity. Conversion of Shields's data involves numerous debatable assumptions. Once converted, it emerges that test-retest scores differ significantly in the samples, and verbal and performance tests correlate rather poorly overall. Males and females consistently differ significantly from each other, and all of the subsamples appear to deviate from normal distributions. Thus, the suggestions that subsamples not be combined and that males and females be analyzed separately have been offered.

Even those strongly in favor of analyzing IQ test scores for degrees of genetic determination may not find fault with the latter argument, since males and females are genetically different, as much or more so than other subpopulations, such as racial subgroups, whose scores have been analyzed elsewhere. Environmentalists also might point to the possibility that the environments relevant to stimulation or inhibition of capacities to score well on IQ tests may differ for the sexes.

Aside from issues surrounding the concept of IQ, our evaluation is that the data in these samples are so fraught with problems, ranging from the construction of the tests, to the conversion of raw scores to IQ, to the nonnormal distributions, that the data do not have prerequisites necessary for pooling of subsamples or for allowing trustworthy estimates of the degree of genetic determination of IQ scores.[20]

However, others may disagree and we estimate that disagreement may stem from two major issues:

First, we used an alpha level of .25 for the tests reported in table 7.3. This is the level suggested as a means of avoiding the error of falsely assuming that data can be pooled in order to give valid tests of and accurate estimates of variance components and correlations (Kirk 1968). We also used the number of individuals rather than the number of pairs in order to estimate the degrees of freedom for the tests reported in table 7.3 and appendix E. Though this is a standard method in twin studies, there is debate over whether the number of sets might not be more appropriate (Loehlin et al. 1975). We considered using the number of individuals to be correct since, under the null hypothesis of no genetic influence, individuals raised in different environments would be considered to be independent. Were a different alpha level or the number of pairs rather than the number of individuals used, fewer significant differences would emerge. Given the importance of the questions asked of these data and the fact that results have been stated to be trustworthy enough to inform public policy and public attitudes, a cautious approach appeared most socially and scientifically responsible (see also Cavalli-Sforza 1975). We realize others may not share our views.

Second, among those who do consider the data questionable and inappropriate for definitive estimates, there may be some who still would like to use it as the only data now available to allow rough estimates of what might be expected were a good sample of twins reared apart found. In particular, while recognizing that precise estimates are not possible, it could be argued that it is worthwhile to pool the samples to estimate the degree of variance associated with various environmental parameters.

Given the possibility of these two sources of disagreement, we therefore offer an analysis of the pooled data.

20. Layzer (1976) makes the same point with the comment that "four sieves will not hold more water than one" (p. 231).

Pooled Data: Heritability Estimates

In this section we assume that data from various studies can be pooled into one large sample of twins reared apart. Prior analyses have made this assumption and, additionally, have analyzed sets irrespective of degree of separation, sex, quality of test, or psychiatric or physical illness that might alter test scores. We have attempted to take these issues into account. We use test scores taken from table 7.1 and do not alter them to fit the variance of the general population. Though such alterations may influence heritability estimates in either direction, in the past they have tended to lower heritability estimates of this data. Again, the material is presented step-by-step so that the reader not versed in statistics may follow the argument intuitively, if not in detail. Pertinent information not included in the text is presented in appendix E.

Full-Scale IQ Scores: Uncorrected Samples

Jensen's original calculations (1970) were based on four large-sample studies: Burt, Shields, Juel-Nielsen, and Newman. Most analyses since then have used the same data and identical IQ conversion methods. Figure 7.1 presents the distribution of full-scale IQ scores from Jensen's 1970 paper, excluding Burt's disputed tests. Figure 7.2 presents the distribution of the same data using the first test scores from sets tested twice and the F-D IQ conversions. Both corrections may be justified on methodological grounds and as such seem not to bias the data toward either heriditarian or environmentalist positions. (See "Issues of Pooling Data.")

Figure 7.3 presents the distribution of *all* IQ data from the literature, using the same corrections noted earlier.[21] It is worth noting that our corrections reduce the variance but appear to shift the data even more to a bell-shaped curve than the calculations used by Jensen and others.

Mean IQ and other information are listed in table 7.4. The intraclass correlation usually is used as an estimate of heritability. With or without our corrections, the results are closely comparable. It is understandable how such results, taken by themselves, are suggestive of substantial genetic contributions to IQ test scores.

Components of Variance

A number of arguments can be made against taking the preceding results at face value. For the moment we will disregard those approaches that estimate portions of variance associated with similar rearing condi-

---

21. Excluding case 186 as explained later in the text.

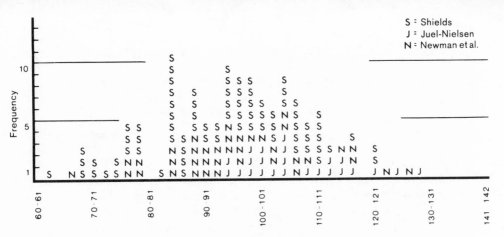

FIGURE 7.1

*Jensen IQ distribution.**

*Based on Jensen's 1970 tables, excluding Burt.

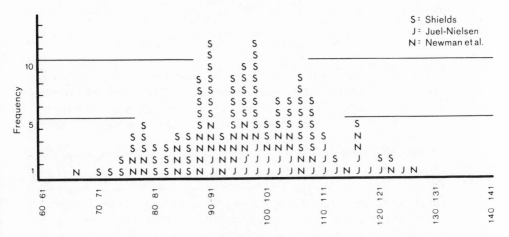

FIGURE 7.2

Same sample as Jensen using first test instead of average and F-D IQ scores for Shields.

O=Other S=Shields J=Juel-Nielsen N=Newman et al.

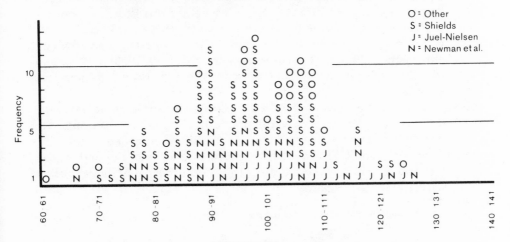

FIGURE 7.3

*Full sample using first test and F-D IQ scores where WAIS unavailable.**

*Excluding cases 180, 186, and 212.

TABLE 7.4
*Analysis of full-scale IQ from Jensen data and
from the full sample of twins reared apart.*

	Mean IQ	Standard Deviation	Absolute Mean Difference	Standard Deviation of Absolute Mean Difference	r'
Jensen conversions (excluding Burt)* (N=69 pairs)	96.1	13.7	7.1	5.8	.78
Full sample (F-D conversions) (N=82 pairs)	96.8	12.8	6.9	5.7	.75

*Slight discrepancies between the figures above and those cited in Jensen's 1970 paper result from the fact that we calculate from rounded IQs while Jensen uses his conversions of Shields's scores taken to several decimal places and uses a standard deviation divided by n rather than n−1. We have been unable to exactly duplicate Jensen's heritability estimates. Apparently he did not use the appropriate analysis of variance method for estimating heritability. (See appendix E.)

tions and the like.[22] Instead, we note that most analyses deal only with full-scale IQ and treat both sexes as one group. Also, whatever portion of variance is associated with mutual contact consistently is confounded with genotype sources and, as such, is neither estimated nor distinguished from the genetic contributions.

In this section we examine verbal and performance test scores in addition to full-scale IQ. Additionally, we examine differences between the sexes and the components of variance associated with degree of contact between twins. There are at least three reasons for examining verbal and performance scores separately: First, in theory, one or the other score, presumably the verbal one, may be more influenced by environmental conditions such as SES, education, and the like. Second, whether or not there are verbal-performance differences in the general population, the analysis of each subsample (see p. 186) suggests that *these twins* differ significantly, though whether this is due to poor test construction or genuine differences in heritability is unknown. Finally, different genetic mechanisms have been implicated for verbal and performance abilities (Jinks and Fulker 1970; Bock 1973) and, as a result, it has been suggested that scores should always be analyzed separately.

The issue of examining by sex also can be supported on at least three grounds: (1) The sexes may differ due to differential environmental conditions; (2) they may differ due to different genetic blueprints (Bock 1973); and (3) *in this sample* (and by inference, in the twin *population* from which they were drawn) the sexes differ, sometimes substantially, in test performance.

22. See Jencks et al. 1972 as an example.

The issue of investigating variance associated with degree of contact is obvious. It has been assumed in all prior studies that these are twins reared apart or that they are close enough to being reared apart to be analyzed as such. Yet in reality almost none of the twins were genuinely reared apart. Almost all had varying degrees of contact and opportunity for mutual influence. Indeed, it is one of the paradoxes that this sample, while it may be a poor indicator of heritability of IQ scores in the general population, is one of the few that offers possibilities of estimating the effects of varying degrees of mutual environments or twinning. If the component of variance associated with degree of contact can be estimated, it should be subtracted from the genetic variance component in the numerator of ratio defining the heritability estimate to allow for more accurate estimates of what heritabilities might look like in a sample of genuinely reared-apart identical twins. Also, the proportion of "mutual contact" variance may provide information on how heritabilities calculated from samples of twins reared together are biased.

The major method of analysis used follows an analysis of variance design known as a "fully nested" or "completely hierarchical design" (see appendix E). The highest level of the hierarchy has degree of separation (alternatively described as degree of contact), followed by pairs nested within levels of separation, followed by individuals nested within pairs. It follows the arrangement of this study's index of cases. The analysis allows for estimates of the components of variance for individuals, for pairs, and for levels of separation.

The sample was all cases with IQ scores listed in table 7.1 with the exception of 186 which was eliminated because of the twins' extremely low scores. Other test scores are questionable on numerous grounds and will be eliminated in a subsequent analysis.

Degree of separation was judged in two ways. The first follows the coding on the index of cases: Groups Ia, b, c, d, e, IIa, b, III, and IV. It is consistent with the way cases have been rank-ordered throughout the study. For ease in communication, we call this "Separation I." In a separate analysis, we additionally examined the degree of contact each twin had during the developmental periods 0–6, 6–10, 10–20 and 20 plus years. This, too, follows the coding on the index of cases (see chapter 3 and appendix E for coding for each twin). The presumption was that the scoring of each developmental unit, including adulthood, might inform not only on whether degree of separation accounted for part of the variance but also might allow inference of when, developmentally, the impact of contact was influential.

The second method of judging degree of separation was based on the assumption that degree of separation might be globally influential during the developmental period from birth through adolescence, irrespective of degree of contact in later life. Accordingly, all sets with no contact from birth through age twenty were placed in one group of no contact, coded "none." Sets with intervals of little contact interspersed with predominantly no contact through age twenty were placed in a group labeled "little" contact. Sets with mixtures of much, little, and no contact to age twenty were placed in a "some" contact group. Finally, sets with much contact through age twenty were placed in the last group, labeled "much" contact. The "little" and "some" groups represented attempts to rank-order separation that evidently fluctuated throughout life. The two extreme groups, "much" contact and "none," probably are ranked according to the most stringent criteria and may prove satisfactory even for those who question the ratings of less clearly delineated degrees of contact. We called this method of judging degree of separation "Separation II." (Index numbers of cases in each group are listed in appendix E.)

The results of the reanalysis are presented in table 7.5. The correlations printed in lighter type are those obtained when separation is not taken into account, while those in darker type are figures obtained when separation is included in the analysis. An F-test was used to judge whether the mean IQs of twins with greater or lesser degrees of contact differed significantly from each other.

Overall, the results are consistent in suggesting that when degree of separation is taken into account, heritability estimates are lowered substantially. For example, correlations for full-scale IQ of .74 and .76 for males and females, respectively, which are almost identical to those reported by Jensen and others for combined samples of males and females, drop to .45 and .48 when separation is taken into account. Under Separation I conditions, the difference in mean IQ when separation is taken into account is significant at the .05 level for males and at the .01 level for females. Similarly, under Separation II conditions, the differences in mean IQ under varying degrees of separation are significant at the .01 and .05 level for males and females respectively.[23]

Using the figures from the Separation I analysis, *it appears that environmental factors associated with degree of contact between twins accounts for approximately 20 to 25 percent of the variance in IQ test scores. If G-E correlation were taken into account (our analysis assumes no G-E correlation), as well as other factors such as prematurity, selection procedures, and so forth, the correlations or heritability estimates would be even lower than the approximately 48 percent suggested here.*

Though the figures in table 7.5 suggest that the amount of variance associated with degree of contact is in roughly the same range for

23. Similar results emerge when one compares other components of variance using these methods. For example, the variance component for pairs, which may be interpreted as the most direct estimate of genotype variance using our design, is significant at the .0001 level for differences associated with degree of contact for males under Separation I groupings. (See appendix E for a full listing.)

TABLE 7.5

Heritabilities of IQ test scores of identical twins reared apart for male and female verbal, performance, and full-scale IQ when variance associated with degree of separation is taken into account and not taken into account. (Separation I: degree of contact scored by grouping in twin index; Separation II: degree of contact scored by global assessment of high, moderate, minimal, or poor separation from birth through age twenty. Ancillary information is listed in appendix E.) Heritabilities would be lowered further if genotype-environment correlation (the similarity between biological and adoptive family environments) was considered.

	VERBAL		PERFORMANCE		FULL-SCALE	
	Separation I	Separation II	Separation I	Separation II	Separation I	Separation II
MALES						
Separation taken into account	.44	.49	.59	.60	.45	.48
Separation not taken into account	.76		.77		.74	
FEMALES						
Separation taken into account	.71	.64	.55	.72	.48	.60
Separation not taken into account	.78		.82		.76	
COMBINED MALE AND FEMALE						
Separation taken into account	.77	.77	.79	.80	.67	.76
Separation not taken into account	.77		.80		.75	

males and females, the relation between degree of separation and IQ is not similar for males and females (appendix E). When both sexes are combined and analysed for Separation I and Separation II, the correlations are .67 for Separation I conditions and .76 for Separation II. As with the mixture problem earlier, combining subsamples of males and females obscures differences that are present and may give a misleading impression of normality and high heritability.

On the assumption that contact might be particularly potent at specific developmental levels and/or that contact might have different impact for each sex, we analyzed the developmental periods when contact occurred (ages 0–6, 6–10, 10–20, 20 plus; see appendix E). For males, the effect appears to be coming from contact during the ages six to ten and ten to twenty but not from contact prior to age six or after age twenty.

For females, the effects were significant in the twenty-plus category and approached significance at ten to twenty years. Whether the interaction between sex, ages of contact, and IQ test scores are genuinely different for males and females or whether the problem lies with a coding system that does not catch the important interaction or with the generally poor IQ data available is open to speculation. Our impression is that since there is such severe question whether subsamples should be combined, the heritability estimates from the combined sample are in doubt. Thus, even less weight should be given to estimates about when, developmentally, twin interaction impacts on IQ scores. However, those who place more faith in the trustworthiness of the combined sample may find it necessary to investigate not only the effect of mutual contact but also the implication that mutual contact will have to be controlled and investigated for each sex separately in any future work on this sample or those that follow it.

The "Pure" Sample: Heritability Estimates

Given the severe problems that beset these data versus the important questions asked of them and their implications for public policy and public attitude, it seems appropriate to attempt to deal with the data in the most cautious and rigorous manner possible. For some, the issues of noteworthy bias in the subsamples may be sufficient to throw heritability estimates based on this data into doubt. For those who favor suspension of judgment or who find our analysis of subsamples too conservative, the pooled data has been analyzed. We propose that factors associated with degree of contact between twins accounts for about 20 to 25 percent of the variance in IQ test scores, more if the sample was corrected for the limited variance imposed by the G-E correlation. This latter analysis still might be judged as insufficiently rigorous since, although it excludes a few questionable cases, it still includes most sets with illnesses, all sets with language problems, all IQ data on sets with late separations, and all of Shields's test scores. The latter are problematic on a number of grounds ranging from questions of test validity to the problem that the variance of the composite IQs always will be less than 15^2 as long as the MH and Dominoes are imperfectly correlated. Accordingly, as "pure" a sample as possible was formed from the pooled twins-reared-apart data. Sets were excluded on the basis of separation past the age of four years, psychosis, any form of illness at the time of testing that conceivably might affect the IQ test score (irrespective of whether the ill twin scored higher or lower), first language other than the language of the test, and IQ tests not in current usage. The latter criteria eliminates all Otis and Kuhlmann scores plus all of Shields's data except his one set with a WAIS score at age fifty-two. The "pure" sample of thirty-four pairs is indicated in table 7.1 by all sets whose data is not shaded. Figure 7.4 gives the distribution of the "pure" sample. Though the distribution no longer appears normal, it may be argued that this is the single best sample now available to estimate heritability of IQ test scores among twins reared apart. It was chosen on the basis of neither hereditarian nor environmentalist criteria, but, insofar as possible, only on the basis of testing considerations. Its analysis is based on the assumption that data can be pooled and that IQ scores from the Danish version of the WAIS and from outdated Stanford-Binet tests still may be trustworthy. Were these assumptions not allowed, *no* data on twins reared apart could be used for estimates.

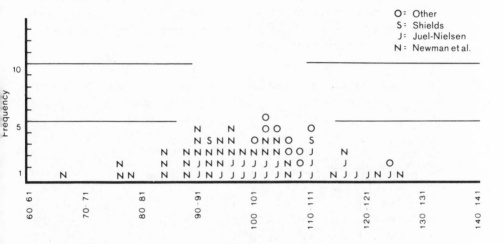

FIGURE 7.4

IQ scores of the "pure" sample of MZ twins reared apart.

The results of the analysis of the "pure" sample of twins reared apart are presented in table 7.6. Though none of the correlations between most and least separated twins differ significantly (because of the small sample), the correlations are substantially lower than those usually reported in the literature. Corrections for G-E correlation, prematurity, selection procedures, and so forth, which are not done here, would lower them still further.

Twin-Reared-Apart Heritability Estimates: Other Issues

Similarity Method of Selection.   In chapter 1 it was noted that the sample of twins reared apart is biased toward those twins who were so alike that they came to each other's and the investigator's attention. Strongly divergent sets presumably were not mistaken for each other and may not have met. In addition, many studies selected sets for zygo-

TABLE 7.6

Heritabilities of full-scale IQ scores for male and female MZ twins reared apart when markedly questionable tests have been excluded and degree of separation has been taken into account. (Heritability estimates generalizable to the population at large would be lower than the figures cited because of similar rearing environments, similarity method of selection, prematurity, and other confounding factors.)

	Full-scale IQ	
	Separation I	Separation II
Males (N=12 sets)	.43	.14
Females (N=22 sets)	.67	.55

sity determination only *after* the twins indicated they were so similar that they might be considered identical. Further, the zygosity determinations that were based on similarity methods, including fingerprints, patently bias toward selection of sets who are extremely alike (McNemar 1938). The question arises of whether the phenotypic similarity in appearance and personality that permeates the sample also bias toward greater resemblance in IQ scores than would be found in a randomly selected sample of MZ twins reared apart *irrespective of similarity or difference in rearing environments*. Put another way, perhaps "intelligence" is a component of personality and affects appearance enough that the similarity method has given us a sample of twins also very alike in IQ.

The only estimate of the relationship between personality similarity and IQ test scores now available suggests that this is exactly the case. In chapter 9, global assessments of similarity within sets are analyzed. The assessments were made by Shields and Juel-Nielsen on their own sets and were informed but subjective ratings of *overall* similarity between partners, particularly in personality. This, presumably, is close to if not exactly the type of subjective rating that would lead twins to be mistaken for each other or would lead them to rate themselves as very similar on questionnaires. When twins are rank-ordered in this way into most, less, and least alike in global assessment, the rank-orderings also hold for within-pair differences in IQ (mean difference: most alike = 4.07 points; less alike = 5.78 points; least alike = 8.58 points; $p < .05$).[24]

In the absence of other information it must be assumed that the sample of MZ twins reared apart *is* biased toward greater within-pair simi-

24. Most alike, IQ = 98.96; less alike, IQ = 99.6; least alike, IQ = 96.5. Linear correlation of IQ difference and degree of similarity = .38, $p < .01$. Mean IQs are not significantly different. Dropping one questionable case (174) from this analyses raises difference scores to more than 9 points in the least alike group.

larity in IQ test scores than would be found in the population of twins reared apart. Further, since the differences in global assessment do not appear to be directly related to differences in SES or to mean IQ level (see chapter 9), it must be presumed that this bias is present *in addition to* the limitations on variance imposed by the G-E correlation as it usually is discussed. The effect probably would lead to a lowering of heritability estimates in a more representative sample.

Rearing Status.   Analyses were performed on the full sample to determine if being reared with parents, relatives, or nonfamily members accounted for any portion of the variance in IQ test scores. Significant effects were found for males in verbal and full-scale IQ, and for females in performance IQ. However, the pattern of IQ or difference scores associated with various rearing environments was not immediately comprehensible. Interested readers are referred to appendix E.

Asymmetry.   Asymmetry, or mirror imaging was rated by handedness. On the assumption that mirror imaging might be reflective of differences in hemispheric dominance which, in turn, might lead to greater differences in full-scale IQ or in verbal versus performance IQ, opposite-handed sets were compared with symmetric pairs. We found no patterns in this sample suggestive of a relationship between laterality and IQ test scores. Given the limited number of pairs with information, and the questionable evaluations of both laterality and IQ, the lack of results is not informative.

Birth Order, Birth Weight.   Pencavel (1976) found that birth order as a probable indicator of birth weight was significantly correlated with raw score IQ in Shields's sample. However, Wilson (1977) found no significant effect of birth order on IQ of twins reared together.

We did not consider the sample of MZ twins reared apart suitable for rigorous analysis of birth-order or birth-weight effects, as almost all of the information regarding birth order or weight came from Shields's sample with its questionable IQ scores. However, though conflicting reports exist on the relationship between prematurity and later IQ, studies such as those by Wiener (1962, 1968), Lubchenco et al. (1963), Strang (1974), and Tilford (1976) suggest that prematurity may lower later IQ and adaptive capacities. Wilson (1977) studied the birth-weight-IQ relationship in young MZ twins reared together and found that pairs of twins with lower birth weights had lower IQs than pairs of twins with higher birth weights. However, the same pattern was not consistent within pairs where partners differed markedly. Overall, the heavier-lighter comparison for MZ twins reared together in Wilson's study accounted for about 2.7 IQ points, or less than 1 percent of the variance in test scores $(.10 > p > .05)$ *in childhood.*

Since Wilson's study was on young twins reared together with both sexes combined, it is possible that age or sex interactions with IQ scores and/or the effects of mutual contact obscure patterns. Until the evidence is in, caution dictates that prematurity continue to be regarded as a potential contaminating factor in the sample of MZ twins reared apart. The focal issue probably would be prematurity's effect on limitations of variance. Contrasting to this is the observation that these are twins who survived despite poor medical care and thus may be drawn from the robust end of the spectrum. Either way, the possibility remains that congenital but nongenetic effects may be influencing heritability estimates.

Age at Separation.   Johnson (1963) analyzed age of separation and later IQs in a sample from Newman plus four individual case histories (twenty-three pairs) and found that sets with early separations were more similar in IQ score than sets with later separations. Vandenberg and Johnson (1968) added Juel-Nielsen and Shields's samples plus a few additional individual case histories and repeated the analysis. The relationship between early separation and small within-pair differences in IQ was significant for all but Shields's sample. Since the majority of cases analyzed in this chapter were covered in the Vandenberg and Johnson paper, the analysis was not repeated here. The errors in IQ in the two papers may be corrected by reference to table 7.1. Neither study corrected for differing standard deviations of various tests.

Degree of Separation: Effects on IQ.   Using our Separation I and Separation II groupings, we examined the relationship between overall degree of separation and IQ. The same was done for difference scores. On the basis of the larger literature, we would expect IQ to decrease the more contact twins have, since it has been found that twins reared together tend to have mean IQs below 100, while twins whose partner died at birth and who, thus, were raised as singletons, have IQs similar to the rest of the population (Record et al. 1970; Zajonc 1976).[25] Figure 7.5 presents the mean full-scale IQs of the full sample under Separation I and II classifications. Decreasing IQ with increasing contact is not characteristic of both sexes. The lack of replication of patterns found by other investigators may be further evidence of the untrustworthiness of the data.

Degree of Separation: Effects on Difference Scores.   Difference scores, in general, follow a more predictable pattern with both sexes having larger absolute mean differences in the no contact groups than they have

25. Myrianthopoulos et al. (1972) did not replicate Record et al.'s findings, which leaves open the possibility that prenatal damage may limit IQ and IQ variance among twins.

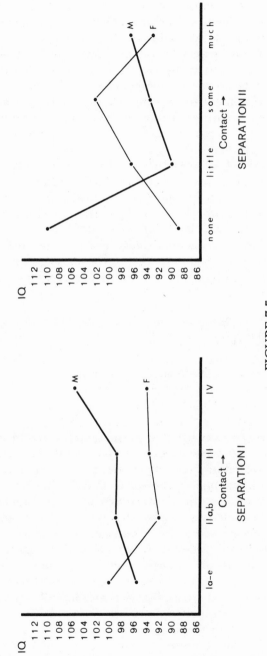

FIGURE 7.5

IQs of MZ twins reared apart and degrees of separation.

in the much contact categories. (The large 13-point difference in the Separation I grouping may be atypical since it is based on only one pair.) Paradoxically, verbal and performance IQ difference scores often increase with increasing contact (appendix E). Figure 7.6 is a condensed version of the patterns for full-scale IQ.

Following the argument that correlation and difference scores are more important than actual mean IQ (Jensen 1976), the data suggest that not only does correlation drop when degree of contact is taken into account, difference scores also increase. By the same argument, if actual IQ scores are questionable (whether due to sampling bias, test construction, or for other reasons), then actual number of points in difference scores also are questionable. This is particularly evident when one considers that twins rated most different in global assessment (see chapter 9), and who are therefore probably more representative of twins eliminated from the sample in the first place, differ by an average of approximately 9 points.

For these reasons we place no faith in the absolute mean differences reported for various separation categories, but offer instead the observation made by McNemar more than forty years ago about Newman et al.'s sample. It remains the most accurate observation on all of the sets analyzed since then:

With regard to measures of intelligence it is safe to say that . . . the only evidence which approaches decisiveness . . . rests ultimately upon the fact that *four* pairs reared in really different environments were undoubtedly different in intelligence. This fact can neither be ignored by the naturite nor deemed crucial by the nurturite. [McNemar 1938, pp. 248–249]

Summary

Though there is evidence that the subsamples should not be pooled into one large sample from which heritability estimates are derived, an analysis of the combined sample is presented. Since those most favorably disposed to analyzing pooled data argue that intraclass correlations and difference scores—but particularly intraclass correlations—are the fundamental issue rather than mean IQ (Jensen 1976; Wolff 1979), the results are presented in terms of intraclass correlations. Verbal, performance, and full-scale IQ are analyzed for males and females separately as well as for both sexes combined. The results consistently support the hypothesis that males and females must be analyzed separately since, in this sample at least, differential relationships between sex and IQ scores are present and are obscured when the sexes are combined.

For economy, only the results on full-scale IQ are summarized here. If one analyzes the full sample with both sexes combined, the heritability for full-scale IQ is .75. If one analyzes by sex, the heritability for IQ

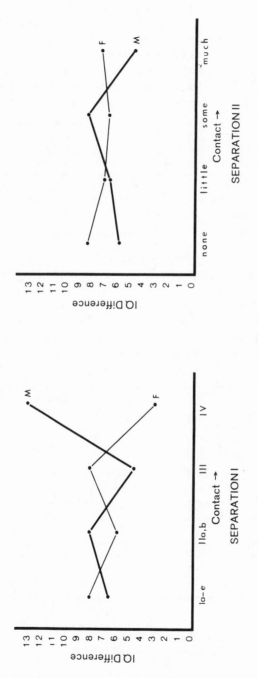

FIGURE 7.6

IQ difference scores of MZ twins reared apart and degrees of separation.

score are .74 for males and .76 for females. All of these correlations are similar to those found in prior studies of pooled data before corrections for G-E correlation and the like are introduced. The similarity exists despite corrections in IQ conversion and a larger sample analyzed here. The following bar graphs may be considered typical of the type of uncorrected heritability estimates usually obtained from these data.[26] One can understand how, at face value, such estimates would lead to the hypothesis of a high degree of genetic contribution to IQ.

Males	G 74 %	E 26%

Females	G 76%	E 24%

G = variance due to genotype   E = variance due to environment.

GRAPH 7.1
Uncorrected heritability estimates for IQ of male and female MZ twins reared apart.

However, a number of environmental interactions are hidden in the uncorrected heritability estimates. We chose to analyze only one, the effect on IQ scores of the degree of mutual contact between partners within sets. Though data were poor for most other analyses of IQ, this is one of the only samples on which such an analysis can be made. Two methods of judging degree of separation were used. The results indicate that approximately 20–25 percent of the total variance is due to factors associated with mutual contact between these twins who usually are assumed to be genuinely reared apart. This variance is hidden in the "genetic" side of the estimates. The following bar graphs indicate

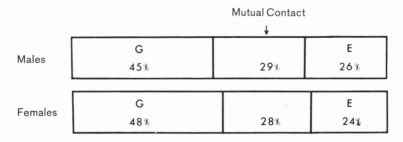

GRAPH 7.2
Heritability estimates for full-scale IQ of male and female twins reared apart corrected only for degree of contact.

26. In the following bar graphs, G stands for genotype influences and E stands for environmental influences.

the altered heritability estimates for males and females when only this single correction is made.

All of the preceding analyses were done on a pooled sample from which the clearest atypical cases were removed. However, a number of questionable sets remained, such as those who had language problems, illness at the time of testing, separations past the age of four years, and all of Shields's, sets who were tested with short forms of tests whose conversion into IQ even Shields himself disapproved. To avoid these problems, a sample was formed in which *all* questionable cases were excluded, though outdated Stanford-Binet scores and Danish standardization of the WAIS remained. This "pure" sample still requires further correction for G-E correlation (see chapter 1), the limitation on variance imposed by similarity methods of selection,[27] interactions between the genotype and the environment, plus those associated with mutual contact, prematurity, and measurement error, to name only a few. Almost all of these would act to lower heritability estimates, with the G-E correlation (the similarity in environments) probably lowering heritability considerably (Jencks et al. 1972). The following bar graphs repre-

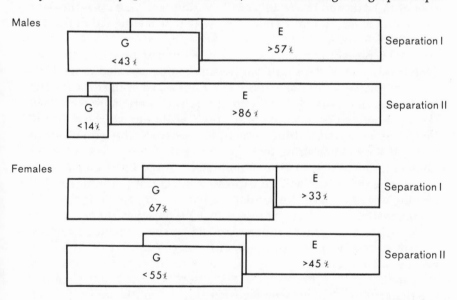

GRAPH 7.3.

Heritability estimates of full-scale IQ scores of male and female MZ twins reared apart based on a sample in which questionable cases have been eliminated and analyzed under two conditions of judging degree of separation. (The "hidden" portion of the "environment" bar represents additional sources of environmental variance that would be subtracted from the genetic side and added to the environmental. The lengths do not represent proportions known at this time and are used for illustrative purposes only.)

27. See earlier in this chapter, also chapters 1 and 9, and McNemar 1938.

sent the analysis of the "pure" sample under two methods of coding degree of separation. They probably are the most trustworthy estimates that can be offered from twin-reared-apart data.

Discussion: IQ Versus Cognition

In the preceding sections it was suggested that the IQ data on identical twins is of highly questionable quality. It is debatable whether it should be analyzed as a single sample of "twins reared apart." Even if it is analyzed as such, the heritability estimate with no correction other than for mutual contact is on the low side. Speculation about a genetic contribution to IQ test scores remains possible, but hypotheses that IQ is determined primarily by heredity appear untenable. The questions asked of the data and the results of the various analyses open the door to a number of issues. Only a few of these will be mentioned in the discussion that follows.

First, the preceding analyses utilized a number of statistical tests. Given this, many of the significant results can be assumed to have occurred by chance. Since none of the questions asked of the data appears superfluous, the reader will have to decide which are more worthy of consideration than others. However, if one wishes to use these data in discussions about racial differences in IQ test score, the issues of analyzing by sex and analyzing by degree of contact appear essential. For example, if one wishes to assume that racial groups differ on a genetic level in a manner that will be expressed in IQ test performance, the same logic would make it essential to analyze *any* sample for genetic distinctions that might be expressed in IQ scores. Sex differences are decidedly based on genetic differences and, as such, would be a necessary part of any rigorous discussion of the argument. We do not, however, maintain that the sexes genuinely differ in cognitive capacities. While it may emerge that each sex, as a group, is better at one cognitive style than another, we have no evidence one way or the other and suggest only that, if one uses the logic of assuming racial differences in IQ test scores to be based on genetic differences, the same logic of examining by groups that differ genetically (and environmentally) should be applied to these data. The results should be more precise from both hereditarian and environmentalist views, and the results in this sample would indicate a lowering of heritability.

Possibly more interesting and fruitful are the results suggesting that mutual contact between twins accounts for about 20–25 percent of the variance in IQ test scores. While better samples may give more precise and trustworthy estimates, these twins are one of the only samples presently allowing approximation. The implications lead in several directions. First, they raise severe and serious question about the accuracy of heritability estimates based on samples of MZ-DZ twins reared together. The effect of mutual contact may be noteworthy and, for the MZ twins at least, appears to act in the direction of making IQ scores more alike. Until a widely acceptable estimate of the portion of variance attributable to mutual interaction emerges, it appears wisest to approach twin studies with substantial caution. Fostering and adoption studies may be the best sources of data and safeguards for the time being.

However, even though we lack the precise estimate of the effects of mutual contact, we do have every reason to assume that the effects are substantial. This in itself allows for a more accurate delineation of the meaning of "environment." Most studies define environment in macroscopic terms such as SES, intact families, and the like. However, if one reflects on how "mutual contact" would be operationalized, it would seem to have to include the way parents and siblings treat twins in a similar manner, plus the effect the twins have on each other. The latter effect could be broken down into mutual identification or modeling. To the degree that motivation is a part of the process of twins reacting to each other, the intrapsychic arena would have to be included in any definition of the environment. In short, mutual contact probably reflects the microscopic environment and that, in twins, includes the nuances of interaction of the individual with his external *and* internal world. Is this not precisely what the child development literature illustrates when it points to parental attention and nuances of interaction as significant in affecting IQ levels? And is it not precisely what disparaged subpopulations, whether racial, ethnic, or sexually defined, describe as the phenomenological impact of discrimination? It is not just living in poverty that takes the toll, it also is being treated with nuances of distaste, anger, and fear, and internalizing these into one's own intrapsychic realities that leads to a failure to realize one's potential. To the degree that "mutual contact" in this study reflects on the microscopic environmental world of the individual, one has an empirically derived estimate that interaction and factors associated with it rival in impact the more typically described parameters of environmental classification.

Those empiricists who find this argument overly removed from the data may find themselves, of necessity, confronting two issues. First, they will have to find some method of defining mutual contact that does not include nuances of interaction plus motivation and the internal psychological world of the individual. Second, if they allow that intrapsychic factors are present but believe they cannot be discussed because they cannot be seen and measured, they also must deal with the logical inconsistency of then wishing to discuss IQ test scores as some index of "intelligence." "Intelligence" is not a trait that can be seen and measured directly. It is a construct used to explain patterns of behavior in testing situations and, presumably, patterns of behavior in the external world. By the same token, "intrapsychic events" or even "unconscious processes" are constructs used to explain behaviors in therapeutic sessions and, presumably, patterns of behavior in the external world. The bottom line is that there is no more reason to believe in one construct than the other if one insists on discussing only observable, quantifiable acts. The methods of collecting data about the two differ, but the inferential logical leaps from observed data to theoretical construct are the same in both cases.

Indeed, because of this problem, we have consistently used only the term "IQ test scores" rather than the term "intelligence." Whether or not there is such a trait and how well or badly our tests tap it, we leave to others to discuss. What seems more germane is the distinction between "IQ test scores" and "intelligence" versus "cognition." The latter, one could argue, is what we really are trying to study, and, if we begin to speak of cognition, we automatically must begin to speak in developmental terms. This raises issues not only about IQ as an index, but also about the concept of heritability. For example, we know that cognition develops in stages (Piaget 1963) and that component parts, such as the utilization of symbols or methods of classification, change as the individual matures. If, indeed, we wish to study the genetic determination of cognitive development, an approach wholly different from the one used in this chapter and in most discussions of IQ would be required. Instead of pooling together different age groups, as has been done here, age groups would have to be studied separately. Presumably heritabilities might be different at different times in life, while a pooled sample offers only an average that may not reflect the true degree of genetic determination accurately at all. Also, component parts of cognition would have to be delineated and studied as they emerge. It might be that the timetable of emergence is substantially influenced by the unfolding of the genetic blueprint, while the stabilization of any component part depends on the environmental reinforcements and psychological network that hold it in place. Developmental psychologists are familiar with numerous such situations, as when a child is maturationally ready to display a behavior but does not do so or does so only erratically because the environmental and psychological reinforcements are lacking. The propositions speak directly to the issues of genetically determined sensitive periods in development *and* to the possibility of informed estimates of when environmental intervention may be most effective. As Bronfenbrenner points out,

The heritability coefficient should be viewed not solely as a measure of the genetic loading underlying a particular ability or trait, but also as an index of the capacity of a given environment to evoke and nurture the development of that ability or trait. [1975, p. 98]

In short, if the study of the genetic influences on either intelligence or cognition is to have any useful meaning, it probably should be phrased in developmental terms and probably should be geared more to the unfolding blueprint of development than to overall estimates of a given ability or cluster of abilities (Schaie et al. 1975).

Wilson (1971, 1977, 1978) offers the opening toward such approaches. Using data from the Louisville Twin Study, he examined repeated tests on MZ and DZ twins reared together from birth through age six. He found that intraclass correlations shift over time in the MZ and DZ groups, which, in itself, suggests different heritability estimates at different ages *on the same children*.[28] More important, he found that the pattern of repeated scores was more similar in MZ than DZ sets. Figure 7.7 is taken from his material.

Though some have criticized too literal an interpretation of infant test data (Scarr-Salapatek 1976; Nichols and Broman 1977; Lewis 1976) and though this study would lead one to speculate that the similarity in actual DQ or IQ scores is related to being reared in the same family, a different issue is illustrated by Wilson's material. Specifically, why is it that the MZ patterns of ebb and peak are so much more similar than the DZ ones? It may be that the identical genotypes of the MZ twins are determining not so much the traits being measured as the sequence and timing of their emergence. Were we to study *patterns* of emergence of cognitive abilities in children rather than whether the children obtain test scores higher or lower than the mean, we might indeed begin to learn something useful about how the genetic blueprint determines the unfolding of the *potentials* of cognition. This, in turn, could instruct on how to provide useful environments to sustain and stabilize the potential that is there at the optimal stages in development.

The sample of identical twins reared apart cannot take us to that point. It only suggests that there is something worth studying. However, the implication is strong that those who have used these data to minimize discussion of the effects of environment on cognitive abilities have misconstrued the data. Both the information that is present and more, the information that is not, paradoxically serve best to broaden the question of environmental influences on intellectual abilities.

28. McCall (1970) found similar and even more striking fluctuations in an older sample of nontwin family members.

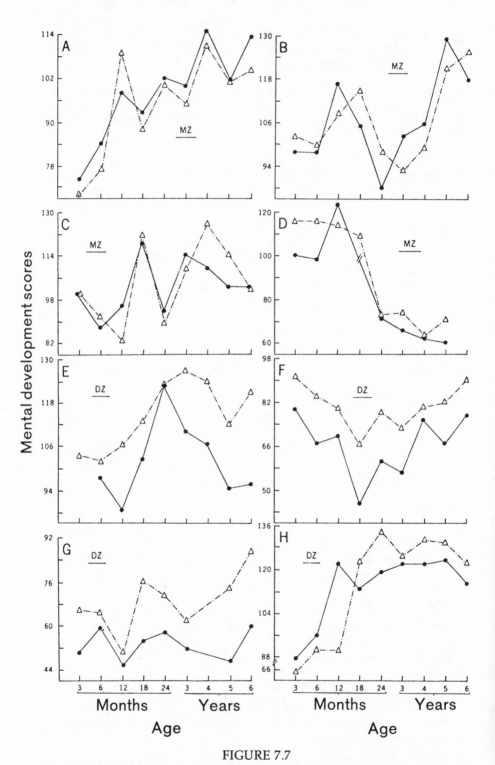

FIGURE 7.7

Illustrative mental development curves for monozygotic (MZ) and dizygotic (DZ) twins.

NOTE: Reprinted by permission of the publisher from "Synchronies in Mental Development: An Epigenetic Perspective," by R. S. Wilson (*Science* 202, 1 Dec 1978, p. 942).

Chapter 8

Personality I: Traits

All studies of separated twins were undertaken for the purpose of examining possible genetic contributions to personality structure and functioning. Some investigators limited their sphere to psychosis or retardation, but most studies had broader scopes. Unfortunately, while all come to the same accurate but uninformative conclusion that both heredity and environment make significant contributions, few go beyond this to discuss specific areas that are more or less permeable by external influence. No overriding construct of personality formation or functioning organizes the literature, and, though I agree with those who argue that such a construct would be premature, its absence is felt.

Psychoanalytic theory may have the potential to build a model of the links between soma and psyche and to clarify how the interaction of the two results in what we call personality or character structure. However, psychoanalysis has moved away from its roots in biology and neurology, and the current state of analytic literature is unsatisfying. Constructs are almost exclusively psychological, and those referring to the innate blueprint of the individual—aggression, anlagen, autonomous ego functions, synthetic functions of the ego, and so forth—are incomprehensible at times even for those educated within the fold. The analytic child development literature offers a few extraordinary exceptions to this rule. Leites (1971) outlines a devastating critique of the imprecise conceptualization and application of terms in psychoanalytic writings (and by extension in all psychodynamic work as well). At the moment, what seems important is only that for the objective but well-disposed nonanalyst who wishes to make rigorous, predictive use of formulations derived from intensive clinical work, the task is almost impossible.

By contrast, the empirical work in behavior genetics is straightforward, operationalized, subject to validation or disproof, and without metapsychological pretense. Alas, it also seems sometimes to study only what can be measured rather than what is interesting, and frequently it is strangely removed from what is most human and compelling about humans. The development of sophisticated statistical techniques has opened areas previously unanalyzable, but the techniques also have been seized upon with the same gusto, and occasional narrowmindedness, once shown for the discovery of the unconscious. Resulting papers seem sometimes to ignore that people think and feel and that cognition and affect can alter attitudes and behavior at all levels. A few of the debates over the finer points of statistical procedure are as hair-splitting, obtuse, and divorced from roots in substantive data as any on drive or death instinct produced by unreconstructed Freudians. Almost none of the studies are developmental.

At this point in the narrative, there usually occurs the requisite statement that what is needed is a bridge between empiricist and psychodynamic traditions. But everyone knows this, and this book makes only a small attempt to straddle that fundamental tension. Instead, this chapter opens with critiques for simpler reasons. In the course of investigating this literature it has become evident that the study of degrees of genetic determination to human functioning, particularly those using reared-apart twins, is a rich topic—intellectually stimulating and with a potential for contributing to refined interventions in clinical work. It also has become evident that it is open to massive abuse from unconscious and conscious bias and limitations of investigators and readers alike.

The abuse of IQ data is known to the professional community and the public at large. There is as great a potential for abuse of personality studies, if not a greater one. For example, IQ tests have been subjected to statistical treatments resulting in statements that genetic variance accounts for such-and-such portion of the total variance while environment claims a different amount. Some of the problems with these conclusions are discussed in chapter 7. Magnify every problem in the IQ data—tests, sampling bias, and so forth—a hundredfold for the measurement of personality differences. At least, whatever one's misgivings with IQ tests, there is a rough idea of what it is we are trying to measure; we have some idea of the validity and error of the tests; and we have a large and reputable literature on how a variety of individuals function when given the same instrument. Personality tests outnumber any other tool of investigation in the twin-reared-apart literature, and all of them are open to serious question. Most have been discarded over the years, sometimes because they were not reliable, more often because agreement could not be reached on what they were supposed to measure, or even that they were measuring anything worthwhile. Those tests remaining in use tend to be employed by small segments of the psychiatry-psychology community, frequently those engaged in academic research and not responsible for direct patient care.

If the tests are questionable, the sample is worse. Bias in the direction of poverty, low socioeconomic rearing conditions, and mutual contact between partners has been mentioned repeatedly. Along with these problems go the necessary assumptions of a higher degree of pre- and perinatal hazard than in the general population and the assumption of greater intrapair similarity in phenotype than would be expected in the entire class of MZ twins reared apart. Additional problems become salient when the issue is personality development. Thirty-six cases were placed with their foster or adoptive families past the age of nine months, an age that would be considered late placement by current child development schemes. Most of these cases were placed considerably past nine months. In addition to perinatal hazard, there is nothing in the case histories to suggest that most sets received what would be considered adequate pediatric care by current standards, and there are frequent references to suggest the reverse. At least three twins were sexually abused in childhood. It would not be surprising to learn that the true figure was double or triple that number. Anywhere from a third to half the cases reported harsh child-rearing attitudes, sometimes including severe beatings (and this estimate is conservative), and alcoholism and mental illness riddled the families in which many twins were raised. In some instances, neglect proceedings were instituted or authorities called in to protect the children. The majority of twins, at some point in their lives, lived in war-torn or occupied countries. Overall, the home life for many of the twins, whether due to poverty, mental illness, alcoholism, or other factors, is below what one would consider optimal, and frequently does not hit even the generous range of what Winnicott (1965) called "average expectable environment."

If one trusts his techniques enough to make estimates about the degree of genetic contributions to specific personality traits from such a sample examined with such instruments, the literature is open and available. I am unwilling to do so, for I suspect that the greatest danger at the present time lies not so much in overt racism or ideological prejudice, but simply in presenting what purports to be a rigorous study when the data cannot support such an analysis at all. In particular, a rigorous statistical study would require so much compensatory weighting that the results probably would be as much speculation as any offered by an armchair analyst without benefit of pocket calculator or computer. However, the study might prove more dangerous, since the awe once reserved for the analyst's couch is now reserved for the scientist who works with numbers. Cavalli-Sforza and Bodmer (1978) offer a brief and lucid discussion on the pitfalls of such an approach to this literature. Considering the sample, those who wish to attempt such a study might do well to focus on adaptability. More than anything else, it would be illuminating to discover what there was in the make-up of these twins that made them able to survive, despite their harsh and often atypical environments and become as complex in personality as they did.

My own approach, and the reason for opening the chapter in this way, is that I wish to use the data differently. In the presence of un-trustworthy instruments, I prefer the evaluations of human instruments rather than paper-and-pencil tests. Thus I focus more on the interviewers' clinical impressions than on test data. The sources of error for either approach are obvious, and it reduces to a matter of taste. Additionally, in the presence of an untrustworthy sample and working merely from written case reports, it seems appropriate to use the material only descriptively and as a source for hypothesis generation, not hypothesis testing. The specificity of conclusions in twin-reared-apart reports have, with few exceptions, changed little over the last fifty years, and frequently I received the impression that early workers may have been closer to pointing out something valuable than many of the later ones. Accordingly, the speculations about specific patterns in the material that follows are just that—speculation. They should be read by the reader with the same spirit of curiosity and skepticism with which they are offered.

Prior Studies

The literature on personality development is vast and, of necessity, references here are brief and highly selective. Citations in this chapter come primarily from two traditions: the psychoanalytic perspective and empirical work in behavior genetics. Within the psychoanalytic framework the study of temperament and developmental styles has a long tradition. Rather than mentioning specific publications, the interested reader is referred to the body of work of authors such as Fries and Wolff; Korner; Escalona; Thomas, Chess, and Birch; Weil; Anna Freud; and Mahler. Rutter, from his own perspective, offers excellent critical reviews. Behavior geneticists have been operating within a different theoretical and methodological framework, one that is nonclinical and less developmental but empirically more rigorous. Fuller and Thompson (1978) offer an excellent review and discussion of the field along with an extensive bibliography. They include the more circumscribed topic of twin studies, and the thoughtful work emerging from the

Louisville Twin Study (Wilson et al. 1971; Wilson 1972, 1974, 1977, 1978) is particularly worthy of note.

Examinations of personality style and development in twins reared apart are few and far between. Newman, Shields, and Juel-Nielsen, working with different populations and different methodological styles, all concluded that there is some substantial similarity in personality between MZ partners reared apart. However, beyond description of individual cases, no one could delineate with any specificity what it was. The two studies that had MZ and DZ control groups (Newman, 1937 and Shields 1962) found the surprising pattern that test scores of the reared-apart twins were in some ways more *alike* than those of reared-together twins. This is the reverse of their findings for IQ. All investigators, including Juel-Nielsen, concluded that although there is some as yet undefined level of similarity, through the broad range of personality style and functioning, the impact of environment shows more strongly on personality than in any other area. This corresponds to the larger literature in behavior genetics, including twin studies, where heritability estimates for personality traits are highly variable from study to study and where almost none of the estimates is of exceptional size (Fuller and Thompson 1978).

All investigators tried to give some rating of family environment to estimate association with later personality development. None found consistent patterns, a result that may not surprise the psychodynamically oriented reader since the environmental ratings typically were based on remarkably narrow criteria. Socioeconomic status was not explanatory for neurosis or personality differences, though Shields discussed rating on both SES and "psychologically" better or poorer homes and found a tendency for the twin from the higher SES and psychologically better home to be less neurotic and more well off as an adult. However, all investigators voiced dissatisfaction with the criteria of their rating systems, and all offered explicit and implicit evidence that wealth, intact families, and the like are not exhaustive enough criteria for estimating personality differences of clinical or nonclinical degree. Newman et al. (1937) were characteristically laconic in writing that ". . . effective factors in determining personality . . . may rather consist in subtle human relations which are revealed only by individual analysis" (p. 341), and they went on to conclude that individual analysis of case histories was a more suitable method of detecting environmental influence than test data (p. 362).

Jinks and Fulker (1970) reanalyzed Shields's data on tests of introversion-extraversion and neuroticism. Though heritability estimates for neuroticism varied depending on method of estimation, they concluded that a simple, additive gene action model was sufficient to explain the data. Heritability can be estimated as about .47 to .61 (Fuller and Thompson 1978). Introversion-extraversion data required more complex explanation, as a mono- or polygenic model did not fit the data. However, they concluded that similar family environment was unimportant in influencing the trait and suggested that introverted genotypes were more susceptible to environmental influence than extraverted ones. The analysis was a sophisticated one and was particularly useful in advancing a hypothesis of genotype-environment interaction that differentiated between genotypes. However, in view of the bias of Shields's sample toward greater contact, low SES, low IQ (see chapter 7), and what I presume must be the greater similarity by virtue of the twins' mode of selection, caution in accepting Jinks and Fulker's results is indicated. A more fundamental problem exists for those who question the validity of paper-and-pencil neuroticism and introversion-extraversion inventories. In a few instances, Shields himself noted divergences between the test scores and his clinical appraisal.

The larger literature on genetic contributions to neurosis is far from revealing. Some have suggested that genetic contributions may be greatest to obsessional neurosis (Marks et al. 1969; Slater and Cowie 1971) but, by and large, two fundamental problems prohibit generalizability of results. One is that the concept of neurosis is inextricably bound up with the concept of intrapsychic conflict, and, by definition, any diagnosis of neurosis involves substantial clinical inference on the part of the observer. The current debate over DSM-III gives ample evidence of the problem. Symptom lists do not offer diagnostic validity since the same symptom may occur in a reactive disorder, a neurosis, or psychosis, and even when it has been determined that a person is nonpsychotic, symptoms or clusters of symptoms give only moderate indication of type of neurosis or character pathology (phobias, for example, occur in a variety of diagnostic classifications). Thus, the need for ratings by multiple judges is greater for evaluations of nonpsychotic disorders than for psychoses, and even then schools of thought vary so widely and shift so rapidly that ratings run the risk of being outdated even before they are published.

A second issue mitigating against using these data to rate neurotic styles or levels of functioning is the question of whether exploring the genetics of neurosis is fruitful at all. Shields (1954) noted in a study of twins reared together that some do not consider it the appropriate question to ask of the data. Rather, the area conceptually more coherent may be the study of personality traits. Whether one agrees with this or not is almost immaterial, for it seems to be one of the only ways to approach the twin-reared-apart literature as it now is constituted. Toward this end, this chapter examines only nonpsychotic twins and begins with the assumption that we know nothing about which traits are more central and which more peripheral to personality development. The material that follows begins with discrete traits, and moves in chapter 9 to global assessment and in chapters 9 and 10 to the question of how to define "environment." Throughout, the information is organized less by what one might wish to study than by what was possible to elicit, even tentatively, from the data.

Gifts and Talents

For centuries, folk wisdom has viewed unusual artistic gifts as anything but environmental. Ranging from the concept that talent is "a gift of the gods" to Freud's opinion that poets know more about human nature than psychologists,[1] talent is viewed as something innate, and talented people themselves often express the idea that they are but repositories of a gift they did not create. Child clinicians are familiar with the experience of watching unusual abilities blossom before their eyes, while signs of the presence of these abilities are often reported since infancy. Galton was one of the first to bring the issue under empirical scrutiny with his studies of pedigrees of gifted families. Since his time, twin studies also have explored the topic, particularly the heritability of musical abilities. Though studies consistently point in the direction of noteworthy genetic determination,[2] the full parameters of giftedness, true to form, continually evade empirical grasp.

In this sample there are no twins of genius, but there are many who seek out music, the plastic arts, or movement despite wide variation in rearing environments. The twins are almost always concordant with each other and almost always choose the same or similar modes of expression. They also seem similar in degree of interest and ability. While there undoubtedly are overriding cultural influences, the similarity is so pervasive that, despite the quality of data, it seems reasonable to offer the hypothesis that there are genetic or congenital contributions to artistic or athletic gifts, even those only moderately out of the ordinary.

If one scores broadly simply for mention of interest or ability in music, drawing, dance, athletics, or drama, thirty-three cases emerge, perhaps only five sets differing enough to score in the discordant range.[3]

1. An attitude to which I wholeheartedly subscribe.
2. See Fuller and Thompson 1978, for an introduction.
3. "Interest" as well as demonstrated ability was scored on the assumption that it might indicate musicality or potential abilities in other areas. See cases 102, 104, 106, 110, 112, 136, 138, 142, 150, 158, 172, 202, 204, 208, 212, 220, 224, 228, 230, 232, 238, 242, 304, 306, 312, 314, 320, 324, 330, 334, 342, and 352.

The figures change, depending on how rigorous the criteria, but discordant sets are always decidedly in the minority. The following cases are meant as an illustrative rather than exhaustive listing.

George and *Millan* (case 102) were both athletic young men and, before becoming aware of each other's existence, each had won boxing championships in his weight class. One was interested in commercial art, the other in music. The fully left-handed twin was the more interested in art. *JJ* and *JB* (case 106) both were mediocre students in school. However, at the age of nine, *JB*, with his mother's encouragement, took up violin and did well. *JJ* took up the trumpet on his own initiative at age fourteen and played in amateur dance bands. Neither boy knew of the other's existence at the time. Tests of musical ability are included in the original articles. *Madeline* and *Lillian* (case 110) are also among the more separated sets. Both were singers, both preferred light music, and both had taken part in amateur theatricals where they liked playing the same kinds of parts. *Earl* and *Frank* (case 204) both took up the violin and, though neither was notably talented, they continued to play the instrument into adulthood. *Berta* and *Herta* (case 136) grew up on different continents and had no face-to-face contact at the time they were examined. Both were talented and fond of performing in public. *Herta* danced in ballet and wrote poems for newspapers. *Berta* sang and accompanied herself on the guitar. *June* and *Clara* (case 224) were the illegitimate children of an actress. Both had dreams of going on the stage as singers. *June*, by far the more privileged, had piano, voice, and dancing lessons. *Clara* was not allowed to touch *June's* piano. However, later she took lessons herself and when not feeling well would say she was "off song." *Victor* and *Patrick* (case 334), despite differences in personality and nervous habits, were both musical and gifted in drawing. *Patrick* did still lifes while *Victor* drew profiles in charcoal. *Esther* and *Elvira* (case 330) both were fond of music and dancing, and *Fanny* and *Odette* (case 342) played piano and violin and were members of a choral society. Their biological mother also was musical.

Mabel and *Mary* (case 318) are one of the few sets scored discordant, and genuine discordance is questionable. *Mary* was raised in a home secure enough to allow her to finish high school. She began music lessons at age ten and continued musical involvement for the next nineteen years until she was seen. She gave piano lessons in the evenings. *Mabel's* family circumstances forced her to leave school just after eighth grade and work left her no time for other pursuits. *Mildred* and *Ruth* (case 150) may be an instance of truer difference. The twins grew up in families from widely differing social strata. *Mildred's* home was the cultural center of her town. She studied music and, when seen at fifteen, played violin in the high-school orchestra. *Ruth* came from a less privileged family and, though exposed to music lessons, did not become proficient.

Olive and *Madge* (case 112) are among the most interesting sets in this regard. They were separated at birth and, past the age of three, had no contact until *after* they were interviewed. Both were markedly musical and both enjoyed dance. They had similar singing voices and similar tastes in clothes, books, and music. One preferred Tchaikovsky, the other Rachmaninov. However, *Olive* liked the *Messiah* best of all and when Shields visited *Madge*, the *Messiah* was on top of the pile of music in her room. Only *Madge* had formal training. On follow-up at age forty-three, both twins were given Wing's Standardized Test of Musical Intelligence. *Madge* scored in the top 10 percent and *Olive*, the twin without training, scored in the top 20 to 30 percent.

Sexual Functioning

Insofar as could be determined, studies of sexual functioning using twins reared together as subjects focus almost exclusively on homosexuality. Since only one case in this sample reported incidence of homosexual preference, though others suggest homosexual experiences, and since the literature on the subject is of questionable methodological quality, no further review is offered here. The interested reader is referred to Fuller and Thompson (1978) or Rosenthal (1971) for discussions.

Homosexuality

One case reported a twin with declared homosexual preference. Though the discordance may be only on the surface, environmental interactions seem the most parsimonious explanation even for the underlying similarities. *Marjorie* and *Norah* (case 128) were one of the most separated in the sample, meeting for the first time at age nineteen and having almost no contact after that. *Marjorie* was adopted by a physician and his wife at age twenty-two months. Their marriage was unhappy, and *Marjorie* and her mother did not get along. She identified strongly with her father and wanted to follow in his footsteps. After her father's death, she went to London with the intention of studying medicine and lived with a woman doctor who financed her medical education. War intervened, stopping both the relationship and the studies. She had what Shields delicately calls "other emotional entanglements with women" and when seen was masculine in her hairstyle and manner of dress.

Norah was adopted at age twenty-eight months by a minister and his wife. He was unsuccessful and, according to *Marjorie*, may have been unfrocked. *Norah* was very attached to him nonetheless. When interviewed at age thirty-six, she was single and, though once engaged, was not greatly interested in marriage. Her close friendships were not exclusively with women.

Palle and *Peter* (case 108) both became attached to older men during adolescence. The family of only one twin suspected him of homosexuality. However, both boys made satisfactory heterosexual adjustments in later life, and there is no evidence of homosexual preference or even activity. The closeness to the older mentors might have been related to the fact that the adoptive fathers of both boys were heavy drinkers and neither was the type of man with whom the twins may have sought to identify during adolescence. Similarly, *Kaj* accused *Robert* (case 206) of making homosexual advances to him after their initial meeting, and *Robert* questioned the interviewer about whether one twin might not be more "feminine" and the other more "masculine" but made no mention of the alleged incident. Each twin was married three times and experienced sexual frustration from what they claimed was high libido. Both were markedly narcissistic and vacillating.

Attitudes/Choice of Mate

People tend to marry people who are similar to themselves in IQ, stature, interests, and the like, one of the reasons geneticists assume assortative mating.[4] Beyond this, however, there is little in this sample to suggest that twins choose highly similar spouses and much, in fact, to suggest the reverse. Sometimes partners have decided tastes, and it does not stretch the imagination to presume them to be environmental, possibly oedipal, in origin. *Kaj* and *Robert* (case 206), for example, liked decidedly different types of women. *Robert* preferred blond homebodies, while *Kaj* liked slim, dark, temperamental types. Each, however, three times married women different from those they preferred.

At other times, the overriding environmental variables seem to be poverty and the attempt to marry out of miserable home conditions, a situation particularly prevalent among the female twins whose options were limited to begin with. Some of these marital partners turned out to be alcoholic, mentally disabled, or intellectually limited, and what Machiavelli calls "fortuna" drastically altered the twins' lives. Indeed, throughout case histories by all investigators there runs the thread of comments on how significantly the choice (or nonchoice) of mate broadens or narrows the course of later life and sometimes leads to

4. See Cavalli-Sforza and Bodmer 1978 or Stern 1973 for discussion.

marked differences in attitude, vitality, taste, and social status within sets. It was this type of observation that led Juel-Nielsen to remark on how much more malleable the middle years of life are than theories that focus almost exclusively on childhood would lead one to expect.

The age at which twins become interested in the opposite sex does not appear notably similar between partners. Again, home environment seems the most parsimonious explanation. *JJ* was interested in girls at age sixteen, *JB* was not (case 106). *Ronald* rather liked girls at age twenty; *Dennis* preferred his motorcycle (case 232). *Palle* and *Peter* (case 108) differed in shyness and sexual experience when seen at twenty-two. Attitudes and sexual license also differ, sometimes leading the twins to be thoroughly disapproving of each other. The most obvious cases are those sets that differ in the number of illegitimate children, though different milieus also shift attitudes even well past adolescence.[5]

Libido/Sexual Dysfunction

The area where there may be a greater degree of underlying similarity is in the intensity of the sexual drive and in the tendency toward disturbance or dysfunction. One is on questionable ground here, however, as clinical experience readily demonstrates how markedly an individual can alter sexual behavior as attitudes change. Still, though the case histories offer information too sparse and inconsistent for even moderate evaluation, the impression remains that this may be an area worth investigating in future studies.

For example, *Ingegerd* and *Monica* (case 188) both included frigidity among their other sexual problems. Neither *Maren* or *Jensine* (case 146) were able to make a satisfactory sexual adjustment, and *Megan* and *Polly* (case 172) had to help each other with some type of unexplained sexual difficulty when first married. *Kaj* and *Robert* (case 206) combined high libido with inability to remain involved with one woman, and *James* and *Robert* (case 228) and *Brian* and *Hubert* (case 336) complained of low or decreasing libido. *Olga* and *Ingrid* (case 104) reported lack of satisfaction, while *Signe* and *Hanne* (case 130) managed to make sexual adjustments to their spouses though each complained that the other flirted with her husband. *Mary* and *Nancy* (case 218) both disliked sex, and one intriguing female set in Shields's sample, *A* and *B* (case 326) refused to be interviewed but both emphatically emphasized that they were "uninterested in the opposite sex" in their record booklets.

Though Freud's concepts of drive and the centrality of libido are open to debate, perhaps no area of functioning combines somatic, intrapsychic, and cultural contributions in as condensed a form as sexual

5. See cases 116 and 178 as examples.

attitudes, activity, and experiences. Were one limited by time or other contingencies, it might be one of the most fruitful topics to explore in any future twin studies.

Drinking

Goodwin (1976) and Fuller and Thompson (1978) offer reviews of the literature on genetic contributions to alcoholism. Several twin studies are included. Case 348 in this sample comes from Kaij's (1960) investigation on alcoholism in Swedish twin pairs. Three other sets from Kaij's study were not included due to insufficient separation or questions of zygosity. The literature in general indicates that MZ twins have higher concordance rates than DZ twins and seem most likely to be concordant when drinking is rated as heavy. Cultural factors sometimes override twin similarity. For example, Conterio and Chiarelli (1962) studied Italian twins and found no significant MZ–DZ difference. Though the Italian preference for wine probably obscured differences, coffee consumption was significantly more concordant in the MZ group.

One of the most interesting twin studies is not on alcoholism per se, but harkens back to the types of basic physiological similarities suggested in chapter 4. Vesell et al. (1971) studied rates of ethanol metabolism in seven MZ and seven DZ reared-together pairs. Individuals were given an oral dose of diluted alcohol, and blood samples were taken at fixed intervals over the next several hours. Metabolism was extremely similar in the MZ sets, five of the seven showing no difference between partners. By comparison, fraternal twins differed notably. The heritability estimate, albeit on a very small sample, approached 100 percent. Fuller and Thompson (1978) noted that the common rearing environments of the sets might be inflating heritability in this experiment. However, the design is simple to replicate and could stand as a model for future twin-reared-apart studies.

As it now stands the twin-reared-apart literature has no definitive information on drinking patterns, but it appears to be in accord with the larger literature on reared-together sets. Partners are predominantly concordant, even to degree of alcohol consumption, as best as could be estimated from the case histories. In particular, the three cases of heavy drinking all were concordant. Nineteen sets reported on presence or

absence of alcohol consumption for both partners.[6] Results are presented in table 8.1.

TABLE 8.1
Drinking habits—MZ twins reared apart.

	Number of Sets
Both nondrinkers	7
Both heavy drinkers	3
Both moderate/light drinkers	6
One moderate/light; one nondrinker	3

Mutual identification was not suggested, as the most separated sets
(predominantly nondrinkers) seemed as similar as the least separated.
Also, in a number of cases alcoholism existed in the rearing family but
did not show in the twins. What happened more often was that twins
reared in homes of relatives or foster parents with drinking problems
became militant nondrinkers in adult life. Roe's (1944) adoption study
is interesting in this regard. She examined adopted-out children of al-
coholics. None of the children in good foster homes became delinquent and none of them drank excessively. Family warmth and solidity
appeared to be of crucial importance in determining whether addiction
occurred or not, and, conversely, one may speculate that disorganized
families may be influential predominantly when susceptibility also is
present as well.

Smoking

Shields studied the smoking habits of his sample and control groups
and found MZ twins significantly more alike, irrespective of rearing
status, than DZ twins, who were alike no more often than could be expected by chance. The similarities went deeper than whether both
twins in a set smoked, and included similarity in the amount of tobacco
consumed per day. Using a scale ranging from 0 through 16 or more
cigarettes per day, Shields found 67 percent of his separated sets closely similar, 19 percent fairly similar, and 14 percent dissimilar (N=42).
The remainder of the literature yields nine other references to smoking

6. Cases 104, 106, 108, 112, 130, 132, 168, 188, 190, 206, 220, 228, 244, 308, 322, 328, 348, 350, and 352.

habits, most of them from Juel-Nielsen's sample.[7] In six of the sets, both partners were smokers, with the amounts consumed usually in the same range. Of the remaining three sets, one described partners who were both militantly antismoking, another included information for only one partner, and the third described a discordant pair. As with Shields's data, this one instance of discordance had the more anxious twin smoking, the more relaxed twin abstinent.

These few additional cases report only sets where smoking occurred and add nothing new to the finding of marked similarity between MZ partners. However, the reorganized listing of separated twins is evidence in support of the hypothesis that mutual identification is not explanatory of this habit. Five of the six most separated sets have information on smoking, and all of them are alike.

TABLE 8.2

Smoking habits—Highly separated MZ twins.

ID	Name	Habit
104	Olga/Ingrid	Both smokers
106	JJ/JB	Both smokers; 10 and 5 per day respectively
108	Palle/Peter	Both light smokers
110	Madeline/Lillian	Neither smoke
112	Olive/Madge	Neither smoke

Nervous Habits, Mannerisms [8]

Throughout the case histories, similarities in gestures, movement, mannerisms, and speech patterns were reported consistently, so much so that zygosity sometimes was questioned in the few discordant cases. The overall similarity in speech patterns is indicated in chapter 4. Here it seems worth noting again the similar manner in which nervousness revealed itself. Though stuttering differed, if one twin became aphonic when touching on emotional subjects, the other usually did as well. If one's voice became high-pitched when she was excited, usually the other's did too. If one had a nervous laugh, the laugh frequently is reported for both. Juel-Nielsen reported the laugh to be one of the most

7. Cases 104, 106, 108, 130, 168, 178, 188, 206, and 244.

8. No one examined mannerisms per se, and the similarity came as a surprise. The similarity (and the tone of surprise) also is present in reports now coming out of the study being conducted at the University of Minnesota (Chen 1979).

consistently similar features in his sample, and reports by other investigators seem to agree.

The similarity in gestures and mannerisms also is a consistently reported observation on almost all twins. The reports, it should be added, are distributed throughout the sample and do not offer the possibility of mutual identification as a satisfactory explanation. The two cases discordantly reporting nervous tics or twitching (118 and 184) are among the few exceptions to the rule. However, in other cases where mannerisms are described (most simply state that twins were alike), the specificity is striking. *Alfred* and *Harry* (case 174), for example, each nodded his head in the same way as he spoke, closed his eyes as he turned his head, and had the same habits such as sprucing up before going out. *Jacqueline* and *Beryl* (case 230) had the same firm handshakes and made the same half-thoughtful, half-humorous face before answering questions. *Adelaide* and *Beatrice* (case 242) had the same limp handshake and manner of turning her head away until one twin consciously tried to change herself in adolescence.

James and *Robert* (case 228) were said to have "remarkable" similarity in gestures. Both tapped on the table to make points, flicked their fingers when unable to think of an answer immediately, and nodded their heads in strong approval of what each other said. *Kathleen* and *Jenny* (case 304) laughed, giggled, and wept over the same things and reported that they often found themselves sitting in the same positions. *Berta* and *Herta* (case 136) had the same nickname of "Pussy" because of their affectionate nature and tendency to purr like a cat when pleased. The nicknames, it is worth adding, were in different languages since the twins lived on different continents and had not met since the age of four. *Olwen* and *Gwladys* (case 214) had the same wild look about them according to Shields, their eyes darting from place to place. Their expressions and gestures mirrored each other, and their hands frequently went to their mouths in a tense finger-biting gesture. Both held their fingers stiffly for fingerprinting. When young twins were examined, they often were noted to giggle at the same time, use the same gestures, and make the same faces when tested. Perhaps one of the more interesting mannerisms is reported for *Madeline* and *Lillian* (case 110), one of the most separated sets in the literature. Their husbands were impressed with the similarities in movements, particularly a habit each twin had of rubbing her nose and rocking when tired. The twins developed the habit without knowledge or contact with each other.

A slightly more concrete way to indicate the similarity, in mannerisms is to score for reports of nail biting. Out of eleven sets, seven are concordant and four discordant.[9] In two of the sets, the habit was severe, one set reporting both partners with less than a quarter of an inch

9. Cases 108, 132, 138, 142, 154, 230, 242, 308, 324, 330, and 334.

of nail left on any finger. Mutual identification is possible for slightly more than half of the cases but is not explanatory for all. Younger sets are overrepresented in the group, and the ubiquity of nail biting among unrelated children in the general population is high enough (MacFarlane et al. 1962) that the habit could be construed more as a common developmental symptom among all children rather than as a noteworthy concordance between twins. However, younger sets are not the only nail biters recorded, and the behavior is similar enough within sets that even those twins who gave up the habit continued with mannerisms of plucking at their eyebrows or cuticles (see cases 108 and 242). *Olwen* and *Gwladys* (case 214), as noted above, even had the same gesture of putting their fingers to their mouths without actually biting their nails.

The similarity in mannerisms and nervous habits seems too consistent to be ignored, nor can the poor rearing conditions be explanatory. Even if twins had ample reason for nervousness, the issue is not why they had nervous habits but why they should express them motorically in such consistently similar ways.

Other Symptoms

Learning Disorders

The diagnostic term *dyslexia* was used in only one case (176; Gottesman and Shields 1972), a set where the twins also were concordant for psychosis. Two other nonpsychotic sets also concordantly report learning disabilities that appear to be dyslexic in nature. *Earl* and *Frank* (case 204) both were poor spellers and transposed letters. *Frank*'s daughter had the same symptoms. *Clara* and *Doris* (case 212) both had severe difficulty in school, and *Clara* learned to read only in adulthood when *Doris* taught her. All four of *Clara*'s children and one of *Doris*'s daughters had reading disabilities.

Criminality

It seems almost ludicrous to question the genetics of criminality, as the concept itself is a sociological rather than psychological or biological one. However, since Lange's (1931) early work there have been repeated studies on whether criminals have some form of "weak-willed" temperament. Rosenthal (1971) offers a brief and lucid critique of the concept and various studies. There is no substantive evidence in the twin-reared-apart data to support the claim that genetic determination is significant in this area, and there is much to support the idea that environment is potent. "Criminal" acts here are defined as those leading to arrest or imprisonment. Arrests due to alcoholism are excluded. Theft is almost the only crime described, since Newman leaves Reese's misdeeds (see case 154) to the reader's imagination.

Neither Lange's set nor Yoshimasu's are included in the case index, though both are mentioned in chapter 2 and are summarized below.

Lange's (1931) well-known case, Ferdinand and Luitpold were separated at eight years when their mother, a "busy, bright, good woman" died. They were sent to different foster homes that even Lange described as appalling and eventually launched into criminal careers. Luitpold had a lesser career, giving up his bigamy, petty larceny, and violence after marrying "a very energetic woman, who took him firmly in hand." Lange credited the possibility that environment might have influenced them, but did not mention the possible effects of the twins' traumatic separation from each other and a mother who had raised them "lovingly" to middle childhood.

Yoshimasu's (1941) set, Kazuo and Takao, were separated soon after birth, Kazuo staying with his parents and Takao going to a slum area in the same city. Kazuo was raised carefully by his educated Christian father and mother. Takao's foster father was alcoholic, and his foster mother died when he was in grade school. At age ten or eleven he tried living with his natural parents, but his mother rejected him. He began a career of petty larceny, including theft of such articles as a Western hat, which, at that time, was a rarity in Japan. Under the influence of his family, Kazuo had a religious conversion while abed with tuberculosis during adolescence. He became a minister. Both were described as gentle, intelligent, and gifted men.

James and Reese (case 154) differed in socially syntonic ways. James was raised by hard-working grandparents and himself became hard-working, respectable, and expert in his trade. Reese was raised by mountaineers and, like them, avoided work, school, and was arrested for unspecified deeds.

Kaj and Robert (case 206) are somewhat more interesting. Though both had a history of minor thefts, Robert, congruent with his rearing environment, was extremely moralistic and conventional as an adult. Kaj, overindulged as a child, was more psychopathic. Both vacillated, had difficulty establishing lasting relationships, and were notably self-centered. However, both also were quite intelligent and hardly could be called impulsive or "weak-willed."

Esther and Elvira (case 330), Mexican-American twins, were reared close to each other amid poverty, alcoholism, and brutality. One would have to presume social discrimination as well. Both were labile and emotionally disturbed, and both began acting-out in adolescence in response to pressure from beatings and drudgery in their homes. Both were sent to correctional schools, where they most wanted to be reunited with each other. *Elvira*, the twin with more parental support, security, and warmth, became acceptably adjusted past adolescence. *Esther* died at age eighteen of a morphine overdose. She was a transient, unregistered in the hotel where her body was found, and was identified only after much investigation.

Environmental trauma and rearing conditions seem convincingly related to both the similarities and differences in this sample. The one minor thread running through the cases is whether there is an overlap in temperamental similarity. If there is, "weak-willed" seems hardly the way to describe it. *Kaj* and *Robert* and *Kazuo* and *Takao* are interesting for the suggestions that the behaviors may, in some cases, be related to good intelligence and endowment channeling itself differently during adolescence. In both cases, one twin became notably moralistic and the other acted in the opposite direction. In *Kaj* and *Robert*'s case there are suggestions of disturbances at the oedipal phase of development showing themselves during adolescence as superego deformation. A psychodynamic approach combining issues of temperament and phase development might prove more fruitful in describing the different channeling than recourse to terms such as "impulsive," "labile," or "easily led," which do not fit the data.

Mood, Affective Lability

The literature suffers from the lack of a rating system for mood or affective style. Barbara Burks, working in the 1940s, was the only investigator to incorporate descriptive, multijudge rating scales, and her series covers only four sets in this sample. From comments throughout case histories, however, it appears that the majority of sets—indeed, almost all sets—were similar in *characteristic* mood, tone, and affective style. If one generally was optimistic, lively, somber, or muted, the other was described in similar terms. Within the broader class of typical style, differences were usually of degree. The following examples are illustrative.

Madeline and *Lillian* (case 110): Both felt lonely as children and wished for a sister (neither knew she was a twin). Both were gigglers, though only *Lillian* was a frightened child and would cry in class. As adults, both were lively, very fond of social interaction, very talkative, and exuberant. Both were excitable and labile. Each had brief fits of depression during which she would sit and sob, though each characteristically was happy.

Brian and *Hubert* (case 336). Both were slow, ponderous, self-contained, and glum. Both had expressive faces that immediately signaled whether they liked a person. *Hubert* was a bit more depressed, and his jaw trembled when he spoke of his unhappy childhood.

Burks's cases are particularly illuminating about the types of variations that occur within a broader picture of similarity. *Adelaide* and *Beatrice* (case 242) are described in chapter 2. The others are summarized below.

Clara and *Doris* (case 212). Both were excitable, easily disturbed if things went wrong, and emotionally expressive. Differences in degree sometimes were slight: *Clara* was spontaneous in her emotional expression; *Dora*, extremely spontaneous and almost lacking inhibition. The differences centered on *Doris* being more somber, pessimistic, and easily upset. Considering that *Clara* had a happy, even indulged childhood, while *Doris* was miserable, unwanted, beaten, and sexually abused, the differences in adult mood seem slight. They appear slighter still in view of the information that *Doris* had two paralytic strokes around the time of interview and a psychiatric disturbance severe enough to require hospitalization. (Diagnosis is unclear, as is degree of organic involvement and even whether it definitely was of psychotic proportions.)

Earl and *Frank* (case 204). Despite considerable differences in education and social standing, both twins were described as generally steady, calm men, though inclined to quick temper flare-ups from which they quickly recovered. Both were toward the reserved end of the spectrum but seemed cheerful. Differences were slight, though *Earl* strained to be superior to his uneducated brother. Thus, *Frank*, lacking in social pretension, was slightly less defensive and warmer and more relaxed in general. Neither seemed labile.

Gertrude and *Helen* (case 186). *Gertrude*'s emotional tone was bleak; *Helen*'s somber and pessimistic. Both were depressed, emotionally inadequate people. They were rated closely alike by observers and family members, the major difference being that one was more sociable.

Sets reporting depressive affects or sets reporting symptoms diagnosed as depressive were predominantly discordant (or concordant only by stretching the limits considerably). Most symptoms were so convincingly related to life-stress situations that judgment of innate susceptibility is unwarranted.[10] Hospitalization or suicide attempts were discordant, although the twins who had nonpsychotic pathology this severe came from sets where both partners were psychiatrically similar in other ways.[11] It may be that similarity increases along with severity of disturbance, but, all in all, discordance is so pervasive that heredity appears minimal or insignificant compared to environmental contributions to reactive, neurotic, or characterologic depressive traits in this sample. Environmental events such as object loss or early trauma could be invoked in almost every case. The problem with using the argument of environmental determinants as exclusively explanatory, however, is that object loss, early trauma, and, in particular, separation from one's sibling(s) permeates the entire sample. One would have to explain why references to depressive affects were not more prevalent throughout the case reports. Nonetheless, there is not enough similarity in this group of twins to warrant a hypothesis of genetic vulnerability.

The situation is somewhat different in the evaluation of affective lability. In almost every instance where one twin was described as emotionally labile, the other was too.[12] The similarity in underlying lability extends even to those cases where the personality structure appears to differ significantly. *Maren* and *Jensine* (case 146) were among the most divergent in defensive style. Though both were in the normal range, *Maren* showed predominantly obsessional and *Jensine* predominantly hysterical patterns. Both, nonetheless, were regarded as having an underlying affective lability. In this and other of the cases mentioning lability, manic-depressive psychosis or marked mood shifts are present in the family pedigree. They are not mentioned in every pedigree, nor is lability mentioned in every set who come from a pedigree with bipolar illness. However, the data is in the direction of Kestenbaum's hypothesis (1979, 1980) of tendencies toward affective lability in the offspring of bipolar parents, tendencies often obscured by the mixed diagnoses given those who require psychiatric intervention and unrecorded for the broad range of offspring who fall within the spectrum of "normality." From samples of psychiatrically ascertained cases of bipolar and unipolar illness, Perris (1973) estimated that the two may be of differ-

10. See cases 114, 118, 130, 132, 146, 148, 156, 168, 170, 186, 218, 338, and 350 as examples.

11. Cases 130, 136, and 156.

12. See cases 108, 110, 136, 330, 344, and 346 as examples. The listing covers only more noteworthy cases.

ent genetic background. The evidence of dissimilarity for depressive traits and similarity for emotional lability in this sample suggests that the hypothesis may be worth testing at the level of subclinical manifestations as well. Studies of twins reared together have not found consistent evidence of noteworthy heritability for cyclothymic traits (Cattell et al. 1955; Vandenberg 1962; Canter 1973; Fuller and Thompson, 1978). However, cyclothymic is more specific than the type of evaluation described in many of these cases. Also, other methodological issues including sample size (Carey et al. 1978) and fluctuations in baseline when inventories rely on self-rating may be clouding the picture. Despite promising early reports, the New York Longitudinal Study (Thomas et al. 1968; Rutter et al. 1970) did not find consistency in temperamental characteristics touching on lability over early childhood. However, again, their categories were both broader and yet required more intense reactions than the type of lability within a predominantly positive mood reported for these twins.

The issue of affective lability touches on the perennial issue of symptom choice or defensive style. Though taking into consideration the questionable labels used in the case reports over the years, still it seems that sets evaluated as having some greater or lesser degree of emotional lability also tended to be described as having either hysterical or obsessional traits. That they would be described as having hysterical styles is not surprising considering the fact that hysteria is often defined, in part, by emotional lability. The obsessional features can perhaps best be understood by the psychoanalytic proposition that obsessive-compulsive traits often are expressions of defenses *against* affect.

In general, one receives the impression of a similarity within sets in *overall* emotional range, tone, and style. Beyond this, differences within sets may sometimes be considerable, though the few rating scales suggest broad commonality. A basic problem is that we lack a precise language of emotion (Davitz 1969) and, lacking the language, have no theory to explain affects.[13] Psychoanalytic theory, for example, has perhaps the most elaborate, multilayered system to describe the control and fate of affects, and includes attempts to track their evolution through the developmental stages. However, it has no coherent explanation of *what* an emotion is or why, observationally and phenomenologically, one differs from another. Claridge's (1967, 1973) work on autonomic arousal and modulation may deal more directly with the problem. If there is some consistency in arousal patterns for each individual, and if the assumption is made that arousal in combination with social contingencies (and internal contingencies, I would add) contrib-

13. See Lewis and Rosenblum (1978) for recent examples of attempts to place affects within a developmental framework.

ute to mood (Schachter 1962, 1964), it might be possible to relate typical mood patterns to the typical level and modulation of arousal patterns of each individual. Claridge (1967) offers a provocative preliminary model along these lines.

Fearfulness, Pattern of Anxiety

Psychoanalysts make distinctions between "fear" and "anxiety." Though both are assumed to stem from the same arousal pattern and carry similar noxious tones, fear is conceptualized as a response to external threats and anxiety as a response to internal ones. Other theoretical frameworks do not make the same distinction and, in this literature, "anxiety," "fear," and "nervousness" were used interchangeably. "Nervousness" usually appeared to describe either a twin who was a worrier or one who was skittish, jumpy, and easily excitable. "Fears" seemed to cover phobias and chronic unpleasant concerns (as when a twin "always feared she would be sent back to her mother").

Numerous "fears" were listed in the case histories, and frequently both partners reported that, during the same periods of life, they both worried about something or both avoided some object or situation. In some cases, the feared objects were the same. For example, both partners in one set were terrified of cats. In another, both partners were frightened of the chain that flushed the toilet. On first reading, it is possible to gain the impression that some people may be more prone to fearful responses or the development of phobias than others. However, further consideration suggests that, while the hypothesis may be a viable one, it is not demonstrated by this sample. Halo effects probably contribute to the similarity in reporting by the twins, and the degree of mutual contact may have contributed to contagion within sets, particularly those sets with more hysterical, suggestible personality traits. Also, fears are prevalent during certain phases of development, even bearing similarities in content in cross-sectional samples of unrelated children (MacFarlane et al. 1962; Freedman and Kaplan, 1967; Sarnoff 1976). However, the fundamental flaw in this sample, or any sample like it, is that the late separations and mutual contact of whatever degree should be assumed to be contributing to a higher level of separation concerns and subsequent phobic reactions than in a randomly selected group of people from the population at large. The content of many of the reported fears suggests this is the case (kidnapping, fear of falling through a trap door, and so forth) and, were one able to do a heritability estimate, it probably would reflect common environmental trauma as much or more than shared genetic susceptibility.

The same problem exists for estimates of what sometimes has been called "proneness to anxiety." Sets frequently were alike in having both partners described as nervous or jumpy. Almost half the case reports in the sample included description or passing reference to nervousness and anxiety level, and a rough scoring indicated that about twice as many sets were alike in description as different. An intuitive grouping suggested that the extreme sets might be classified according to whether they were predominantly worriers, atypically phlegmatic, or skittish and excitable. This grouping overlaps somewhat the more formally and rigorously defined categories of personality and temperament scales,[14] and it is hard to escape the impression of innate temperamental styles of excitability and internal control. Portions of the sample seemed further subclassified into sets that channeled into cognitive styles (the worriers) versus those that were characterized by abrupt reactivity (the jumpy, impulsive pairs). However, to say this is like reinventing the wheel, and not even a particularly modern wheel considering the personality theories passed on from ancient times. Though the impression is strong that there is some striking similarity within sets, even to the style of expression, the massive prevalence of trauma, stress, and poor living conditions suggests that this sample or one like it should not be used to test the hypothesis.

However, although the sample is poor as a vehicle for examining proneness to anxiety, it is extraordinary for the suggestions that when anxiety occurs the *pattern* of experience is unique to the individual. Juel-Nielsen (1965) and Shields (1962) both noted that twins frequently, and independently of each other, described symptoms and phenomenological experiences in identical terms. Juel-Nielsen concluded that the striking similarity must point to some fundamental similarity in the experience of physical and psychical phenomena. Consider the following brief summaries. In each instance, the presence of anxiety symptoms was not surprising considering the family environment. However, the similarity in symptoms and the similarity in description of state (which is better illustrated in the case histories than in these brief vignettes) would be hard to explain on purely environmental grounds. The cases below are meant as examples, but, judging from interviewers' comments, they are not unrepresentative of the thread of similarity running through the sample at large.

Palle and *Peter* (case 108). The twins were reared to the age of twenty-two without knowledge or contact with each other. They were seen three days after they met. *Peter* had just learned he was adopted, *Palle* had learned six months earlier. *Peter* felt he resembled his adoptive family so strongly that he had difficulty accepting the

14. See, as examples, Cattell et al. 1955; and Thomas et al. 1968.

fact that he was not their natural child. *Palle* always had wondered at his lack of similarity to his parents.

Palle was reared in a working-class Danish home. His father drank heavily and his mother was a delicate, reserved but anxious woman. *Peter's* parents ran a newspaper stand and had limited income. His mother, seductive and quarrelsome, was the dominant force in the family. His father was frequently drunk, and the parents often considered divorce. *Palle* left school at age fourteen after an undistinguished career. *Peter* was a student at the university and had spent a year in the United States. Despite macroscopic similarities in the homes, the twins described the psychological atmospheres as very different.

As children, both were nervous and restless. Both suffered from nightmares and picked at their nails. *Palle* also picked his nose and had nocturnal enuresis and stammering. *Peter* plucked at his eyebrows when worried about exams in later life. Both were restless, nervous, and troubled in adolescence, and each chose an older man as a mentor, a fact that led to *Peter's* mother accusing him of homosexual tendencies.

Palle described vague sensations that had been with him since puberty. They consisted of a feeling of internal restlessness lasting for a few hours or days. He felt "partly dead" and had sensations of soreness around his larynx. He felt his voice was "wrong" at these times, and he mumbled and spoke indistinctly, unable to correct himself.

Peter also described vague sensations that had been with him since puberty. He felt "dead," a feeling that would last for a few days before going away. Sometimes he felt he had a lump in the throat localized around his larynx. He felt his voice was "pitched wrongly" at these times and was unable to stop mumbling and speaking indistinctly.

Both were pedantic and limited in insight and emotional responsiveness.

Signe and *Hanne* (case 130). Their case was described earlier (see chapter 5). These women were strikingly similar in the minute details of symptoms and the question of the degree to which emotional factors versus hyperthyroidism could be implicated. The symptoms, which developed without the twins' knowledge of each other, included palpitations, difficulty concentrating, globulus sensations, tremulousness, and depression, to name only a few. Juel-Nielsen noted that they both became aphonic and hoarse when interviews touched on stressful topics, and he commented, "... It was also typical that they described their symptoms in a pe-

culiar, persevering manner and often ended quite gloomy statements with a high snigger" (1965, p. 207).

Alfred and *Harry* (case 174). The twins were separated at birth and
had some sporadic contact throughout life. They were reared in
very different households.

Despite marked differences in height and weights when seen at
age thirty-nine, the twins' movement and mannerisms were similar. As a child, *Alfred* was extremely shy and anxious, which he attributed to the abuse and neglect in his home. Both as a child and
an adult *Harry* was much more relaxed. Both had a fear of heights
but otherwise seemed to differ in psychological symptoms. At age
thirty-six, *Alfred* had a pain in his heels that progressed into conversion symptoms in his legs. His case is described by Slater (1961)
as well as Shields. When first seen, Harry had no noteworthy neurotic traits or history of conversion symptoms. At age forty-two,
following a bus accident, he too was unable to walk for two weeks
because of "shock."

Viola and *Olga* (case 344). The twins had much contact throughout
childhood and were caught in the middle of conflict between the
mother and grandmother. As adults both were nervous and restless, with pronounced hysterical traits and tendencies to somatize.
They were antagonistic to each other, which limited their contact
and, presumably, their mutual confidences. At twenty-five, *Olga*
had sudden attacks of panic with globulus sensations and fears
that she would choke. The symptoms lasted about six months, then
remitted. *Viola* is reported to have known nothing of these symptoms at the time. At age twenty-seven *Viola* began having fainting
fits, with headaches and globulus sensations. They were sometimes accompanied by jerking movements of the limbs and loss of
consciousness. The symptoms were diagnosed at a psychiatric clinic as hysterical. After about nine months the symptoms remitted.
At the age of thirty the globulus sensations returned after a throat
infection and were so severe that she had eaten no solid foods for
seven years prior to interview.

Dora and *Brenda* (case 350). The twins had much contact as children
and adults. Both were hypochondriacs though they had a history
of ill health as well. Temperamentally, both were quiet with little
energy or interests. Both were afraid of falling, though each gave
different reasons. Both were troubled by sleeplessness. The twins
had diametrically opposed strong attitudes toward doctors and
hospitals: *Dora* liked them and *Brenda* feared them. *Brenda*, the

more neurotic of the two, complained additionally of headaches and stomach trouble when nervous.

If one adds to this list other manifestations often thought to have psychological components such as insomnia, menstrual symptoms, or speech patterns (see chapter 4) plus smoking, drinking, and sexual functioning, the suggestion grows that there may be, for each individual, an innate pattern of anxiety arousal that contributes to a circumscribed repertoire of potential symptoms or phenomenological experiencings. Symptom choice within this fixed repertoire would depend on the interaction of genetic and constitutional susceptibility with degree of stress and the intrapsychic meaning ascribed to environmental events. The proposition is more specific than the tabula rasa or "empty child" approach popular in psychiatry through the mid-1960s but is much less specific than one would wish for hypothesis testing. The question remains of how to investigate what these cases suggest, and how to better specify which types of phenomena are more determined by genetic blueprint than others.

Probably one of the most fruitful approaches at the present time is at the physiological level. For example, Lacey and Lacey (1962) have demonstrated that, although autonomic arousal bears certain similarities among all people, each individual has his own pattern that shows considerable stability over time. Others (Duffy 1962; Hume 1973) concluded that there is substantial evidence for genetic control of activation and autonomic arousal patterns. Since activation and, in particular, autonomic arousal are components of anxiety states, workers such as Lacey and Lacey inform not only on the issue of proneness, but also on the more specific issue of symptom choice.

Still, much more than arousal patterns are involved even if environmental events are ignored for the moment. For example, from the case histories one gains the impression that nervous habits such as nail biting, smoking, or drinking were more frequently alike than more psychological traits such as indecision or suspiciousness. Globulus sensations and hysterical loss of voice always were alike,[15] and investigators consistently commented on the similarities of movement, gestures, and nervous mannerisms. It may be that the similarity is noteworthy because these types of behaviors are more easily reported than cognitive or emotional style. However, it seems not unreasonable to wonder if the more a symptom or personality trait includes somatic components, particularly motor activity, in its expression, the more heritable it might be. Studies of temperament include investigation of motor activity level and style (Fries and Wolff 1953; Escalona 1968; Thomas et al. 1968), but the patterns have not been found to be consistent over time.

15. See cases 108, 130, 212, and 344 as examples.

However, these studies focus primarily on style (high or low activity, and so forth) while what is suggested here is not only style but also discrete movements, circumscribed action patterns, and specific parts of the body that are more involved in emotional expression and symptom choice than others.

The idea is speculative, based on impressions, and even based on impressions of data that are questionable in their own right. However, the similarity of experiences and mannerisms have been reported by reputable observers in different countries, with different theoretical orientations and over a span of more than fifty years. Somehow one has to come to grips with why twins should so consistently be alike at this discrete level. How is it that one set rubs their noses when tired, another shuts their eyes, another purrs like kittens when contented, and yet others gnaw their nails to the quick? It may be that in examining style, introversion-extroversion, or "neuroticism," we already move too far away from the somatic substrate.

Neurosis and the Issue of Environment

In theory, a sample of twins reared apart should be the definitive group to inform on the heritability of neurosis (if there is such a thing), and, even better, on the specificity of the genotype. The latter concept (Rosenthal 1971) refers to the issue of whether certain genotypes develop only certain disorders and rarely or never develop others. For example, do affectively labile twins develop hysterical or obsessive traits but never significant schizoid or paranoid features? Unfortunately, the sample under consideration is not illuminating, as the diagnostic evaluations are of variable and highly questionable quality and are never, except for Juel-Nielsen's use of projective tests, based on consensual diagnosis. The problem of diagnosis may be illustrated by the case of *Paul C* and *Paul O* (case 118) whom Newman evaluated as not differing greatly in emotional reactions. *Paul O* was "affable, free and unrestrained" and reported minimal symptoms of lack of love, indecision, irritability, and easily hurt feelings. *Paul C*, by contrast, was "constrained, taciturn and might almost be thought to be sullen." Among his many symptoms were frequent headaches, twitches in the upper part of his body, feelings of being misunderstood, and experiences of derealization. Despite the differences, no further attempt at diagnostic evaluation was made.

Neuroticism scales were included in some of the individual case histories as well as in the series reported by Newman (1937) and Shields (1962). Jinks and Fulker's (1970) analysis of Shields's data was mentioned earlier, as was Shields's estimate that severity of disorder bore some relationship to lower SES. Acceptance of the results depends on one's belief in the usefulness of tallying frequency of "symptoms" and in acceptance of the validity of Eysenck's concept of a unitary "neuroticism" factor. If one does not accept these issues, twin-reared-apart studies offer little information.

However, Shields (1962) also included blind ratings of the family environments and found correspondence with neuroticism scales and with other estimates of differences and severity of disturbance within sets. The assumption of this approach—that the psychological atmosphere of the family is significant—may be more palatable to some schools of thought. It is possible to take this line of inquiry further and examine cases where the rearing environments differed markedly and, yet, the twin from what might seem the poorer environment was not the most disturbed. Three cases are illustrative.

Betty and *Ruth* (case 152) were twelve and one-half years old when seen. *Betty* was reared as the pampered only child of wealthy foster parents. She evidently had the best schools and cultural and material advantages her parents could offer. When she felt like it, she was served breakfast in bed. She was allowed to attend only the most exclusive parties. *Ruth's* foster father lived on a pension from the railroad. Her first foster mother died when she was six, and her second foster mother was described as a plain, uneducated but common-sensical and kind woman. *Ruth* was raised with two foster siblings and was not coddled or restrained.

Though *Ruth* lost her first foster mother at an impressionable age, it was *Betty* who was more worried, atypical in her responses, and "neurotic" on the tests. *Betty* ascribed the difference to the fact that her mother was a nervous woman who had suffered a "nervous breakdown."

Petrine and *Dorthe* (case 184). *Petrine*, the stronger twin at birth, was raised in a well-to-do family with a loving but weak father and dominating, mentally ill mother. *Dorthe* was raised in poverty with her natural mother, who was described as a calm, realistic, and unneurotic woman. In adulthood, *Petrine* displayed more neurotic symptomatology.

Olga and *Ingrid* (case 104). *Olga* was removed from her foster home at age seven, presumably because of neglect and possibly also because of mental illness in the foster mother. She was attached to her foster father. She spent the remainder of her childhood and adolescence in an orphanage where she became attached to the head of the home and his wife, both of whom cared about the children. In adolescence she was placed for work on farms and was sexually abused. *Ingrid* was raised in a well-to-do family. Her foster father died when she was three, but she remained closely attached to her foster mother throughout life. The foster mother was rigidly religious and kept *Ingrid* closely tied to her apron strings. In adulthood, *Olga's* deprived background could be seen in her lower intellectual abilities and aspirations, lower SES, and possibly her more primitive attitude. However, she was rated as less neurotic than *Ingrid*, who had been reared in a stable home but with a rigid and overly protective mother.

In each instance, the "environment" that may have been significant for the development or inhibition of disturbance—without giving specific labels to the type of disturbance except that it is nonpsychotic—was at the level of interaction with significant others. The idea may seem trite to many, but it is offered here to underscore the proposition, developed at length in the next chapter, that the most fruitful approach to the study of personality traits may have to be at the level of examining specific genotypes in interaction with specific environments, particularly at the microscopic and interpersonal levels. While it undoubtedly is true that certain events are stressful for everyone—war, illness, loss of job or family members—and while it is unquestionable that severe deprivation, both physical and psychological, can forever damage and limit a person, not everyone responds to lesser but still harsh events or constraints in the same way. A leitmotif of "physical and psychical acts of violence" runs through Ingmar Bergman's *Passion of Anna*. What is suggested here is only what he, other artists, and our patients always have told us: Sometimes it is the psychical acts that are the cruelest.[16]

16. Summaries for chapters 8 and 9 are included in chapter 10.

Chapter 9

Personality II: Global Assessment and Developmental Issues

There are those who believe that personality is more than the sum of its parts. When the "parts" are as fragmented, biased toward the pathological, and minimally described as the traits in the preceding chapter, one cannot help but agree. Definition may be part of the problem. Terms such as "identity," "mood," "lability," or even everyday words such as "personality," "emotion," or "humor" all describe states or concepts we know well intuitively, but falter in delineating. What is most obvious is often most difficult to study. Leites's quotation from Han Fei Tzu is apt:

Once upon a time there was a traveler drawing for the King of Ch'i. "What is the hardest thing to draw?" asked the King. "Dogs and horses are the hardest." "Then what is the easiest?" "Devils and demons are the easiest. Indeed, dogs and horses are what people know and see at dawn and dusk in front of them. To draw them no distortion is permissible.... Devils and demons have no shapes and are not seen in front of anybody..." [Leites 1971]

In this chapter I assume ignorance of definition and of which traits might be most important to study—not a hard assumption to come by after immersion in this literature. Rather than imposing organizing constructs on the cases, subjective impressions and ratings of the interviewers organize the data.

An attempt also is made to incorporate a developmental perspective. As noted in chapter 7, "genetic determination" or "heritability" is not fixed and immutable from the moment of conception but may change according to the developmental level of the organism or according to environmental events mediated through physiologic processes. Longitudinal data of a type that would allow for repeated heritability estimates are not available for this sample. However, it is possible to examine intratwin contact at various stages of development. The patterns suggest that developmental processes are involved and that we need a broader definition of "environment" that includes stage levels and intrapsychic events.

The chapter begins with brief vignettes of some twin sets arranged in a sequence of increasing personality differences. Some have been described earlier in the book, others are introduced for the first time. Following the listing, which is based on my own subjective impressions, global assessments by various investigators are examined. Chapter 10 offers suggestions on where we might go from here and how we might rephrase questions to more accurately elicit information from future cases.

Anecdotal Summaries

Sometimes similarities seem so pervasive that it is hard to describe any noteworthy area of discordance. Consider the following case of the most highly separated set in the literature.

> *George* and *Millan* (case 102) were separated immediately after birth and adopted by different families. *George* was adopted by a newspaper "make-up" man and his wife and was raised as an only child. The family moved around the country, settling in New York at approximately the time *George* began first grade. He did not know he was adopted, much less that he was a twin, until he was eighteen years old.
>
> *Millan* went to a young couple in Salt Lake City and had a younger sister, also adopted. He completed four years of high school but decided against college. He was interested in music while *George's* profession was commercial art. Shortly before the

age of eighteen, *Millan* learned he had a twin, and the two boys met at age nineteen for the first time. (It was at this time that they were studied.) They were handsome, athletic young men, so similar that neighbors mistook them for one another. Both had won boxing championships. Both showed indications of artistic interest. Physical characteristics were identical or almost so, down to the locations of cavities in the teeth. They impressed the interviewers as markedly similar in personality, and tests of personality were so alike that one of them was rechecked because it was thought a mistake had been made (it had not). The only area in which they appeared to differ was in social attitudes and values. The differences accorded with the divergent social attitudes of the two families.

After a few weeks, the boys parted and did not meet again. *George* became a glider pilot and *Millan* joined the Coast Guard. Within a few months of each other in 1943, each developed signs of ankylosing spondylitis (a progressive crippling disease of the spine). The atypical progression of the disease was the same for both, and each responded similarly to treatment.

Sometimes differences in social attitudes, values, and personal relationships are marked, yet the underlying temperament seems similar.

James and *Reese* (case 154) were separated at less than a year, *James* going to the maternal and *Reese* to the paternal grandparents. The families were on such bad terms that the twins had never spent more than a few hours together before their mutual examination at age twenty-seven. *James's* family were hard-working, steady people who operated a sawmill and sand-and-gravel business. He was good with machinery, was considered expert in some areas, and had steady employment. He was fond of reading "improving literature." *Reese's* family were mountaineers. Like them, he avoided work at all costs and had as little to do with school as possible. He evidently served time in prison and was not industrious or trustworthy.

Their IQs differed markedly (19 points in the uncorrected tests), but their temperaments seemed alike. Newman (1937) describes the only discernible difference as *Reese's* tendency to be slippery and less than forthcoming about his past.

Kaj and *Robert* (Case 206) were raised in homes with very different psychological climates. *Kaj* was the indulged only child of elderly foster parents; *Robert* had a less indulged but still acceptable early childhood with his foster mother. After his father remarried, he became the despised foster child in a perfectionistic military home.

Robert was markedly obsessional and conventional as an adult, though he had an encounter with the law as a young man. *Kaj* was diagnosed psychopathic until he settled down in late middle age, and had numerous early encounters with the law. Both were vain and temperamentally similar, with some of the nuances of interaction astonishingly alike. For example, both cadged cigarettes from the interviewer—*Robert* apologetically, *Kaj* with a flourish and an offer to light them with his fancy lighter. Both were married three times and had periods of sexual frustration in the marriages. *Kaj* suggested prostitutes as the natural outlet. *Robert* was horrified by the idea, a response that only confirmed *Kaj*'s contempt for his brother. The two rationalized, evaded, and, in short, did everything they could not to confront difficulties or conflictual issues, though each did it in his own characterologic style. The two found little in common and remained on bad terms. Only once did one of them confide that he suspected what the interviewer already had concluded, namely that the two had far more in common on some fundamental level than either wished to believe.

On rarer occasions, the twins present pathology suggestive of structural differences in personality configuration, but the case histories also leave the impression of closely similar temperamental blueprints.

Maren and *Jensine* (case 146) were so dissimilar in appearance and interaction that Juel-Nielsen (1965) questioned their zygosity, but blood groups, PTC, fingerprints, and anthropomorphic traits were consistent with monozygosity. The overall impression of differences seemed to stem from their markedly different personality styles. The twins were separated at six weeks and lived with little contact with each other throughout life. Their homes were similar on the macroscopic level but different in psychological atmosphere. Both were problem children, but of different types. *Maren* was shy, withdrawn, and lonely; *Jensine* was dramatic, temperamental, and overtly anxious. The differences persisted into later life. When seen at age thirty-seven, *Jensine* used cosmetics, and dressed and behaved in an overtly sexual way. She mimicked expressions. *Maren* used no cosmetics, did not wave her hair, and was subdued. Neither their movements nor manner of speaking was similar, though the tone and pitch of their voices were alike. Psychiatric interview and psychological testing evaluated *Jensine* as extroverted, impulsive, and though within the normal range, of fundamental hysterical personality organization. *Maren*, by contrast, though also within the normal range, was judged to have minimal hysterical features, tending more toward obsessive-compulsive defensive patterns. Both were emotionally labile (the pedigree includes manic-depressive psychosis), and both had marked sexual difficulties, the details of which were not published. *Maren* remained unmarried and probably never established a sexual relationship. Though she had an illegitimate child at an early age, *Jensine* had a childless union and reported sexual dissatisfaction.

On the rarest of occasions, twins differ in structural personality configuration with differences appearing to go deep enough to link with major divergencies in temperamental style. These are the types of MZ twins probably excluded by the "similarity" method of selection that permeates much of the sample.

Millicent and *Edith* (case 148) were separated at three months and had little contact throughout life. *Millicent* was raised by her maternal grandmother and two prim maiden aunts. *Edith* was reared by her mother along with six other siblings. *Millicent*'s home was Victorian in its emphasis on propriety. *Edith*'s was inconsistent and riddled with mental illness.

Millicent was something of a tomboy in childhood but had no history of neurotic symptomatology. As an adult she was reserved and "not a worrier." *Edith*, the smaller twin, was "high strung" like her biological mother. She had numerous symptoms in childhood and at ages twenty-two and twenty-five had "nervous breakdowns" characterized by depression and anxiety. She improved but remained a worrier up to the time she was seen at age forty. In contrast to her twin, she was livelier overall and the case history reports that her movements were more rapid.

Global Assessment

Juel-Nielsen (1965) and Shields (1962) offered openly subjective global assessments of their subjects that attempted to pull together all the information and impressions in order to say which sets were most alike and which most divergent. It is possible to combine their scales into a three-point rating system with "1" scored for most similar and "3" for least similar. Newman's (1937) sets were not ranked, nor does ranking seem possible since his case histories focus primarily on discussion of test patterns—tests he concluded to be insufficiently illuminating. Individual case histories also defy rating. Halo effects permeate the subjective evaluations of twins and become insurmountable (at least in the numerous attempts tried in this sample) when the data consist of a written case history on a single pair. The exception to the rule is case 138, *Lois* and *Louise*, whom Newman (1937) described as the most similar of the twenty he had seen; in addition, I have attempted to complete the scoring of the most-separated group (see below).

Table 9.1 lists the assessments of the twins. Psychotic twins and those with known organic pathology such as multiple sclerosis, chorea, or severe epilepsy are not included.[1] Though there is little reason to believe the full sample is representative either of MZ twins reared apart or the population at large, this subsample generally is representative of the larger group in terms of ratios of males to females, age, asymmetry, and so forth. The two ratings in parenthesis are my own, made in order to complete the scoring of the most-separated sets. Their accuracy may be checked by going to the original papers. However, these two ratings are *not* used in the analysis that follows.

The immediate impression from table 9.1 is that the sets most separated (Groups Ia, b, c) also are among the more similar in personality. Taking the listing as a whole, it also is evident that similarity or difference in personality is not exclusively linked to overall degree of separation. Other factors, presumably a multitude of other factors, are operating. However, one recalls the conclusions of Shields and Newman who, when comparing scores on personality tests, found tendencies for reared-apart sets to be more similar than reared-together ones. The hint present in their analyses is present here also and is highlighted if the data are reorganized and comparisons are made between those twins considered most alike with those less and those least alike. One method is to compare the percentage of life the twins spent together up to the time of interview. "Contact" has been defined broadly to include letters as well as face-to-face meetings. Graph 9.1 gives the averages for sets rated most to least alike in personality.

The groups seem differentiated by contact/no contact. The percentage of life spent with no contact rank-orders them.

However, this says nothing about the ages in life when contact may be more or less significant. Table 9.2 presents the same data organized into four developmental periods: early childhood, middle childhood, adolescence, and adulthood. Weighting in this scheme is on the importance of the first two decades of life rather than on total years together

1. Shields (1962) suggested that differences in his grade IV sets could be explained by organic impairment and, for the most part, this appears accurate. However, rather than excluding all grade IV subjects, cases were examined one by one out of a concern that the sample already is biased in the direction of greater similarity. Two of Shields's grade IV sets (148, 174) remain in this listing since organic factors that could explain personality differences were not evident. Excluding them probably would strengthen the conclusions discussed in the text.

TABLE 9.1
Personality assessments—twins reared apart.

Group I	ID	Name	Sex	Hand	Age	Contact at ages* 0-6/6-10/10-20/20+	Reared by†	Rating‡
Ia	102	George/Millan	M	L/LR	19	O / O / O	O/O	(1)
	104	Olga/Ingrid	F	R/R	35	O / O / O / O	O/O	2
	106	JJ/JB	M	R/R	16	O / O / O	O/O	(2)
	108	Palle/Peter	M	R/R	22	O / O / O / O	O/O	1
	110	Madeline/Lillian	F	R/L	36	MO / O / O / O	O/O	1
	112	Olive/Madge	F	R/R	35	MO / O / O / O	P/R	2
Ib	114	Kamma/Ella	F	A/AL	50	O / O / OL / OL	O/P	1
Ic	130	Signe/Hanne	F	R/R	54	O / O / O / L	R/O	2
	136	Berta/Herta	F	R/R	43	MO / O / O / OL	O/P	2
Id	138	Lois/Louise	F	R/R	18	L? / L? / L?	O/R	1
	146	Maren/Jensine	F	R/R	37	L / L / L / L	R/R	3
	148	Millicent/Edith	F	L/R	40	L / L / L / L	R/P	3
	168	Martha/Marie	F	R/R	49	?L	O/R	3
	170	Astrid/Edith	F	R/R	72	ML / L / L / L	P/O	2
Ie	172	Megan/Polly	F	R/R	32	O / O / OL /LML	P/O	1
	174	Alfred/Harry	M	R/R	39	MO / L / L / O	P/R	3
	178	Karin/Kristine	F	R/R	64	O / OL / L / OL	O/R	2
	184	Petrine/Dorthe	F	R/L	70	O / O /OML/ L	O/P	1
	188	Ingegerd/Monica	F	R/R	42	ML / M / ML / LO	PR/RP	1
	190	Keith/Edward	M	R/R	38	ML / L /LMO/ O	O/O	3
Group II								
IIa	206	Kaj/Robert	M	R/R	45	O / O / O /OM	O/O	1
	214	Olwen/Gwladys	F	R/R	48	MO / O / O / OM	O/O	1
IIb	216	Joanna/Isobel	F	R/R	50	LM / M / M / M	R/P	2
	218	Mary/Nancy	F	L/R	47	O /OM/ M / M	R/P	1
	220	Rodney/Barry	M	R/R	34	O /OM/ M / M	R/P	3
	224	June/Clara	F	R/R	41	O /OM/ M / M	O/O	3
	228	James/Robert	M	R/R	49	O /OM/ M / ML	P/R	2
	230	Jacqueline/Beryl	F	R/R	41	O / O /OM/ M	R/R	2
	236	Richard/Kenneth	M	R/R	14	O /OM/ M	P/R	3
	238	Jessie/Winifred	F	R/R	8&16	OLM/ LM	O/O	1
	246	William/Stanley	M	R/R	39	M / O / OM / M	O/O	3
Group III								
	302	Bertram/Christopher	M	R/R	17	M / M / M	R/R	3
	304	Kathleen/Jenny	F	R/R	33	M / M / M / M	R/R	2
	306	Laura/Charlotte	F	R/R	45	M / L / M / M	P/R	2
	308	Timothy/Kevin	M	R/R	45	M / M / M / M	P/R	3
	312	Nina/Christine	F	R/R	42	M / M / M / M	R/P	2
	322	Frederick/Peter	M	R/R	30	M / M / M / LM	R/O	1
	324	Foster/Francis	M	R/R	32	M / M / M / M	R/P	1
	328	Benjamin/Ronald	M	R/R	52	M / M / M / M	P/R	1
	334	Victor/Patrick	M	R/R	51	M / M / M / M	P/R	2
	336	Brian/Hubert	M	R/R	51	M / M / M / M	R/P	2
	338	Valerie/Joyce	F	R/L	30	M / M / M / M	O/P	3
	342	Fanny/Odette	F	R/R	51	M / M / M / M	P/R	2
	344	Viola/Olga	F	R/R	39	M / M / M / M	R/P	2
	346	Maisie/Vera	F	R/R	59	M / M / ML / LO	P/R	3
	350	Dora/Brenda	F	R/R	56	M / M / M / M	R/P	2
	352	Joan/Dinah	F	R/R	40	M / M / M / M	P/R	2

* O=none, L=little, M=much; includes correspondence without face-to-face meetings in the L category.
† P=parent, R=relative, O=other.
‡ Rating conversion: 1=most similar; 2=less similar; 3=least similar

Shields	I	IIa,IIb	III,IV
Juel-Nielsen	+	++	+++
Gardner & Newman	case 138		

Most similar	none 32%		little 30%	much 38%	
Less similar	none 17%	little 27%		much 56%	
Least similar	none 13%	little 43%		much 44%	

GRAPH 9.1.

Personality ratings and degree of contact from birth to age of interview—MZ twins reared apart. (N=47)*

* Computed from "Years apart and degree of contact" column, table 3.1.

or apart. The shaded areas indicate segments of life span in which the twins had no contact.[2] Again, the pattern points to the same hypothesis. *As a group, the more time MZ twins spend with no contact with each other, the more similar they seem to become.* If segments blocked-out in table 9.2 are counted as "developmental units," the twins most similar in personality spent about 40 percent of them apart (21/53 segments). The less-similar group spent only 25 percent of their units with no contact, and the least-alike group only 13 percent.

It is possible to be even more specific in estimating which periods of life are more vulnerable to impact from MZ twins having contact with each other. Psychoanalytic theories of child development postulate that the earliest years are most formative, latency a bit less, and adolescence a time of personality reorganization rooted in the foundations of the preschool and latency period. If the data are inspected with this in mind, it appears that lack of contact during the preschool years distinguishes the most-alike twins as a group from all others and offers moderate rank-ordering of groups. Eight of the fourteen most similar twins had no contact to age six (57 percent), while only 39 percent of the middle group and 31 percent of the least-alike twins remained isolated from each other during this period. It is more discriminant to examine lack of contact from birth through the end of latency (0 to 10 years in this scoring system). Half of the most similar twins spent the years from birth to age ten with no contact. Twenty-eight percent of the middle group went through the primary school years completely separated. *None of the twins rated least alike in personality spent the years up through age ten completely apart.*

2. Question arose over how to score twins with separations past age one or who had contact with each other before the final separation took place (those scored MO in the 0–6 category). They are scored as "no contact" here. Scoring "some contact" alters the figures but not the pattern. However, there is ample reason to think late separation has marked consequences on areas more specific than the global level of these ratings. The sections on fearfulness and affect include comments on these cases.

TABLE 9.2
*Personality similarity and degree of contact over life span
—MZ twins reared apart.*

	ID	Reared by*	Degree of separation† 0–6	6–10	10–20	20+
	108	O/O	O	O	O	O
	110	O/O	MO	O	O	O
	114	O/P	O	O	OL	OL
	138	O/R	L?	L?	L?	
	172	P/O	O	O	OL	LML
	184	O/P	O	O	OML	L
MOST SIMILAR	188	PR/RP	ML	M	ML	LO
"1"	206	O/O	O	O	O	OM
	214	O/O	MO	O	O	OM
	218	R/P	O	OM	M	M
	238	O/O	OLM	LM		
	322	R/O	M	M	M	LM
	324	R/P	M	M	M	M
	328	P/R	M	M	M	M
	104	O/O	O	O	O	O
	112	P/R	MO	O	O	O
	130	R/O	O	O	O	L
	136	O/P	MO	O	O	OL
	170	P/O	ML	L	L	L
	178	O/R	O	OL	L	OL
	216	R/P	LM	M	M	M
LESS SIMILAR	228	P/R	O	OM	M	ML
"2"	230	R/R	O	O	OM	M
	304	R/R	M	M	M	M
	306	P/R	M	L	M	M
	312	R/P	M	M	M	M
	334	P/R	M	M	M	M
	336	R/P	M	M	M	M
	342	P/R	M	M	M	M
	344	R/P	M	M	M	M
	350	R/P	M	M	M	M
	352	P/R	M	M	M	M
	146	R/R	L	L	L	L
	148	R/P	L	L	L	L
	168	O/R	L?	L?	L?	L?
	174	P/R	MO	L	L	O
LEAST SIMILAR	190	O/O	ML	L	LMO	O
"3"	220	R/P	O	OM	M	M
	224	O/O	O	OM	M	M
	236	P/R	O	OM	M	
	246	O/O	M	O	OM	M
	302	R/R	M	M	M	
	308	P/R	M	M	M	M
	338	O/P	M	M	M	M
	346	P/R	M	M	ML	LO

* P=parent, R=relative, O=other
† O=none, L=little, M=much.

If one examines rearing status (whether with parents, relatives, or unrelated individuals) or knowledge of twinship, the patterns are similar. Since, in this sample close contact and knowledge of twinship are associated with being raised in branches of the same family, more specific evaluation was not done. It would be valuable if future twin-reared-apart studies could disentangle the various effects.

Thus, we are confronted with a paradox. The usual assumption is that being reared in the same family and having one's twin present for mutual identification acts in the direction of making sets more alike. Yet evidence suggests opposite effects. Twins with the least overlap in family environment and interaction often seem more similar. Degree of separation is in no way an exhaustive criteria for defining differences. However, the pattern is the same as hints from MZ-DZ test scores in Newman's and Shields's samples—samples studied on different continents, with different methodologies, more than thirty years apart. Further, the ratings in this regrouping *exclude* all of Newman's original sets, using Juel-Nielsen's instead, and they are based on subjective global assessment rather than the test scores used in the original studies. The hypothesis of less contact/more similarity is also supported by Canter's (1973) results, where twins who had separated for varying periods of time in adolescence or adulthood were studied.

Some might use this paradox as an argument for denying the influence of environment on personality development. However, on reflection, it probably implies the opposite. It implies, first and foremost, that it is necessary to define *levels* of environment. At the macroscopic level are socioeconomic status, intactness of family, culture, and the like. These factors have been emphasized in this and other studies, the effect in this study probably acting primarily to limit the variance. What is now thrown into clearer focus is the potential for extraordinarily potent impact at the microscopic or psychological level. With a better sample and more rigorous design it would not be surprising to discover that the effect the twins have on each other rivals that shown by any other variable, whether social or perinatal. I can only construe this effect to include an intrapsychic element expressing itself through the channels of personality style. Also, since those twins who had more contact also had parents who knew they were twins and had seen the partner (usually relatives were parents moreover), there may be some overlap with the types of nuances of interaction shown by parents trying, artificially, to differentiate between identical twins reared in the same family. In the reared-apart data, we would speak of identical children being reared in the same extended family. The pattern, even at the level suggested here, raises serious questions about using twins reared together as subjects for personality studies. Rating parental attitude, even observing parent-child interaction, may be insufficient safeguards. The crux of the problem is that twins may have profound impact on each other, particularly during the early and middle years of childhood when they are least articulate about self-observation. Child clinical work also suggests that parents may be unaware of the subtle biases in their interaction.

Still, though mutual contact has some effect, though far from the exclusive one, how can it be explained that some sets with much contact throughout life also are in all three groups of similarity and account for half of the sets in the intermediate range? Again, there must be a multitude of factors operating, but one worth investigation is the issue of *consistency* of contact. Hinted at in table 9.2 and suggested in the case histories is the fact that the twins in the extreme groups tended to have more inconsistent contact. The middle group, by and large, either lacked contact or had a great deal. Perhaps the assumption of a direct relationship between lack of contact and degree of similarity oversimplifies psychological functioning. If twinning is at issue, the problem may center on how much of a chance parents and twins have to digest, check, and recheck impressions rather than intermittently being subjected to a psychologically stressful and novel situation. If this is the case, possibly twins in the middle group most resemble twins reared together.

It probably has been noticed that nothing yet has been said about *how* these groups of twins are similar or different in personality—an interesting omission in a discussion of this type. However, once started on this road, let us follow it a bit longer. For example, granting that intrapsychic effects of contact with one's twin may be potent, still it is possible that the most similar twins also have the most similar homes. Even if they lack similar homes, perhaps the ranking has to do with education, neurosis, or personality type. Following Jinks and Fulker's (1970) suggestion, perhaps extraverts are most similar and introverts, most influenced by environment, are most different. Insofar as I am able to tell, nothing in the macroscopic environment distinguishes one group from another, and if there is a personality type that remains more or less unaffected by environment, it is not evident from inspection of either these subgroups or the full sample.[3] It seems more reasonable to assume that different genotypes are influenced differently by the environment, not that one is influenced more.

For example, twins in group 1 sometimes come from very different homes in terms of social standing, family configuration, and child-rearing attitudes. The same is true for twins in group 3. Among most similar sets, *Kamma* (case 114) grew up in an intact family while *Ella* was left with her father and neglected almost to the point of death. *Kaj* and *Robert* (case 206) had markedly different family experiences. The values

3. Newman said the same thing, though Juel-Nielsen and I both have the impression that twins may grow more and more alike in old age (Juel-Nielsen 1979; personal communication).

the twins held, their beliefs, or social standing do not differentiate between most or least alike. Neither do differences in education explain the ranking. For example, *Palle* and *Peter* (case 108) were among the most similar but differed by many years in amount of education. Given the imbalance of women to men in the sample, it could not be said that women were more similar than men, nor can it be said that children were more similar or different than adults.[4] Even differences in neurotic style do not exclusively distinguish the groups. *Kaj* and *Robert* (case 206) were different in neurotic traits yet were ranked as highly similar, while *Maren* and *Jensine* (case 146), who also differed markedly, were ranked among most different.

If none of these variables distinguishes the groups, what does? Though differences in neurotic styles are not exclusively discriminant, differences appear to occur somewhat more often among group 3 than among group 1 twins. Also, it seems that sets with only one partner notably in the "nervous" or neurotic range occurred slightly more among "different" twins than among those rated most similar. IQ differences increase with the global assessment of personality difference (group 1, mean difference = 3.07; group 2 = 5.78; group 3 = 8.58.)[5] Other than this, however, it appears that the subjective ratings of the interviewers were not based on the usual psychodiagnostic criteria. Instead, they probably registered some common denominator at the level of tempo, lability, impulsivity, mood, and nuances of relatedness and interaction. Carriage, movement, and mannerisms also seem a common thread, and narcissism may have a place. In short, the pairs seem to share a common style, a little more similar among the most alike, a little less similar in those rated most different. The "style" described here overlaps considerably with definitions of temperament (Thomas et al. 1968; Chess and Hassibi 1978), adding to it the circumscribed but highly differentiated units of behavior falling under the category of "mannerisms." To put it another way, I suspect that the interviewers intuitively registered similarities or differences in those "psychological" traits most imbued with expressions of neurobiological patterns. If my speculation is correct, the irony is that those twins who had the least opportunity to influence each other were the most similar at this fundamental level—a level, moreover, that one would think would be least altered, except temporarily, by cognitive or emotional events.[6]

4. The middle group is somewhat older than the rest but, given the distribution, lack of children is probably based on chance.

5. $p < .05$, $F(2, 41) = 3.55$. It is worth underscoring that the three groups do *not* differ significantly in mean IQ (group 1 = 98.96; group 2 = 99.61; group 3 = 96.46). The linear correlation between IQ differences and degree of similarity is .38, N = 44, $p < .01$. If one highly questionable case is eliminated (174), the difference in the least alike group rises to more than 9 points.

6. A summary for chapter 9 is included in chapter 10.

Chapter 10

Paradoxes and Speculations

The material on the twins' personality patterns suggests a number of conclusions, some of them paradoxical. For example, it appears that the clearest signs of genetic determination may occur in traits closest to neurobiological functioning—arousal, sensory patterning, tempo, units of movement, lability, and so forth. It also is implied that the effects of twinning may be most pronounced at the level of temperament—and temperament usually is defined in the same or similar terms. Thus there is the paradox that minute interpersonal and intrapsychic events may be the most potent in altering at least some traits fundamentally linked to the somatic blueprint of the individual. If nothing else the pattern suggests the need to broaden the usual definition of "environment."

A second paradox emerges from the suggestion that twins with the least contact may most frequently be the most alike. Again it speaks to the power of minute interpersonal and intrapsychic events. Since twins with contact appear the most different, the differences also speak eloquently to the need of each individual to be an individual—unique and clearly bounded. And, since twins evidently make themselves different as well as being made different by external forces, the pattern suggests that an approach that views the individual as an active participant in the creation of his reality is essential to understand the data.

Finally, there is the problem of substantial ambiguity in this data. Some of the problem undoubtedly stems from incomplete reporting and poor instruments. However, I suggest that the major problem is that we may be asking the wrong questions of the material. In looking for "heritabilities" of specific traits we ignore the developmental approach, which may more accurately portray the processes we are trying to unravel. The most fruitful issue may not be genetic determination of discrete units of behavior but genetic determination of the pattern of development itself. As with cognition (chapter 7), I suggest that traits may be highly determined at some points in development but may be maintained by the psychological apparatus and subject to psychological influence at others.

Twinning and Temperament

The conclusion that these monozygotic twins differ in temperament as one consequence of early contact is based more on inference and a process of elimination than on direct evidence. One method of testing the hypothesis would be to obtain matched samples of genuinely separated and reared-together MZ twins and to compare them, using clearly defined and operationalized tests. Lacking this, one might follow a form of reverse logic and examine reared-together MZ and DZ twins to see which traits are more alike among DZ twins than MZ. According to my speculation, DZ twins might sometimes be more similar, despite different genotypes, in areas where MZ twins make themselves artificially different. In other words, for some traits twinning might work toward similar identifications in DZ twins and dissimilar identifications in MZ ones. A rough approximation, which indicates that temperament may be a salient issue, is obtained from inspection of Shields's (1962) and Newman's (1937) data. It is emphasized that I do not speak here of patterns that have been found to differ from chance but only of a consistent direction in raw scores and correlations. In both studies, there was a slight tendency for reared-together sets to be more different in personality tests than reared-apart sets. In Newman's data, one test, which has a surprisingly modern ring, was designed specifically to tap temperamental traits. The Downey Will-Temperament test uses tasks performed with an examiner (not self-rating scales) and attempts to rate impulsivity, motor control, finality of judgment, and the like. On the Downey, in contradistinction to every other test, fraternal twins almost always tended to be more alike than identical twins reared in the same home.

The suggestion, again, is that there may be a subtle but noteworthy effect specifically on temperamental traits from the interaction of parents with identical twins and the interaction of identical twins with each other. A major problem with the Downey test, however, is that it

TABLE 10.1

*Raw intraclass correlations and z-transformations on the Downey Will-Temperament Test for identical and fraternal twins reared together.**

	IDENTICAL		FRATERNAL	
	r'	z-transformation	r'	z-transformation
Downey:				
Speed of decision	.497	0.555	.694	0.866
Finality of judgment	.311	0.332	.367	0.395
Motor inhibition	.513	0.577	.575	0.665
Coordination of impulses	.819	1.164	.786	1.071

* Differences between correlations are statistically insignificant.
NOTE: Reprinted by permission of the publisher from *Twins: A Study of Heredity and Environment*, by H. H. Newman, F. N. Freeman, and K. J. Holzinger (Chicago: University of Chicago Press, 1937), p. 98. © 1937 by The University of Chicago, renewed 1965 by Marie E. Newman

is not reliable. Individuals are not consistent in their scores in repeated retestings. The problem was severe enough that Newman and his colleagues essentially dropped the Downey scores from the majority of their analyses. By the logic of my speculation, however, perhaps even the unreliability in itself is of interest. Undoubtedly we need to better define what we are looking for and construct tests that accurately tap it. However, perhaps we err in assuming that traits with high degrees of genetic determination always are constant. Some may be, but the capacity to adapt to minute changes in the interactional sphere also is innate and is perhaps the bedrock of personality structure and functioning. In other words, instability in the service of adaptation may be the core issue.

The proposition speaks to the issue of the low and inconsistent heritability estimates obtained in many studies of temperamental traits in twins reared together. By inspection of these data and by face validity of inventories used in other studies, many of these traits *should* be strongly interrelated with the innate somatic blueprint of the individual. The problem may be that the type of environmental interactions most likely to modify them also are present in samples of twins reared together. They also are present in samples of nontwins where it is found that temperamental variables are not constant over time (Thomas et al. 1968).

Personality and a Developmental Approach

Earlier I suggested that two paradoxes—temperament affected by twinning and lack of contact contributing to more similarity—may be explained by a developmental approach. Indeed, on reflection, the explanations are so simple and straightforward that they seem to be no more than logical extensions of developmental theory. One might predict the results rather than find them perplexing.

For example, the first issue—that temperament may be affected by contact between identical twins—seems paradoxical since temperament also appears to be fundamentally interrelated with innately determined response patterns. The clarification may reside in the dictum, common to embryology as well as developmental psychology, that intervention affects an organism according to its level of developmental organization. German measles impacts differently according to the stage of pregnancy; separation from a parent is experienced differently by children according to their age and stage of development, and so forth. In this twin-reared-apart sample, "contact" or "lack of contact" focused primarily on degree of contact during early life. In early childhood, sensorimotor functioning is paramount, and, presumably, intervention at this stage expresses itself primarily in sensorimotor modes. It is not hard to make a correspondence between "sensorimotor" and traits usually described under the rubric of "temperament." Similarly, as development proceeds and the individual becomes more differentiated, contact with one's twin would be presumed to affect more differentiated and probably more "psychological" traits. Thus, contact through early childhood might express primarily through sensorimotor channels, while contact in latency might show more in identifications, ideals, industry, and so forth. The expected areas of impact could be broken down quite finely using psychoanalytic, Piagetian, or other developmental schemes. The ideal experiment would compare groups of separated twins who had no contact other than some intensive meetings at only certain points in development. This sample is coded in a way that should allow an analysis to be done, but the data were too sparse to allow it. However, it may be useful to maintain the twin-reared-apart index according to when twins met and how much and what type of contact they had. Though this sample was unsuitable, future ones may not be.

The issue then arises of what environmental events subsumed under the label "contact" are impacting on the twins. Without detracting from the effect of macroscopic environmental variables, it appears that "contact" must include minute interactions between parent and child and child and child during various developmental periods. As noted, in chapter 9, "twinning" probably refers, in part, to parents interacting in subtle but tellingly different ways with children they know or sense are identical. Clinical experience suggests that parents often are unaware of nuances of their interactions with twin or nontwin children alike. Thus, self-rating inventories used in some studies to tap this effect may not catch the essential components. Other effects of twinning probably are bound up in the twins' interactions with each other. Since the form of "identification" described here moves in a negative direction, motivation would appear to be an essential component. If motivation is involved, it implies that the intrapsychic world must be included in the definition of "environmental influence." In short, "environment" exists at the macroscopic, microscopic, and intrapsychic levels, and the "significant environment" that will produce change depends on the developmental level of the child. It is not only *what* the environment is, but *when* the interaction takes place. Some children even seem to have more recoverability from unpleasant or traumatic interactions at vulnerable periods than others (see Mahler 1968). The flexibility appears to be innate and surely could be more discriminantly characterized in future work.[1]

The seeming paradox that twins who have no contact often seem to be the most alike, despite families and cultures that sometimes seem very different, also is a logical extension of some currents in psychodynamic developmental theory. The core of the explanation rests on the inference that even though the environments appear dissimilar to us, the twins must be making them similar or experiencing them similarly nonetheless. If this is the case, the only construct applicable is one that views the child as an active participant in the developmental process rather than as a largely passive, shaped and molded bit of protoplasm. Both Piagetian and psychodynamic developmental theories make the assumption of the child actively creating his interactions and reality. Escalona's (1968) work is one example from the psychodynamic tradition that speaks directly to the issue.

Though Escalona makes no direct reference to genotype-environment interaction, her work is clinically descriptive of it. For example, she illustrates how autoerotic activities stem from areas of innate sensitivity in the infant that also must be stimulated by the parent. A child insensitive to tactile stimulation may not stroke himself for pleasure no matter how much his mother touches him. A child sensitive to touch may stroke himself tenderly when alone, but only if his mother also has stimulated him, even minimally.[2] For the first child, the experience of "good mothering" may have little to do with how much his mother cuddles him. For the second child, it has everything to do with it. As outside observers, we might rate both mothers as adequate, even optimal in overall caretaking. The children nonetheless could experience them as less than optimal: One because she doesn't do what he experiences best, the other because she doesn't do it enough.

---

1. See Papoušek (1967; 1977) for insightful methods of investigating adaptability in infant research.
2. This also may be an initial clue toward understanding the similarity in mannerisms suggested for this sample.

A similar example stems from Escalona's observation that some active children become overwhelmed with active parents and shift into dedifferentiated states unsuitable for attention and learning. Some passive children, conversely, require active parents to bring them to the optimal level to display their capacities. Again, one child might experience an active parent as poor, the other might experience the same parent as excellent.

Escalona drew a conclusion that is worth underscoring. It is neither the innate blueprint nor the environment that is laid down as memory traces and as basic building blocks from which the child will respond with new behaviors. What is laid down is the *experience* of the child—the phenomenological experience of how the blueprint interacted with the environment and was interpreted through the psychic level of organization. Children with different genotypes may experience the same or similar mothers differently. Conversely, children with similar response patterns—such as identical twins—may experience even different environments in similar ways.

Still, the explanation does not speak fully to the issue of why degree of contact might be an important variable. If MZ twins filter even moderately dissimilar environments in similar ways, contact should have little effect. I suggest that part of the explanation lies in another observation of those who study early child development. Escalona noted that most parents instinctively alter their behavior to bring the child to an optimal level of comfort and alertness. These are the states most conducive for learning for the infant. Parents appear to do it automatically, evidently not out of an awareness of the value for the child but because these states are the most pleasant for the parents. Spitz (1965) echoed the thought in speaking of the "intricate ballet" of adjustment between parent and child, as did Mahler (1968) with her comment that most children are able to elicit needed nutriments from the environment, no matter how different the environments appear to our eyes. Perhaps identical twins reared apart in effect "seduce" their environments into acting in accord with their needs, and what they cannot seduce into similarity, they tend to experience in roughly similar ways anyway. When parents have contact or awareness of another identical child, I suspect that it limits their "seducibility" in probably subtle and largely unconscious ways. Considering the wealth of experiments from all areas of psychology indicating the degree to which information or misinformation alters attitudes and shifts behaviors, the hypothesis does not seem farfetched. The similarities in temperament, thus, possibly, *are* based on interactional phenomena as much as later divergences within sets that stem convincingly from twins identifying or rebelling against parental beliefs and stances. The issue is the level and channels of parental and environmental interactions—some minute, others easily observable and quantifiable.

Developmental Psychology and Behavior Genetics

There is much that is ambiguous in these data. Though poor reporting undoubtedly is implicated, the confusion may stem as well from our own ambiguity and confusion in methodological approaches. Calculations of heritability or statistical approaches that attempt to delineate degrees of various environmental influences are rooted in the methodologies of the physical sciences. Though grossly oversimplified, it seems that many studies approach the issue of environment as if sufficient outside force will alter the direction of the organism. Thus, breast-feeding should result in contentment, stimulation in higher mental abilities, and so forth. While there are demonstrable degrees of accuracy in such assumptions and approaches, they are insufficiently explanatory and sometimes produce results incongruent with clinical or everyday observation and experience. There is, in effect, an analogy between such approaches and a view of the individual as a particle shifted about in a chamber.

A developmental approach rooted in biology rather than the physical sciences makes different assumptions. The individual is viewed as an active and changing organism undergoing hierarchical reorganizations in the movement toward increasing differentiation. As suggested earlier, intervention is sometimes elicited by the child and is discriminantly filtered and acted upon according to the level of organization. Effects sometimes show not at all, and sometimes show markedly but in widely varying ways. Thus clinical observation indicates that there is no direct correspondence between the form of childhood neurotic symptoms and the form of adult neurosis (Blos 1972). Temperamental variables may be unstable over time, and a child who is very active early in life may turn out to be very much master of his own behavior and impulses only a few years later (Thomas et al. 1968; Bell et al. 1971; Fuller and Thompson 1978), though evidently even this is not always the case (Yang and Halverson 1976). Thus, although developmentally informed studies may produce results that are confusing and sometimes not subject to rigorous statistical analysis, they may be describing the organism more faithfully.

Within the field of behavior genetics, developmental genetics is being cited more and more frequently.[3] As noted in chapter 7, different genes may be switched on and off during the developmental process, making invalid the implicit assumption in many studies that genetic determination or "heritability" is constant throughout life. McClearn's (1970) observation that "developmental processes are subject to continuing genetic influence, and different genes are effective at different times" (p. 61) bears continual repetition. Gottesman (1974) elaborates:

It cannot be overemphasized that it is *environmental* factors acting through such extracellular metabolic intermediates as hormones, vitamins, and toxins that determine *which* genes get switched on and how long they function. . . . Since only a small portion of the genome (perhaps 5 to 20 percent) is activated at any one time, the *effective* genotype upon which environmental forces are acting is constantly changing. [pp. 63, 66]

The propositions suggest several corollaries, all of them compatible with developmental psychology and all exquisitely enticing for a revised view of data and more refined research and interventions. For example, if genetic determination (or penetrance) for a given trait is higher at some points in development than at others, the converse also must be true: Environmental impact must be greater at some points than at others. Developmental psychology offers numerous examples to support the point, ranging from issues of critical periods, to concepts of specific vulnerabilities at specific stages, to issues of early versus late intervention. Examples from the fields of medicine and psychology are widely known. Rather than repeat them, it seems more germane to underscore several propositions that emerge from the concept.

First, if developmental psychologists are true to their traditions, the study of heritability would focus on different heritabilities at different stages of development. The issue is the degree of genetic determination of a trait *at a particular stage of psychological and maturational organization*, not some simple estimate of heritability overall. Polygenic traits, such as cognition or personality attributes, emerge through the complex interaction of many genes and many environments, and the weighting of their interrelationships must be presumed to shift and reshift over time. Accordingly, if our goal in studying these traits is to form more refined intervention programs, it makes more sense to study the components that combine to form complex traits rather than the traits overall. Authors often describe genes as "building blocks." There is a crucial analogy in the metaphor. Over the millenia bricks and mortar have been used to build structures widely divergent in function and architectural design. Right now we seem to be studying the human equivalent of "heritability" of a limited number of completed buildings

3. See Waddington 1957, 1962; McClearn 1970; Gottesman, 1971; Fishbein 1976; Caspari 1977; and Wilson 1978 as examples.

when actually we should be studying the materials that form the structures and the creative processes that make them so different.

Thus, it may be more fruitful to begin to break down traits such as cognition and personality into component parts. The point in development where a component is newly emergent may be the point where genetic determination is most significant. Following the principle of hierarchical reorganization, it might be most useful to study those traits newly emergent at the beginning of phase reorganizations (such as psychosexual or Piagetian stages). It may be that through a genetically determined sequence of maturational development, genetic determination of the trait is important then. However, a trait may be substantially maintained by the psychic apparatus after that time and be open to environmental manipulation. For example, one might consider the difference between stepping as a reflex versus walking under increasing volitional control. Similarly, one might consider the similar sequence of sounds that emerge in infants' babbling in divergent cultures versus the many different ways sounds are put together to form words and language under environmental influence. Though language acquisition and linguistic structure may be innately determined, this implies different things when considering a two-year-old putting together sounds and sentences for the first time and a forty-year-old learning a second language. Yet another example is the differentiation of various affects during the course of development. To a substantial degree, the early differentiation probably is associated with innately determined maturational sequences, such as increasing neurological differentiation (Izard, 1978). The expression of increasingly differentiated affects later in life, however, may have quite different roots. Consider the affect of contempt as an example. It is both attitudinal and can be expressed in emotional nuances. Infants do not display contempt. School-age children may do it crudely, while some adults are capable of fine-honed innuendo. I doubt if there are "contempt genes" that switch on in the course of development, though heritability estimates in some subpopulations undoubtedly would be high. Instead, a more reasonable explanation is that contempt is rooted in elementary emotions such as anger and fear, but that it emerges out of recombinations of increasingly psychological components and is maintained by psychological and cultural structures. As such, it is open to environmental manipulation, however difficult such interventions may be to design. The trait itself probably is not genetically determined in any meaningful sense. However, the capacity for recombination of increasingly psychological components probably is.

The building metaphor again comes to mind. The form and timing of emergence of some individual bricks may well be determined by a genetic mason. However, stones are maintained in place by their relationship with other parts of the building and, after the building has been erected, individual parts or even whole sections of the building may be removed and replaced.

What the building metaphor eventually points to is the importance of the infrastructure and the sequence of the unfolding of the design plans. In developmental terms, this speaks to the blueprint of development and unfolding timetables. I agree with Juel-Nielsen that we probably are asking the wrong questions of the data. Heritability estimates for specific traits have only limited usefulness, and, in the long run, with their emphasis we may be missing the forest for the trees. The important issue is why the blueprint of development unfolds in a roughly similar sequence throughout the almost incomprehensible diversity of families and cultures that exist or have existed throughout history. Again, developmental theory may provide guideposts for hypothesis formation. For example, it would be hard to dispute that child-rearing patterns affect the form of adult personality, or that personality is intimately bound up in cultural factors (Erikson 1968; Mead 1928, 1930). In this sample of MZ twins reared apart, cultural issues are partially controlled by the fact that interviewers and subjects almost always were from the same milieu. However, some of the similarities within sets may be accounted for by cultural issues. I suspect, for example, that few of the Danish sets were as emotionally flamboyant as some of the American or South American ones, no matter what their innate propensities. At the macroscopic level, with but few exceptions, both partners in all sets were reared in broadly similar ways.

Perhaps more pertinent to issues of developmental unfolding and reorganization, however, would be the issue of timetable of vulnerability to environmental influence of whatever type. Twin studies suggest that timetables may be more similar among twins than nontwins, and I suggest that some of the similarity in specific traits is not so much because the trait itself is strongly predetermined but because the twins were susceptible to environmental influence when they were in similar stages of psychological and maturational organization. In more psychodynamic terms, I believe that the environment broadly accommodated to the twins' similar timetables, and the twins themselves interpreted and integrated stimuli when their psychic structures were in similar stages of formation.

For example, it has been reported that maturational landmarks are more similar in onset for MZ than DZ twins (Stern 1973). Test-retest profiles of infant development and IQ scores are more similar among MZ than DZ. Reports from the Louisville Twin study (see chapter 7 and Wilson 1972, 1974, 1978) offer provocative examples of similar ebbs and peaks in test performance in MZ twins. As noted in chapter 7,[4] it probably is incorrect to assume as high a degree of genetic influence over

4. See also Scarr-Salapatek 1976; Nichols and Broman 1976; and Lewis 1976.

test performance, much less cognition, as the profiles suggest. What seems more interesting is whether the cognitive bursts, attentional shifts, or the plain and simple joy of children show in exploration and problem solving is tied in to some timetable and whether this in turn provokes the environment to respond in more pleasurable and stimulating ways, ways that the children themselves then interpret according to their overall level of organization.

However, the study that may be most provocative to psychodynamic child development theorists is Freedman's (1965) examination of smiling response and fear of strangers. In psychoanalytic theory, particularly object-relations theory, smiling response and stranger anxiety (which is different from stranger fear, but Freedman's study touches on the important point) are considered to be ego organizers (Spitz 1965). As such, they give information about levels of psychic organization, structure, attachment, affective development, and object relations. Indirectly, they also may also point toward forms of later pathology and character structure (Blank and Blank 1974). Freedman's observation that smiling response and stranger fear had more similar timetables between MZ than DZ twins may thus, from a psychoanalytic perspective, begin to suggest why MZ twins so frequently appear to have almost eerie likenesses in personality. Similarly, I am not aware of twin studies of separation-individuation (Mahler et al. 1975). However, if the timetable of moving through subphases was found to be similar in MZ twins, it also would suggest that some traits that are similar are alike not because the trait is determined but because stimuli were sought out, perceived, and integrated by children in the same asynchronous equilibrium of maturational and psychological development. For example, a child (or MZ twins) who moved into practicing (Mahler and La-Pierre 1965) at an early age might interpret the experiences differently from a child (or MZ twins) who moved into practicing when either cognition or motility was more advanced. After all, in the long run, it is not discrete traits we wish to examine, but rather it is the human organism and how it *interacts* with the environment to produce observable characteristics.

Psychology has a great deal to learn from genetics, and behavior genetics may have something to learn from the discontinuity theories of developmental psychology. What would be useful would be longitudinal studies informed by developmental issues, or, at minimum, cross-sectional studies at different ages. Were it possible, better data on childhood timetables and developmental patterns in separated twins might provide many answers. Until then, we probably do the issues justice only if we regard one-shot heritability estimates or concordance rates with a good deal of caution, for they represent only an end-product or static measurement of an organism that, among all creatures, is typified best by capacities for adaptation, change, and creativity. This study began as an attempt to learn what was stable in separated MZ twins. I end by suggesting that we will begin to come to grips with the problem when we study the instability that led to their similarities.

Toward Psychotherapy

In his introduction to Leites's critique of psychoanalytic conceptualizations (1971) Robert Stoller offered the indisputably correct observation that most psychoanalytic papers are essays rather than scientific reports. Toward the end of this book I have moved increasingly away from the data and into conjecture. This last section is unabashedly an essay, but one informed, I believe, by data that most psychotherapists do not consider. Students, friends, and colleagues, knowing I was studying this literature, frequently questioned me on how it affected my attitude toward child and adult psychotherapy. The assumption, sometimes stated, almost always implied, was that the remarkable similarities between twin partners led in a direct line to a form of nihilism about verbal psychotherapy. In truth, the first impact this literature had on me and appears to have on my students is precisely that. It is more provocative than almost anything I have come across. Once past the shock, however, and given a chance to reflect and digest, I do not think this is the accurate conclusion; nor does it seem to be the one left with my students. The core problem, I suspect, is that it is unconscionably difficult to hold in mind *at the same time* the interaction of two processes—genetic and psychic determinism—both of which are invisible to the naked eye and known only by inference. It is not too hard to comfortably, albeit unwittingly, fit onself into a basically hereditarian or environmentalist position, giving lip service to the interaction but viewing the data essentially from one's accustomed position. Nor is it difficult to examine studies that quantify "environment" according to socioeconomic status, sibling position, intact-nonintact family, and the like. One can *see* manifestations of those variables and believe in their impact. What seems to cause problems is when, in effect, we are asked to assume that the "environment" that may be significant is the environment inside our heads. This "environment" is almost impossible to quantify and, at one and the same time, is the best and least known to our senses. In effect, I suggest that we artificially see genetic determinism and *multileveled* environments as dichotomous concepts. To put them together requires coming to grips with the fact that each of us has a blueprint that constrains our construction of reality in ways we do not know; yet at the same time, our construction of reality may shift that blueprint, also in ways we may not know. We like to play with paradoxes, but I don't know how much most of us like to live with them.

If one speaks of patient care, the data, above all else, speak to the individuality of each patient. If MZ twins reared apart tend to remain similar because of their innate endowments, then each individual in the general population must also be assumed to be unique. Similarly, if MZ twins reared apart become more dissimilar after contact, is there any more striking example of the need of each individual to be an individual? This realization leads to a certain kind of respect that, without direct statement, somehow probably is communicated to patients. It also is a valuable concept for child psychotherapy, since it ineluctably leads to a conviction that the child is influencing the parents in greater or lesser degree, and it is somehow easier for the parents to deal with how they handle *this* child at *this* point in their lives rather than with the usual idea of damaging a passive victim.

These may be the only firm therapeutic concepts to come from the limited data of this study. However, on a speculative level, more is suggested. For example, I suspect that each individual has a discrete repertoire of possible "symptoms" or forms of pathology. His pattern of anxiety arousal is unique and probably is a contributory factor, even for nonpsychosomatic symptoms. Environmental explanations that such-and-such causes a given pathology are probably as overly simplistic as a firm hereditarian position. Individuals probably are more susceptible to certain environmental events, depending on genotype, as they are differentially susceptible to toxins or infectious agents. The difference between susceptibility to infectious agents versus psychological susceptibility is that the individual may have had a hand in shaping the helpful or pathological psychological environment. Continuing the analogy to medical genetics, some events may be so potent that they almost invariably result in disturbance (such as deprivation or battering) or, conversely, some individuals may be so innately at risk that environmental factors have little influence (psychosis).

The question of psychosis raises a number of interesting issues. At the moment, the genetic contribution appears most noteworthy and biochemical interventions appear most promising. However, as Gottesman and Shields (1972) note, the issue is not a simple one of genetic load, for environmental events appear to increase resistance. Concordance in identical twins still remains somewhere around 50 percent for the schizophrenias, and one wonders not only what environmental events precipitate breakdown in one twin but not the other but also what events *protect* vulnerable individuals. Following a developmental approach, one would ask not only what environmental interactions protect, but at what stage in development they impact most.

Similarly, for lesser forms of pathology and even for the broad range of well-being, one need ask not only what the interaction between genotype and environments was, but at what point it occurred. The genotype may remain the same in the nucleus of each cell, but the effective genetic substrate and the effective psychological and maturational organization shift. Moreover, the two shift each other, and this may be one of the areas that broaches on insight psychotherapy. Emotions, stress, and the like are psychological terms that also eventually will be described in biochemical terms. It is a peculiar form of logic, however, that assumes that a biochemical description closes the case. A two-year-old seeing a Halloween mask may scream with fright; a six-year-old, shriek with glee; and an adult, warm in fond remembrance of earlier pleasures. One person may recoil from work as loathsome imposition on his individuality while another may approach the same job as a challenge to be met with pleasure and enthusiasm. The perception shifts the emotion, and what is insight other than a process of shifting perceptions and, hence, responses at whatever level one wishes to describe them?

Still, the problem remains that only some of our patients get better. Some retain their symptoms but feel better anyway, others remain the same, and a few get worse. Freud's (1937) recourse to hereditarian nihilism is, I suggest, premature. We need to delineate more clearly what symptoms or syndromes we are competent to treat, and at what stage in development we wish to intervene if we are treating children.

The problem also exists of what, in genetics, would be called phenocopies; that is, phenotypic expressions that mimic those that have a genetic base. Both issues, I suggest, may be approached by exploring the developmental sequence of the emergence of any given trait. At some points in development, genetic determination may be noteworthy for all individuals, while later the trait may persist by being maintained by psychological factors. Similarly, while complex traits may persist and appear highly similar as consanguinity increases, this may be an expression of the individual responding to component parts that once had a noteworthy genetic determination but either no longer do or now have a number of psychological filterings and rearrangements along the way to expression. Were we able to distinguish which traits become maintained by the psychic world of the individual, and when they begin to be thus maintained, we might begin to know when and how to make better interventions. Interestingly, this does not necessarily mean that the symptom will more easily be removed. Earlier I hypothesized that direct genetic influence may be most noteworthy when a trait is newly emergent. Subsequent to this, it may be maintained by the psychic apparatius or even elaborated. Developmentalists, however, know that it is *easiest* to disrupt a trait when it is newly emergent. It is only when it has been fixed in place by numerous interconnec-

tions that it becomes difficult to alter. Should my hypothesis have validity, it also may emerge that the most psychologically maintained
traits are the *most difficult* to change. This offers consolation to those of
us who believe there is a kernel of validity in insight approaches to
some disorders, yet who are troubled by the time and painstaking unraveling involved.

Summary

I have tried throughout this book to indicate how questionable any
conclusions drawn from these data are. Reservations are particularly
strong when one broaches the subject of the degree of genetic determination of IQ and personality traits. Two issues have been stressed repeatedly: the biased and limited sample and the inconsistent quality of
data. To these issues at least two others should be added: "Environment" must be redefined to include intrapsychic and minute interpersonal events, and, more important, our methods and questions probably should be restructured.

Lest it be thought that I am dismissing the issue of genetic determination, let us begin with a review. Throughout this sample one receives a pervasive impression of remarkable similarities, sometimes so
striking as to be unnerving. Appearance, voice, gestures, and even onset of landmarks such as menstruation or menopause certainly are under a noteworthy degree of hereditary control. So also is susceptibility
to symptoms and disorders ranging from menstrual complaints, to dental caries, to cardiovascular disease, to psychosis, to musculoskeletal
disorders. It is possible that even if the specific disorder is not determined, the system in which it occurs may be; and this may hold for
psychological systems as well as somatic ones, if only we knew how to
define them. Some symptoms that occur with low frequency and high
discordance, such as enuresis or sleepwalking, still may stem from a
congenital if not genetic base. Others, such as some forms of cancer,
may have little if any contributions except from the environment.

I have been particularly cautious in discussing IQ, not because it appears to be lacking in genetic components, but because of the grotesque
conclusions drawn from these data. If one wants to say that intelligence—whatever it is—includes some transmission from parent to
child, some will demur, but perhaps not the majority of psychologists

or even the majority of parents. Questions of scientific accuracy arise only when data as poor as these are used to give heritability estimates of highly specific values. To say that these data close the case on environmental effects on IQ is a scientific farce. They do not close the case; they open it. The limitations discussed in chapter 7, plus suggestions of effects from macroscopic environmental factors, constitutional factors, and even effects related in some way to the amount of contact the twins have with each other, should be sufficient to lead the objective reader to suspend judgment until results from a more rigorously designed study are in. Those who persist in maintaining that an accurate heritability estimate can be obtained from these data and who extend the estimate to discuss racial differences in IQ (which are problematical in their own right) should question their own motivation and commitment to a dispassionate search for full understanding.

The same limitations exist for studies of personality using these data, only more so. Therefore, I have not even attempted to offer heritability estimates. Investigators who have studied series of separated twins are unanimous in concluding that personality is more affected by environment than any other area of human functioning. The challenging question is to begin to define what traits to study and how to define environment.

For example, why should most of these twins laugh alike, describe symptoms in the same way, smoke similar numbers of cigarettes, choose similar creative pursuits, and sometimes even marry the same number of times? Someone will have to examine if, in fact, the similarity in mannerisms described in this sample exists in another sample, and, if it does (and I suspect it will) someone will have to fathom why twins reared in different environments should so frequently bite their nails, grimace, snicker, tap their fingers, and even have "neurotic" symptoms such as globulus hystericus in such similar ways. That activity levels might have innate components is not hard to envision, but the suggested specificity at the level of mannerisms and nervous habits is hard to comprehend.

It is easier to conceptualize temperament as the important area to study. I have been cautious in suggesting particular temperamental traits from this sample, not because I doubt noteworthy genetic/constitutional contributions to temperamental variables, but because I do not think that this sample, as it is constituted, is the one from which to draw firm conclusions. The similarities in characteristic mood, lability, and the suggested similarity in the pattern of anxiety seem noteworthy. Proneness to anxiety, fearfulness, and depressive tendencies also bear similarities but probably are not worthy of interpretation in this sample, given the massive environmental traumas pervading the lives of almost all twins. They may show more clearly in other studies, as would tempo, sociability,[5] impulsivity, activity levels, and a multitude of other variables.

In short, the data are firmly instructive on the involvement of hereditary determination in all levels of human functioning. To this must be added those nongenetic contributions present from such an early stage in development and so fundamentally part of the structure of the organism that they determine as much as genetic. The data are equally instructive on the potency of environmental influences. I do not mean this as a middle-of-the-road fuzzing of boundaries. As noted earlier, many people unwittingly fall more toward the hereditarian or environmentalist camps, not necessarily because they firmly believe in either, but because it simplifies matters in areas far from simple. In these data, macroscopic environmental variables probably show in an overall limiting of the full potentials of any of the individuals, and they may be presumed to have contributed to the generally limited range of occupations, aspirations, and financial resources of the twins. By and large, these were poor or struggling people whose lives were lived within a narrower scope than one could envision for them. Achievement as we usually judge it in societal terms was not high. Their human capacities in the midst of war, poverty, and misfortune may be another matter altogether and cannot be judged by rating systems or numerical criteria.

Family influences show clearly in attitudes, values, choice of mate, and in presence of nonpsychotic psychiatric symptomatology. The cultural or regional influences transmitted by the family and social nework also are present and probably show in general personality traits ranging from emotional expressivity to drinking habits. However, since in almost every instance investigators were from the same culture, there is some control for cultural influences; there is also some obscuring of the full degree of differences that exist among Danes, Englishmen, Japanese, and Americans reared in different decades and different social milieus. Indeed, everything in these data points toward the massive and perhaps predominant influence of family and culture on attitudes and psychological traits, particularly traits increasingly removed from direct somatic involvement (such as the difference between suspiciousness or indecision versus the experienced state of anxiety arousal).

Few probably would dispute the influence of macroscopic, family, or cultural pressures. Where these data may offer a singular contribution is not only in underscoring the influence of heredity, but also in suggesting the power of minute interpersonal and intrapsychic events to

5. Sociability frequently is mentioned as similar in twins. I could find no way to score for it in this sample, and, subjectively, had the impression that it was not one of the more similar characteristics within sets. Juel-Nielsen specifically discounted similarity in social approach and interaction in his series.

alter personality patterns at a level so fundamental as to be almost in-distinguishable from where constitutional or genetic contributions also may be clearest. By this I refer to the consistent finding in prior studies of series of MZ twins reared apart that the more separated the twins, the more similar they appeared to be on personality tests. Using differ-ent data (global assessments rather than test scores) and different sam-ples of twins (Shields and Juel-Nielsen rather than Newman and Shields), the same pattern emerged in this study. Twins with no con-tact were more frequently alike than twins with ample opportunity to "identify" with each other. Lack of contact through childhood, rather than lack of overall contact, may be one of the most discriminant crite-ria. The issue is confounded by the possibility that consistency or in-consistency of contact in addition to quantity may be what is impor-tant, plus related environmental variables such as being reared in the same extended family.

By a process of elimination, it appears that "similarity" in global as-sessment may rest substantially on attributes we usually term "tem-peramental" rather than on education, psychiatric diagnosis, or social class. If this is the case, it seems inescapable to suggest that both hered-ity *and* early parent-child and child-child interactions exert their influ-ence on the same cluster of personality traits most closely tied to the in-dividual's somatic substrate of rhythms and patterns of evoking and assimilating experience. Twins may be most similar when they are most separated because they have the unfettered opportunity to seduce the environment into matching their style. Conversely, if parents alter or limit their "seductability" out of a need to make twins different, by extension it must be assumed that parental stance and psychologically motivated limits or biases on interaction would have to affect funda-mentally the style of any child, twin or nontwin alike. Also, if one ef-fect MZ twins have on each other is to alter fundamental personality styles, I can think of no more powerful indication of the need of an in-dividual to be his own person—unique, and clearly defined. Though having a partner who is an identical image of oneself may be peculiarly stressful for separation-individuation, the need for uniqueness and the capacity to alter oneself in the service of individuation must be pre-sumed to exist in everyone.

Finally, one issue—that of a trait's stability—became more and more intriguing as my work progressed. Naively, one would think that the more genetically determined a trait, the more stable it would be over time. Yet it is a fallacy to assume that genetic determinism implies im-mutability. Mental retardation from phenylketonuria can be eliminat-ed entirely by environmental intervention. Height is strongly deter-mined, but nutrition, mental stress, or emotional deprivation alters it remarkably. Personality may be influenced by genetic and congenital factors (laterality and so forth), but do we really need any more than to contemplate the diversity of cultures to tell us that we shape ourselves and our realities?

The real issue, I suggest, is not to study stability of traits but to study the broadly stable blueprint of instability. By this I mean the overall pattern of development through hierarchical stages and the emergence of traits within those stages. Similarity or low variance among twins reared apart automatically leads one to suspect that the trait in question has been altered little over time and is similar because of the genetic identicality of the pairs. Cross-sectional studies that utilize heritability estimates make this assumption. The cross-sectional approach may be useful in delineating areas that are more worthy of investigation than others. It is the approach used, of necessity, in this study. However, in addition to flaws in the concept of heritability, there are flaws in the assumption of stability as a necessary feature. I have suggested that a developmental approach may more fruitfully investigate how a trait, in combination with experience and the emergence of other innate capacities, transforms and reorganizes into a new configuration. Not until we know this, will we begin to have an accurate picture of "personality."

Indeed, on the broadest scale, the single most important attribute that distinguishes us from all other creatures is precisely our change-ability and synthetic creativity. It is a product of evolution and has to be related to changes in our genetic blueprint. More than consistency, our capacity for inconsistency—for creativity and change—is the truly fundamental issue.

In chapter 1 I used the metaphor of the artist asking what genetic contributions there are to the brush and palette with which we represent reality to ourselves. If I have interested someone enough to think about the subject, challenge, refine, or alter my conclusions, I will have succeeded in my task. There is room for all in a field still in its infancy, and the issues require investigation from a variety of disciplines. However, to continue my metaphor, I would suggest that we will really begin to learn something worth knowing when we delineate not only *how* we paint our image of the world, but *why* we paint it so differently at different stages of life.

Epilogue

Though there is little that is unambiguous in this study, one thing is very clear. We need a comprehensive and rigorous study of twins reared apart. The most accurate description of this sample is "MZ twins partially reared apart." The sample's degrees of separation allowed speculation about the effects of contact (and by extension, of the effects of similarly psychologically stressful events on nontwins), but mitigated against estimates of degrees of heritability. Since the literature is, and probably will continue to be, international and substantially based on individual case studies, I would like to offer a few suggestions based on my own frustration in dealing with these data. First, certain basic information should be included in every case study. Laconic reporting may be essential in scientific communication, but omission when dealing with such an unusual population is a disservice.

Undoubtedly, workers with widely varying theoretical orientations will continue to provide material, which is as it should be. However, cases consisting predominantly if not exclusively of outmoded tests have been a grievous source of difficulty in this sample. Whatever one's theoretical persuasion, a descriptive profile of each twin and his history is an invaluable source of data and may well prove to be the most valuable overall source of information in the long run. Subjective impressions *should* be included—our tests are nowhere near the point of perfection that they eliminate the human instrument. Consensual validation would be of use in this regard. Test profiles should be reported in full and should include reputable and widely known tests as well as whatever more specialized or experimental ones the investigator wishes. This request for reputable testing seems almost ludicrous, but repeatedly in these data one comes across obscure tests, "quickies," or profiles based on constructs accepted by only small portions of the psychology community. Needless to say, biographical outlines, raw test profiles, and case summaries are the best safeguards against the dis-

reputable claims and use of data that have occurred in the past and undoubtedly will occur in the future.

Probably the most fruitful avenue would be to have a central registry
for all such cases. The World Health Organization or the International
Society for Twin Studies would be a good choice for a central library of
raw case data. This registry need not infringe in any way on an investigator's ability to publish part or all of his data under his own name in
any way he sees fit or to continue to use the information from his study
in whatever way he wishes. However, access to a core of explicit, detailed, and reputable data might contribute greatly to unraveling issues
touching on many aspects of human development and functioning. A
central library also could help with the issues of privacy and disguise
that, by right, we owe to our subjects.

Appendices

TABLE A1

Height and Weight

Trait	N pairs	Mean	Standard Deviation	Absolute Mean Difference	Standard Deviation	r′
Height (cm)*						
Female	21	160.04	5.40	1.47	1.82	.96
Male	10	165.64	14.14	1.37	1.02	.99
Weight (kg)*						
Female	21	59.75	15.31	5.28	4.82	.89
Male	9	65.85	15.94	3.11	3.10	.96

* Excluding Shields.

TABLE A2
EEG

ID	Sex	Age	Handedness	Clinical features	Dominant activity			Response to		Abnormal features
					frequency per sec.*	voltage microvolt*	Range†	hyperventilation	flicker lamp	
104	F	35	R	1) enuresis as child wetting on stress as adult	9.5	35–75	++++	amplitude and diffusion increased	activity suppressed	occasional trains of 6hz potentials (frontal)
			R	2) wetting on stress as adult	9.5	35–75	++++	same as twin	same as twin	occasional trains of 6hz potentials (frontal)
108	M	22	R	1) none	11	50	++	none		5 per sec. activity (occipital)
			R	2) febrile convulsions in infancy enuresis as child	11	50	+++	none		5 per sec. activity (occipital)
114	F	49	R	1) hemicrania	8–9	120	++		voltage increased	none
			L	2) hemicrania	10	120	++++		same as twin	none
126	M	18	R	1) none	11–12			theta and slow wave increase (rt. posterior)	20c/sec: voltage increase, massive generalized spike and wave	spike & wave on flicker (generalized, no locus)
			R	2) idiopathic epilepsy right hemiplegia	10–11			not done	increase in spike-wave bursts	5–6c/sec. activity (parietal) bursts of mixed spike, sharp wave, slow wave (generalized with paroxysmal features, possible left fronto-central locus)
130	F	56	R	1) ECT treatment	10	75	++	none		small 8 per sec. paroxysms
			R	2) none	10	75	++++	none		small 8 per sec. paroxysms
146	F	37	R	1) none	9	75	++++	voltage increase	voltage suppressed	6 per sec. activity (frontal)
			R	2) enuresis as child	9–10	75	++++	voltage increase	voltage suppressed	none

Case	Sex	Age	Side	History	Frequency	Voltage	Registration	Change	Activity / Reaction
156	F	42	R	1) none	9–10	75	++	voltage increased	none
			R	2) none.		75	++	voltage increased	none
170	F	72	R	1) none	9–11	50	+++		none
			R	2) none	9–11	50	+++		none
184	F	71	L	1) none	9–10	50	+		none
			R	2) none	9–10	50	++		none
206	M	46	R	1) enuresis as child	10	120	++++	none	none
			R	2) none	10	70	++++	none	none
240	M	38	?	1) convulsions as infant enuresis, encopresis as child schizophrenia as adult	normal EEG as adult				
			?	2) none	not done				
330	F	18	?	1) none	11.5		++	slight increase	random 5–7 per sec. slow-wave activity (all areas)
			?	2) none	11.5		++	slight increase	random 5–7 per sec. slow-wave activity (all areas)
332	M	16	?	1) late development; enuresis; at age 6: a grand mal; schizophrenia in adolescence				activity increased	dysrhythmical, photoconvulsive reaction
			?	2) retarded development at 12 & 16; low school achievement				activity increased	dysrhythmical, photoconvulsive reaction

* Known to be measured in right occipital region in cases 104, 108, 114, 130, 146, 156, 170, 184, and 206.
† + = 0–25% of total period of registration, ++ = 25–50%, +++ = 50–75%, ++++ = 75–100%; known to be measured in right occipital region in cases 104, 108, 114, 130, 146, 156, 170, 184, and 206.

Circulatory System: Symptoms, Examination, ECG, and Blood Pressure.

ID	Sex	Age	Symptoms or Diagnosis	Examination	ECG	Blood Pressure
102	M	19	1) none	normal		138/86
			2) none	normal		134/92
104	F	35	1) none	normal	normal	normal
			2) none	normal	normal	normal
106	M	16	1) none	normal	normal (splintering of QRS complex)	normal
			2) none	normal	normal (sinus arrhythmia)	normal (few mm higher)
108	M	22	1) none	normal (same subclinical abnormalities)	normal (slight Q&T wave deviations)	normal
			2) none	normal (same subclinical abnormalities)	normal (slight Q&T wave deviations)	normal
112	F	35	1) age 15: mycarditis suspected			
			2) none			
114	F	50,73	1) age 50: none; >50 arteriosclerosis; hypertension; coronary occlusions at 59 and 60	normal (age 50)	normal (age 50) "very similar"	135/55–130/55 (age 50) (>50: hypertension)
			2) age 50: none; age 73: arteriosclerosis, mild hypertension	normal (age 50)	normal (age 50) "very similar"	155/100–155/95 (age 50) (age 73: mild hypertension)
130	F	54	1) hemorrhoids; palpitations (Graves disease?)	normal	normal (low Q_1)	155/85–155/90
			2) palpitations (Graves disease?)	normal	normal (low Q_1 left dominance)	155/100–155/95
132	F	55	1) varicose veins			
			2) no diagnosis			
136	F	43	1) age 39: low BP, tachycardia, "vascular spasm"			
			2) none			
146	F	37	1) none	normal		normal
			2) none	normal		normal
156	F	42	1) hemorrhoids	normal	normal "similar"	normal
			2) none	normal	normal "similar"	normal
168	F	49,68	1) hemorrhoids	normal (age 49)		normal (age 49) (elevated past age 59)
			2) hemorrhoids; died age 68 of intracerebral bleed	normal (age 49)		normal (age 49) (elevated past age 62)
170	F	72,83	1) age 27: rheumatic fever and endocarditis; age 32: varicose veins; age 62: hypertension (180mm); age 76: angina, coronary occlusion; age 83: died of stroke	normal (age 72)	normal (age 72) (left dominance; slight depression ST_1 and neg T)	165/105–165/105 (age 72)
			2) ages 14 and 16: rheumatic fever; age 26: varicose veins; died age 80: lung edema; arteriosclerosis	normal (age 72)	normal (age 72) (same deviations)	145/80–145/65 (age 72)

Circulatory System: Symptoms, Examination, ECG, and Blood Pressure.

ID	Sex	Age	Symptoms or Diagnosis	Examination	ECG	Blood Pressure
172	F	32	1) hypertension in pregnancy			hypertension–pregnancy
			2) hypertension in pregnancy			hypertension–pregnancy
178	F	64,77	1) age 20: varicose veins; age 40: phlebitis; age 77: arteriosclerotic heart disease	normal (age 64)		normal (age 64) died heart disease (77)
			2) age 18: varicose veins; ages 50–60: transient mild hypertension	normal (age 64)		normal (age 64) mild hypertension ages 50–60
184	F	70	1) age 38: hypertension (180/80); age 70: labile BP	normal	slight left dominance; changes due to obesity, hypertension, and old age	185/80–130/75 (age 70)
			2) hypertension not diagnosed: age 70: labile BP	normal	same: less abnormal	170/70–130/75 (age 70)
186	F	52	1) ankle edema			
			2) ankle edema; died of "dropsy" at 52			
206	M	45,68	1) none at 45: age 52: angina, arteriosclerosis	normal (age 45)		normal (age 45) (>52: arteriosclerosis)
			2) none at 45: mild angina; age 65: died of sudden coronary infarct	normal (age 45)		normal (age 45) (not diagnosed or treated for later angina, etc.)
218	F	47	1) ages 44-45: slight hypertension			elevated
			2) ages 44-45: slight hypertension			elevated
228	F	49	1) rheumatic heart pains			
			2) rheumatic heart pains			
246	M	39	1) none			
			2) rheumatic fever "many times"			
334	M	51	1) none			
			2) child: rheumatic fever and suspected valve disease; pain around heart and fainting			
344	F	39	1) varicose veins			
			2) varicose veins			
346	F	59	1) none			unknown
			2) symptoms unknown			elevated since age 57
350	F	56	1) ages 56-59: hypertension			hypertension (ages 56–59)
			2) unknown			unknown
354	M	33	1) >25: chest pain			
			2) age 32: "acceleration of heart"			

Ophthalmic Traits

ID	Sex	Age	Handed-ness	Data on Vision
102	M	19	L	1) right 10/100, left 20/100
			L/R	2) right 20/100, left 20/50
104	F	35	R	1) normal, same subclinical anomalies
			R	2) normal, same subclinical anomalies
106	M	16	R	1) astigmatism; pronounced cupping both eyes (see original report); visual acuity without glasses—both eyes 5/5
			R	2) astigmatism; pronounced cupping both eyes (see original report); visual acuity without glasses—both eyes 5/6
110	F	36	R	1) "glasses for eyestrain"—gave them up
			L	2) "glasses for eyestrain"—kept them
112	F	35	R	1) double vision from age 15, "due to illness"
			R	2) glasses since age 9, type unspecified
114	F	50	L/R	1) severe myopia: R=6/6-0.75 cyl. 175° L=6/6-0.25-1.5 cyl. 0°
			L/R	2) severe myopia: R=6/6-0.25 sph.-0.75 cyl. 0° L=6/6-0.25 sph.-0.75 cyl. 0°
116	F	30	L	1) same iris color and pattern
			L	2) same iris color and pattern
128	F	36	L	1) age 20: lost vision, "interstitial keratitis" age 21: partial vision in left eye; decreasing
			R	2) age 28: glasses, "blepharitis" (no keratitis)
130	F	54	R	1) glasses since age 42; at 54, exam = − 2.25
			R	2) glasses since age 39; at 54, exam = − 3.25
132	F	55	R	1) "needs glasses," type unspecified
			R	2) "needs glasses," type unspecified
146	F	37	R	1) age 24: "longsighted," wore glasses for years
			R	2) ages 21–24: "longsighted," wore glasses; resumed wearing them at age 34
148	F	40	L	1) "eye trouble subsequent to chickenpox as child"
			R	2) no disturbance
150	F	15	L	1) "right eye badly crossed," poor vision
			R	2) "left eye badly crossed," poor vision
154	M	27	L	1) left eye: "strabismic, no image-forming power, registers only light and dark"
			R	2) left eye: "strabismic, no image-forming power, registers only light and dark"
160	F	29	L/R	1) right eye: slight strabismus
			R	2) left eye: slight strabismus
162	M	14	R	1) normal: "right eye is master eye"
			L/R	2) normal: "left eye is master eye"
168	F	49	R	1) no cataract; age 49: slightly hypermetropic, slight convergent strabismus
			R	2) age 38: "heterochromia iridis, cataracta o. dext." (surgery) age 49: slightly hypermetropic, slight convergent strabismus
170	F	72	R	1) "glasses for reading"
			R	2) "glasses for reading"

ID	Sex	Age	Handed-ness	Data on Vision
178	F	64	R R	1) glasses; "longsighted last few years" 2) glasses; "longsighted last few years"
184	F	70	R L/R	1) ages 50–73: "glasses for longsightedness" 2) ages 50–73: "glasses for longsightedness"
186	F	52	R R	1) age 52: uses glasses for reading 2) age 52: uses glasses for reading
188	F	42	R R	1) normal; slight converging strabismus 2) normal; somewhat more converging strabismus
204	M	37	R R	1) normal vision 2) normal vision
206	M	45	R R	1) myopia: right=2.00; left=4.00 2) myopia: right=2.00; left=4.25
212	F	39	R L/R	1) severe astigmatism since age 5 2) "needed glasses as child but had none"; glasses for farsightedness as adult
222	M	36		1) right eye: limited visual field; dx. conversion 2) no mention of visual disturbance
232	M	20	R R	1) no glasses 2) glasses
242	F	12	AR A	1) "when 9 or 10 wore glasses for myopia" 2) "never wore glasses; probably myopic"
246	M	39	R R	1) color-blind 2) color-blind
304	F	33	R R	1) squint in left eye; corrected 2) squint in right eye; corrected
312	F	42	R R	1) age 13: glasses for shortsightedness 2) no glasses, no mention of visual disturbance
334	M	51	R R	1) glasses as adult—type unknown—"weaker than twin's" 2) glasses as child and adult—type unknown
336	M	51	R R	1) no visual problems mentioned 2) age 20: "film of skin grew over eye—successfully treated" (cataract?)
346	F	59	R R	1) glasses: type unknown 2) no glasses or mention of visual problems
352	F	40	R R	1) "eye infection" in childhood 2) no symptoms reported

TABLE A5

Hearing

ID	Sex	Age	Data on Hearing*	Concordance*
102	M	19	1) normal	++
			2) normal	
106	M	16	1) normal	++
			2) normal	
132	F	55	1) "a little hard of hearing"	++
			2) "a little hard of hearing"	
134	F	52	1) slight deafness probably due to otosclerosis	++
			2) "about same degree of deafness" (refused ear exam)	
136	F	43	1) no symptom noted	+−
			2) deaf for 3 hours, aphonic for 1 week following "vascular spasm" at age 39	
186	F	52	1) "fair"	++
			2) "fair"	
204	M	37	1) "good"	++
			2) "good"	
212	F	39	1) occasional problems	++?
			2) occasional problems	

* Cases 102, 106, 186, 204, and 212 are the only cases in the series where an evaluation of hearing was part of the standard workup.

TABLE A6
Dental Traits

ID	Sex	Age	Handedness	Data on Dental Structure and Disorder
102	M	19	L	1) normal; same deviations; identical cavities
			L/R	2) normal; same deviations; identical cavities
104	F	35	R	1) total upper denture; defective lower teeth; many fillings
			R	2) partial upper denture; defective lower teeth; many fillings
106	M	16	R	1) first tooth: 11 months; identical structure including subclinical anomalies; two extractions, left upper 6 and right upper 6
			R	2) identical structure including subclinical anomalies; one extraction, right upper 6 (dentist who did examination thinks no extractions were necessary)
108	M	22	R	1) closely resemble in configuration of teeth
				2) closely resemble in configuration of teeth
114	F	50	A	1) age 40: severe paradentosis, lower teeth loose, lost many. Age 50: upper denture, 6 teeth with severe paradentosis in lower jaw
			AL	2) age 40: denture. Age 50: upper denture, 6 teeth with severe paradentosis in lower jaw
116	F	30	L	1) same fillings; same structure and anomalies
			L	2) identical
118	M	23	R	1) 3 lower molars filled
			R	2) 2 lower molars filled
120	F	39	L	1) widely spaced in front; upper first premolars never lost
			R	2) widely spaced in front; upper first premolars never lost; one decayed and was removed
124	F	35	R	1) 6 fillings; molars and bicuspids: same shape
			R	2) 6 fillings; molars and bicuspids: same shape
138	F	18	R	1) same: 2–3 small molar fillings
			R	2) same: 2–3 small molar fillings; upper incisors overlap a bit more than twin's
142	M	19	R	1) almost identical in size, shape, and arrangement: 2 decayed molars
			R	2) almost identical in size, shape, and arrangement: 4 decayed molars
144	M	13	R	1) same shape and arrangement: lower-right first and second molars beginning to decay
			R	2) same shape and arrangement: lower-right first and second molars beginning to decay
146	F	37	R	1) many cavities as child; upper and lower front teeth capped
			R	2) many cavities as child; upper denture by age 18
148	F	40	L	1) many teeth extracted by age 25
				2) many teeth extracted by age 25
150	F	15	L	1) same "peculiar" teeth: front teeth are too small and widely spaced, poor dentition
			R	2) same "peculiar" teeth: front teeth are too small and widely spaced, poor dentition but better than twin's

ID	Sex	Age	Handedness	Data on Dental Structure and Disorder
152	F	12	R	1) same: large and in good condition; right lower second molar filled; lower incisors almost regular
			A	2) same: large and in good condition; right and left lower second molars filled; lower incisors irregular
154	M	27	R	1) extremely similar in shape and arrangement: first and second right lower molars extracted
			L	2) extremely similar in shape and arrangement: second lower left molar lost
158	F	38	R	1) upper incisors discolored and worn to half length; half of other teeth are decayed or extracted
			R	2) perfect teeth; no decay
160	F	29	A	1) same; overbite of lower incisors; upper left canine out of line; decay in lower left wisdom tooth
			R	2) same; overbite of lower incisors; upper left canine out of line; no decay
162	M	14	R	1) same; two fillings in molars; upper canines very sharp
			L/R	2) same; no fillings; upper canines very sharp
164	F	11		1) same size and shape teeth but narrow dental arch; two molars filled
				2) same size and shape teeth but wide dental arch; two molars filled
168	F	49	R	1) lost all her teeth in her 30s; complete dental prosthesis by age 40
			R	2) lost all her teeth by age 40
178	F	64	R	1) age 35; upper denture; age 55: lower denture
			R	2) by age 30: upper denture; shortly after 30: lower denture
182	M	26	R	1) teeth are irregular and in same condition; upper middle incisors turned inward in middle line; right upper supernumerary canine too high in gum: extracted
			R	2) teeth are irregular and in same condition; upper middle incisors turned inward in middle line; left upper supernumerary canine too high in gum: not extracted
186	F	52	R	1) teeth described as "yellow"; gums as "red"
			R	2) teeth described as "yellow"; gums as "red"

Dental Traits

ID	Sex	Age	Handedness	Data on Dental Structure and Disorder
188	F	42	R	1) poor, many cavities
			R	2) poor, many cavities
204	M	37	R	1) imperfect overlap
			R	2) slightly better overlap
206	M	45	R	1) "much work" on teeth
			R	2) paradentosis
208	F	27	R	1) lower front teeth have pronounced overbite; median line distinctly on left
			R	2) lower front teeth have pronounced overbite; median line distinctly on left
232	M	20	R	1) very good, strong, white teeth; identical in shape, size, etc.
			R	2) same
242	F	12	AR	1) same structure, color, etc.; healthy gums; 5 fillings
			A	2) same structure, color, etc.; slightly inflamed gums; 9 fillings
244	F	59	R	1) complete false teeth
			R	2) most of original teeth but in poor condition
320	M	19	L	1) "unusually similar in all particulars"
			R	2) "unusually similar in all particulars"
330	F	18		1) same conformation and alignment; more secondary grooves and more decay
				2) same conformation and alignment; less secondary grooves and less decay
332	M	16		1) high-arched palate; caries
				2) same palate; no caries mentioned
352	F	40	R	1) age 22: dentures
			R	2) age 22: dentures

TABLE A7
*Menstruation and Menopause**

ID	Name	Age Menarche	Months Difference	Regular, Normal	Irregular Menstruation	Dysmenorrhea (painful, difficult)	Menostas (suppressi of flow)
104	Olga	12		✔	"early" and 32	✔ 19	✔ 18
	Ingrid	12		✔	✔	✔	✔ 18
110	Madeline	12:6	12		✔	✔	
	Lillian	13:6			✔	✔	
114	Kamma	11	24				✔
	Ella	13			✔		
128	Marjorie					?	
	Norah					✔ 11–34	
130	Signe	14		✔	✔	✔	✔ 39
	Hanne	14		✔	✔	✔	
136	Herta						
	Berta						
146	Maren	14		✔		✔	
	Jensine	14		✔		✔	
148	Millicent	14:6	1				
	Edith	14:6					
152	Betty		≈ 12				
	Ruth						
156	Ingegerd	14					
	Monica	14				✔ 31	
168	Marthe	15	12		✔ 49		
	Marie	16			✔ 49		
170	Astrid	14				✔	
	Edith	14				–	
178	Karin	13	24	✔			
	Kristine	11		✔			
184	Petrine	13	12	✔			
	Dorthe	12		✔			
186	Gertrude						
	Helen						
212	Clara	11					
	Doris	11					
214	Olwyn	12	42				
	Gwladys	15/16					
218	Mary	14					
	Nancy	14					
224	June	14:6/15					
	Clara	14:6/15					

Headache connected w/cycle	Migraine connected w/cycle	Emotionality, mood shifts	Age Menopause	Other
				fainting, better after pregnancy
				fainting, same after pregnancy
	✔			vomiting, nausea
	✔			vomiting, nausea
			(49)	menopausal symptoms
				from mid-30s
			51	some menopausal symptoms
✔		✔		
✔		✔		
✔ sinus	✔			
✔ sinus	✔			
			54	no menopausal symptoms
			52	menopausal symptoms
			51	no menopausal symptoms
			51	no menopausal symptoms
			42	no menopausal symptoms
			43	no menopausal symptoms
			36	
			34	
✔			(38)	
✔			(29)	ovaries removed
			46	
			48	
			36	

Menstruation and Menopause

ID	Name	Age Menarche	Months Difference	Regular, Normal	Irregular Menstruation	Dysmenorrhea (painful, difficult)	Menostasis (suppression of flow)
226	Kaete	12	0				
	Lise	12					
230	Jacqueline	15	12				
	Beryl	16					
234	A	14:10	(31 weeks) 7¾ mo.				
	B	15:5					
242	Adelaide	10:4	14		✔ 11–18	✔	
	Beatrice	11:6			✔ 11–18	✔	
304	Kathleen						
	Jenny						
306	Laura	14					
	Charlotte	14	3				
312	Nina	12					
	Christine	12					
314	Annie	13	2–3				
	Trixie	13					
338	Valerie		2–3				
	Joyce						
340	A	16	24				
	B	14					
342	Fanny	13	12				
	Odette	12					
344	Olga	13	48				
	Viola	17					
350	Dora	14	1				
	Brenda	14					
352	Joan	13				✔	
	Dinah	13	1			✔	

Headache connected w/cycle	Migraine connected w/cycle	Emotionality, mood shifts	Age Menopause	Other
✔				
✔				
				symptoms decrease after age 18
				symptoms decrease after age 18
				mittleschmerz
				mittleschmerz
			40	
	✔		38	
				periods regular at 48
			48	
		✔		insomnia/fatigue 16–17
		✔		excitement, loneliness
			46	
			45	
	✔			
	✔			
			(49)*	49—"menopausal symptoms"
	✔ 56		>59	56–59—no symptoms but headache

es of onset. Parentheses indicate estimates.

ID	Name	Nightmares	Insomnia	Disturbed/ Very light Sleep	Sleepwalk/ Sleeptalk/	Comment
108	Palle	−				
	Peter	+				
130	Signe	(−)?C	+A	+A		both afraid of dark
	Hanne	+C	+A	+A		as child; only *H* reported nightmares
132	Amy		+A	+A		neither can sleep
	Teresa		+A	+A		alone
134	Florence	+A		+A	+A	*F* has recurrent
	Edith	−		−	+C	dream
136	Berta	+C	+A		+A	*B*: sleepwalk as adult;
	Herta	+C	?		+C	*H*: sleepwalk as child
146	Maren	−				*J*: nightmares from
	Jensine	+C				7–14 years
148	Millicent				−	*E*: sleepwalk until
	Edith				+C	age 14
156	A		+A			*A*: clinically depressed
	B		?			since 40; *B*: depressed since 25
166	A		?			*A*: insomnia at schizophrenic
	B		+A			onset age 18
168	Martha		+A			*Martha*: insomnia in
	Marie		+A			"later years"; *Marie*: insomnia at 48
176	Herbert				+CA	*H*: talked in sleep frequently;
	Nicholas				+CA	*N*: walked in sleep frequently
184	Petrine		−			*D*: insomnia due to
	Dorthe		+A			pain from "lumbago"
186	Gertrude			+A		
	Helen			+A		
188	Ingegerd			+A		*I*: disturbed sleep
	Monica			+A		at 42; *M*: disturbed sleep at 22
190	Keith	−				*E*: nightmares at age
	Edward	+A				30
204	Earl			+A		
	Frank			+A		
210	Alice	+−				one had bad dreams
	Olive					but not the other
212	Clara			+A		
	Doris			+A		
214	Olwen			+A		both epileptic?
	Gwladys			+A		
218	Mary			+A		*M*: sleep disturbance
	Nancy			+A		after breast surgery; *N*: more severe sleep disturbance after sister's surgery
222	A		+A			insomnia whether
	B		?			drinking or not
228	James	+C				both had severe nightmares
	Robert	+C				in 1929

	Name	Nightmares	Insomnia	Disturbed/ Very light Sleep	Sleepwalk/ Sleeptalk/	Comment
●	A		+A			A: insomnia at 27 with schizophrenic onset; B: insomnia at 20, probably mild schizophrenia
	B		+A			
4	Foster	+C				both had frequent nightmares as children
	Francis	+C				
4	Victor	?				V: "irrational fear later in life" (sleep?); P: nightmares as child
	Patrick	+C				
6	Brian		?			H: after age 2, difficulty falling asleep
	Hubert		+CA			
8	Valerie				−	J: occasional sleepwalking
	Joyce				+	
0	A		+A			A: insomnia age 16, premenstrual and preschizophrenic; B: insomnia at 18, schizophrenic
	B		+A			
4	Viola				−	V: never sleepwalk; O: one episode of sleepwalking
	Olga				+	
4	A		?			A: afraid of dark, no other information; B: sleepless one night per month
	B		+A			

C=child; A=adult.

ID	Name	Stammer/Lisp	Accent/Dialect	Style (e.g., Talkative/Taciturn)	Tone/Pitch	Comment
104	Olga			+		*O:* more talkative;
	Ingrid			−		*I:* tried to be "warmer"
108	Palle	+		+	+	same voice; both hoarse;
	Peter	−		+	+	Palle stammers
110	Madeline		+	+	+	both loud; same
	Lillian		+	+	+	"manner"
112	Olive			+	+	similar voices; weak
	Madge			+	+	singing voices; spoke in short phrases
114	Kamma		+		+	similar voices; same
	Ella		+		+	accent
116	Bessie				+	voices indistinguishable
	Jessie				+	
120	Esther			+		*Esther:* gentle speech;
	Ethel			−		*Ethel:* more aggressive and vigorous speech
126	Tristram			+		*T:* normal speech;
	Russell			−		*R:* epileptic, retarded, slow development
130	Signe			+	+	same voices; aphonic
	Hanne			+	+	when discussing emotional subjects; both very talkative
138	Lois			+	+	same voice; same tone
	Louise			+	+	often same words
146	Maren	+			+	same tone and pitch for
	Jensine	−			+	both; *M* stammered and mumbled; *J* did not
150	Mildred	−		+		*M:* no lisp, spoke freely;
	Ruth	+		−		*R:* pronounced lisp, very timid speech
168	Martha		+		+	same voice and dialect
	Marie		+		+	
170	Astrid		+		+	voices alike; *A:* talkative;
	Edith		−		+	*E:* taciturn then all right
172	Megan				+	same low-pitched flat
	Polly				+	voices
174	Alfred		+			both had marked accent
	Harry		+			from childhood; *A:* was absent from childhood environs for 22 years
178	Karin		+		+	same low voices and
	Kristine		+		+	dialect
184	Petrine		−	+		*P:* no dialect, more elegant speech;
	Dorthe		+	−		*D:* dialect; less elegant speech
186	Gertrude			+ +		*G:* not talkative, more clipped speech;
	Helen			+ −		*H:* not talkative, less clipped speech

ID	Name	Stammer/ Lisp	Accent/ Dialect	Style (e.g., Talkative/ Taciturn)	Tone/ Pitch	Comment
188	Ingegerd		+		+	extremely similar
	Monica		+		+	voices and dialect
190	Keith	+				K: severe stammer as
	Edward	−				child, still showed; E: no stammer
204	Earl			+		both quite talkative
	Frank			+		
212	Clara			+		C: extremely talkative,
	Doris			+		chattered constantly; D: very talkative; insisted on speaking loudly
220	Rodney	+				R: stammer as child; still
	Barry	−				showed; B: no stammer
230	Jacque-line			+	+	voices alike; both
	Beryl			+	+	talkative; both became high-pitched when excited
232	Ronald			+	+	identical voices; parents
	Dennis			+	+	could not distinguish them; same animated expression
242	Adelaide			+		similar talkativeness
	Beatrice			+		
304	Kathleen		+		+	same voices despite
	Jenny		−		+	distinct regional accents
312	Nina			+	+	voices alike; laughs
	Christine			+	+	alike; both talkative
314	Annie			+		A: normal speech;
	Trixie			−		T: indistinct speech (ill)
328	Benjamin			+		both had loud voices
	Ronald			+		when drunk
330	Esther					both spoke at 11 months
	Elvira					
336	Brian	−				B: no stammering
	Hubert	+				reported; H: tended to stammer when describing arguments with parents
338	Valerie			+		both had quiet, tense,
	Joyce			+		confiding manner of speaking
342	Fanny		+		+	different voices;
	Odette		−		−	different accents
344	Viola			+	+	same voices; husbands
	Olga			+	+	couldn't tell them apart
350	Dora			+	+	voices alike,
	Brenda			+	+	high-pitched; both spoke slowly and in a monotone
352	Joan				+	voices alike
	Dinah				+	
354	A			−		A: speech disturbed—
	B			+		presumed organic after concussion; B: normal speech

Appendix A

Case 180: Twins A and B and Brother C [1]

This case, mentioned by Rosanoff et al. (1935) consists of male twins, A and B, who may be the only set of separated MZ twins with manic-depressive psychosis now reported in the literature. Because of their rarity, the report here, with the exception of a few introductory remarks, follows the sequence of the chart notes and does not attempt to reorganize or evaluate the information.[2] Where discrepancies were encountered, the uncertainty is indicated.

A and B's family lived in a remote area, a distance of over one hundred miles over poor roads from the nearest major town. Much of the area is rocky with thin soil, and the region is primarily dependent on lumbering and farming. Although poor farmsteads abound, many of them have returned to bushland. The twins' father was born in Canada around 1860 of Irish, Roman Catholic parentage. His early history is unknown, and although he may have had some schooling, the records indicate doubt about his ability to read and write. He was a farm or lumbering laborer, and moved about with seasonal jobs. He was described as sociable, likable, too fond of drink, and a poor provider for his family. He married late in life, in 1905 at age forty-five, and settled down on a small farm one and one-half miles from any road and about seven miles from the nearest hamlet. In 1914 the farm was sold to pay debts, and the family moved to a small community where he continued

1. The summary was prepared by W. C. Craig, Ph.D., with the cooperation of the Kingston Psychiatric Hospital.
2. As far as can be determined the family was interviewed personally by hospital staff only twice, once after the death of one of the brothers. However, considering the time (1925–1935) and staff available, the records are surprisingly complete. The material has been disguised slightly and certain dates and nonpertinent information have been omitted to protect anonymity.

to work as a hired hand and laborer, though dependent to some extent on assistance from his wife's relatives. He died in 1924 of "heart disease" but had been ill for three to five years and "wasted away" during the six months prior to his death. There is no record of mental illness, but a brother is recorded as having become "queer" after the death of his wife and was drowned about a year later, a suspected suicide.

The twins' mother also was born of Irish, Roman Catholic parentage in the same district in about 1870 or 1878. Her amount of schooling is unknown, but she came from a large family, at least some of whom prospered modestly. She was about thirty-five when she married. After the farm was sold she worked according to the availability of jobs to assist the family income. During this time, the family appears to have moved about the general area of the community, not having a fixed address. After her husband died, it appears that her brother took over the family affairs since some of the hospital correspondence was with him. Prior to the mother's death in 1942,[3] she kept in touch at least annually with her sons. The remoteness of the area, poor transportation, and general poverty of the time probably precluded anything else.

Five children were born while the family resided on their own farm. Two died—a girl at one month and a boy at eleven months. Three survived, twins A and B and brother C. The twins were described by Rosanoff as identical in physical characteristics and almost indistinguishable. A photograph recently found in the files also indicates them to be extremely alike.

Brother C

C was born in 1906.[4] His early life was uneventful. At age seven he moved with his family to a small hamlet, but he did not begin school until age eleven. Although the records state that he had "public school education," which ordinarily means eight years, it seems certain he did not go that far as he "did not learn well." He worked on farms and perhaps at home. His illnesses consisted of influenza in 1922 and sunstroke in 1923. (However, the significance of this information may be open to question since it was elicited during a structured interview and one question specifically asked about sunstroke.) Supposedly at the time of the sunstroke he became excited, confused, and restless, with impaired memory. For the next two years he did not work (ages seventeen to nineteen) and instead rambled around the countryside at night, sleeping during the day, and getting into trouble with others due to his behavior. He would get up and eat at night and "kick up a row." At

3. Rosanoff states that the mother died in the early 1930s and adds that she suffered from involutional melancholia. He evidently confused the mother with her sister-in-law.
4. Rosanoff also mistakenly makes C three years younger than the twins rather than three years older.

times he would be well, then suddenly he would become violent if crossed by his parents. He gradually became worse. He imagined some big development for himself, such as an important job, then acted the part, swaggering around, talking, and twitching constantly.

Events precipitating his admission to the mental hospital in 1925 included his threatening to kill his parents and his attempts to knock down the house with an axe. He was taken from the jail of a small town, where he was confined for vagrancy (a typical means at the time of sending a patient to a mental hospital), to the hospital. A brief history had been taken by a local doctor, and certificates had been made out at the jail. When the constable delivered C to the hospital he was quiet and cooperative, but was so filthy and verminous that the hospital superintendent was dismayed and protested about the jail and its methods of handcuffing and transporting a sick man in such condition. The amount of time C spent in jail prior to his arrival at the hospital is not known, but he was in poor physical shape and had two small bedsores.

C had auditory hallucinations of voices and whistles at night plus visual hallucinations about people carrying lanterns moving around in the dark. He reported that he felt something strike him in the ribs and back of the neck. When asked about his home, he gave various locations, his speech was confused, his attention wandered, and little things made him laugh. However, he was cooperative, stating that the hospital was a fine place, that he was there for rheumatism and a cure for the pains in his back and neck. He spoke to everyone at great length in a very disconnected manner. In conference he was given a diagnosis of disturbed defective. He was no trouble on the ward and remained well behaved although restless at night. He was placed in the shoe-repair shop where he took some interest in the work. Emotionally he was in a state of elation all the time, talking to others almost continually, but by January, he was back on the ward. The hospital's monthly notes for 1926 indicate that he was physically weak and had foolish conversations that were rambling, cheerful, good humored, and full of often extravagant, unrealistic ideas. Notes for 1927 indicate little change in his condition. He gave the impression of being a "defective" (mentally retarded). In 1928 and 1929 the same situation continued, but in 1930 the notes become fewer. One note indicated a change, describing him as filthy in his habits, continually laughing and talking to himself, disoriented for time, place, and sometimes person as well. He frequently postured, holding out his hands in a peculiar manner and dementia was evident. His face was covered with acne vulgaris. In 1931, entirely uncooperative, filthy, and demented, he was transferred to a bed-care ward, but he did go on walking parties and helped with some light work on the ward. Rosanoff reported his diagnosis at this time as dementia praecox, hebephrenic type.

In 1932, C was observed to have a hugely distended abdomen. When it was learned that he had had no bowel movement for many days, he was operated on for intestinal obstruction. He recovered very well physically. A note later that year (1933) indicated that he would eat rubbish and paper and so had to be carefully watched. At times, abdominal distention was noted; bed care would be used to reduce this. By 1935, he was markedly deteriorated; he could not participate in sensible conversation and would sit or stand around the ward. An abdominal parencetesis was required to draw off fluid. In 1936, C was failing rapidly, running a temperature and exhibiting signs of abdominal infection without remission despite medical and nursing care. Subacute peritonitis was the diagnosis. Mentally there was absolutely no improvement. C died in 1936. A visit by his mother was recorded after his death.

Twin A

A was born in March 1909. At two months of age he was given to an uncle to rear because the parents were too poor to care for A and his twin. The uncle, also a farmer, lived in a community about one hundred miles away from the family farm. Poor roads between the two places limited communication. At seven years of age, A was sent to a church-operated school, where he proved to be clever and progressed well. He stayed out of school a year to work on the farm, then returned for one year of high school. Feeling he had sufficient education, he then returned to farm work and laboring jobs. In 1929, he left the farm to move to another town closer to his mother where he felt he could get work and help her financially (an indication that he knew and had been in touch with his natural parents and siblings). The uncle then heard nothing further from A until his hospitalization in 1930. The uncle reported A to be hard-working, truthful, fond of social activities, with many friends in the community. He added that A did not drink or get into any trouble.

From the records it appears that A was promised a job several times but, when jobs were available, he was not given one, so he obstructed a railway track in retaliation, which led to his arrest. His behavior in jail—he talked constantly, tore up two suits of clothing, was violent and had to be restrained, boasted of fights, swore, and would not reply to questions—led to a certificate for hospitalization. Brought to the hospital from over one hundred miles away, he still was violent and attempted to kick the attendant and destroy furnishings. He was restrained and placed in a continuous bath until the next day, when he was quieter but still tore up clothing and had to be kept in his room. Treatment continued with continuous baths and sodium barbitol. By the end of the month he had quieted down and a history was taken from him. Records indicate that he had had some delusions while in jail and, though his behavior was manic on admission, it had partially calmed down. By the time of the interview, he was indifferent, although he showed occasional peculiar behavior such as smiling to himself or hitting the wall with his fist. He said he had no plans for the future and had a tendency to play tricks and be mischievous with others. The diagnosis was manic depressive, manic reaction. It was felt that he could get along at home if he was supervised, but the family had to be informed about his illness and preparations made for readmission in case of recurrence, which was thought likely. However, the prognosis for the present episode was good. A was placed in occupational therapy doing basketry. In four months his uncle was informed that improvement was such that he could go home. A month later the uncle came for him, and a family history was obtained at that time. A was released on probation, which expired in 1931, when a book discharge was entered.

Readmission took place in 1933. A constable was called to a farm where A was found running around, singing, talking, and laughing. He was still excited when he was brought to the hospital and was extremely filthy, apparently not having had a haircut or bath for weeks. He seemed pleased to be back and greeted staff and patients he remembered. Continuous baths and sedatives were resumed. It seemed that the excited stage had developed about two weeks earlier. A had not slept and roamed around bothering neighbors and getting into trouble. Finally, as the uncle became more alarmed, the constable was called. By the end of a month's hospitalization, A had become quieter and was sleeping fairly well at night, but there was a recurrence of excited behavior. Further exacerbations of similar behavior were noted about every six weeks.

In 1934 A was described as noisy, restless, talking along religious lines, with intervals of quiet behavior between attacks. Continuous baths and paraldehyde were the treatment. Occupational therapy notes for 1935 indicate that A was quiet; his movements were slow, his mood depressed. He did little work but found sufficient energy to run away in November, taking shelter in the local general hospital. The excited phase began again at that time, then diminished. From January until March 1936, he was in an excited manic phase, which subsided in July. He was judged to be sufficiently recovered to leave the hospital at this time, but due to the high probability of relapse, he was kept there. The next note in 1937 indicated that A was again thinking along religious lines. Later he was allowed to go to his uncle's home, but this probation lasted only two weeks. While on leave, he caused considerable annoyance to others with daily visits to priests and relatives. He was returned to the hospital after threatening to burn down buildings. He attempted to run away in June, expressing many religious delusional ideas, and became excited and dirty in his habits. Notes from September 1937 indicate that A was confused at times, stared into space when asked a question, and always asked about going home. A year later a note indicated that he was in excellent physical health, though quiet, preoccupied, and presenting delusional material in conversations. He did some light duties such as floor polishing. When he was transferred to a more open ward in 1939, his behavior was unchanged. A note in 1941 indicated a depressive phase, with tube feeding required for a few days. In August 1941 a manic phase reappeared: A was excited and talkative, mostly about religious matters. This lasted about two weeks. In September hyperactivity and unclean habits were again noted, but by October, A was much improved and treatments in use at the time were discontinued. He was now a good worker on the wards.

In October 1942 A was described as schizophrenic, requiring supervision because of his inability to pay attention to things. He usually was preoccupied, grinning and smiling inappropriately, and he enjoyed being called "Father" because of his delusion about being a priest. In August 1943 he was hallucinating, disorganized, and disconnected in conversation. In April 1944 he was again noted to be excited, euphoric, restless, and was treated with mild sedatives.

In May 1943 A had a hernia repair and was slightly euphoric. In September 1945 he was in a state of considerable excitement, which continued until January 1946. By May 1946 he was again slow, quiet, and seldom spoke but assisted with ward work. In July 1946 he was taking part in sports programs, but in December he was again excited and talkative. This phase lasted until sometime in February or March 1947.

In April 1947 he was quiet, smiling to himself. The next note was in February 1948, when A was again in a manic stage that lasted until April, but in May he again was very quiet and slow, assisting with light duties. The notes indicate that A had recurring excited spells but was a good worker when well. Notes in the chart continue in the same manner. It is difficult to know from them how long the excited spells lasted. Apparently records were made only when A was disturbed. In 1954 A was noted as being cooperative in spite of his incoherent conversation. The treatment now was two ECT which promptly ended each manic attack. He was regularly employed in the laundry. In 1962 he complained of chest pain, which was diagnosed as a myocardial infarction. Treatment for hypertension was begun plus Mellaril and Diaril, with continued light duties. Mellaril appeared to control his behavior satisfactorily. The diagnosis now was manic-depressive. The last attack noted, the excited stage, was in 1958. One hundred mg. Mellaril q.h.s. provided control. A was neat, tidy, and physically well with no delusions or hallucinations. In 1966 he was sent to a community home where, still on Mellaril, he remained in stable condition to the time this summary was written.

Twin B

B was born in March 1909. His early years were spent on the family farm. He went to school at age six (after the family left the farm) but did not like school and left at age thirteen (approximately grade seven, so his progress was normal). At age fourteen he was working at mills in the vicinity as a laborer or in the woods at lumbering operations. Rosanoff described him as always having been somewhat unstable and never having held a job for long.

At age twenty-one B lost a job and a few weeks later attacked a man for no apparent reason, so he was placed in jail and charged with vagrancy. There he was very filthy in his habits. He tore up all his clothing and went naked, was irritable and combative with guards, and expressed religious ideas. (Rosanoff described the ideas as a belief that B's hometown was somehow connected with Noah's Ark. In early 1930 he began to roam the countryside searching for the Garden of Eden and assaulted those who contradicted him.) After being seen by two physicians, B was certified. He was brought to the hospital, handcuffed and disheveled, by a driver and two guards with whom he fought all the way over one hundred miles of poor roads. He was admitted in 1930, about ten weeks after twin A. He exhibited much the same behavior as his twin. He could converse on arrival, was noted to be properly oriented with his memory intact, but had disconnected thoughts and ideas, with religious concepts, was overactive, making religious signs with his hands, and was cheerful and euphoric. He could not remember the jail. In conference, he was diagnosed manic depressive, manic phase. Notes taken at the time of the conference indicate that he now remembered jail and described events there. Considerable nervous tension was observed. He was quite disturbed on the ward, attempting to strike others, and he had to be placed in continuous baths. This treatment continued until August, when he was allowed to get up and dressed and be on the ward. His wages had been the main support to his family, and he and twin A had combined their salaries to pay off debts. It was suggested that having his two brothers ill in the hospital was too much of a strain, resulting in an acute maladjustment in B very similar to that of his brothers. The notes indicate a typical manic state. He had a room by himself, which was as disheveled as he was. He continually talked, laughed, swore, and often repeated words and phrases. He was overactive, distracted, jumped over furniture, and made religious signs. His habits were very filthy. By mid-September he was quite and sensible. He also daydreamed, was dejected, depressed, and said little. He cried several times but a few days later became excited again. In November he was physically ill with a high temperature and was very difficult to examine since he would not cooperate. The excited phase continued throughout the illness. By December he was quiet. Notes cease abruptly, with a brief note in 1931 stating that he was discharged from probation in August.

In 1933 he was returned,[5] again by a constable and again in an excited, unstable, unkempt state, as on his first admission. For a few days B was quiet, then on September 1 he became violently excited and continuous baths were prescribed. A series of excited phases followed, each of about ten-days duration, with a few days of quiet behavior between each episode.

In 1934 a note indicates that B was quiet and lacked energy to work although he answered questions relevantly and intelligently. Later in the same month that the note was entered on his depressed period, he was again overactive and excited. Continuous bath treatment was instituted. During 1934 the excited spells lasted three weeks, after which there would be a period of retardation of movement and disinterest in things. A number of notes about excited spells appear throughout 1935 and 1936. There were six such notes in 1937 but only one in 1938. A January 1941 note stated that B lay in bed depressed, not speaking to anyone, refusing food for some days, and had shown no mental improvement for a long time. This depression lasted until March of that year. By September he assisted with minor ward duties in a slow manner. In March 1942 he was noted to be a good, steady worker when well and would remain at a monotonous task for hours, but he was kept to ward work, not outside activities. He ran away in April 1942 at night. A careful search did not locate him anywhere in the hospital, on the grounds, or in nearby areas. His body was found later. The cause of death was not given exactly but probably was exposure.

Additional Information

In 1934 twins A and B (but not their brother C) were given an intelligence test, the early form of the Stanford edition of the Binet-Simon. B was found to be cooperative and willing. His IQ was given as 66, but this particular test was designed for educational use and has levels up to fourteen years, then average adult. Intelligence was calculated by using a chronological age of sixteen years as the maximum. A person under sixteen could achieve an IQ of over 100 by correctly answering some of the items above his age level. A sixteen-year-old with a perfect score would have an IQ of 100. Anyone sixteen or over who failed any items would have a score of less than 100. There were no norms or adjustments for age at this stage of the test's development. A primitive correction by taking fifteen as the maximum would adjust B's IQ of 66 to 73. Given that the patient was disabled by his mental illness to some

5. Seven weeks after his twin.

extent, it seems likely that his intelligence would have been higher than this normally, so no suggestion of mental retardation can be made.

A, tested at the same time, was noted to be persistent, willing, and attentive. Using sixteen as the maximum age, his IQ was calculated to be 84; corrected to fifteen years, the result would have been 95. A did better at school but he also had much greater opportunity for education and better circumstances in his home, so he would be expected to have better performance, all else being equal.[6]

6. Dr. Craig and I both agree that the test scores should best be disregarded.

Appendix B

Case 310:
Twins *A* and *B*[1]

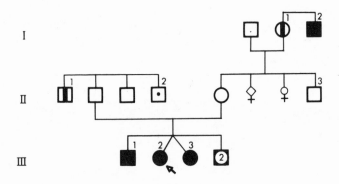

Pedigree

    I-1 died in psychotic state
    I-2 chronic schizophrenia
    II-1 transient psychotic episode
    II-2 committed suicide
    III-1 died in chronic schizophrenic state
    III-2 proband (*A*)
    III-3 co-twin (*B*)
Zygosity determination: *A* and *B*: B, MN, CDe, Secretor, ear wax (d), PTC (+), MDH (−), fingerprint (conc.). Pr (MZ)> 0.987

---

1. Information for this case history was provided by Dr. E. Inouye of the University of Tokyo School of Medicine. His informants were two hospitals and twin *B*. The case is number MZ4138 in his 1972 listing and appears to be case number 10 in Mitsuda's (1967) series.

Birth

A and *B* were female twins born in K. city on November 15, 1925. *A*, the firstborn, weighed less than *B*. Both were forceps deliveries.

Life History

At age seven days, *A* was separated from her biological parents to be raised by adoptive parents. Her adoptive father, a carpenter, was a stiff man who loved *A*, but, nonetheless, she felt constraint. The family economic state was bad. At age thirteen, *A* left senior primary school and got a job with a spinning factory. At age nineteen (September 1945), she changed her job. At age twenty-two (February 1948), she entered into an illegal marriage. She hated her husband because of his venereal disease, and they were divorced after two months. After that, she developed mysophobia.

B was reared by her biological parents. The family economic state was good and her biological parents were indulgent towards *B*. At age sixteen (March 1942) she graduated from a supplementary course of senior primary school. At age eighteen (1943), she got a job with a bank. At age twenty (August 1945), she resigned from the bank and stayed at home. At age twenty-four (February 1950) her father died, and in 1952 her mother died.

The Twin Relationship

A first lived one hundred meters away from *B*'s home. It is possible they met once a month during their early years. Later, at an unknown age, *A* moved to a more remote place. *A* and *B* were regarded as cousins. *A* knew of her twinship at age seven, *B* at age ten.

Premorbid Personality

A was asociable, nervous, obsessive, mysophobic, and more introverted than *B*. *B* was asociable, nervous, introverted, and more obsessive than *A*. *B* also was irritable, egocentric, mysophobic, and possibly sexually phantastic.

History of Schizophrenic Psychosis

At age twenty-seven (November 1952), *A* suffered from insomnia, was mutistic, autistic, abulic, negativistic, and had ideas of reference. She visited a university hospital. She was admitted to a mental hospital in June 1954. The diagnosis was depression. She was incoherent and suffered from hallucinations. Occasionally she was excited and sang, cried, and walked around. She exhibited a tendency toward homosexuality. She received seventeen electric shock treatments. She was interviewed at age thirty (November 1955 and March 1956). At age thirty-two (October 1958) she was interviewed again. At the time of interview, she was in a stupor with moderate to marked deterioration. At age thirty-six (August 1962), she was interviewed again. She appeared stiff, her symptoms fluctuated, she had occasional guilt feelings, hallucinations, and homosexual tendencies, but there was a slight improvement. In February 1966 at age forty, another interview found that she was in a hebephrenic state with catatonic features. There was a thought disorder, echo symptoms, and moderate to marked deterioration.

At age twenty, B suffered from insomnia. At age twenty-two (February 1948), it is possible that she was occasionally emotionally unstable. In 1949 (age twenty-three) she was occasionally irritable. By February 1950 (age twenty-four), B was abulic, expressed suicidal ideas, cried, had ideas of reference, hallucinations, "passivity phenomena," felt depersonalized, and had other ego disturbances. She felt sexually "neutralized." Gradually, she improved without treatment. At age twenty-seven (March 1953), B entered into an illegal marriage but was divorced after six months. She had an abortion because her husband was not working and was found to have a criminal record. At age twenty-eight (November 1953), she worked at a thread and yarn shop for four months, then worked as a hotel maid. Her mental state continued to improve. B was interviewed at age thirty (November 1955 and March 1956) and again at age thirty-two (October 1958). The latter interview indicated slight deterioration. Final information was obtained when she was thirty-nine (September 1965). It was learned that she changed jobs often.

Diagnosis

    A—chronic progressive schizophrenia
    B—chronic mild or transient schizophrenia

Appendix C

Case 340:
Twins *A* and *B*[1]

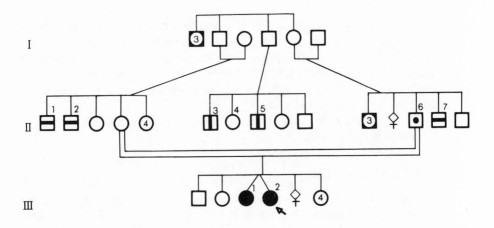

Pedigree

II-1,2 childhood convulsions
II-3, 5 psychotic (general paresis?)
II-4 adoptive mother of B
II-6 father, alcoholic
II-7 childhood convulsions with loss of consciousness until age six or seven
III-1 co-twin (*A*)
III-2 proband (*B*)

1. Information for this case history was provided by Dr. E. Inouye of the University of Tokyo School of Medicine. His informants were the biological parents, a brother, *B*'s adoptive mother, teachers at *A*'s primary school and *B*'s junior high school, and two hospitals. The case is number MZ4192 in his 1972 listing, and appears to be case number 9 in Mitsuda's (1967) series.

Zygosity determination: *A* and *B*: B, MN, p. Secretor, ear wax (d), PTC
(+), MDH (−), fingerprint (conc.). Pr (MZ)>0.973

Birth

A and *B* were female twins born August 29, 1937. *A* was the firstborn
and weighed 1500 grams. *B* weighed 1300 grams.

Illnesses

A's development was better than *B*'s. *A* had measles at age seven, *B* at
age eight. At age 12, *A* had left otitis media while *B* reported the same
at age six. Until age twelve, *B* had convulsions followed by fever, one
to three times a year (though this was denied by her father). *B* also had
acute pneumonia at age ten.

Life History

At age two years eight months, *B* was separated from her biological
parents and sent to be raised by adoptive parents. The adoptive mother
hated *B*. After the death of her adoptive father (when *B* was nine), *B*
quarreled frequently with her adoptive mother. At age fifteen, *B*
graduated from junior high school. The family was poverty-stricken
after the adoptive father's death.

No information is available on *A*'s family. She graduated from high
school at age eighteen.

The Twin Relationship

A and *B* were born in a small harbor town. *B* moved to K. city after
her adoption. *B* visited *A* once or twice a year while they were young.
In the summer she stayed about ten days to swim in the sea. *B* knew of
her adoption at age fifteen and of her twinship at age seventeen. There
is no information on *A*'s awareness of being a twin.

Premorbid Personality

A and *B* were both reserved and shy. *A* was stubborn, hot-tempered,
and sensitive. *B* was cranky, selfish, and cynical. At age eleven, *A*'s IQ
was 94; at age twelve, 90. *B*'s IQ was 106 at age twelve.

History of Schizophrenic Psychosis

At age sixteen (during the fall and winter of 1953), *A* complained of
insomnia and fatigue. She became anxious for five days and was prescribed sleeping pills. Menarche occurred later that year (February

1954). At age seventeen (July–August 1955) and on one other occasion, she had similar episodes of anxiety. After graduation from senior high school at age eighteen, A moved to Tokyo (March 1956). In April of that year she entered a dressmaking school. She soon became mutistic, abulic, refused food, suffered from insomnia, had ideas of reference, was hypochondriacal, possibly carried on monologues, and displayed "autochthones Denken." She visited a psychiatric clinic and was diagnosed as catatonic. She exhibited lack of facial expression, incoherence, blocking of thoughts, anxiety, auditory hallucinations, "gedankenver-standenwerden," and lack of insight. She received eight electric shock treatments. She was interviewed at age nineteen (July 1957) and still was autistic, reticent, and sensitive. There was a slight deterioration in her condition.

At age twelve (April 1950), B entered junior high school. She complained of occasional headaches. At age fourteen, in the fall of 1951, she was excited, hypocondriacal, had a fear of death, complained of ascariasis, and had an occasional fever and convulsions. She improved after three months. Menarche occurred in August 1952. From that time, she was occasionally excited and danced and sang. It is possible that she had a sexual trauma. After graduation from junior high, she changed jobs often. At the age of eighteen (September 1955), she became excited during menstruation and complained of loneliness. It is possible that a boyfriend proposed to her at this time. Two months later (November 1955), she may have quarreled with her adoptive mother. She left home, went to A's house, and stayed for a week. One month later (December 1955), she became excited, cried, walked around, and had ideas of reference after a night when she may have been drinking. In January 1956 she was excited again. In February 1956, she went to Tokyo and visited a psychiatric clinic complaining of headache and insomnia. She was diagnosed as hebephrenic. She suffered from abnormal body sensations, feelings of telepathy, and had auditory hallucinations and "passivity phenomena." She received one ECT, went back home, but was admitted to a university hospital in K. city where she was diagnosed as "Degenerationspsychose." She was heboid, impulsive, showed "pseudologisch," and had a fear of death. During the admission, A visited B at the hospital. B was discharged after a twenty-day stay. Soon B visited A's home, where she quarreled with, harassed, and was negativistic toward her grandmother. It is possible that she once became sexually uncontrolled. She was interviewed three times at age nineteen (April to July 1957) and still was autistic, abulic, heboid, negativistic, "verschroben und gehoben." There was a slight deterioration in her condition.

Diagnosis: A and B—relapsing schizophrenia

Appendix D

Case 404: Twins *A* and *B*[1]

Mother:	age 24 at twins' birth
Father	age 35 at twins' birth
Siblings:	female, 7 years older
	female, 5 years older
	female, 2 years older
	A and *B*
	female, 1 year younger
	male, 2 years younger
	female, 7 years younger
Half-sibs:	male, 14 years younger
	female, 15 years younger
(by mother)	

Birth

A and *B*, females, were born at home. The attending physician pronounced them to be "identical." Birth order or weights are unknown, and complications were not mentioned. In subsequent hospitalizations physicians pronounced the twins "monozygotic" without giving specifics of evaluation in the written record. All those who came in contact with the twins viewed them as identical, with the exception of one social worker in *B*'s late adolescence who was zealously protective of her separation from her sister, then hospitalized, and who kept trying to

---

1. Dr. John Rainer of the New York State Psychiatric Institute provided the file of raw data used in the Kallmann and Roth (1956) study of these twins and subsequently checked the accuracy of the report given here.

find ways to emphasize differences without ever specifying them. Though zygosity diagnosis is not unambiguous, the weight of evidence strongly suggests them to be identical.

Separation

The children lived with their parents and siblings until age five, when the home was broken up due to the father's desertion. The children were placed in a series of foster homes. It is unclear if the twins were placed together or separately, or at what times they may have been together or separate. At approximately age fourteen (not later, likely to have been thirteen) A was placed in a residential home following two unsuccessful foster placements. At this point she clearly was separated from her sister, though the number of foster placements for A prior to this suggests some degree of separation in the period from age five to thirteen. Kallmann's formal investigation began when the twins were fifteen and continued until they were eighteen. They did not live together from age thirteen or fourteen through eighteen, when the last contact is recorded. They appear to have had some type of at least minimal contact during this period, however, for they were aware of each other's vicissitudes.

Family Background

Their mother and father were first cousins. The mother's first recorded pregnancy occurred when she was sixteen and the father twenty-seven. The mother disclaimed any history of mental illness in family and background. Psychiatrists who took a history from her when the twins were fifteen made no note of any remarkable features in her behavior or reporting. The father was said to have been a drunkard and violent. By the time the twins were five he had become excessively abusive and had deserted the family, though evidently only temporarily. Throughout the twins' life, the family appears to have been on relief. The mother reported their religion as "Protestant," but no overtly religious themes are noted in the record.

History of A[2]

A and her sister were born at home and, as the family was large and on relief, there sometimes was not enough to eat, though the mother recalled that the children always had a good appetite. A had several illnesses in childhood, including a severe asthmatic attack requiring hos-

2. Information on history is taken primarily from psychiatric interviews with the mother when A was an inpatient at age fifteen. Some material also seems to come from A herself and from child-care workers who had contact with her.

APPENDIX D

pitalization when she was less than a year old and pneumonia when she was about two years old. The latter required a stay in the hospital and left her with crossed eyes. In subsequent years (ages not given) she had several operations to correct this, and note is made of an operation at age five to remove a cyst from her eye. As an adolescent, A expressed a good deal of worry that her eyes were going bad.

Other than this, the mother could recall no problem from A's early life. She specifically ruled out temper tantrums, enuresis, and nightmares. Asthma was not mentioned by mother or physicians as occurring past the episode in infancy.

At age fifteen, when A was admitted to a psychiatric ward, she included persistent right lower quadrant pain among her many complaints and, after nine weeks was transferred to a medical ward for work-up on suspicion of appendicitis. The physical examination was negative except for strabismus in the right eye: urine was negative, blood count negative, and Wassermann negative.

At age eighteen and one-half, after being in a family-care home for over a year, A was reported to be in excellent health with regular menstrual periods. Height at this age: 5 feet 2 inches; weight: 124 pounds.

In the years prior to age five, the mother reported A to have been the passive twin, always taking the back seat to her sister. She was especially generous to her sister and never made a fuss about things. The mother felt that the children got little attention from their father since he usually came home intoxicated and abused them. A, as the youngest, was "blamed for many things and punished unduly." The mother reported that A still remembered several of these incidents and whenever she saw her father, she became angry and mentioned them to him.

At age five, the father's abuse and desertion led to the children being placed in foster homes. Since A had always been so much the passive twin, the mother was surprised when she seemed to take this harder than any of the other children. A was always sad when her mother visited, becoming more upset when the mother had to leave. Despite this, the mother felt that A had always seemed good-natured and close to her twin, although with a good many other friends. She felt that A had a very affectionate nature and seemed to require a great deal of affection. Nonetheless, she added that A had a fierce temper and was practically uncontrollable when angry.[3]

When A was thirteen or fourteen she was placed in a residential home following two unsuccessful foster placements. At this point she was said to have only two friends, a social worker and a four-year-old blind girl. Just before A's fifteenth birthday and about six weeks prior to hospitalization, the social worker got married and A became depressed, anorexic, fearful, restless, and subject to nightmares. She be-

3. Compare this to the mother's denial of temper tantrums, at least in early childhood.

gan to hear voices when alone and, at age fifteen years one month, was admitted to a psychiatric hospital on a certified basis.

Hospitalization: On admission *A* was violently resistive, screaming and claiming that she heard voices. She had to be kept in restraint. She was a continuous management problem, abusive, demanding, boister-ous, and impulsive. She received six electric shock treatments without significant change. Her affect was at all times appropriate. She related well to many of the personnel in the hospital. After six weeks there was no improvement and she was transferred to the state psychiatric hospital.

On admission to the state hospital, she quieted down within twenty-four hours, seeming subdued and sad but still with occasional attacks of provocative, impulsive behavior. She reported that while still at the residential home, she had had a bad dream in which the little blind girl appeared and told her bad things about herself and her family. The lit-tle girl had said that people were going to kill her family and so forth. *A* complained of hearing voices from some time around and subse-quent to this dream, but the staff of the home had considered her to be acting. She had been unable to sleep because of bad dreams.

Four days after admission, after she had quieted somewhat more, the mental examination was reported as follows:

Cooperative with the examiner and related well. Her stream of mental activity showed no disorder, she was always relevant and coherent with logical pro-gression. Her emotional reaction was that of a lively young adolescent, always understandable and appropriate. She was often cheerful, laughing spontane-ously, and yet at other times she showed self-pity, and at still other times a hos-tility. Underneath was an affect of sadness and resignation. Her mental trend included visual and auditory hallucinations, which *A* stated bothered her al-most constantly. She also expressed concern with her impulsive, uncontrolla-ble behavior. She discussed her difficult life situation, her hatred and distrust of men, and her inability to trust anyone. *A*'s expression of a desire for secure human relationships and her disappointment in them seemed very persuasive and sincere. Her sensorium and intellectual functions seemed to be intact.

In the hospital she soon quieted and was able to be in the ward. Re-ports described her as a lively young adolescent, obviously in good contact but still full of hostility and mistrust, clearly searching for some kind of security and approval. She soon claimed that the hallucinations were merely her own inventions in order to obtain attention. (Staff at both hospital and residential center had always been of mixed opinion in their reactions to the hallucinations.) She said all her troubles start-ed when her social worker got married and she felt deserted. She seemed to have a good superficial insight into the causes of her upset but she stated that she seemed to have no control over her periods of hyperactivity.

She continued to show occasional temper tantrums and childish demanding behavior, and constantly expected special considerations. She continued to complain of not sleeping well and felt very badly. Right lower quadrant pain was persistently mentioned. After three weeks she was transferred to a medical ward, where examination was negative.

Psychological testing indicated above-average IQ, good contact with reality, and "strong ego." There were many malignant responses in the record that the tester reported as pointing to a schizoid pattern, but the tester felt the patient seemed to be functioning on a compensated "neurotic" level.

Two years after her initial hospitalization she was placed in a family-care home. One year after this placement, when she was eighteen and one-half, she was reported to be in school, physically healthy, holding a part-time job, and "happy to be away from her twin."

History of B[4]

B was born at home and, as with A, grew up in an environment where the father was drunk and abusive and where sufficient food was not always available. The mother's reference to A receiving the brunt of the father's aggression "because she was the youngest" suggests that B was less abused and raises the possibility of her being the firstborn. She was not reported as having an asthmatic attack, nor is there any record of asthma. However, at age two she and her sister had to be hospitalized for pneumonia and, like her sister, she was left with crossed eyes. No mention of subsequent operations or cysts is made, but this may be an omission.

In the years prior to age five, B seems to have been the more active, assertive twin. The mother said she had a good appetite, "not many problems" in early life, and no enuresis, temper tantrums, or nightmares. When the children were placed in foster homes at age five, B seems to have shown less overt upset and clinging than A. It is not stated whether the twins were placed together or separately.

By age thirteen to fourteen, the twins appear definitely to have been separated. A went to a residential home; B's location was indicated only as "somewhere else." B's initial response to A's hospitalization during this period is unknown.

A few weeks prior to B's sixteenth birthday (when A was in the state hospital), the investigators attempted to make contact. B's social worker refused to allow her to be seen and offered only the following information: "Both are cross-eyed and show some facial resemblance and can be told easily apart and are definitely dissimilar in personality."

By the time B was eighteen and one-half the content of the social

4. Information on B is taken from the mother's report when A was hospitalized and from what could be gleaned from child-care workers on her case.

worker's report changed though the tone of seeing B as "not sick" re-mained the same. The report states: "B is imitating the behavior of A in every respect in order to be admitted to the hospital to be given to a foster home from there." (It should be noted that the "imitation," if such it was, was of A's behaviors of three and one-half years earlier, not of A's adjusted behavior reported from her family-care placement at this age.) Further contact was made difficult, and later events are not reported in the record.

Summary

A and B were the fourth and fifth births to parents who produced eight children in fairly rapid succession, and two additional half-sibs by the mother when the twins were in adolescence. The girls were pro-nounced identical at birth by the attending physician, and the family and physicians who had contact with them subsequently continued to evaluate them as MZ without stating criteria. The one exception to this evaluation was B's social worker, who insisted on B's differences from her twin, who was at that time committed to the state psychiatric hos-pital. Although zygosity determination is far from unambiguous, the weight of evidence by the similarity method suggests monozygosity.

The separation of the twins took place, at the earliest, at five years, and with any certainty at about thirteen to fourteen years. At the time of Kallmann's investigations, with the literature as sparse as it was, this was sufficient to allow the girls to be reported as "separated" twins without much further elaboration. In the present literature, and with more stringent criteria for separation, the case falls into the least sepa-rated group (my 400 category).

Keeping this in mind, the following points appear salient from the history. The twins were the product of mating between first cousins. Familial mental illness was denied by the mother, but the environment was chaotic and the father was alcoholic and prone to violence, particu-larly against A, the twin who first displayed overt signs of psychiatric disorder. Given that the twins were reared together in this environ-ment for the first five years of their life, it seems that some differential attitudes existed toward them, particularly if A was indeed the youn-ger, passive member of the set.

The medical histories are similar, with A having had somewhat more illnesses as an infant, but with both showing the unique pattern of pneumonia at age two with crossed eyes as a sequela.

The children lived in a series of foster homes from age five, and A developed her first flagrant psychiatric symptoms at age fifteen in di-rect response to loss of a significant adult in her environment. B began showing identical symptoms at age eighteen and one-half, when the twins were not in direct contact and when A was recompensated. It is interesting that, for both girls, the response of the environment was to question the authenticity of deep pathology in the symptoms, including hallucinations, reported by the girls. *A* was thought to be "just acting" and *B* later was said to be "manipulating." Even though the reader, like some of those who had contact with the girls at the time, may remain unconvinced of an ongoing schizophrenic process, the similarity of the reported symptomology *and* the mixed response of the caretakers are suggestive of similarity in signals emitted by the girls that led to similar bafflement in the response of persons directly dealing with them.

Further evaluation of the case, including the role of potential pathological mourning reactions to the loss of a twin, other sibs, and parents, is left to those who evaluate twin-reared-together material.

Appendix E[1]

Statistical Analysis of IQ Data from Identical Twins Reared Apart

Selection and Construction of Measures of IQ

In most of the studies of identical twins reared apart there were administrations of multiple tests of intellectual ability, sometimes on more than one occasion. In order to combine the data from these studies, an equivalent measure of IQ had to be found. The first section of this technical appendix describes the measures of IQ selected or developed for each sample.

Newman, Freeman, and Holzinger

As stated in chapter 7, we chose the Stanford-Binet score to serve as the measure of IQ for Newman et al.'s nineteen twin pairs. The scores were taken from the tables presented in the case studies found in their

1. Prepared by Noel Dunivant, Ph.D., New York University, New York, New York and National Center for State Courts, Williamsburg, Virginia.

book. McNemar (1938) suggested that the scores should be adjusted for age differences. He and Jencks et al. (1972) reported results of analyses of Newman et al.'s data with IQ scores adjusted to control for age effects. Rather than making age corrections to the Stanford-Binet scores initially, we decided to delay our evaluation of age differences until the combined sample had been formed. (It emerged later that age effects proved to be minimal or nonexistent, and age corrections were not made.) The Stanford-Binet IQ scores from Newman et al.'s sample are presented in table E1.

Shields

Because of the limited time available to test each twin, Shields used two brief tests of mental ability: The synonyms section of the Mill Hill Vocabulary Test, and the Dominoes Test. Unfortunately, a reliable IQ conversion has not been established for either of these tests. Indeed, Shields (1978) argued that his Mill Hill and Dominoes scores could not be accurately transformed into an IQ metric. Most previous investigators, e.g., Jensen (1970), have performed a linear transformation of the raw scores using the standard psychometric formula (Magnusson, 1966). There are two problems with this approach. First, to our knowledge, estimates of the population standard deviations from normative samples have not been published, and second, the test manual indicates that mean (median) performance varies greatly as a function of age. The former problem leads one to create transformed scores which are forced to have a standard deviation of 15 points. This eliminates one's ability to test for variance differences between samples and can adversely affect components of variance (and heritabilities) estimation using pooled data. The second problem causes gross inaccuracies in estimating IQ scores in age heterogeneous samples when the general population mean is employed in the conversion formula. To illustrate: Shields's sample spanned an age range from eight to fifty-nine. A raw score of 40 on the Mill Hill represents an IQ of 100 for a fifteen-year-old. However, the same score translates into an IQ of 90 for someone fifty-five years of age. This situation can also cause problems for heritability estimation in age heterogeneous samples.

In an effort to deal with these potential problems, we converted the raw Mill Hill synonyms and Dominoes scores to IQs as follows: For the Mill Hill we entered the raw synonyms score (plus 10 for all except those who had been administered the Junior Form) into Tables III and IV (page 10) of the 1950 version of the test manual; we then read off or interpolated an expected total score. Using the twin's age and expected total score we obtained a percentile from Table 2 in Peck's paper (1970). Finally, an IQ equivalent to the percentile was found in Peck's Table 3. The interested reader will find these IQ scores, as well as the raw scores

TABLE E1
Newman, Freeman, and Holzinger twin data

PAIRID	TWIN	SEX	SBIQ
118	A	1	99
118	B	1	101
120	A	2	85
120	B	2	84
124	A	2	92
124	B	2	116
142	A	1	94
142	B	1	95
144	A	1	105
144	B	1	106
150	A	2	92
150	B	2	77
152	A	2	122
152	B	2	127
154	A	1	96
154	B	1	77
158	A	2	89
158	B	2	93
160	A	2	116
160	B	2	109
162	A	1	115
162	B	1	105
164	A	2	90
164	B	2	88
182	A	1	91
182	B	1	90
208	A	2	66
208	B	2	78
210	A	2	85
210	B	2	97
244	A	2	102
244	B	2	94
318	A	2	89
318	B	2	106
320	A	1	102
320	B	1	96
408	A	2	88
408	B	2	79

List of Variables

Variable	Label
PAIRID	Twin Pair Identification Number
TWIN	Individual Member of Twin Pair
SEX	Sex of Twin Pair
SBIQ	Stanford-Binet IQ Score

TABLE E2
Shields Twin Data

PAIRID	TWIN	SEX	RAWMH	FDMHIQ	RAWDOM	FDDOMIQ	MEANFDIQ
110	A	2	14	89	27	98	94
110	B	2	13	88	24	93	91
112	A	2	25	114	35	112	113
112	B	2	26	115	30	103	109
126	A	1	14	95	30	103	99
126	B	1	6	81	23	91	86
128	A	2	24	110	32	107	109
128	B	2	16	93	18	83	88
132	A	2	9	88	12	72	80
132	B	2	7	87	9	67	77
136	A	2	14	89	28	100	95
136	B	2	8	82	16	79	81
148	A	2	21	102	33	109	106
148	B	2	14	89	24	93	91
172	A	2	20	99	33	109	104
172	B	2	22	106	32	107	107
174	A	1	10	85	•	•	85
174	B	1	10	85	•	•	85
176	A	1	11	90	10	69	80
176	B	1	6	81	13	74	78
190	A	1	13	88	24	93	91
190	B	1	11	86	20	86	86
214	A	2	13	89	4	58	74
214	B	2	7	84	2	55	70
216	A	2	27	118	41	123	121
216	B	2	28	122	40	121	122
218	A	2	13	89	32	107	98
218	B	2	17	94	28	100	97
220	A	1	15	91	26	97	94
220	B	1	7	82	17	81	82
224	A	2	15	91	23	91	91
224	B	2	11	86	21	88	87
228	A	1	21	103	26	97	100
228	B	1	14	90	20	86	88
230	A	2	25	114	38	117	116
230	B	2	22	106	27	98	102
236	A	1	19	96	22	90	93
236	B	1	19	96	12	72	84
238	A	2	11	100	23	91	96
238	B	2	12	103	21	88	96
246	A	1	22	106	26	97	102
246	B	1	25	114	30	103	109
302	A	1	11	95	36	114	105
302	B	1	15	104	34	110	107
304	A	2	19	98	30	103	101
304	B	2	21	102	34	110	106

TABLE E2 *(continued)*
Shields Twin Data

PAIRID	TWIN	SEX	RAWMH	FDMHIQ	RAWDOM	FDDOMIQ	MEANFDIQ
306	A	2	20	99	27	98	99
306	B	2	17	94	25	95	95
308	A	1	22	106	35	112	109
308	B	1	17	94	29	102	98
312	A	2	14	89	33	109	99
312	B	2	16	93	26	97	95
314	A	2	12	88	19	84	86
314	B	2	6	82	9	67	75
322	A	1	10	85	25	95	90
322	B	1	5	76	30	103	90
324	A	1	20	99	32	107	103
324	B	1	23	107	28	100	104
328	A	1	10	87	4	58	73
328	B	1	6	82	13	74	78
334	A	1	22	106	22	90	98
334	B	1	25	114	28	100	107
336	A	1	19	99	27	98	99
336	B	1	21	103	21	88	96
338*	A	2	17	94	•	•	111
338*	B	2	11	86	•	•	92
342	A	2	17	95	40	121	108
342	B	2	21	103	38	117	110
344	A	2	19	98	9	67	83
344	B	2	19	98	15	77	88
350	A	2	12	90	13	74	82
350	B	2	10	89	22	90	90
352	A	2	14	89	10	69	79
352	B	2	14	89	6	62	76
410	A	2	11	86	22	90	88
410	B	2	10	85	23	91	88
416	A	2	19	98	27	98	98
416	B	2	16	93	28	100	97
422	A	2	23	110	29	102	106
422	B	2	23	110	30	103	107

*MEANFDIQ is WAIS full-scale IQ obtained at age 52.

List of Variables

Variable	Label
PAIRID	Twin Pair Identification Number
TWIN	Individual Member of Twin Pair
SEX	Sex of Twin Pair
RAWMH	Raw Mill Hill Vocabulary Score
FDMHIQ	Farber-Dunivant Mill Hill IQ Score
RAWDOM	Raw Dominoes Score
FDDOMIQ	Farber-Dunivant Dominoes IQ Score
MEANFDIQ	Mean Farber-Dunivant Mill Hill–Dominoes IQ Score
•	Missing Values

(plus 10 as appropriate) in Table 2, labelled FDMHIQ (Farber-Dunivant Mill Hill IQ). In order to convert the Dominoes scores to IQs, we used the percentiles provided in the test manual used by Shields (these are presented in chapter 7) to estimate the population standard deviation. Assuming that the Dominoes raw score follows a normal distribution, an optimal estimate of its standard deviation is 8.62 (this does not differ substantially from the sample sigma of 9.2 that Jensen used in his conversion). The population mean is 28; thus, our IQ conversion formula was

$$\text{FDDOMIQ} = (15 \div 8.62)\,(\text{RAWDOM} - 28) + 100.$$

See table E 2 for the raw and transformed scores. Of course, if mean Dominoes performance varies as a function of age, then this linear transformation is subject to the same difficulties identified above.

Having constructed two IQ scores for each twin, we now confronted the problem of combining them to form a "full-scale" IQ score. Given the content of the two tests, it is reasonable to think of this as combining verbal and performance scores as is done with the WAIS. However, here we met an insoluble problem since there are no norms or percentiles available for combined Mill Hill and Dominoes scores. The most obvious method is simply to average the two IQ scores as Jensen (1970) did in his analysis of these data. However, if both of the component scores have standard deviations of 15, the standard deviation of the average of the component scores will equal 15 only under very limited circumstances. While we could have arbitrarily fixed the standard deviation at 15 for the combined Mill Hill-Dominoes IQ score, we opted instead to form the composite IQ score as the mean of FDMHIQ and FDDOMIQ; this appears in table E 2 as MEANFDIQ.[2] The question of the psychometric efficacy of combing these verbal and performance scores will be deferred until we consider the same issue with respect to Juel-Nielsen's WAIS scores.

Juel-Nielsen

The text discusses problems associated with Juel-Nielsen's use of a Danish version of the WAIS. In this section we take up the problems of choosing an IQ score when test and retest scores are available and of

2. We performed some exploratory analyses with a combined Mill Hill and Dominoes IQ score that was constructed to have a standard deviation of 15 for each sex. These IQ scores were generally more extreme (in terms of distance above and below the mean) and their distributions exhibited greater nonnormality than the MEAN FDIQ scores. The correlation between the two types of composite IQ was very high and it seems unlikely that they would perform differently in the types of linear models analyses we conducted later. For this reason, and because it is highly questionable that Shields's male and female samples were drawn from a population with a standard deviation of 15, we selected the mean of the Mill Hill and Dominoes IQ scores as the measure of full-scale IQ.

combining verbal and performance scores. Since the ultimate objective of this research was to pool the IQ scores from the various samples, we wanted to choose a test or retest score (or their average) as a twin's IQ measure that would be comparable with the scores from other samples. While the mean of the test and retest scores will usually be more reliable than either of the tests used individually, there may be a practice effect so that the second test and, to some extent, the mean will not be equivalent to the tests in the samples that were administered only once. This is precisely the result that was found when we evaluated the significance of the difference between the test and retest means for the verbal, performance, and full-scale IQ scores in Juel-Nielsen's sample. (See table E3). These findings suggest that it is the first administration

TABLE E3

*Mean test and retest WAIS performance for
Juel-Nielsen's sample.*

	WAIS Verbal		WAIS Performance		WAIS Full-Scale	
	Test	Retest	Test	Retest	Test	Retest
Mean	102.2	104.1	109.7	114.8	105.4	108.6
df		17		17		17
t		7.22		6.53		2.73
p		.001		.001		.01

of the WAIS that produces the comparable scores. Furthermore, test-retest differences in mean absolute pair difference all failed to reach to significance, indicating that heritability estimates would not be affected by using scores from the first administration instead of the average of the test and retest scores. The WAIS scores used in our analyses appear in table E 4.

Now we consider the psychometric and genetic implications of combining verbal and performance scores to form a composite called full-scale IQ or, simply, IQ. Psychometric theory holds that different tests can be combined when they measure the same underlying attribute or factor, or in psychometric terminology, when they are congeneric. From other large-scale investigations we know that the WAIS verbal and performance scales are not congeneric (i.e., the WAIS consists of more than a *single* factor.) Indeed, in Juel-Nielsen's sample the correlation of .59 does not differ much from the .60 to .70 correlation estimate typically reported. WAIS verbal and performance scales measure related, but clearly distinct, psychological attributes. The same statement may be made concerning the Mill Hill and Dominoes, which correlate .56 for males and females combined. Even when corrected for attenuation, the hypothesis that the correlation is 1.0 is easily rejected by a

TABLE E4
Juel-Nielsen twin data.

PAIRID	TWIN	SEX	VERBIQ	PERFIQ	FULLIQ
104	A	2	94	103	99
104	B	2	99	105	103
108	A	1	114	121	119
108	B	1	120	117	121
114	A	2	94	109	100
114	B	2	93	98	94
130	A	2	86	100	91
130	B	2	93	105	98
146	A	2	104	110	108
146	B	2	96	98	97
188	A	2	88	97	91
188	B	2	96	105	100
168	A	2	95	116	105
168	B	2	85	113	97
170	A	2	109	115	111
170	B	2	111	124	117
178	A	2	101	108	104
178	B	2	101	106	103
184	A	2	119	127	125
184	B	2	109	115	111
206	A	1	110	111	111
206	B	1	118	114	117
406	A	1	102	103	99
406	B	1	110	116	112

List of Variables

Variable	Label
PAIRID	Twin Pair Identification Number
TWIN	Individual Member of Twin Pair
SEX	Sex of Twin Pair
VERBIQ	WAIS Verbal IQ Score
PERFIQ	WAIS Performance IQ Score
FULLIQ	WAIS Full-Scale IQ Score

likelihood ratio test. Thus, one must be careful in interpreting the full-scale IQ score since it may be a psychological aggregate rather than a unitary process. This is especially consequential for heritability studies since the genetic bases (if any) of verbal and performance ability may be different (cf. Bock 1973). What is particularly perplexing about the Shields and Juel-Nielsen data sets is the fact that the magnitude of the correlation between the verbal and performance scores differs significantly between males and females. (The correlations were presented in chapter 7.) The result implies that either that the tests measure different attributes in men and women or that they measure the same constructs with differential precision. It is reasonable to infer from these findings that when analyzing the components of variance of these tests, particular interest should be focused on the individual component (verbal and performance) scores instead of the composite (full-scale) score and on interactions with sex or on within-sex analyses. (As the presentation of results proceeds, the reader will observe how fruitful this approach proved and how frequently-made erroneous conclusions were prevented.)

Other (Miscellaneous) Sample

Table E 5 presents the full-scale IQ scores for pairs of identical twins whose case studies were found scattered throughout the psychological and medical literatures. The scores were taken directly from the published reports and used without modification.

In table E 6 the complete set of data on the 83 pairs of twins used in our analyses is laid out. Complete variable descriptions appear in the footnote to table E 6.

TABLE E5
Other miscellaneous twin data.

PAIRID	TWIN	SEX	IQ
102	A	1	97
102	B	1	104
106	A	1	124
106	B	1	107
138	A	2	107
138	B	2	110
180	A	1	84
180	B	1	66
202	A	1	108
202	B	1	109
204	A	1	96
204	B	1	83
212	A	2	70
212	B	2	61
232	A	1	100
232	B	1	104
242	A	2	103
242	B	2	102
330	A*	2	99
330	B†	2	88
332	A	1	108
332	B	1	104

* VIQ = 94; PIQ = 103.
† VIQ = 83; PIQ = 96.

List of Variables

Variable	Label
PAIRID	Twin Pair Identification Number
TWIN	Individual Member of Twin Pair
SEX	Sex of Twin Pair
IQ	Scores from Various IQ Tests

TABLE E6

Twin data from combined samples.

CASEID	PAIRID	TWIN	SEX	SAMPLE	VALID	PAURE	VIQ	PIQ	IQ	IQTEST	AGETEST	DSIMI	DESIMI	AGESEP	DSICB	DC610	DC120	DC20	RELREAR	REARR	HAND	SYM	BWT1	BWT2
1	102	A	1	4	1	0	·	·	97	4	19	1	1	0	1	1	1	·	1	3	2	2	·	·
2	102	B	1	4	1	0	·	·	104	4	19	1	1	0	1	1	1	·	1	3	3	2	·	·
3	104	A	2	3	2	1	94	103	99	1	35	1	1	2	1	1	1	1	1	3	1	1	·	·
4	104	B	2	3	1	1	99	105	103	1	35	1	1	2	1	1	1	1	1	3	1	1	·	·
5	106	A	1	4	1	1	·	·	124	2	17	1	1	3	1	1	1	·	1	3	1	1	·	·
6	106	B	1	4	1	1	·	·	107	2	17	1	1	3	1	1	1	·	1	3	1	1	·	·
7	108	A	1	3	1	1	114	121	119	1	22	1	1	10	1	1	1	1	1	3	1	1	·	·
8	108	B	1	3	1	0	120	117	121	1	22	1	1	10	1	1	1	1	1	1	1	1	·	·
9	110	A	2	2	2	0	89	98	94	3	36	1	1	16	1	1	1	1	1	3	2	2	1	·
10	110	B	2	2	2	0	88	93	91	3	36	1	1	16	1	1	1	1	1	1	1	2	2	·
11	112	A	2	2	2	0	114	112	113	3	35	1	1	0	1	1	1	1	3	2	1	1	·	·
12	112	B	2	2	2	0	115	103	109	3	35	1	1	0	1	1	1	1	3	3	3	1	·	·
13	114	A	2	3	2	1	94	109	100	1	50	2	2	0	2	1	2	2	2	1	3	1	·	·
14	114	B	2	3	2	1	93	98	94	2	50	2	2	0	2	1	2	2	2	3	1	1	·	·
15	118	A	1	1	1	1	·	·	99	2	23	1	2	2	1	1	1	2	1	3	1	1	·	·
16	118	B	1	1	1	1	·	·	101	1	23	1	1	2	1	1	1	2	1	3	1	1	·	·
17	120	A	2	1	2	1	·	·	85	2	39	1	1	6	1	1	1	2	1	3	2	2	·	·
18	120	B	2	1	2	1	·	·	84	2	39	1	1	6	1	1	1	2	1	3	1	2	·	·
19	124	A	2	1	2	1	·	·	92	2	35	1	1	18	1	1	1	2	1	3	1	1	·	·
20	124	B	2	1	2	1	·	·	116	2	35	1	1	18	1	1	1	2	1	3	1	1	·	·
21	126	A	1	2	1	0	95	103	99	3	18	2	2	20	2	2	3	·	2	1	2	1	1	2608
22	126	B	1	2	1	1	81	91	86	3	18	2	2	20	2	2	3	·	2	3	2	1	2	2041
23	128	A	2	2	2	0	110	107	109	3	36	2	2	22	2	1	2	2	1	3	2	2	·	·
24	128	B	2	2	2	0	93	83	88	3	36	2	2	22	2	1	2	2	1	3	1	2	·	·
25	130	A	2	3	1	1	86	100	91	1	54	3	1	1	1	1	2	3	2	2	1	1	·	·

CASEID	PAIRID	TWIN	SEX	SAMPLE	VALID	PURE	VIQ	PIQ	IQ	IQTEST	AGETTEST	DSIMM	DSIMI	AGESEP	DCB6	DC610	DC1020	DC20	RELREARER	REARER	DNAHAS	ASYM	BWT1	BWT2
26	130	B	2	3	1	1	93	105	98	1	54	3	1	1	1	1	1	3	2	3	1	1	•	•
27	132	A	2	2	1	0	88	72	80	3	55	3	2	6	1	1	2	3	3	2	1	1	•	•
28	132	B	2	2	1	0	87	67	77	3	55	3	2	6	1	1	1	3	3	1	1	1	•	•
29	136	A	2	2	1	0	89	100	95	3	43	3	1	48	1	1	1	2	2	3	1	1	•	•
30	136	B	2	2	1	0	82	79	81	3	43	3	1	48	1	1	1	2	2	1	1	1	•	•
31	138	A	2	4	1	1	•	•	107	2	18	4	3	0	3	3	3	•	3	3	1	1	1	2722
32	138	B	2	4	1	1	•	•	110	2	18	4	3	0	3	3	3	•	3	2	1	1	2	2268
33	142	A	1	1	1	1	•	•	94	2	19	4	2	1	2	1	2	•	3	3	1	1	•	•
34	142	B	1	1	1	1	•	•	95	2	19	4	2	1	2	1	2	•	3	3	1	1	•	•
35	144	A	1	1	1	1	•	•	105	2	13	4	3	1	3	3	3	•	3	3	1	1	•	•
36	144	B	2	1	1	1	•	•	106	2	13	4	3	1	3	3	3	•	2	2	1	1	•	•
37	146	A	2	3	1	1	104	110	108	1	37	4	3	2	3	3	3	3	2	2	1	1	2	•
38	146	B	2	3	1	1	96	98	97	3	37	4	3	2	3	3	3	3	2	2	1	1	1	•
39	148	A	2	2	1	0	102	109	106	3	40	4	3	3	3	3	3	3	2	2	1	1	•	•
40	148	B	2	2	1	0	89	93	91	3	40	4	3	3	3	3	3	3	1	1	2	2	•	•
41	150	A	2	1	1	1	•	•	92	2	15	4	3	3	3	3	3	•	2	2	1	2	1	2722
42	150	B	2	1	1	1	•	•	77	2	15	4	3	3	3	3	3	•	2	2	1	2	2	1588
43	152	A	2	1	1	1	•	•	122	2	12	4	3	11	3	3	3	•	3	3	3	2	•	•
44	152	B	2	1	1	1	•	•	127	2	12	4	3	11	3	3	3	•	3	3	2	2	•	•
45	154	A	1	1	1	1	•	•	96	2	27	4	2	6	2	2	2	2	2	2	1	2	•	•
46	154	B	1	1	1	1	•	•	77	2	27	4	2	6	2	2	2	2	2	3	1	2	•	•
47	158	A	2	1	1	1	•	•	89	2	38	4	1	14	1	1	1	4	1	1	1	1	1	•
48	158	B	2	1	1	1	•	•	93	2	38	4	1	14	1	1	1	4	3	3	1	1	2	•
49	160	A	2	1	1	0	•	•	116	2	29	4	3	18	3	3	3	3	3	1	1	2	•	•
50	160	B	2	1	1	0	•	•	109	2	29	4	3	18	3	3	3	3	3	1	3	2	•	•

TABLE E6 (continued)

Twin data from combined samples.

51	162	A	1	1	1	1	•	•	115	2	14	3	4	3	25	3	3	3	•	1	3	2	2	•	•
52	162	B	1	1	1	1	•	•	105	2	14	3	4	3	25	3	3	3	•	1	3	1	2	•	•
53	164	A	2	1	1	1	•	•	90	2	11	3	4	3	30	3	3	3	•	1	3	•	•	•	•
54	164	B	2	1	1	1	•	•	88	2	11	3	4	3	30	3	3	3	•	1	3	•	1	•	•
55	168	A	2	3	1	1	95	116	105	1	49	3	4	3	42	•	•	•	•	2	3	1	1	1	2500
56	168	B	2	3	1	1	85	113	97	1	49	3	4	3	42	•	•	•	•	2	2	1	1	1	2000
57	170	A	2	3	1	1	109	115	111	1	72	3	4	3	42	3	3	3	3	2	1	1	1	1	•
58	170	B	2	3	1	1	111	124	117	1	72	3	4	3	42	3	3	3	4	2	3	1	1	2	•
59	172	A	2	2	1	0	99	109	104	3	32	2	5	1	0	1	1	2	4	2	1	1	3	•	•
60	172	B	2	2	1	0	106	107	107	3	32	2	5	1	0	1	3	3	4	2	3	1	1	•	•
61	174	A	1	2	1	0	85	•	85	3	39	3	5	1	0	1	3	3	•	3	1	1	1	•	•
62	174	B	1	2	1	0	85	•	85	3	39	3	5	1	0	1	3	3	1	3	2	1	1	2	•
63	176	A	1	2	1	0	90	69	80	3	22	3	5	4	0	4	4	3	3	2	2	1	1	1	•
64	176	B	1	2	1	0	81	74	78	3	22	3	5	4	0	4	4	3	3	2	3	1	1	1	•
65	178	A	2	3	1	1	101	108	104	1	64	2	5	1	1	1	2	2	2	2	2	1	2	2	•
66	178	B	2	3	1	1	101	106	103	1	64	2	5	1	1	1	2	2	2	2	2	1	•	•	•
67	180	A	1	4	1	0	•	•	84	2	23	3	5	4	2	4	4	4	5	3	2	•	•	•	•
68	180	B	1	4	1	0	•	•	66	2	23	3	5	4	2	4	4	4	5	3	1	•	•	•	•
69	182	A	1	1	1	1	•	•	91	2	26	2	5	1	6	2	2	1	2	1	3	1	1	•	•
70	182	B	1	1	1	1	•	•	90	2	26	2	5	1	6	2	2	1	2	1	3	1	1	•	•
71	184	A	2	3	1	1	119	127	125	1	70	3	5	3	12	1	1	4	3	2	3	2	2	1	•
72	184	B	2	3	1	1	109	115	111	1	70	3	5	3	12	1	1	4	3	2	1	1	2	2	1360
73	186	A	2	4	1	0	•	•	66	5	52	3	5	1	12	1	1	4	4	2	3	1	1	2	1360
74	186	B	2	4	0	0	•	•	51	5	52	3	5	1	12	1	1	4	4	2	1	1	1	2	1375
75	188	A	2	2	1	1	88	97	91	1	42	3	5	3	12	3	5	4	2	2	2	1	1	1	1125
76	188	B	2	3	1	1	96	105	100	1	42	3	5	3	12	3	5	4	2	2	2	1	1	2	•
77	190	A	1	3	0	1	88	93	91	3	38	3	5	3	24	3	3	4	1	3	3	1	1	•	•
78	190	B	1	4	0	1	86	86	86	3	38	3	5	3	24	3	3	4	1	3	3	1	1	•	•
79	202	A	1	4	1	1	•	•	108	1	29	1	6	1	1	1	1	1	1	1	1	2	1	•	•
80	202	B	1	4	1	1	•	•	109	1	29	1	6	1	1	1	1	1	1	1	1	1	1	2	•
81	204	A	1	4	0	1	•	•	96	2	37	3	6	4	6	1	4	4	4	2	3	1	1	1	•
82	204	B	1	4	0	1	•	•	83	2	37	3	6	4	6	1	4	4	4	2	2	1	1	1	•
83	206	A	1	3	1	1	110	111	111	1	45	1	6	1	9	1	1	1	4	2	3	1	1	•	•
84	206	B	1	3	1	1	118	114	117	1	45	1	6	1	9	1	1	1	4	1	3	1	1	•	•
85	208	A	2	1	1	1	•	•	66	2	27	1	6	1	18	1	1	1	4	1	3	1	1	•	•

CASEID	PAIRID	TWIN	SEX	SAMPLEX	VAPLIRED	PURERE	VIQ	PIQ	IQ	QTEST	AGETEST	DSIMI	DSIMEP	AGESEP	DCB6	DC610	DCIO20	DCO20	RELREAR	REARR	HAND	ASYM	BWT1	BWT2
86	208	B	2	1	1	1	•	•	78	2	27	6	1	18	1	1	1	4	1	3	1	1	•	•
87	210	A	2	1	1	1	•	•	85	2	19	6	1	18	1	1	1	4	1	3	1	2	•	•
88	210	B	2	1	1	1	•	•	97	2	19	6	1	18	1	1	1	4	1	3	2	2	•	•
89	212	A	2	4	1	0	•	•	70	5	39	6	1	24	1	1	1	4	1	3	1	2	•	•
90	212	B	2	4	1	0	•	•	61	5	39	6	1	24	1	1	1	4	1	3	3	1	•	•
91	214	A	2	2	1	0	89	58	74	3	48	6	1	30	1	1	1	4	1	3	1	1	•	•
92	214	B	2	2	1	0	84	55	70	3	48	6	1	30	1	1	1	4	1	3	1	1	•	•
93	216	A	2	2	1	0	118	123	121	3	50	7	3	0	4	5	5	5	3	2	1	1	•	•
94	216	B	2	2	1	0	122	121	122	3	50	7	3	0	4	5	5	5	3	1	1	1	•	•
95	218	A	2	2	1	0	89	107	98	3	47	7	3	0	1	4	5	5	3	2	2	2	•	•
96	218	B	2	2	1	0	94	100	97	3	47	7	3	0	1	4	5	5	3	1	1	2	•	•
97	220	A	1	2	1	0	91	97	94	3	34	7	3	0	1	4	5	5	3	2	1	1	1	2722
98	220	B	2	2	1	0	82	81	82	3	34	7	3	0	1	4	5	5	1	1	1	1	2	1134
99	224	A	2	2	1	0	91	91	91	3	41	7	3	0	1	4	5	5	1	1	1	1	•	•
100	224	B	1	2	1	0	86	88	87	3	41	7	3	0	1	4	5	5	3	3	1	1	•	•
101	228	A	1	2	1	0	103	97	100	3	49	7	3	1	1	4	5	4	3	1	1	1	•	•
102	228	B	2	2	1	0	90	86	88	3	49	7	3	1	1	4	5	4	3	2	1	1	•	•
103	230	A	2	2	1	0	114	117	116	3	41	7	3	1	1	1	4	5	3	2	1	1	•	•
104	230	B	1	2	1	0	106	98	102	3	41	7	3	1	1	1	4	5	3	2	1	1	•	•
105	232	A	1	4	1	1	•	•	100	2	20	7	3	1	3	4	5	•	3	2	1	1	•	•
106	232	B	1	4	1	1	•	•	104	2	20	7	3	1	3	4	5	•	3	1	1	1	•	•
107	236	A	1	2	1	0	96	90	93	3	14	7	3	3	1	4	5	•	3	2	1	1	1	1361
108	236	B	1	2	1	0	96	72	84	3	14	7	3	3	1	4	5	•	3	1	1	1	2	1134
109	238	A	2	2	1	0	100	91	96	3	8	7	3	3	4	4	•	•	3	2	1	1	2	•
110	238	B	2	2	1	0	103	88	96	3	8	7	3	3	4	4	•	•	1	3	1	1	1	•

TABLE E6 (continued)
Twin data from combined samples.

111	242	A	2	4	1	1	•	•	2	103	12	7	3	30	1	4	5	•	1	3	3	1	•	•
112	242	B	2	4	1	1	•	•	2	102	12	7	3	30	1	4	5	•	1	3	3	1	•	•
113	244	A	2	1	1	1	•	•	2	102	59	7	3	36	1	1	4	5	3	2	1	1	•	•
114	244	B	2	1	1	1	•	•	2	94	59	7	3	36	1	1	4	5	3	2	1	1	•	•
115	246	A	1	2	1	0	106	97	3	102	39	7	3	48	5	4	4	5	1	3	3	1	•	•
116	246	B	1	2	1	0	114	103	3	109	39	7	3	48	5	4	4	5	1	3	1	1	•	•
117	302	A	1	2	1	0	95	114	3	105	17	8	4	0	5	1	5	•	3	2	1	1	•	•
118	302	B	1	2	1	0	104	110	3	107	17	8	4	0	5	5	5	•	3	2	1	1	•	•
119	304	A	2	2	1	0	98	103	3	101	33	8	4	0	5	5	5	5	3	2	1	1	1	2948
120	304	B	2	2	1	0	102	110	3	106	33	8	4	0	5	5	5	5	3	2	1	1	2	1588
121	306	A	2	2	1	0	99	98	3	99	45	8	3	0	5	3	5	5	3	1	1	1	1	•
122	306	B	2	2	1	0	94	95	3	95	45	8	3	0	5	3	5	5	3	2	1	1	2	•
123	308	A	1	2	1	0	106	112	3	109	45	8	4	0	5	5	5	5	3	1	1	1	2	•
124	308	B	1	2	1	0	94	102	3	98	45	8	4	0	5	5	5	5	3	2	1	1	1	•
125	312	A	2	2	1	0	89	109	3	100	42	8	4	1	5	5	5	5	3	2	1	1	•	•
126	312	B	2	2	1	0	93	97	3	95	42	8	4	1	5	5	5	5	3	1	1	1	•	•
127	314	A	2	2	1	0	88	84	3	86	48	8	4	1	5	5	5	5	3	2	1	1	1	•
128	314	B	2	2	1	0	82	67	3	75	48	8	4	1	5	5	5	5	3	1	1	1	2	•
129	318	A	2	1	1	1	•	•	2	89	29	8	4	5	5	5	5	5	3	2	1	1	•	•
130	318	B	2	1	1	1	•	•	2	106	29	8	4	5	5	5	5	5	3	1	1	1	•	•
131	320	A	1	1	1	1	•	•	2	102	19	8	4	6	5	5	5	•	3	2	1	1	•	•
132	320	B	1	1	1	1	•	•	2	96	19	8	4	6	5	5	5	•	3	2	2	2	•	•
133	322	A	1	2	1	0	85	95	3	90	30	8	4	6	5	5	5	4	3	2	1	2	1	•
134	322	B	1	2	1	0	76	103	3	90	30	8	4	6	5	5	5	4	2	2	1	1	1	•
135	324	A	1	2	1	0	99	107	3	103	32	8	4	6	5	5	5	5	2	2	1	1	•	•
136	324	B	1	2	1	0	107	100	3	104	32	8	4	6	5	5	5	5	3	3	1	1	•	•
137	328	A	1	2	1	0	87	58	3	73	52	8	4	9	5	5	5	5	3	2	1	1	•	•
138	328	B	1	2	1	0	82	74	3	78	52	8	4	9	5	5	5	5	3	1	1	1	•	•
139	330	A	2	4	1	0	94	103	1	99	18	8	4	9	5	5	5	•	3	1	1	1	•	•
140	330	B	2	4	1	0	83	96	1	88	18	8	4	9	5	5	5	•	3	2	•	•	•	•
141	332	A	1	4	1	0	•	•	1	108	16	8	4	9	5	5	5	•	2	2	•	•	•	•
142	332	B	1	4	1	0	•	•	1	104	16	8	4	9	5	5	5	•	2	3	1	•	•	•
143	334	A	1	2	1	0	106	90	3	98	51	8	4	12	5	5	5	5	3	1	1	•	2	•
144	334	B	1	2	1	0	114	100	3	107	51	8	4	12	5	5	5	5	3	2	1	1	1	•
145	336	A	1	2	1	0	99	98	3	99	51	8	4	12	5	5	5	5	3	2	1	1	•	•

CASEID	PAIRID	TWIN	SAMPLEX	VALIDE	VALID	PURE	VIQ	PIQ	IQ	IQTEST	AGEATTEST	DSIMEST	DSIMI	AGEDSIMEST	DCB6	DC610	DC1020	DCI20	RELEAR	REAARR	HAND	ASYM	BWT1	BWT2
146	336	B	1	2	1	0	103	88	96	3	51	8	4	12	5	5	5	5	3	1	1	1	.	.
147	338	A	2	2	1	1	94	.	111	1	52	8	4	13	5	5	5	5	2	3	1	2	.	.
148	338	B	2	2	1	1	86	.	92	1	52	8	4	13	5	5	5	5	2	1	2	2	.	.
149	342	A	2	2	1	0	95	121	108	3	48	8	4	0	5	5	5	5	3	1	1	1	2	.
150	342	B	2	2	1	0	103	117	110	3	48	8	4	0	5	5	5	5	3	2	1	1	1	.
151	344	A	2	2	1	0	98	67	83	3	39	8	4	0	5	5	5	5	3	2	1	1	2	.
152	344	B	2	2	1	0	98	77	88	3	39	8	4	0	5	5	5	5	3	1	1	1	1	.
153	350	A	2	2	1	0	90	74	82	3	56	8	4	9	5	5	5	5	3	2	1	1	.	.
154	350	B	2	2	1	0	89	90	90	3	56	8	4	9	5	5	5	5	3	1	1	1	.	.
155	352	A	2	2	1	0	89	69	79	3	40	8	4	0	5	5	5	5	3	1	1	1	.	.
156	352	B	2	2	1	0	89	62	76	3	40	8	4	0	5	5	5	5	3	2	1	1	.	.
157	406	A	1	3	1	0	102	103	99	1	77	9	3	72	5	3	3	3	3	1	.	.	.	.
158	406	B	1	3	1	0	110	116	112	1	77	9	3	72	5	3	3	3	3	1	.	.	.	.
159	408	A	2	1	1	0	.	.	88	2	41	9	3	72	5	3	4	3	3	1	2	2	.	.
160	408	B	2	1	1	0	.	.	79	2	41	9	3	72	5	3	4	5	3	1	3	2	2	1588
161	410	A	2	2	1	0	86	90	88	3	38	9	4	84	5	5	5	5	3	1	1	1	1	2041
162	410	B	2	2	1	0	85	91	88	3	38	9	4	84	5	5	5	5	3	2	1	1	.	.
163	416	A	2	2	1	0	98	98	98	3	38	9	4	96	5	5	5	5	3	1	1	1	.	.
164	416	B	2	2	1	0	93	100	97	3	38	9	4	96	5	5	5	5	3	1	1	1	.	.
165	422	A	2	2	1	0	110	102	106	3	59	9	3	108	5	5	3	2	3	1	1	1	.	.
166	422	B	2	2	1	0	110	103	107	3	59	9	3	108	5	5	3	2	3	1	1	1	.	.

TABLE E6 (continued)

Twin data from combined samples.

Variable descriptions for combined twin sample.

Variable Name	Variable Label
CASEID	Individual Case Identification Number
PAIRID	Twin Pair Identification Number
TWIN	Individual Member of Twin Pair A. Twin A B. Twin B
SEX	Sex of Twin Pair 1. Male 2. Female
SAMPLE	Sample Twin Pair is in 1. Newman et al. 2. Shields 3. Juel-Nielsen 4. Other
VALID	Is case unreliable test 0. Invalid 1. Valid
PURE	Selected Sample-Not Ill, Valid test, Sep 0. Not Sep, Invalid or Ill 1. Separated, Valid
VIQ	Verbal IQ Score
PIQ	Perfor-Quant IQ Score
IQ	Full-Scale IQ Score
IQTEST	Test Used to Assess IQ 1. WAIS 2. Stanford-Binet 3. Mill Hill-Dominoes 4. Otis 5. Kuhlmann
AGETEST	Age of IQ Testing in years
DSIMI	Degree of Contact I Measure 1. IA 2. IB 3. IC 4. ID 5. IE 6. IIA 7. IIB 8. III 9. IV
DSIMII	Degree of Contact II Measure 1. None 2. Little 3. Some 4. Most
AGESEP	Age of Separation in Months
DCB6	Degree of Contact: Birth-6 Years 1. None or MO 2. None-Little 3. Little 4. Little-Much-OM 5. Much
DC610	Degree of Contact: 6-10 Years 1. None 2. None-Little 3. Little 4. Little-Much-OM 5. Much
DC1020	Degree of Contact: 10-20 Years 1. None 2. None-Little 3. Little 4. Little-Much-OM 5. Much
DC20	Degree of Contact: 20+Years 1. None 2. None-Little 3. Little 4. Little-Much-OM 5. Much
RELREAR	A & B Reared by Relatives 1. Other-Other 2. Par-Oth Rel-Oth 3. P-P P-R R-R
REAR	Person who Reared Twins 1. Parent 2. Relative 3. Other
HAND	Handedness 1. Right 2. Left 3. Ambidextrous
SYM	Symmetry of Laterality of A and B 1. R-R L-L A-A 2. R-L R-A L-A
BWT1	Birth Weight Rank 1. Heavier or Stronger 2. Equal, Lighter, or Weaker
BWT2	Birth Weight in Grams
BO	Birth Order 1. First 2. Second
.	Missing Values

Representativeness of Twin Samples

There has been a great deal of discussion about the special characteristics of twins and the degree to which twins (especially identical twins) are representative of the general population. In table E 7 are presented statistics characterizing the distributions of the full-scale IQ scores for each sample. It will be noted that the distributions are primarily platykurtic ($\hat{\beta}_2 < 3$), several significantly so. Pearson skewness index $\sqrt{\hat{\beta}_1}$, shows that some of the distributions are significantly positively skewed while others are significantly negatively skewed. Table E 8 reports the results of the Anderson-Darling (1954) test of normality. Using an alpha level of .25 as is appropriate in this case (see chapter 7), we find that each sample shows a significant departure from normality. The various samples, thus, do not appear to be distributed normally. Table E 9 confirms what is apparent from the sample variances and means shown in the last two columns of table E 7. It is very unlikely that these samples were drawn from a population with variance 15^2 and mean 100. (Robust statistical tests were employed because of distribution non-normality and variance heterogeneity.) The twins are less variable and less able than the general population. These facts should make one very cautious about generalizing results from twin studies and the general population. Finally, we inquired if the male and fe-

TABLE E7

Full-scale IQ distribution characteristics by sex for twin samples.

Sample	Sex	N	$\hat{\beta}_2$†	$\sqrt{\hat{\beta}_1}$†	$\hat{\sigma}^2$	$\hat{\mu}$
	Males	14	4.53	− .49	81.8*	98.0
Newman et al.	Females	24	2.96	.60	228.0	94.3
	Combined	38	3.16	.30	173.7	95.7
	Males	30	2.00*	− .14*	104.2**	93.3
Shields	Females	50	2.46	.03	156.1*	95.5
	Combined	80	2.45	.04	137.1	94.7
	Males	6	1.67*	−1.26	63.4	113.2
Juel-Nielsen	Females	18	.90	.92	78.7**	103.0
	Combined	24	−.78**	.37	92.2	105.5
	Males	14	1.59	− .92	200.4	99.6
Other (Misc.)	Females	8	−.36**	−1.04	325.4	92.5
	Combined	22	.59	− .99	244.7	97.0
	Males	64	2.91	− .24	144.0	97.6
All	Females	100	2.91	− .10	177.4	96.3
	Combined	164	2.91	− .16	163.7	96.8

*$p<.05$
**$p<.01$

†$\sqrt{\hat{\beta}_1}$ and $\hat{\beta}_2$ are the Pearsonian skewness and kurtosis coefficients, respectively, which were estimated by the SAS UNIVARIATE procedure. The significance of the departures from normality were determined using the formulas and methods devised by D'Agostino and Pearson (1973).

TABLE E8
Tests of hypothesis that sample was drawn from a normal population.[1]

		Males			Females		
		N	A^2	p	N	A^2	p
I.	Newman et al.						
	SBIQ	14	.28	ns	24	.62	.10
II.	Shields						
	RAWMH	30	.62	.10	50	.38	ns
	FDMHIQ	30	.41	ns	50	1.46	.001
	RAWDOM	26	.41	ns	50	.59	.12
	FDDOMIQ	26	.46	.24	50	.59	.12
	MEANFDIQ	30	.33	ns	50	.18	ns
III.	Juel-Nielsen						
	VERBIQ	6	.23	ns	18	.36	ns
	PERFIQ	6	.26	ns	18	.34	ns
	FULLIQ	6	.35	ns	18	.37	ns
IV.	Other						
	IQ	12	.52	.15	6	.43	.25

[1]Probabilities for the A^2 statistic were computed by the method given in Pettitt (1977).

List of Variables

Variable	Label
SBIQ	Stanford-Binet IQ Score
RAWMH	Raw Mill Hill Vocabulary Score
FDMHIQ	Farber-Dunivant Mill Hill IQ Score
RAWDOM	Raw Dominoes Score
FDDOMIQ	Farber-Dunivant Dominoes IQ Score
MEANFDIQ	Mean Farber-Dunivant Mill Hill–Dominoes IQ Score
VERBIQ	WAIS Verbal IQ Score
PERFIQ	WAIS Performance IQ Score
FULLIQ	WAIS Full-Scale IQ Score
IQ	Scores from Various IQ Tests

TABLE E9
Tests of population variance and mean.

		$H_0 : \sigma^2 = 15^2$			$H_0 : \mu = 100$		
		df	χ^2	p	df	t	p
Newman	Males	13	4.73	.04	13	−.83	ns
	Females	23	23.30	ns	23	−1.84	.08
Shields	Males	29	13.42	.01	29	−3.59	.001
	Females	49	33.20	.08	49	−2.85	.01
Juel-Nielsen	Males	5	1.41	.15	5	4.05	.01
	Females	17	5.95	.01	17	1.43	ns
Other (Misc.)	Males	13	11.58	.12	13	−.11	ns
	Females	7	10.12	ns	7	−1.18	ns

male subsamples are comparable. For most of the hypotheses concerning equality of sex means and variances we find that the weight of the evidence indicates that the male and female twins were drawn from different populations. The male twins tend to have lower mean IQ scores and to have smaller variances than their female counterparts (table E 10).

We close this section by concluding that the data do not suggest that the samples of twins were drawn from the normal IQ population with mean 100 and variance 225. In contrast to Jensen (1970), who analyzed most of the present data plus questionable samples from Burt, our results do not imply that the samples can be pooled for a more powerful analysis. Indeed, we interpret these findings as suggesting that combining the samples will introduce serious distortions in the data analysis. That this is in fact the case will be seen in the variance components analysis, to which we now turn.

TABLE E10

Test of equality of male and female variances and means.

Sample/	$H_0:\sigma^2_M=\sigma^2_F$				$H_0:\mu_M=\mu_F$		
Test	df_N	df_D	F^*	p	df	$t\dagger$	p
Newman et al.							
Stanford-Binet IQ	1	36	2.14	.08	34	.94	ns
Shields							
RAWMH	1	78	.99	ns	54	−.96	ns
RAWDOM	1	74	3.57	.06	63	.39	ns
FDMHIQ	1	78	.59	ns	68	−.67	ns
Juel-Nielsen							
VERBIQ	1	22	.52	ns	10	4.05	.002
PERFIQ	1	22	.93	ns	10	1.58	.15
FULLIQ	1	22	.10	ns	7.5	2.63	.03
Other							
Various Full-Scale IQ	1	14	.39	ns	10	.95	ns

*Brown-Forsythe (1974) analysis of variance F for mean absolute differences. This robust test was used since most of the distributions were non-normal.
†Behrens-Fisher t with Welch degrees of freedom (Winer 1971, p. 42).

IQ Variance Components and Heritability Analyses

Several previous studies, e.g., Jensen (1970), Jinks and Fulker (1970) and Loehlin et al. (1975), have estimated the heritability of IQ on the bases of one or more of these samples. If certain assumptions are met, very simple components of variance model can be used to estimate the heritability of IQ as an intraclass correlation. Some of the most important of these assumptions are: (1) members of each individual twin pair are assigned at random to different environments which, for purposes of generalizability, should represent the full range of environments available to a population (thus, no correlation between pairs can be attributed to environmental effects or overlap); (2) the linear model relating phenotypic IQ to genetic and environmental causes is correctly specified (e.g., no genotype x environment interaction is present); and (3) the assumptions of the linear model are satisfied, e.g., the components of variance are distributed normally.

When these and other conditions hold, the phenotypic twin variance in IQ can be partitioned into two orthogonal components representing genetic and environmental sources. If one conceives a data matrix in which each row represents a twin pair (genotype) and the two IQ scores from the individuals in each pair constitute the columns (assigned arbitrarily), the variance of the IQ scores in the matrix can be divided into between pairs (rows) and individuals within pairs (columns) sources. The variation in IQ between pairs represents the effects of different genotypes. The variation within pairs (or between individuals within pairs) results from nongenetic factors, e.g., environmental effects and measurement error. The linear model relating genetic and environmental causes to phenotypic IQ can be written as

$$y = p + i\,(p) \tag{1}$$

where y represents phenotypic intelligence (IQ), p symbolizes the effects of pairs (genotypes) and $i\,(p)$ indicates the effects of individuals within pairs (environments). Since p and i are taken to be uncorrelated, the total y variance can be partitioned into two nonoverlapping subsets corresponding to genetic and environmental components:

$$\sigma_y^2 = \sigma_p^2 + \sigma_{i\,(p)}^2 \tag{2}$$

The two quantities on the right are referred to as components of variance and may be estimated by standard analysis of variance techniques. Under the model assumptions a variance ratio or intraclass correlation representing heritability may be formed as

$$h_y^2 = \frac{\sigma_p^2}{\sigma_p^2 + \sigma_{i\,(p)}^2} \tag{3}$$

While this ratio can be given several behavioral and statistical interpretations, most patently it represents the proportion of total y (IQ) variance that is accounted for by the between pairs (genotypes) component.

For each sample of the four twin samples we estimated the components of IQ variance and formed the variance ratio representing the heritability of IQ. The results of these analyses, which were performed using the SAS (Statistical Analysis System) computer package (SAS, 1979), are presented in tables E 11 through E 20. Inspection of these tables reveals close correspondence with results previously published by various authors. Certain differences are apparent (e.g., with some of Jensen's (1970) results) because we developed slightly different methods for scaling IQ. The important statistics from all these tables are summarized in table E 21. The reader will observe that the heterogeneity in variance components across types of ability, sample, and sex is considerable. These variance components are all based on small samples and can be expected to have rather large sampling errors. Although it would be desirable to perform a statistical test of the variance homogeneity of the genetic and environmental components across sex and sample combinations, the evidence that scores are not normally distributed cautions against taking the results of such a test seriously. (It is well established in the statistical literature that non-normality of distributions can greatly affect [bias] variance [components] estimators and hypothesis tests, cf. Scheffé, 1959, ch. 10.) Furthermore, robust variance testing procedures, e.g., the Brown-Forsythe (1974) test, have not been extended to the components of variance situation. We are persuaded by the magnitude of the differences among the variance components that the samples were probably drawn from different populations of genetic and environmental effects. The fact that most of the genetic and environmental components sum to something less than the expected 225 indicates to us that these twin samples may not be representative of the range of genotypes and environments in the general population. The weight of these findings reinforces our earlier conclusions based on analyses of the IQ test distributions that the data from the males and females in the various samples can be pooled and analyzed collectively only at the risk of making serious errors of inference.

Within-sample analysis of these data can be very perplexing on the other hand. Consider the extreme example presented by Juel-Nielsen's twin sample: For males, the heritabilities of verbal and performance IQs are estimated to be .41 and .19 respectively. However, the heritability estimate for the full-scale IQ rises to .51. For females, the situation reverses. The verbal and performance heritabilities are .74 and .56, while the full-scale heritability takes an intermediate value of .59. If we combine the male and female data and estimate the heritability of the full-scale IQ, a value of .64 is obtained: It may well be that in the combined sample many random errors cancel each other, so that the best estimate of the population heritability is determined by this method. There is no way to know with certainty whether this or something else accounts for the discrepancy between the within-sample and pooled results. We are very receptive to the hypothesis that the discrepancy may indicate inadequate normalization of the Danish version of the

TABLE E11
Components of variance analysis of Newman et al.'s Stanford-Binet IQ Scores.

	Males				Females				Males and Females			
Variance Source	df	Mean Square	Variance Component	Variance Ratio	df	Mean Square	Variance Component	Variance Ratio	df	Mean Square	Variance Component	Variance Ratio
Pairs	6	135.3	49.7	.58	11	403.1	167.9	.71	18	298.1	121.1	.68
Individuals	7	36.0	36.0	.42	12	67.4	67.4	.29	19	55.8	55.8	.32
Total	13	81.8	85.7	1.00	23	228.0	235.3	1.00	37	173.7	176.9	1.00

TABLE E12
Components of variance analysis of Shields's Raw Mill Hill Vocabulary Scores.

	Males				Females				Males and Females			
Variance Source	df	Mean Square	Variance Component	Variance Ratio	df	Mean Square	Variance Component	Variance Ratio	df	Mean Square	Variance Component	Variance Ratio
Pairs	14	68.7	29.0	.73	24	57.2	25.0	.78	39	60.7	26.1	.76
Individuals	15	10.6	10.6	.27	25	7.1	7.1	.22	40	8.5	8.5	.24
Total	29	38.7	39.7	1.00	49	31.6	32.2	1.00	79	34.2	34.6	1.00

TABLE E13
Components of variance analysis of Shields's Farber-Dunivant Mill Hill IQ Scores.

	Males				Females				Males and Females			
Variance Source	df	Mean Square	Variance Component	Variance Ratio	df	Mean Square	Variance Component	Variance Ratio	df	Mean Square	Variance Component	Variance Ratio
Pairs	14	183.6	73.9	.67	24	186.0	83.3	.81	39	182.1	78.3	.75
Individuals	15	35.7	35.7	.33	25	19.4	19.4	.19	40	25.5	25.5	.25
Total	29	107.1	109.6	1.00	49	101.0	102.7	1.00	79	102.8	103.8	1.00

TABLE E14
Components of variance analysis of Shields's Raw Dominoes Scores.

	Males				Females				Males and Females			
Variance Source	df	Mean Square	Variance Component	Variance Ratio	df	Mean Square	Variance Component	Variance Ratio	df	Mean Square	Variance Component	Variance Ratio
Pairs	13	109.5	45.1	.70	23	181.9	81.3	.81	37	151.7	66.2	.77
Individuals	14	19.3	19.3	.30	24	19.3	19.3	.19	38	19.3	19.3	.23
Total	27	62.7	64.4	1.00	47	98.8	100.6	1.00	75	84.6	85.5	1.00

TABLE E15

Components of variance analysis of Shields's Farber-Dunivant Dominoes IQ Scores.

	Males					Females					Males and Females			
Variance Source	df	Mean Square	Variance Component	Variance Ratio	Variance Source	df	Mean Square	Variance Component	Variance Ratio	Variance Source	df	Mean Square	Variance Component	Variance Ratio
Pairs	13	328.4	134.9	.70	Pairs	23	548.8	245.6	.81	Pairs	37	457.1	199.6	.77
Individuals	14	58.6	58.6	.30	Individuals	24	57.6	57.6	.19	Individuals	38	58.0	58.0	.23
Total	27	188.5	193.5	1.00	Total	47	298.0	303.2	1.00	Total	75	254.9	257.6	1.00

TABLE E16

Components of variance analysis of Shields's Composite Farber-Dunivant Mill Hill and Dominoes IQ Scores (Mean FDIQ).

	Males					Females					Males and Females			
Variance Source	df	Mean Square	Variance Component	Variance Ratio	Variance Source	df	Mean Square	Variance Component	Variance Ratio	Variance Source	df	Mean Square	Variance Component	Variance Ratio
Pairs	14	185.3	78.4	.73	Pairs	24	281.4	122.9	.78	Pairs	39	242.0	104.5	.76
Individuals	15	28.6	28.6	.27	Individuals	25	35.6	35.6	.22	Individuals	40	32.9	32.9	.24
Total	29	104.2	106.9	1.00	Total	49	156.0	158.5	1.00	Total	79	136.1	137.4	1.00

TABLE E17

Components of variance analysis of Juel-Nielsen's WAIS Verbal IQ Scores.

	Males					Females					Males and Females			
Variance Source	df	Mean Square	Variance Component	Variance Ratio	Variance Source	df	Mean Square	Variance Component	Variance Ratio	Variance Source	df	Mean Square	Variance Component	Variance Ratio
Pairs	2	64.7	18.7	.41	Pairs	8	151.4	64.4	.74	Pairs	11	200.1	88.2	.79
Individuals	3	27.3	27.3	.59	Individuals	9	22.6	22.6	.26	Individuals	12	23.8	23.8	.21
Total	5	42.3	46.0	1.00	Total	17	83.2	87.0	1.00	Total	23	108.1	112.0	1.00

TABLE E18

Components of variance analysis of Juel-Nielsen's WAIS Performance IQ Scores.

	Males					Females					Males and Females			
Variance Source	df	Mean Square	Variance Component	Variance Ratio	Variance Source	df	Mean Square	Variance Component	Variance Ratio	Variance Source	df	Mean Square	Variance Component	Variance Ratio
Pairs	2	47.2	7.4	.19	Pairs	8	118.3	42.6	.56	Pairs	11	105.3	36.2	.??
Individuals	3	32.3	32.3	.81	Individuals	9	33.1	33.1	.44	Individuals	12	32.9	??	??
Total	5	38.3	38.3	1.00	Total	17	73.2	75.7	1.00	Total	23	67.5	69.1	1.00

TABLE E19

Components of variance analysis of Juel-Nielsen's WAIS Full-Scale IQ Scores.

Males

Variance Source	df	Mean Square	Variance Component	Variance Ratio
Pairs	2	106.2	35.7	.51
Individuals	3	34.8	34.8	.49
Total	5	63.4	70.5	1.00

Females

Variance Source	df	Mean Square	Variance Component	Variance Ratio
Pairs	8	129.8	48.2	.59
Individuals	9	33.3	33.3	.41
Total	17	78.7	81.5	1.00

Males and Females

Variance Source	df	Mean Square	Variance Component	Variance Ratio
Pairs	11	156.0	61.1	.64
Individuals	12	33.7	33.7	.36
Total	23	92.2	94.8	1.00

TABLE E20

Components of variance analysis of other (miscellaneous) sample Full-Scale IQ Scores.

Males

Variance Source	df	Mean Square	Variance Component	Variance Ratio
Pairs	6	362.2	150.3	.71
Individuals	7	61.7	61.7	.29
Total	13	200.4	212.0	1.00

Females

Variance Source	df	Mean Square	Variance Component	Variance Ratio
Pairs	3	724.0	348.8	.93
Individuals	4	26.5	26.5	.07
Total	7	325.4	375.3	1.00

Males and Females

Variance Source	df	Mean Square	Variance Component	Variance Ratio
Pairs	10	460.0	205.5	.81
Individuals	11	48.9	48.9	.19
Total	21	244.7	254.4	1.00

TABLE E21
Summary of variance components analyses.

| | Variance Components | | Variance Ratio |
	Pairs	Individuals	for Pairs
Verbal IQ			
Shields's Mill Hill (FDMHIQ)			
Males	73.9	35.7	.67
Females	83.3	19.4	.81
Juel-Nielsen WAIS Verbal			
Males	18.7	27.3	.41
Females	64.4	22.6	.74
Performance IQ			
Shields's Dominoes (FDDOMIQ)			
Males	134.9	58.6	.70
Females	245.6	57.6	.81
Juel-Nielsen WAIS Performance			
Males	7.4	32.3	.19
Females	42.6	33.1	.56
Full-Scale IQ			
Newman et al. Stanford-Binet			
Males	49.7	36.0	.58
Females	167.9	67.4	.71
Shields's Mill Hill-Dominoes (MEANFDIQ)			
Males	78.4	28.6	.73
Females	122.9	35.6	.78
Juel-Nielsen WAIS Full-Scale			
Males	35.7	48.2	.51
Females	34.8	33.3	.59
Other (Various IQ Scores)			
Males	150.3	61.7	.71
Females	348.8	26.5	.93

WAIS employed by Juel-Nielsen. Scrutiny of the results in tables E 11 through E 21 will give the reader an appreciation for the substantial differences which exist among the samples.

In order to provide as thorough an analysis as possible, we have conducted components of variance analyses for the pooled male, female, and total[3] samples, and present the results in tables E 22 through E 24. Many of the inconsistencies are no longer apparent. (Whether they have been removed or simply hidden is the important but unanswered question.) The heritabilities all lie in the interval between .74 and .82, and the genetic and environmental variance components are not as grossly discrepant across sex or ability as they appeared across samples. Consideration of only these tables would lead one to virtually the same

3. Pair 186 (see table E6) was excluded from all analyses reported in this appendix. Both members of this pair had I Q scores below 70 (51 and 66); no other set in any of the samples had comparably low scores. By several statistical criteria this pair was judged to be an outlier.

TABLE E22

Components of variance analysis of Verbal IQ Scores from combined sample.

Males

Variance Source	df	Mean Square	Variance Component	Variance Ratio
Pairs	17	255.5	110.6	.76
Individuals	18	34.3	34.3	.24
Total	35	141.7	144.9	1.00

Females

Variance Source	df	Mean Square	Variance Component	Variance Ratio
Pairs	34	173.0	75.8	.78
Individuals	35	21.4	21.4	.22
Total	69	96.1	97.2	1.00

Males and Females

Variance Source	df	Mean Square	Variance Component	Variance Ratio
Pairs	52	196.9	85.5	.77
Individuals	53	25.8	25.8	.23
Total	105	110.5	111.3	1.00

TABLE E23

Components of variance analysis of Performance IQ Scores from combined sample.

Males

Variance Source	df	Mean Square	Variance Component	Variance Ratio
Pairs	16	411.1	178.6	.77
Individuals	17	53.9	53.9	.23
Total	33	227.1	232.5	1.00

Females

Variance Source	df	Mean Square	Variance Component	Variance Ratio
Pairs	33	500.0	224.9	.82
Individuals	34	50.2	50.2	.18
Total	67	271.7	275.1	1.00

Males and Females

Variance Source	df	Mean Square	Variance Component	Variance Ratio
Pairs	50	462.6	205.6	.80
Individuals	51	51.4	51.4	.20
Total	101	255.0	257.0	1.00

TABLE E24

Components of variance analysis of Full-Scale IQ Scores from combined sample.

Males

Variance Source	df	Mean Square	Variance Component	Variance Ratio
Pairs	31	253.4	107.7	.74
Individuals	32	38.0	38.0	.26
Total	63	144.0	145.7	1.00

Females

Variance Source	df	Mean Square	Variance Component	Variance Ratio
Pairs	49	315.4	136.6	.76
Individuals	50	42.2	42.2	.24
Total	99	177.4	178.7	1.00

Males and Females

Variance Source	df	Mean Square	Variance Component	Variance Ratio
Pairs	81	288.5	124.0	.75
Individuals	82	40.6	40.6	.25
Total	163	163.8	164.5	1.00

conclusions reached by Jensen in 1970 when he performed a similar analysis that included Burt's twins.

In previous analyses of these data and up to this point in our own analysis, the assumption has been made implicitly that the sole source of variation, represented by differences among rows in the pairs x individuals data matrix, is genotypic. Thus all of the phenotypic variance accounted for by the between pairs (rows) effect has been labeled genetic in origin. However, it is conceivable that some of the between pairs effect is due to nongenetic sources. For example, pairs may be nested within other factors which represent environmental causes of IQ test performance, such as socioeconomic status, ethnicity, and sex. In general, any system of measuring or classifying the environment can be used to impose a structure on the rows of the data matrix. Then a variance components analysis will provide estimates of the effects of all the environmental and genetic sources. A variety of variance components ratios can be formed with this approach.

One might expect the degree of contact that two "separated" twins have had to reflect something about the similarity of the environments they have experienced, the effects of twinning, or other environmental factors. Farber's index allows two ways of coding the degree to which two separated twins actually had been in contact with each other. These were described in the text and will be referred to in this appendix as DSIMI and DSIMII. DSIMI consists of nine levels (corresponding to separation groups Ia-e, IIa-b, III, and IV of the twin index). DSIMII has four levels based on the degree of contact between birth and age twenty. Both of these code in ascending order the degree of contact the twins had. (See chapters 3 and 7 for detailed descriptions.) In addition, Farber applied a similar scoring scheme separately to four chronological age periods of development producing measures of the degree of contact from birth to age six (DCB6), from six to ten years of age (DC610), from age ten to twenty (DC1020), and in the interval beyond age twenty (DC20). (See table E 6 and the text for variable descriptions.) We hypothesized that if degree of contact actually represented the operation of nongenetic effects on IQ test performance, then differentiating the degree of contact and the between pairs variance components would yield a more accurate estimate of the true genotypic effect. In addition, since degree of contact indexes the similarity of the environments that the two twins in a pair have experienced, similarity of IQ scores within pairs would be expected to increase with degree of contact to the extent that environments uniformly affect IQ. (Equivalently, absolute within pair difference in IQ should decrease as degree of contact increases.) On the other hand, if the effect of twinning is to accentuate differences between identical twins (as was suggested with respect to personality development in chapter 9), then increasing contact may lead to increasing differences in within pair IQ or academic achievement. Conceivably, whatever processes are at work may differentially affect males and females. Several types of statistical analysis were undertaken in order to fully explore these possibilities.

The linear model specifying the effects of sex, degree of contact, pairs, and individuals within pairs of IQ may be written:

$$y = s + c + p(s*c) + i (p (s*c)) \tag{4}$$

where s symbolizes sex, c the degree of contact, and the parentheses indicate the nesting of an effect within one or more other effects. Total phenotypic intelligence variance can be decomposed into orthogonal components as:

$$\sigma_y^2 = \sigma_s^2 + \sigma_c^2 + \sigma_{p\,(s*c)}^2 + \sigma_{i\,(p\,(s*c))}^2 \tag{5}$$

An intraclass correlation representing the proportion of IQ variance determined by between-pairs-within-sex-by-degree-of-contact may be interpreted as a heritability coefficient:

$$h_y^2 = \frac{\sigma_{p\,(s*c)}^2}{\sigma_s^2 + \sigma_c^2 + \sigma_{p\,(s*c)}^2 + \sigma_{i\,(p\,(s*c))}^2} \tag{6}$$

(Please note that the effects of sex and degree of contact are fixed rather than random effects and have been estimated and tested as such in the analyses to follow; however, following usual procedure they have been symbolized as variances rather than sums of squares.)

We used the GLM and VARCOMP procedures of SAS to estimate and test the parameters of this model for the combined sample for verbal, performance, and full-scale IQ. table E 25 presents the results for DSIMI and table E 26 gives comparable data for DSIMII. The main effects of sex and degree of contact are not significant except for the effect of DSIMI on full-scale IQ ($p < .05$). However, the interaction of sex x degree of contact is significant ($p < .05$) for both DSIMI and DSIMII on verbal, performance, and full-scale IQ. The variance ratio (heritability) for the between-pairs-within-sex x degree-of-contact effect is about .45 for most of the variables. Given the magnitude and significance of the sex x degree-of-contact interaction, further analyses were conducted for males and females separately.

In tables E 27 through E 32 appear the results from variance components analyses which estimated the completely nested model:

$$y = c + p (c) + i (p (c)) \tag{7}$$

and the following variance components:

$$\sigma_y^2 = \sigma_c^2 + \sigma^2{}_{p\,(c)} + \sigma_{i\,(p\,(c))}^2 \tag{8}$$

TABLE E25

Variance components analysis of the effects of sex and degree of contact (DSIMI).

		Verbal IQ					Performance IQ					Full-Scale IQ			
Variance Source	df	Mean Square	F	Variance Component	Variance Ratio	df	Mean Square	F	Variance Component	Variance Ratio	df	Mean Square	F	Variance Component	Variance Ratio
Sex	1	12.4	.08	−12.5	.00	1	51.0	.14	−34.8	.00	1	59.3	.29	−13.1	.00
DSIMI	8	190.5	1.16	−28.6	.00	8	471.4	1.33	−83.8	.00	8	504.0	2.47*	−24.7	.00
Sex × DSIMI	6	439.6	2.68*	50.2	.35	6	1143.0	3.21**	151.5	.43	7	861.5	4.23**	74.9	.38
Pairs	37	163.9	6.36**	69.1	.48	35	355.7	6.92**	152.1	.43	65	203.8	5.02**	81.6	.41
Individuals	53	25.8		25.8	.17	51	51.4		51.4	.14	82	40.6		40.6	.21
Total	105	110.5		104.0	1.00	101	255.0		236.4	1.00	163	163.7		159.3	1.00

‡ p<.10
* p<.05
** p<.01

TABLE E26

Variance components analysis of the effects of sex and degree of contact (DSIMII).

		Verbal IQ					Performance IQ					Full-Scale IQ			
Variance Source	df	Mean Square	F	Variance Component	Variance Ratio	df	Mean Square	F	Variance Component	Variance Ratio	df	Mean Square	F	Variance Component	Variance Ratio
Sex	1	12.4	.08	−22.6	.00	1	51.0	.02	−36.6	.00	1	59.3	.25	−25.9	.00
DSIMII	3	184.9	1.13	−34.5	.00	3	283.9	.67	−59.0	.00	3	196.7	.82	−42.9	.00
Sex × DSIMII	3	779.8	4.79**	60.8	.39	3	1308.4	3.07*	90.6	.28	3	1681.5	7.04**	79.4	.36
Pairs	45	162.9	6.32**	68.6	.44	43	425.6	8.28**	187.1	.57	74	238.8	5.89**	99.1	.45
Individuals	53	25.8		25.8	.17	51	51.4		51.4	.16	82	40.6		40.6	.19
Total	105	110.5		98.1	1.00	101	255.0		233.5	1.00	163	163.7		150.3	1.00

‡ p<.10
* p<.05
** p<.01

TABLE E27

Variance components analysis with effects of degree of contact (DSIMI) on Verbal IQ for the combined sample.

		Males					Females					Males and Females			
Variance Source	df	Mean Square	F	Variance Component	Variance Ratio	df	Mean Square	F	Variance Component	Variance Ratio	df	Mean Square	F	Variance Component	Variance Ratio
DSIMI	6	408.2	2.37‡	51.8	.33	8	214.0	1.33	7.3	.07	8	191.4	.97	−.6	.00
Pairs	11	172.2	5.02**	69.0	.44	26	160.4	7.49**	69.5	.71	44	197.9	7.67**	86.0	.77
Individuals	18	34.2		34.2	.22	35	21.4		21.4	.22	53	25.8		25.8	.23
Total	35	141.7		155.0	1.00	69	96.1		98.1	1.00	105	110.5		111.8	1.00

‡ p<.10
* p<.05
** p<.01

Pursuing the same logic as above a variance ratio defined as:

$$h_y^2 = \frac{\sigma_{p\,(c)}^2}{\sigma_c^2 + \sigma_{p\,(c)}^2 + \sigma_{i\,(p\,(c))}^2} \tag{9}$$

can be regarded as a heritability estimate. Examination of tables E 27 through E 32 reveals that the effects of degree of contact appear more pronounced for the verbal and full-scale IQ scores than for performance IQ and slightly more pronounced for males than females. The proportion of IQ variance which can be attributed to this source (within sex) is about .20–.25. DSIMI and DSIMII show comparable patterns and magnitudes of effect. As would be expected from the significant sex x degree-of-contact interaction, the heritability estimates are lower for males and females separately than when they are combined. Although the $p(c)$ variance ratio varies across the analyses, most of the values are in the .40–.60 range.

Comparable analyses were conducted on a subset of the total sample (coded as PURE = 1 in table E 6) selected by Farber. This group had the least questionable IQ tests, was relatively free of serious psychopathology, and was in good physical health at the time of testing. Twins with grossly inadequate separations (coded as Group IV in the twin index in chapter 3) were excluded. The results presented in tables E 33 and E 34 show lower heritability estimates for males than for females, with both male estimates being less than .45. (The reduced sample size rendered it impossible to analyze the verbal and performance scores.)

Variance components analyses were also conducted for each of the indices of degree of contact during various developmental periods in an effort to identify any age periods where contact or separation seemed especially potent. Tables E 35 through E 37 summarize the results of these analyses. Briefly one can glean from the tables that degree of contact had an identifiable effect for males in the six to ten and ten to twenty age ranges and for females after the age of ten years. Although the overall degree of contact measure indicates greater effect than those within developmental periods, the age at which the twins are together seems to be an important factor. Apparently the time of separation affects male and female twins differently. A similar analysis was performed to ascertain the effects of being reared by a parent or other relative as opposed to an unrelated adult (see footnotes to table E 6 for the definition of the RELREAR variable). Significant effects were found for males on verbal and for females on performance IQ scores. The results may be found in tables E 38 and E 39. Means are presented in tables E 48 and E 49.

The mean verbal, performance, and full-scale IQ scores for males and females are broken down by degree of contact (DSIMI and DSIMII) in tables E 39 through E 44. A similar breakdown is given in tables E 45 through E 46 for degree of contact in the significant age periods for males and females.

TABLE E28

Variance components analysis with effects of degree of contact (DSIMII) on Verbal IQ for the combined sample.

Males

Variance Source	df	Mean Square	F	Variance Component	Variance Ratio
DSIMII	3	555.8	2.91‡	47.8	.30
Pairs	14	191.1	5.58**	78.4	.49
Individuals	18	34.3		34.3	.21
Total	35	141.7		160.5	1.00

Females

Variance Source	df	Mean Square	F	Variance Component	Variance Ratio
DSIMII	3	408.9	2.72‡	15.5	.15
Pairs	31	150.2	7.01**	64.4	.64
Individuals	35	21.4		21.4	.21
Total	69	96.1		101.3	1.00

Males and Females

Variance Source	df	Mean Square	F	Variance Component	Variance Ratio
DSIMII	3	183.3	.93	-.6	.00
Pairs	49	197.7	7.67**	86.0	.77
Individuals	53	25.8		25.8	.23
Total	105	110.5		111.7	1.00

‡ p<.10
* p<.05
** p<.01

TABLE E29

Variance components analysis with effects of degree of contact (DSIMI) on Performance IQ for the combined sample.

Males

Variance Source	df	Mean Square	F	Variance Component	Variance Ratio
DSIMI	6	530.8	1.56	45.2	.19
Pairs	10	339.2	6.29**	142.6	.59
Individuals	17	53.9		53.9	.22
Total	33	227.1		241.8	1.00

Females

Variance Source	df	Mean Square	F	Variance Component	Variance Ratio
DSIMI	8	930.5	2.57*	78.4	.28
Pairs	25	362.3	7.22**	156.1	.55
Individuals	34	50.2		50.2	.18
Total	67	271.7		284.6	1.01

Males and Females

Variance Source	df	Mean Square	F	Variance Component	Variance Ratio
DSIMI	8	477.3	1.04	1.7	.01
Pairs	42	459.8	8.94**	204.2	.79
Individuals	51	51.4		51.4	.20
Total	101	255.0		257.3	1.00

‡ p<.10
* p<.05
** p<.01

TABLE E30

Variance components analysis with effects of degree of contact (DSIMII) on Performance IQ for the combined sample.

Males

Variance Source	df	Mean Square	F	Variance Component	Variance Ratio
DSIMII	3	673.7	1.92	44.3	.18
Pairs	13	350.4	6.50**	148.2	.60
Individuals	17	53.9		53.9	.22
Total	33	227.1		246.5	1.00

Females

Variance Source	df	Mean Square	F	Variance Component	Variance Ratio
DSIMII	3	918.6	2.00	28.4	.10
Pairs	30	458.2	9.13**	204.0	.72
Individuals	34	50.2		50.2	.18
Total	67	271.7		282.6	1.00

Males and Females

Variance Source	df	Mean Square	F	Variance Component	Variance Ratio
DSIMII	3	291.1	.61	-7.7	.00
Pairs	47	473.5	9.21**	211.1	.80
Individuals	51	51.4		51.4	.20
Total	101	255.0		262.5	1.00

‡ p<.10
* p<.05
** p<.01

In these tables also appear the mean absolute pair differences for verbal, performance, and full-scale IQ by degree of contact. As was explained previously, if one of the hypotheses concerning effects of environmental similarity was correct, the mean absolute pair IQ differences would be expected to show a decreasing trend across levels of contact (i.e., as degree of contact increases). Inspection of the means in the various tables reveals that both of these trends may be present, especially for DSIMI. However, the patterns are difficult to evaluate because of the large number of categories and consequent small number of pairs at some levels. To facilitate analysis we collapsed DSIMI into its four superordinate levels (corresponding to Roman numerals I-IV in the footnotes to table E 6 and in the twin index in chapter 3). The absolute difference means are given for these collapsed levels (referred to as DSIMIC) in tables E 47 through E 49. In these tables the tendency for those pairs which experienced the greatest contact to have the least difference in IQ scores, i.e., to be most similar in IQ, is readily observed for females. The opposite trend is noted for males. Multivariate and univariate analyses of variance performed for the absolute pair differences are reported in tables E 53 and E 54. The significant interaction effects inform us that the patterns are different for males and females. In our opinion, these results suggest a complex pattern of environmental effects on IQ which have not been detected by previous investigators.

In sum, the components of variance analyses generally indicate that there is an effect for degree of contact, that it varies by sex, and that an estimate of heritability which adjusts for this effect is about .50. This value is about .25 lower than comparable estimates which do not take into account degree of contact and sex. Environmental factors appear to exert somewhat stronger influence on verbal than performance IQ. The estimate of .50 may be even lower in future samples which take into account the similarity method of twin recruitment and selection and the similarity in rearing environments (G-E correlation).

It should be reiterated that we continue to question the value of these twin data for estimating heritability. However, we wanted to conduct as extensive analyses as possible since these were the only data available. In undertaking this thoroughgoing analysis, we were well aware that far too many parameters were being estimated and tested for the number of observations available. However, it seemed to us that given the uniqueness of this data set and the significance it has attained in the IQ controversy, we should be more concerned about evaluating characteristics of the scores and identifying potential sources of variance than about preserving an experiment-wise alpha rate near .05. Of course, others will disagree. Needless to say, we emphatically would welcome a replication of our analyses in a new and better sample.

Variance components analysis with effects of degree of contact (DSIMI) on Full-Scale IQ for the combined sample.

	Males						Females						Males and Females				
Variance Source	df	Mean Square	F	Variance Component	Variance Ratio	Variance Source	df	Mean Square	F	Variance Component	Variance Ratio	Variance Source	df	Mean Square	F	Variance Component	Variance Ratio
DSIMI	7	520.9	2.97*	45.3	.30	DSIMI	8	802.0	3.64**	54.2	.29	DSIMI	8	505.7	1.91‡	13.8	.08
Pairs	24	175.4	4.61**	68.7	.45	Pairs	41	220.3	5.22**	89.1	.48	Pairs	73	264.7	6.53**	112.1	.67
Individuals	32	38.0		38.0	.25	Individuals	50	42.2		42.2	.23	Individuals	82	40.6		40.6	.25
Total	63	144.0		152.0	1.00	Total	99	177.4		185.4	1.00	Total	163	163.8		166.4	1.00

‡ p<.10
* p<.05
** p<.01

Variance components analysis with effects of degree of contact (DSIMII) on Full-Scale IQ for the combined sample.

	Males						Females						Males and Females				
Variance Source	df	Mean Square	F	Variance Component	Variance Ratio	Variance Source	df	Mean Square	F	Variance Component	Variance Ratio	Variance Source	df	Mean Square	F	Variance Component	Variance Ratio
DSIMII	3	851.5	4.50**	44.0	.28	DSIMII	3	1026.6	3.82*	32.5	.17	DSIMII	3	192.8	.66	-2.6	.00
Pairs	28	189.4	4.98**	75.7	.48	Pairs	46	268.9	6.38**	113.4	.60	Pairs	78	292.1	7.20**	125.8	.76
Individuals	32	38.0		38.0	.24	Individuals	50	42.2		42.2	.22	Individuals	82	40.6		40.6	.24
Total	63	144.0		157.7	1.00	Total	99	177.4		188.1	.99	Total	163	163.7		166.3	1.00

‡ p<.10
* p<.05
** p<.01

Variance components analysis with effects of degree of contact (DSIMI) on Full-Scale IQ for the selected (PURE) sample.

	Males						Females						Males and Females				
Variance Source	df	Mean Square	F	Variance Component	Variance Ratio	Variance Source	df	Mean Square	F	Variance Component	Variance Ratio	Variance Source	df	Mean Square	F	Variance Component	Variance Ratio
DSIMI	6	268.4	1.84	38.0	.30	DSIMI	7	252.5	.91	-5.0	.00	DSIMI	7	169.8	.61	-13.6	.00
Pairs	5	146.0	4.12**	55.3	.43	Pairs	14	277.7	4.97**	110.9	.67	Pairs	26	276.4	5.68**	113.9	.70
Individuals	12	35.4		35.4	.27	Individuals	22	55.9		55.9	.33	Individuals	34	48.7		48.7	.30
Total	23	120.3		128.7	100.0	Total	43	160.1		166.8	1.00	Total	67	149.7		162.5	1.00

‡ p<.10
* p<.05
** p<.01

TABLE E34

Variance components analysis with effects of degree of contact (DSIMII) on Full-Scale IQ for the selected (PURE) sample.

	Males						Females						Males and Females				
Variance Source	df	Mean Square	F	Variance Component	Variance Ratio	Variance Source	df	Mean Square	F	Variance Component	Variance Ratio	Variance Source	df	Mean Square	F	Variance Component	Variance Ratio
DSIMII	3	580.2	7.74**	90.9	.62	DSIMII	3	435.8	1.80	21.0	.12	DSIMII	3	243.9	.96	−.7	.00
Pairs	8	75.0	2.12	19.8	.14	Pairs	18	241.5	4.32**	92.8	.55	Pairs	30	254.8	5.24**	103.1	.68
Individuals	12	35.4		35.4	.24	Individuals	22	55.9		55.9	.33	Individuals	34	48.7		48.7	.32
Total	23	120.2		146.1	1.00	Total	43	160.1		169.7	1.00	Total	67	149.7		151.7	1.00

‡ p < .10
* p < .05
** p < .01

TABLE E35
Variance ratios for degree of contact during various periods of development:
Verbal IQ

Variance Source	Males			Females			Males and Females		
	Contact	Pairs	Individuals	Contact	Pairs	Individuals	Contact	Pairs	Individuals
DCB6	.00	.77	.23	.14‡	.66	.20	.00	.78	.22
DC610	.37*	.41	.22	.00	.80	.20	.00	.77	.23
DC1020	.31‡	.48	.21	.12	.67	.20	.00	.78	.22
DC20	.00	.84	.16	.00	.82	.18	.00	.81	.19

For F-tests associated with Contact Variance Ratios:
 ‡ p<.10
 * p<.05
** p<.01

TABLE E36
Variance ratios for degree of contact during various periods of development:
Performance IQ

Variance Source	Males			Females			Males and Females		
	Contact	Pairs	Individuals	Contact	Pairs	Individuals	Contact	Pairs	Individuals
DCB6	.06	.72	.23	.00	.81	.19	.00	.80	.20
DC610	.21	.57	.22	.00	.82	.18	.01	.79	.20
DC1020	.13	.65	.22	.03	.78	.19	.00	.80	.20
DC20	.00	.82	.18	.00	.82	.18	.00	.82	.18

For F-tests associated with Contact Variance Ratios:
 ‡ p<.10
 * p<.05
** p<.01

TABLE E37
Variance ratios for degree of contact during various periods of development:
Full-Scale IQ

Variance Source	Males			Females			Males and Females		
	Contact	Pairs	Individuals	Contact	Pairs	Individuals	Contact	Pairs	Individuals
DCB6	.19‡	.56	.25	.09	.69	.23	.01	.75	.24
DC610	.24*	.51	.25	.00	.77	.23	.00	.75	.24
DC1020	.16‡	.59	.25	.12‡	.65	.23	.00	.76	.24
DC20	.00	.80	.20	.16*	.61	.24	.00	.75	.25

For F-tests associated with Contact Variance Ratios:
 ‡ p<.10
 * p<.05
** p<.01

TABLE E38

Components of variance analysis for males reared by relative (RELREAR).

Verbal IQ

Variance Source	df	Mean Square	F	Variance Component	Variance Ratio
RELREAR	2	855.5	4.88*	68.8	.40
Pairs	15	175.5	5.12**	70.6	.41
Individuals	18	34.3		34.3	.20
Total	35	141.7		173.6	1.00

Performance IQ

Variance Source	df	Mean Square	F	Variance Component	Variance Ratio
RELREAR	2	497.0	1.25	10.2	.04
Pairs	14	398.8	7.39**	172.4	.73
Individuals	17	53.9		53.9	.23
Total	33	227.1		236.5	1.00

Full-Scale IQ

Variance Source	df	Mean Square	F	Variance Component	Variance Ratio
RELREAR	2	704.5	3.17‡	24.0	.16
Pairs	29	222.3	5.85**	92.2	.60
Individuals	32	38.0		38.0	.25
Total	63	144.0		154.2	1.00

‡ $p < .10$
* $p < .05$
** $p < .01$

TABLE E39

Components of variance analysis for females reared by relative (RELREAR).

Verbal IQ

Variance Source	df	Mean Square	F	Variance Component	Variance Ratio
RELREAR	2	52.5	.29	−6.3	.00
Pairs	32	180.5	8.43**	79.6	.79
Individuals	35	21.4		21.4	.21
Total	69	96.1		101.0	1.00

Performance IQ

Variance Source	df	Mean Square	F	Variance Component	Variance Ratio
RELREAR	2	1441.4	3.28*	51.9	.18
Pairs	31	439.3	8.76**	194.6	.66
Individuals	34	50.2		50.2	.17
Total	67	271.7		296.7	1.00

Full-Scale IQ

Variance Source	df	Mean Square	F	Variance Component	Variance Ratio
RELREAR	2	666.0	2.22	11.6	.06
Pairs	47	300.4	7.12**	129.1	.71
Individuals	50	42.2		42.2	.23
Total	99	177.4		182.9	1.00

‡ $p < .10$
* $p < .05$
** $p < .01$

TABLE E40

Mean twin pair means and absolute differences classified by degree of overall contact (DSIMI) for males and females.

			Verbal IQ			Performance IQ			Full-Scale IQ		
			Number of Pairs	Pair Mean	Absolute Pair Difference	Number of Pairs	Pair Mean	Absolute Pair Difference	Number of Pairs	Pair Mean	Absolute Pair Difference
	(1)	IA	4	104.1	3.25	4	106.5	5.0	6	106.8	6.2
	(2)	IB	3	94.3	10.7	3	98.5	15.7	6	95.4	9.8
Degree	(3)	IC	3	87.5	5.0	3	87.2	10.3	3	87.0	8.0
of	(4)	ID	4	98.9	8.3	4	109.8	10.0	14	101.6	7.6
Overall	(5)	IE	7	95.3	5.1	6	99.7	6.0	9	93.4	5.9
Contact	(6)	IIA	2	98.5	3.0	2	85.5	5.0	7	87.5	8.1
(DSIMI)	(7)	IIB	9	100.1	6.1	9	97.1	9.4	12	99.4	5.9
	(8)	III	17	94.4	6.0	16	93.4	9.3	20	95.6	6.5
	(9)	IV	4	99.3	3.5	4	100.4	4.3	5	96.2	4.8

TABLE E41

Mean twin pair means and absolute differences classified by degree of overall contact (DSIMII) for males and females.

			Verbal IQ			Performance IQ			Full-Scale IQ		
			Number of Pairs	Pair Mean	Absolute Pair Difference	Number of Pairs	Pair Mean	Absolute Pair Difference	Number of Pairs	Pair Mean	Absolute Pair Difference
Degree of	(1)	None	8	98.6	4.1	8	98.6	7.0	18	95.9	7.4
Overall	(2)	Little	6	95.7	6.7	6	96.7	9.3	9	93.7	6.7
Contact	(3)	Some	21	98.7	6.2	20	100.2	8.7	34	99.0	7.1
(DSIMII)	(4)	Much	18	93.9	5.7	17	93.4	8.7	21	95.3	6.0

TABLE E42

Mean twin pair means and absolute differences classified by degree of overall contact (DSIMI) for males.

			Verbal IQ			Performance IQ			Full-Scale IQ		
			Number of Pairs	Pair Mean	Absolute Pair Difference	Number of Pairs	Pair Mean	Absolute Pair Difference	Number of Pairs	Pair Mean	Absolute Pair Difference
	(1)	IA	1	117.0	6.0	1	119.0	4.0	3	112.0	8.7
	(2)	IB	1	88.0	14.0	1	97.0	12.0	2	94.3	3.5
Degree of	(3)	IC	—	—	—	—	—	—	—	—	—
Overall	(4)	ID	—	—	—	—	—	—	4	99.1	7.8
Contact	(5)	IE	3	85.8	3.7	2	80.5	6.0	5	83.6	5.2
(DSIMI)	(6)	IIA	1	110.5	1.0	1	114.5	7.0	3	104.0	6.7
	(7)	IIB	4	97.3	7.5	4	90.4	12.8	5	95.6	8.8
	(8)	III	7	96.9	7.9	7	96.5	9.3	9	98.2	4.6
	(9)	IV	1	106.0	8.0	1	109.5	13.0	1	105.5	13.0

TABLE E43

Mean twin pair means and absolute differences classified by degree of overall contact (DSIMII) for males.

		Verbal IQ			Performance IQ			Full-Scale IQ		
		Number of Pairs	Pair Mean	Absolute Pair Difference	Number of Pairs	Pair Mean	Absolute Pair Difference	Number of Pairs	Pair Mean	Absolute Pair Difference
Degree of Overall Contact (DSIMII)	(1) None	2	113.8	3.5	2	116.8	5.5	6	109.8	5.8
	(2) Little	1	88.0	14.0	1	97.0	12.0	4	90.0	6.5
	(3) Some	8	94.1	6.1	7	90.3	10.9	13	93.5	8.2
	(4) Much	7	96.9	7.9	7	96.5	9.3	9	98.2	4.6

TABLE E44

Mean twin pair means and absolute differences classified by degree of overall contact (DSIMI) for females.

		Verbal IQ			Performance IQ			Full-Scale IQ		
		Number of Pairs	Pair Mean	Absolute Pair Difference	Number of Pairs	Pair Mean	Absolute Pair Difference	Number of Pairs	Pair Mean	Absolute Pair Difference
Degree of Overall Contact (DSIMI)	(1) IA	3	99.8	2.3	3	102.3	5.3	3	101.5	3.7
	(2) IB	2	97.5	9.0	2	99.3	17.5	4	96.0	13.0
	(3) IC	3	87.5	5.0	3	87.2	10.3	3	87.0	8.0
	(4) ID	4	98.9	8.3	4	109.8	10.0	10	102.6	7.6
	(5) IE	4	102.4	6.3	4	109.3	6.0	4	105.6	6.8
	(6) IIA	1	86.5	5.0	1	56.5	3.0	4	75.1	9.3
	(7) IIB	5	102.3	5.0	5	102.4	6.8	7	102.1	3.9
	(8) III	10	92.7	4.7	9	91.1	9.2	11	93.5	8.1
	(9) IV	3	97.0	2.0	3	97.3	1.3	4	98.9	2.8

TABLE E45

Mean twin pair means and absolute differences classified by degree of overall contact (DSIMII) for females.

			Verbal IQ			Performance IQ			Full-Scale IQ		
			Number of Pairs	Pair Mean	Absolute Pair Difference	Number of Pairs	Pair Mean	Absolute Pair Difference	Number of Pairs	Pair Mean	Absolute Pair Difference
Degree of Overall Contact (DSIMII)	(1)	None	6	93.5	4.3	6	92.6	7.5	12	88.9	8.2
	(2)	Little	5	97.2	5.2	5	96.6	8.8	5	96.6	6.8
	(3)	Some	13	101.5	6.2	13	105.5	7.5	21	102.4	6.5
	(4)	Much	11	91.9	4.4	10	91.3	8.3	12	93.1	7.2

TABLE E46

Mean twin pair means and absolute differences in Verbal IQ classified by degree of contact during ages 6 to 20 years for males.

			6 to 10 Years (DC610)			10 to 20 Years (DC1020)		
			Number of Pairs	Pair Mean	Absolute Pair Difference	Number of Pairs	Pair Mean	Absolute Pair Difference
Degree of Contact During Age Periods	(1)	None	3	112.5	5.0	2	113.8	3.5
	(2)	None-Little	1	88.0	14.0	–	–	–
	(3)	Little	3	92.7	3.3	4	91.1	7.8
	(4)	Little-Much-OM	4	91.1	7.8	2	98.5	5.0
	(5)	Much	7	96.9	7.9	10	95.8	7.7

TABLE E47

Mean twin pair means and absolute differences in performance IQ classified by degree of contact after age 10 years for females.

		10 to 20 Years (DC1020)			20 Years and Above (DC20)		
		Number of Pairs	Pair Mean	Absolute Pair Difference	Number of Pairs	Pair Mean	Absolute Pair Difference
Degree of	(1) None	6	92.6	7.5	3	102.3	5.3
Contact	(2) None-Little	4	94.0	10.5	6	99.8	11.2
During	(3) Little	5	106.8	8.0	6	102.9	9.8
Age	(4) Little-Much-OM	3	109.8	13.0	2	82.3	2.5
Periods	(5) Much	14	94.6	7.0	14	95.1	7.9

TABLE E48

Mean twin pair means and absolute differences classified by relation of persons rearing twins (RELREAR) for males.

		Verbal IQ			Performance IQ			Full-Scale IQ		
		Number of Pairs	Pair Mean	Absolute Pair Difference	Number of Pairs	Pair Mean	Absolute Pair Difference	Number of Pairs	Pair Mean	Absolute Pair Difference
Relation of Persons Rearing Twins (RELREAR)	(1) Other-Other	4	106.1	4.3	4	105.8	6.0	11	104.0	5.4
	(2) Parent-Other Relative-Other	3	84.7	10.7	3	89.1	8.3	6	93.6	4.2
	(3) Parent-Parent Parent-Relative Relative-Relative	11	97.1	6.9	10	94.8	11.5	15	94.1	8.3

TABLE E49

Mean twin pair means and absolute differences classified by relation of persons rearing twins (RELREAR) for females.

		Verbal IQ			Performance IQ			Full-Scale IQ		
		Number of Pairs	Pair Mean	Absolute Pair Difference	Number of Pairs	Pair Mean	Absolute Pair Difference	Number of Pairs	Pair Mean	Absolute Pair Difference
Relation of Persons Rearing Twins (RELREAR)	(1) Other-Other	6	93.8	6.0	6	88.3	6.7	16	92.8	7.1
	(2) Parent-Other Relative-Other	9	97.3	5.7	8	108.2	8.1	10	103.2	8.1
	(3) Parent-Parent Parent-Relative Relative-Relative	20	96.9	4.7	20	96.4	8.3	24	95.8	6.7

TABLE E50

Mean twin pair means and absolute differences classified by degree of overall contact—collapsed (DSIMIC) for males and females.

			Verbal IQ			Performance IQ			Full-Scale IQ		
			Number of Pairs	Pair Mean	Absolute Pair Difference	Number of Pairs	Pair Mean	Absolute Pair Difference	Number of Pairs	Pair Mean	Absolute Pair Difference
Degree of Overall Contact— Collapsed (DSIMIC)	I	(1–5)	21	96.4	6.1	20	101.0	8.7	38	98.3	7.4
	II	(6–7)	11	99.8	5.5	11	95.0	8.6	19	95.0	6.7
	III	8	17	94.4	6.0	16	93.4	9.3	20	95.6	6.5
	IV	9	4	99.3	3.5	4	100.4	4.3	5	96.2	4.8

TABLE E51

Mean twin pair means and absolute differences classified by degree of overall contact—collapsed (DSIMIC) for males.

			Verbal IQ			Performance IQ			Full-Scale IQ		
			Number of Pairs	Pair Mean	Absolute Pair Difference	Number of Pairs	Pair Mean	Absolute Pair Difference	Number of Pairs	Pair Mean	Absolute Pair Difference
Degree of Overall Contact— Collapsed (DSIMIC)	I	(1–5)	5	92.5	6.2	4	94.3	7.0	14	95.6	6.4
	II	(6–7)	5	99.9	6.2	5	95.2	11.6	8	98.8	8.0
	III	8	7	96.9	7.9	7	96.5	9.3	9	98.2	4.6
	IV	9	1	106.0	8.0	1	109.5	13.0	1	105.5	13.0

TABLE E52

Mean twin pair means and absolute differences classified by degree of overall contact—collapsed (DSIMIC) for females.

		Verbal IQ			Performance IQ			Full-Scale IQ		
		Number of Pairs	Pair Mean	Absolute Pair Difference	Number of Pairs	Pair Mean	Absolute Pair Difference	Number of Pairs	Pair Mean	Absolute Pair Difference
Degree of Overall Contact— Collapsed (DSIMIC)	I (1–5)	16	97.6	6.1	16	102.7	9.1	24	99.9	7.9
	II (6–7)	6	99.7	5.0	6	94.8	6.2	11	92.3	5.8
	III 8	10	92.7	4.7	9	91.1	9.2	11	93.5	8.1
	IV 9	3	97.0	2.0	3	97.3	1.3	4	93.9	2.8

TABLE E53

Multivariate analysis of variance of absolute pair differences in IQ by degree of contact (DSIMIC).

Variance Source	Hypothesis df	Error df	F^*	p
DSIMIC	3	119	1.32	.23
Sex	1	41	3.53	.02
DSIMIC × Sex	9	119	3.16	.002

*F approximation to the Hotelling-Lawley Trace statistic.
Dependent Vector: VIQ, PIQ, IQ

TABLE E54

Analysis of variance of absolute pair differences in IQ by degree of contact (DSIMIC).

Variance Source	Absolute Difference Verbal IQ				Variance Source	Absolute Difference Performance IQ				Variance Source	Absolute Difference Full-Scale IQ			
	df	Mean Square	F	η^2		df	Mean Square	F	η^2		df	Mean Square	F	η^2
DSIMIC	3	8.3	.46	.03	DSIMIC	3	27.4	.90	.05	DSIMIC	3	11.3	.35	.01
Sex	1	38.9	2.17#	.04	Sex	1	27.3	.89	.02	Sex	1	7.9	.25	.00
DSIMIC × Sex	3	11.0	.62	.04	DSIMIC × Sex	3	56.6	1.85#	.10	DSIMIC × Sex	3	59.9	1.87#	.07
Error	45	17.9			Error	43	30.5			Error	74	32.1		
Total	52	17.4			Total	50	31.9			Total	81	32.0		

#p<.15

Bibliography

Aire, I.; Bentall, H. H.; and Fraser Roberts, J. A. 1953. A relationship between cancer of stomach and the ABO blood groups. *British Medical Journal* 1:799–801.

Allen, M. G. 1976. Twin studies of affective illness. *Archives of General Psychiatry* 33:1476–1478.

Anderson, P. W., and Darling, D. A. 1954. A test of goodness of fit. *Journal of the American Statistical Association* 49:765–769.

Annett, M. 1978. Genetic and nongenetic influences on handedness. *Behavior Genetics* 8 (3):227–250.

Badalian, L. O.; Oradovskaia, I. V.; and Lipovetskaia, N. G. 1971. Nocturnal enuresis in twins (Clinico-genetic analysis). *Urol. Nefrol. (Mosk.)* 36(2):44–48. (In Russian with English summary.)

Bakwin, H. 1970. Sleep-walking in twins. *Lancet* 2(670):446–447.

———. 1971. Enuresis in twins. *Am. J. Dis. Child* 121(3):222–225.

Ballenger, J. J. 1977. *Diseases of the nose, throat and ear* 12th ed. Philadelphia: Lea & Febiger.

Bane, M. J., and Jencks, C. 1976. Five myths about your IQ. In *The IQ controversy*, ed. N. J. Block, and G. Dworkin, pp. 325–328. New York: Pantheon Books.

Beeson, P. B., and McDermott, W. 1975. *Textbook of medicine*. 14th ed. Philadelphia: W. B. Saunders.

Bell, R. O.; Weller, G. M.; and Waldrop, M. F. 1971. *Newborn and preschooler: Organization of behavior and relations between periods.* Monographs of the Society for Research in Child Development 36, 1–2.

Bellone, F.; Pecorari, D.; and Trovati, G. 1975. Menarche and menstruation disorders in girls with birth weight lower than 2500 grams. *Minerva. Ginecol.* 27(7):515–522.

Bertelsen, B.; Harvald, B.; and Hauge, M. 1977. A Danish study of manic-depressive disorders. *British Journal of Psychiatry* 130:330–351.

Blank, G., and Blank, R. 1974. *Ego psychology: Theory and practice.* New York: Columbia University Press.

Block, N. J., and Dworkin, G. 1976. *The IQ controversy.* New York: Pantheon Books.

Blos, P. 1972. The epigenesis of the adult neurosis. In *The psychoanalytic study of the child*, ed. R. S. Eissler et al., vol. 27, pp. 106–135. New Haven: Yale University Press.

Bock, R. D. 1973. Word and image: Sources of the verbal and spatial factors in mental test scores. *Psychometrika* 38:437–457.

Bodmer, W. T., and Cavalli-Sforza, L. L. 1976. *Genetics, evolution, and man.* San Francisco: W. H. Freeman.

Boklage, C. E. 1974. Embryonic determination of brain programming asymmetry: A neglected element in twin-study genetics of mental development. Paper presented to the First International Congress of Twin Studies, October 30, 1974, Rome.

*Bouterwek, H. 1936. Erhebungen an eineiigen Zwillingspaaren uber Efbanlage und unwelt als characterbildner. *Z. Menschl. Vererb-u. Konstit-Lehre* 20:265–275.

Brandborg, L. L. 1975. Malignant neoplasms of the stomach. In *Textbook of medicine*, ed. P. B. Beeson and W. McDermott, pp. 1293–1296. Philadelphia: W. B. Saunders.

Bronfenbrenner, U. 1975. Is 80% of intelligence genetically determined? In ed. U. Bronfenbrenner and M. A. Mahoney. *Influences on human development.* 2nd ed. pp., 91–100. Hinsdale, Ill.: Dryden Press.

Brown, A. M.; Stafford R. E.; and Vandenberg, S. G. 1967. Twins: Behavioral differences. *Child Development* 38(4):1055–1064.

Brown, M. B., and Forsythe, A. B. 1974. Robust tests for the equality of variances. *Journal of the American Statistical Association* 69:364–370.

1. Citations preceded by an asterisk (*) are case references.

Bulmer, M. G. 1970. *The biology of twinning in man.* Oxford: Clarendon Press.
*Burks, B. S. 1942. A study of identical twins reared apart under differing types of family relationships. In *Studies in personality,* ed. Q. McNemar and M. R. Merrill, pp. 35–69. New York: McGraw-Hill.
*Burks, B. S., and Roe, A. 1949. *Studies of identical twins reared apart.* Psychol. Monogr. 63.
Buros, O. K. 1965. *The sixth mental measurements yearbook.* Highland Park, N. J.: Gryphon Press.
———. 1974. *Tests in print II.* Highland Park, N. J.: Gryphon Press.
Cancro, R., ed. 1971. *Intelligence: Genetic and environmental influences.* New York: Grune & Stratton.
Canter, S. 1973. Personality traits in twins. In *Personality differences and biological variations: A study of twins,* ed. G. Claridge, S. Canter, and W. I. Hume, pp. 21–51 Oxford: Pergamon Press.
Carey, G.; Goldsmith, H. H.; Tellegren, A.; and Gottesman, I. I. 1978. Genetics and personality inventories: The limits of replication with twin data. *Behavior Genetics* 8 (4):299–313.
Carter-Saltzman, L.; Scarr-Salapatek, S.; Barker, W. B.; and Katz, I. 1976. Left-handedness in twins: Incidence and patterns of performance in an adolescent sample. *Behavior Genetics* 6(2):189–203.
Carter-Saltzman, L., and Scarr, S. 1977. MZ or DZ? Only your blood grouping laboratory knows for sure. *Behavior Genetics* 7:273–280.
Caspari, E. W. 1977. Genetic mechanisms and behavior. In *Genetics, environment and intelligence,* ed. A. Oliverio, pp. 3–22. New York: Elsevier/North-Holland Biomedical Press.
Cattell, R. B.; Blewett, D. B.; and Beloff, J. R. 1955. The inheritance of personality. A multiple variance analysis determination of approximate nature-nurture ratios for primary personality factors in Q-data. *Am. J. Hum. Genet.* 7:122–146.
Cavalli-Sforza, L. L. 1975. Quantitative genetic perspectives: Implications for human development. In *Developmental human behavior genetics,* ed. K. W. Schaie, V. E. Anderson, G. E. McClearn, and J. Money, pp. 123–138. Lexington, Mass.: Lexington Books, D. C. Heath.
———, and Bodmer, W. T. 1978. *The genetics of human populations.* San Francisco: W. H. Freeman.
Cederlof, R.; Friberg, L.; Jonsson, E.; and Kaij, L. 1961. Studies on similarity diagnosis with the aid of mailed questionnaires. *Acta Genet. Stat. Med.* 11:338–362.
———, and Kaij, L. 1970. The effect of childbearing on body-weight: a twin control study. In *Studies dedicated to Erik Essen-Möller. Acta Psychiat. Scand.* Suppl. 219, pp. 47–49. Copenhagen: Munksgaard.
Chen, E. 1979. Twins reared apart: A living lab, *The New York Times Magazine,* Dec. 9, 1979, New York, pp. 112–126.
Chess, S., and Hassibi, M. 1978. *Principles and practice of child psychiatry.* New York: Plenum Press.
Christian, C. C. 1975. Diseases of the joints. In *Textbook of medicine,* ed. P. B. Beeson and W. McDermott, pp. 140–163. Philadelphia: W. B. Saunders.
Claridge, G. S. 1967. *Personality and arousal.* Oxford: Pergamon Press.
———; Canter, S.; and Hume, W. I. 1973. *Personality differences and biological variations: A study of twins.* Oxford: Pergamon Press.
Cohen, D. J.; Dibble, E.; Grawe, J. M.; and Pollin, W. 1975. Reliably separating identical from fraternal twins. *Archives of General Psychiatry* 32(11):1371–1375.
Conterio, F., and Chiarelli, B. 1962. Study of the inheritance of some daily life habits. *Heredity* 17:347–359.
*Craike, W. H., and Slater, E. 1945. Folie a deux in uniovular twins reared apart. *Brain* 68:213–221.
D'Agostino, R., and Pearson, E. S. 1973. Tests for departure from normality. Empirical results for the distributions of b_2 and $\sqrt{b_1}$. *Biometrika* 60:613–622.
Davidson, E. H. 1976. *Gene activity in early development.* 2d ed. New York: Academic Press.
Davitz, J. 1969. *The language of emotion,* New York: Academic Press.
DeGroot, L. J. 1975. Diseases of the endocrine system: the thyroid. In *Textbook of medicine,* ed. P. B. Beeson and W. McDermott, pp. 1703–1732. Philadelphia: W. B. Saunders.

*Dencker, S. J. 1958. A follow-up study of 128 closed head injuries in twins using co-twins as controls. *Acta Psychiat. Scand., Suppl. 123.* Copenhagen: Munksgaard.

Deutsch, M.; Katz, I.; and Jensen, A., eds. 1968. *Social class, race and psychological development.* New York: Holt, Rinehart & Winston.

Dobzhansky, T. 1973. *Genetic diversity and human equality.* New York: Basic Books.

Duffy, E. 1962. *Activation and behavior.* New York: Wiley.

Dustman, R. E., and Beck, E. C. 1965. The visual evoked response in twins. *Electroencephalogr. Clin. Neurophysiol.* 19:570–575.

Erikson, E. 1968. *Childhood and Society.* 2d ed. New York: W. W. Norton.

Escalona, S. 1963. Patterns of experience and the developmental process. In *The psychoanalytic study of the child,* ed. R. S. Eissler et al., vol. 8, pp. 197–244. New York: International Universities Press.

————. 1968. *The roots of individuality,* Chicago: Aldine.

*Essen-Möller, E. 1941. Psychiatrische Untersuchungen an einer Serie von Zwillingen. *Acta Psychiatrica et Neurologica Scandinavica,* Suppl. 23. Copenhagen: Munksgaard.

Eysenck, H. J. 1976. Genetic factors in personality development. In *Progress in human behavior genetics,* ed. S. Vandenberg, pp. 198–229. Baltimore: Johns Hopkins Press.

Fishbein, H. D. 1976. *Evolution, development, and children's learning.* Pacific Palisades, Calif: Goodyear.

Fraser Roberts, J., and Pembry, M. E. 1978. *An introduction to medical genetics.* Oxford: Oxford University Press.

Fraumeni, J. F. 1975. *Persons at high risk of cancer: An approach to cancer etiology and control.* New York: Academic Press.

Freedman, A. M., and Kaplan, H. J. 1967. *Comprehensive Textbook of Psychiatry.* Baltimore: Waverly Press. (Reprinted 1974.)

Freedman, D. 1965. An ethological approach to the genetical study of human behavior. In *Methods and goals in human behavior genetics,* ed. S. Vandenberg, pp. 141–161. New York: Academic Press.

Freud, S. 1900. The interpretation of dreams. In *The standard edition of the complete psychological works of Sigmund Freud,* ed. J. Strachey, vols. 4 and 5. London: Hogarth Press, 1975.

————. 1937. Analysis terminable and interminable. In *The standard edition of the complete psychological works of Sigmund Freud,* ed. J. Strachey, vol. 23, pp. 209–254. London: Hogarth Press, 1975.

Fries, M. 1977. Longitudinal study: Prenatal period to parenthood. *J. Am. Psychoanalytic Assn.* 25(1):115–140.

————, and Wolff, P. 1953. Some hypotheses on the role of the congenital activity type in personality development. In *The psychoanalytic study of the child,* ed. R. S. Eissler et al., vol. 8, pp. 48–64. New York: International Universities Press.

Frieze, I. H.; Parsons, J. E.; Johnson, P. B.; Ruble, D. N.; and Zellman, G. L. 1978. *Women and sex roles, a social psychological perspective.* New York: W. W. Norton.

*Fukuoka, C. 1937. In T. Komai and C. Fukuoka. Studies on Japanese twins, 9–47. *Contributions to the genetics of the Japanese race II.* Kyoto, Japan.

Fulker, D. W. 1975. Review of L. J. Kamin, science and politics of IQ. *Journal of Psychology* 88:505–519.

Fuller, J. L., and Thompson, W. R. 1978. *Foundations of behavior genetics,* St. Louis: C. V. Mosby.

*Gardner, I. C., and Newman, H. H. 1940. Mental and physical traits of identical twins reared apart: The twins Lois and Louise. *J. Hered.* 31:119–126.

Gedda, L. 1961. *Twins in history and science.* Springfield, Ill.: Charles C Thomas.

Goldsmith, H. H., and Gottesman I. I. 1977. An extension of construct validity for personality scales using twin-based criteria. *Journal of Research in Personality* 11:381–397.

Goodwin, D. W. 1976. *Is alcoholism hereditary?* New York: Oxford University Press.

Gottesman, I. I. 1965. Personality and natural selection. In *Methods and goals in human behavior genetics,* ed. S. Vandenberg, pp. 63–80. New York: Academic Press.

————. 1968. Biogenetics of race and class. In *Social class, race and psychological development,* ed. M. Deutsch, L. Katz and A. Jensen, pp. 11–51. New York: Holt, Rinehart & Winston.

————. 1972. Heredity and intelligence. In *The Young Child,* ed. W. Hartup, pp. 25–52. Washington D.C.: National Association for the Education of Young Children

————. 1974. Developmental genetics and ontogenetic psychology: Overdue détente and propositions from a matchmaker. In *Minnesota Symposium on Child Psychology*, ed. A. Pick, pp. 55–80. Minneapolis: University of Minnesota Press.

*————, and Shields, J. 1972. *Schizophrenia and genetics: A twin study vantage point.* New York: Academic Press.

————. 1976. A critical review of recent adoption, twin and family studies of schizophrenia: Behavioral genetic perspectives. *Schizophrenia Bulletin* 2:360–453.

Gough, H. G., and Domino, G. 1963. The D 48 test as a measure of general ability among grade school children. *Journal of Consulting Psychology* 27(4):344–349.

Grossman, M. I. 1975. Peptic ulcer: Pathogenesis and pathophysiology. *Textbook of Medicine*, ed. P. B. Beeson and W. McDermott, pp. 1198–1201. Philadelphia: W. B. Saunders.

Hanson, D. R.; Gottesman, I. I.; and Heston, L. C. 1976. Some possible childhood indicators of adult schizophrenia inferred from children of schizophrenics. *British Journal of Psychiatry* 129:142–154.

Harvald, B., and Hauge, M. 1965. Hereditary factors elucidated by twin studies. In *Genetics and the epidemiology of chronic diseases*, ed. J. V. Neel, M. W. Shaw, and W. J. Schull, pp. 61–76, Public Health Service Publication #1163. Washington, D.C.: Department of Health, Education and Welfare.

Hearnshaw, L. S. 1979. *Cyril Burt: Psychologist.* Ithaca, N.Y.: Cornell University Press.

Hirsch, N. D. M. 1930. *Twins, heredity and environment.* Cambridge, Mass.: Harvard University Press.

Howard, R. G., and Brown, A. M. 1970. Twinning: A marker for biological insults. *Child Development* 41:519–530.

Huhey, J. E. 1977. Concerning the origin of handedness. *Behavior Genetics* 7 (1):29–32.

Hume, W. I. 1973. Physiological measures in twins. In *Personality differences and biological variations: A study of twins*, ed. G. Claridge. S. Canter, and W. I. Hume, Oxford: Pergamon Press.

ICDA, *International classification of diseases, 8th Revision, U.S. Adaptation,* vols. 1–2, Public Health Service Publication #1693, Washington, D.C.: Department of Health, Education and Welfare.

ICD-9. 1979. *International classification of diseases, 9th revision, clinical modification,* Jan. 1, 1979, vols. 1–2, Commission on Professional and Hospital Activities. Ann Arbor, Mich.: Edwards Brothers.

Inouye, E. 1970. Twin studies and human behavioral genetics, *Jap. J. of Human Genet.* 15(1):1–25.

*————. 1972. Monozygotic twins with schizophrenia reared apart in infancy. *Jap. J. Human. Genet.* 16(3):182–190. (Additional information in appendices B and C of this text.)

Izard, C. E. 1978. On the ontogenesis of emotions and emotion-cognition relationships in infancy. In *The development of affect*, ed. M. Lewis, and L. A. Rosenblum, pp. 389–413. New York: Plenum Press.

Janowitz, H. D. 1975. Chronic inflammatory diseases of the intestine. In *Textbook of medicine*, ed. P. B. Beeson and W. McDermott, pp. 1256–1273. Philadelphia: W. B. Saunders.

Jencks, C.; Smith, M.; Acland, H.; Bane, M. J.; Cohen, D.; Gintis, H.; Heyns, B.; and Michelson, S. 1972. *Inequality: A reassessment of the effect of family and schooling in America.* New York: Basic Books.

Jensen, A. R. 1970. IQs of identical twins reared apart. *Behavior Genetics* 1:133–148.

————. 1973. *Educability and group differences.* London: Methuen.

————. 1976. Twins' IQs: A reply to Schwartz and Schwartz. *Behavior Genetics* 6(3):369–371.

Jinks, J. L., and Fulker, D. W. 1970. Comparison of the biometrical genetical, MAVA, and classical approaches to the analysis of human behavior. *Psychological Bulletin* 73:311–349.

Johnson, R. C. 1963. Similarity in IQ of separated identical twins as related to length of time spent in same environment. *Child Development* 34:745–49.

*Juel-Nielsen, N. 1965. Individual and environment: A psychiatric-psychological investigation of MZ twins reared apart. *Acta Psychiat. Scand.*, Suppl. 183. Copenhagen: Munksgaard. Reprinted 1980, with epilogue, by International Universities Press, New York.

————, and Harvald, B. 1958. The electroencephalogram in uniovular twins brought up apart. *Acta Genet.* 8:57-64.

*Kaij, L. 1960. *Alcoholism in twins.* Stockholm: Almquist & Wiksell.

*Kallmann, F. J. 1938. *The genetics of schizophrenia.* Locust Valley, New York: J. J. Augustin.

*————, and Roth, B. 1956. Genetic aspects of preadolescent schizophrenia. *American Journal of Psychiat.* 112:599-606. (For further information see appendix D of this text.)

Kamin, L. J. 1974. *The science and politics of IQ.* New York: Wiley.

Kaplan, A. 1976. *Human behavior genetics.* Springfield, Ill.: Charles C Thomas.

Katz, W. 1977. *Rheumatic diseases: Diagnosis and management.* Philadelphia: J. B. Lippincott.

Kestenbaum, C. J. 1979. Adolescents at risk for manic depressive illness: Possible predictors. *American Journal of Psychiatry* 136:9.

————. 1980. Adolescents at risk for manic depressive illness. In manuscript.

Kety, S. S.; Rosenthal, D.; Wender, P. H.; and Schulsinger, F. 1976. Studies based on a total sample of adopted individuals and their relatives: Why they were necessary, what they demonstrated and failed to demonstrate. *Schizophrenia Bulletin* 2:413-428.

Kirk, R. E. 1968. *Experimental design procedures for the behavioral sciences.* Belmont, Calif.: Brooks/Cole.

Kohler, W. C. 1969. Sleep EEG patterns in identical twins with developmental disturbance. *South. Med. J.* 62(1):17-22.

Kraus, B. S.; Jordan, R. E.; and Abrams, L. 1969. *Dental anatomy and occlusion.* Baltimore: Williams & Wilkins.

————; Wise, W.; and Frei, R. 1959. Heredity and the craniofacial complex. *Amer. J. Orthodont.* 45:172-217.

*Kringlen, E. 1964. Schizophrenia in male monozygotic twins. *Acta Psychiat. Scand.,* Suppl. 178. Copenhagen: Munksgaard.

*————. 1967. *Heredity and environment in the functional psychoses.* London: Heinemann.

*————. 1967. Case histories supplement, *Norwegian Monographs on Medical Science.* Universitetsforlaget.

Lacey, J. I., and Lacey, B. C. 1962. The law of initial value in the longitudinal study of autonomic constitution: Reproducibility of autonomic response and response patterns over a four-year interval. *Ann. N.Y. Acad. Science* 98:1257-1290.

*Lange, J. 1931. *Crime as destiny.* London: George Allen and Unwin, Ltd.

Layzer, D. 1976. Science or superstition? A physical scientist looks at the IQ controversy. In *The IQ controversy,* ed. N. J. Block, and G. Dworkin, pp. 194-241. New York: Pantheon Books.

Leites, N. 1971. *The new ego.* New York: Science House.

Lennox, W. G.; Gibbs, E. L.; and Gibbs, F. A. 1945. The brain-wave pattern: An hereditary trait: Evidence from 74 "normal" pairs of twins. *J. Heredity* 36:233-243.

Levitan, M. 1977. *Textbook of human genetics.* 2d ed. New York: Oxford University Press.

Levy, J. 1976. A review of evidence for a genetic component in the determination of handedness. *Behavior Genetics* 6(4):429-454.

Lewis, E. G.; Dustman, R. E.; and Beck, E. C. 1972. Evoked response similarity in monozygotic, dizygotic and unrelated individuals: A comparative study. *Electroencephalogr. Clin. Neurophysiol.* 32:309-316.

Lewis, M., ed. 1976. *Origins of intelligence: Infancy and early childhood.* New York: Plenum Press.

————, and Rosenblum, L., eds. 1974. *The effect of the infant on its caregiver.* New York: Wiley.

————. 1978. *The development of affect.* New York: Plenum Press.

Liljefors, I., and Rahe, R. H. 1970. An identical twin study of psychosocial factors in coronary heart diseases in Sweden. *Psychosomatic Medicine* 32:523-542.

*Lindeman, B. 1969. *The twins who found each other.* New York: Morrow.

Linder, D.; McCaw, B. F.; and Hecht, F. 1975. Parthenogenic origin of benign ovarian teratomas. *New Eng. J. Med.* 292:63-69.

Loehlin, J. C. 1975. Empirical methods in quantitative human behavior genetics. In *Developmental Human Behavior Genetics,* ed. K. W. Schaie, V. E. Anderson, G. E. McClearn, and J. Money, pp. 41-54. Lexington, Mass.: Lexington Books, D. C. Heath.

————; Lindzey, G.; and Spuhler, J. N. 1975. *Race differences in intelligence.* San Francisco: W. H. Freeman.

Lubchenco, J.; Horner, F.; Reed, L.; Hix, I.; Metcalf, D.; Cohib, R.; Elliott, H.; and Borg, M. 1963. Sequelae of premature birth. *American Journal of the Diseases of Children* 106:101–115.

Lundstrom, A. 1963. Tooth morphology as a basis for distinguishing monozygotic and dizygotic twins. *Amer. J. Human Genet.* 15:34–43.

Lynch, H. T. 1976. *Cancer genetics.* Springfield, Ill.: Charles C Thomas.

McCall, R. B. 1970. Intelligence quotient pattern over age: Comparisons among siblings and parent-child pairs. *Science* 170:644–48.

McClearn, G. E. 1970 Genetic influences on behavior and development. In *Carmichael's Manual of Child Psychology,* ed. P. H. Mussen, pp. 39–76. New York: Wiley.

————, and Defries, J. C. 1973. *Introduction to behavioral genetics.* San Francisco: W. H. Freeman.

MacFarlane, J. W.; Allen, L.; and Honzik, M. P. 1962. *A developmental study of behavior problems of normal children between 21 months and 14 years.* Berkeley: University of California Press.

MacGillivray, I.; Nylander, P. P. S.; and Corney, G. 1975. *Human multiple reproduction.* Philadelphia: W. B. Saunders.

McKusick, V. A. 1978. *Mendelian inheritance in man.* 5th ed. Baltimore: Johns Hopkins University Press.

McNemar, Q. 1938. Special review: Newman, Freeman and Holzinger's twins: A study of heredity and environment. *Psychological Bulletin* 35(4):237–249.

Magnusson, D. 1966. *Test theory.* Reading, Mass.: Addison-Wesley.

Mahler, M. 1968. *On human symbiosis and the vicissitudes of individuation,* vol. 1. New York: International Universities Press.

————, and LaPerriere, K. 1965. Mother-child interaction during separation-individuation. *Psychoanalytic Quarterly* 34:483–498.

————, Pine, F.; and Bergman, A. 1975. *The psychological birth of the human infant.* New York: Basic Books.

Malkoff, D. B., and Mick, B. A. 1970. Sleepwalking in twins. *Lancet* 2(674):664.

Marks, I. M.; Crowe, M.; Drewe, E.; Young, J.; and Dewhurst, W. G. 1969. Obsessive-compulsive neurosis in identical twins. *British Journal of Psychology* 115:991–998.

Mead, M. 1928. *Coming of age in Samoa,* New York: Morrow and Co.

————. 1930. *Growing up in New Guinea.* New York: Morrow and Co.

*Mitsuda, H. 1967. *Clinical genetics in psychiatry.* Tokyo: Igaku Shoin.

*Muller, H. J. 1925. Mental traits and heredity. *Journal of Heredity* 16:433–448.

Myrianthopoulos, N. C.; Nichols, P. L.; Broman, S. H.; and Anderson, V. E. 1972. Intellectual development of a prospectively studied population of twins and comparison with singletons. *Human genetics: Proceedings of the fourth international congress of human genetics.* Amsterdam: Excerpta Medica.

Neel, J. V.; Shaw, M. W.; and Schull, W. J. 1965. *Genetics and the epidemiology of chronic diseases,* Public Health Service Publication #1163. Washington, D. C.: Department of Health, Education and Welfare.

Newman, H. H. 1928. Studies on human twins: II. Asymmetry reversal, or mirror imaging in identical twins. *Biological Bulletin* 55(4):298–315.

*————; Freeman, F. N.; and Holzinger, K. J. 1937. *Twins: A study of heredity and environment.* Chicago: University of Chicago Press.

Nichols, P., and Broman, S. H. 1977. Infant mental development: Letter to the editor. *Behavior Genetics* 7(4):347–348.

Novitski, E. 1977. *Human genetics.* New York: Macmillan.

Ongaro, A., and Manzoni, A. 1974. Menstruation in twins. *Riv. Ostet. Ginecol. Prat. Med. Perinat.* 54(4):187–194.

Osborne, R. H., and De George, F. V. 1959. *Genetic basis of morphological variation.* Cambridge: Harvard University Press.

Osborne, R. T. 1970. Heritability estimates for the visual evoked response I. *Life Sci.* 9:481–490.

————; Horowitz, S.; and DeGeorge, F. 1958. Genetic variation in tooth dimensions: A twin study of permanent anterior teeth. *Amer. J. Hum. Genet.* 10:350–356.

Papoušek, H. 1967. Genetics and child development. In *Genetic diversity and human behavior*, ed. J. N. Spuhler, pp. 171–186. Chicago: Aldine.

———. 1977. Individual differences in adaptive processes of infants. In *Genetics, environment and intelligence*, ed. A. Oliverio, pp. 269–84. New York: Elsevier/North-Holland Biomedical Press.

Peck, D. F. 1970. The conversion of progressive matrices and Mill Hill vocabulary raw scores into deviation IQs. *J. Clinical Psychology* 26(1):67–70.

Pencavel, J. H. 1976. A note on the IQ of monozygotic twins raised apart and the order of their birth. *Behavior Genetics* 6:455–460.

Perris, C. 1973. The genetics of affective disorders. *Biological psychiatry*, ed. J. Mendels, pp. 383–415. New York: Wiley.

———, and d'Elia, G. 1966. A study of bipolar (manic-depressive) and unipolar recurrent depressive psychoses. *Acta Psychiat. Scand.* Suppl. 194(42):172–183. Copenhagen: Munksgaard.

Petri, E. 1934. In *Zeitschr. Morph. u. Anthropol.*, 33. Cited in *Principles of human genetics*, by C. Stern. San Francisco: W. H. Freeman, 1973.

Pettigrew, T. 1964. *A profile of the negro american*, Princeton: Van Nostrand.

Pettit, A. N. 1977. Testing the normality of several independent samples using the Anderson-Darling statistic. *Applied Statistics* 26:156–161.

Piaget, J. 1963. *The origins of intelligence in children*. New York: W. W. Norton.

*Popenoe, P. 1922. Twins reared apart. *J. Hered.* 5:142–144.

Price, J. 1968. The genetics of depressive behavior. In *Recent developments of affective disorder*. British Journal of Psychiatry, special publication no. 2.

*Prokop, H., and Druml, W. 1973. Diskordantes auftreten einer depressiv gefarbten Katatonie bei eineiigen zwillingen im jugendalter. *Wien. Z. Nervenheilkunde* 31:156–166.

Raney, E. T. 1938. Reversed lateral dominance in identical twins. *J. Exp. Psychol.* 23:304–312.

Raven, J. C. 1938–1979. Manuals for *Raven's progressive matrices and Mill Hill vocabulary scale*. London: H. K. Lewis.

Record, R. G.; McKeown, T.; and Edwards, J. H. 1970. An investigation of the difference in measured intelligence between twins and single births. *Annals of Human Genetics* 34:11–20.

Riccardi, V. M. 1977. *The genetic approach to human disease*. New York: Oxford University Press.

Rieder, R. O.; Broman, S. H.; and Rosenthal, D. 1977. The offspring of schizophrenics II. Perinatal factors in IQ. *Archives of General Psychiatry* 34:789–799.

Roe, A. 1944. The adult adjustment of children of alcoholic parents raised in foster-homes. *Quarterly Journal of Studies on Alcohol* 5:378–393.

Rome, H. P., ed. 1979. Genetics and schizophrenia. *Psychiatric Annals* 9:3–116.

*Rosanoff, A. J.; Handy, L. M.; and Plesset, I. R. 1935. The etiology of manic-depressive syndromes with special reference to their occurrence in twins. *Am. J. Psychiat.* 91:725–762. (Additional information in appendix A of this text.)

*———. 1937. The etiology of mental deficiency with special reference to its occurrence in twins. *Psychol. Monogr.* 48(4).

Rosenthal, D. 1971. *Genetics of psychopathology*. New York: McGraw-Hill.

Rutter, M. 1970. Psychological development: Predictions from infancy. *J. of Child Psychology and Psychiatry* 11:49.

———; Graham, P.; and Yule, W. 1970. *A neuropsychiatric study in childhood*. Philadelphia: J. B. Lippincott.

Rybo, G., and Hallberg, L. 1966. Influence of heredity and environment on normal menstrual blood loss. A study of twins. *Acta Obstet. Gynecol. Scand.* 45(4):389–410.

Sarnoff C. 1976. *Latency*. New York: Jason Aronson.

SAS Institute, Inc. 1979. *SAS user's guide: 1979 edition*. Raleigh, N.C.: SAS Institute.

*Saudek, R. 1934a. Identical twins reared apart. *Character & Personality* 2:22–40.

*———. 1934b. A British pair of identical twins reared apart. *Character & Personality* 3:17–39.

Scarr, S., ed. 1979. Psychology and children: Current research and practice. *American Psychologist*. Special issue 34:10.

Scarr-Salapatek, S. 1976. An evolutionary perspective on infant intelligence: Species patterns and individual variations. In *Origins of intelligence,* ed. M. Lewis, pp. 165–197. New York: Plenum Press.

Schachter, S. 1964. The interaction of cognitive and physiological determinants of emotional state. In *Psychobiological approaches to social behavior,* ed. P. H. Leiderman and D. Shapiro, Stanford: University of California Press.

———, and Singer, J. E. 1962. Cognitive, social and physiological determinants of emotional state. *Psychological Review* 69:379–399.

Schaie, K. W.; Anderson, V. E.; McClearn, G. E.; and Money, J., eds. 1975. *Developmental human behavior genetics.* Lexington, Mass.: Lexington Books, D. C. Heath.

Scheffé, H. 1959. *The analysis of variance.* New York: Wiley.

Schienfeld, A. 1967. *Twins and supertwins.* Philadelphia: J. B. Lippincott.

Schwartz, M., and Schwartz, J. 1976. Comment on "IQs of identical twins reared apart." *Behavior Genetics* 6(3):367–368.

*Schwesinger, G. 1952. The effect of differential parent-child relations on identical twin resemblance in personality. *Acta Genet. Med.* (Roma) 1:40–47.

Scott, J. T., ed. 1978. *Copeman's textbook of the rheumatic diseases.* 5th ed. New York: Churchill-Livingstone.

Shields, J. 1954. Personality differences and neurotic traits in normal twin school-children. *Eugenics Review* 45:213–246.

*———. 1962. *Monozygotic twins brought up apart and brought up together.* London: Oxford University Press.

———. 1978. MZA twins: Their use and abuse. In *Twin Research Psychology and Methodology,* ed. W. Nance, pp. 79–93. New York: Alan R. Liss.

———, and Gottesman, I. I., eds. 1971. *Man, mind, and heredity: Selected papers of Eliot Slater on psychiatry and genetics.* Baltimore, Maryland: Johns Hopkins University Press.

*Slater, E. 1961. Hysteria 311. *J. Ment. Sci.* 107:359–381.

———, (with the assistance of J. Shields). 1953. Psychotic and neurotic illness in twins. *Medical Research Council Report,* Series No. 278. London: Her Majesty's Stationery Office.

———, and Cowie, V. 1971. *The genetics of mental disorders.* London: Oxford University Press.

Sorsby, A. 1970. *Ophthalmic genetics.* 2nd ed. New York: Appleton-Century-Crofts.

Spitz, R. 1965. *The first year of life.* New York: International Universities Press.

*Stenstedt, A. 1952. A study in manic-depressive psychosis. *Acta Psychiat. Scand.,* Suppl. 79. Copenhagen: Munksgaard.

*Stephens, F. E., and Nunemaker, J. C. 1950. Spondilytis in identical twins reared apart. *J. Hered.* 41(11):282–286.

*Stephens, F. E., and Thompson, R. B. 1943. The case of Millan and George, identical twins reared apart. *J. Hered.* 34:109–114.

Stern, C. 1973. *Principles of human genetics.* San Francisco: W. H. Freeman.

Strang, J. S. 1974. A comparative study of full term and prematurely born children, aged 10–13, on factors of intelligence, personality, and perceptual-motor development. Doctoral dissertation, University of Alabama.

Sulloway, F. 1979. *Freud, biologist of the mind.* New York: Basic Books.

Thomas, A.; Chess, S.; and Birch, H. G. 1968. *Temperament and behavior disorders in children.* New York: New York University Press.

*Tienari, P. 1963. Psychiatric illnesses in identical twins. *Acta Psychiat. Scand.,* Suppl. 171. Copenhagen: Munksgaard.

Tilford, J. A. 1976. The relationship between gestational age and adaptive behavior. *Merrill-Palmer Quarterly* 22(4):319–326.

Tisserant-Perrier, M. 1953. Etude comparative de certains processus de croissance chez les jumeaux. *J. Genet. Hum.* 2:87–102.

Vandenberg, S. G. 1962. The hereditary abilities study: hereditary components in a psychological test battery. *Am. J. Hum. Genet.* 14:220–237.

———. 1965. *Methods and goals in human behavior genetics.* New York: Academic Press.

———, and Johnson, R. C. 1968. Further evidence on the relation between age of separation and similarity in IQ among pairs of separated identical twins. In *Progress in human behavior genetics,* ed. S. Vandenberg, pp. 215–219. Baltimore: Johns Hopkins University Press.

Vesell, E. S.; Page, J. G.; and Passanti, G. T. 1971. Genetic and environmental factors affecting ethanol metabolism in man. *Clin. Pharmacol. Ther.* 12:192–201.

Waddington, C. H. 1957. *The strategy of the genes.* London: Allen and Unwin.

———. 1962. *New patterns in genetics and development.* New York: Columbia University Press.

*Wagenseil, F. 1931. Zwei mitteilungen uber die erbbiologische bedeutung der eineiigen mehrlinge. *Z. fur Konstitutionslehere* 15:632–645.

Wiener, G. 1962. Psychologic correlates of premature birth: A review. *J. Nerv. and Mental Diseases* 134:129–144.

———. 1968. Scholastic achievement at age 12–13 of prematurely born infants. *J. of Special Education* 2(3):237–250.

Wilde, G. J. S. 1964. An experimental study of mutual behavior imitation and person perception in MZ and DZ twin pairs. *Acta Genet. Med. Gemellol.* (Roma) 19:273.

Wilson, R. 1972. Twins: Early mental development. *Science* 175:914–917.

———. 1974. Twins: Mental development in the preschool years. *Develop. Psychol.* 10:580–588.

———. 1977. Mental development in twins. In *Genetics, environment and intelligence,* ed. A. Oliverio, pp. 305–334. New York: Elsevier/North-Holland Biomedical Press.

———. 1978. Synchronies in mental development: An epigenetic perspective. *Science* 202:939–948.

———; Brown, A. M.; and Matheny, A. P. 1971. Emergence and persistence of behavioral differences in twins. *Child Development* 42(5):1381–1398.

Winer, B. J. 1971. *Statistical principles in experimental design.* 2nd ed. New York: McGraw-Hill.

Winnicott, D. W. 1965. *The maturational processes and the facilitating environment.* New York: International Universities Press.

Winokur, G.; Clayton, P. J.; and Reich, T. 1969. *Manic Depressive Illness.* St. Louis: C. V. Mosby.

Wolff, J. L. 1979. A critique of Milkman's (1978) "A simple exposition of Jensen's error." *Journal of educational statistics* 4(3):197–205.

Yang, R. K., and Halverson, C. F., Jr. 1976. A study of the "inversion of intensity" between newborn and preschool-age behavior. *Child Development* 47:350–359.

*Yates, N., and Brash, H. 1941. An investigation of the physical and mental characteristics of a pair of like twins reared apart from infancy. *Ann. Eugen.* 11:89–101.

*Yoshimasu, S. 1941. Psychopathie und kriminalitat. *Psychiat. Neurol. Jap.* 45:455–531. (In Japanese with German summary.)

Young, J. P. R., and Fenton, G. W. 1971. An investigation of the genetic aspects of the alpha attenuation response. *Psychol. Med.* 1:365–371.

Zajonc, R. B. 1976. Family configuration and intelligence. *Science* 192 (4236): 227–235.

Zung, W. W., and Wilson, W. P. 1966. Sleep and dream patterns in twins: Markov analysis of a genetic trait. In *Recent Advances in Biological Psychiatry,* ed. J. Wortis, vol. 9, pp. 119–130. New York: Plenum Press.

Case Index

Name Index

Subject Index

Myocardial infarction, 302
Myocarditis, 103, 106
Myoma, 99–100
Myopia, 74
Myxedema, 135

Nail biting, 41, 227–28, 238
Narcissism, 52
Nasal polyps, 126, 129
Neoplasms: benign, 99–100; malignant, *see* Cancer
Nervous habits, 226–28
Nervous system, disorders of, 116–20, 122
Nervousness, 234
Neuritis, 120
Neurosis: childhood versus adult patterns of, 260; genetic contributions to, 218; in global personality assessment, 253; issue of environment and, 239–41; SES and, 217
Nevi, 99
New York Longitudinal Study, 233
Nightmares, 82–84
Normative traits, 64–90
Nutritional disorders, 135–38

Object loss, 232
Object-relations theory, 264
Obsessional traits, 218, 232, 233, 239, 245
Occupational therapy, 301
Oedipal phase, 230
Oocytic twins, 9
Ophthalmic features, 73–76, 89; data on (table), 282–83
Osteomyelitis, 111
Otis test, 180, 198
Otosclerosis, 121–22

Paraldehyde, 301
Paranoid psychosis, 156–57, 161
Parasitic diseases, 138–39
Pathological mirror imaging, 11
Pedigree, *see* Family pedigree
Perimetritis, 134
Pernicious anemia, 98
Personality, 45–46, 48–50; ambiguity of data on, 253–54; anecdotal summaries of cases illustrating, 243–46; developmental approach to investigation of, 256–60; genetic components of, 269; global assessment of, 246–53, 271; IQ and, 200; marital status and, 82; neurological functioning and, 253; prior studies of, 216–19; problems in definition of, 242–43; traits, 213–41; twinning and, 253–56
Personality tests, 38–39, 247; inadequacy of, 246; questionable validity of, 214–16; similarity indicated in, 244

Petty larceny, 229
Phenotype, IQ and, 180, 200
Phenylketonuria, 271
Phlebitis, 102, 105, 106
Phobias, 218, 234
Physical disorders, 91–141; allergies, 129; benign neoplasms, 99–100; cancer, 95–99; circulatory, 100–6; digestive, 111–16; endocrine, metabolic, and nutritional, 135–38; genitourinary and reproductive, 129–35; infective and parasitic, 138–40; musculoskeletal, 106–11; of nervous system and sense organs, 116–22; respiratory, 122–26; of skin and subcutaneous tissue, 126–28
Piagetian developmental theory, 258, 262
Placenta, evaluation of to determine zygosity, 17
Pleurisy, 125
Pneumonia, 125
Polio, 120, 122
Postpartum fever, 134
Practicing subphase of development, 264
Pregnancy, 82; breast cancer risk and, 95; toxemia in, 133–34; weight gains and, 68
Prematurity, 14–15; affective disorders and, 150–51; indicated in sample, 62; IQ and, 201–2
Projective tests, 239
Pseudocyesis, 80
Psoriasis, 128; arthritis and, 109
Psychoanalytic theory, 213, 216; of child development, 249, 257, 264; critique of, 265; description of emotion in, 233; fear and anxiety in, 234–39
Psychodynamic developmental theory, 258
Psychological asymmetry, 11–12
Pscychosis, 143, 165–66; awareness of twinship and, 20; case summaries of, 297–318; encopresis and, 85; genetic contribution to, 266; studies of, 36–37; symptoms in, 218; *see also* Affective disorders; Schizophrenia
Psychotherapy, 265–68
Pubertal development, 78
Pulmonary edema, 105
Purigo, 128
Pyelonephritis, 131

QRS complex, splintering of, 72

Ravens Progressive Matrices, 49, 171, 181
Reactive disorders, 218
Reading disabilities, 228
Rearing status, 65; adult height and, 66; EEG patterns and, 71; IQ and, 201; personality traits and, 225, 251